BRITISH ARCHITECTURE AND ITS BACKGROUND

John B. Nellist

BRITISH ARCHITECTURE AND ITS BACKGROUND

MACMILLAN & CO. LTD
ST MARTIN'S PRESS
1967

MACMILLAN AND COMPANY LIMITED
Little Essex Street London WC2
also Bombay Calcutta Madras Melbourne

THE MACMILLAN COMPANY OF CANADA LIMITED
70 Bond Street Toronto 2

ST MARTIN'S PRESS INC
175 Fifth Avenue New York NY 10010

Library of Congress Catalogue No. 67 – 11466

To the VIth Form
at
ASHVILLE COLLEGE
for whom this book
was written

Printed in Great Britain by Jarrold and Sons Ltd, Norwich

INTRODUCTION

The study of architecture, like all worth-while pursuits, is not easy. Perhaps more than any other art form, buildings reflect the social conditions of the period which produced them, and to really understand the architecture of any given period it is necessary to read something of the period's social and economic history as well as the more specialist books on its architecture; in this way it is possible to get the 'feel' of a period in depth and so enhance one's appreciation of the buildings being studied.

Not that reading books is enough. A good recording can reveal the secrets of a Mozart symphony and a good modern colour reproduction can give a fair idea of a painting, but a photograph or drawing is a very poor substitute for an actual building. Buildings must be experienced in the round; they must be walked round and through, and examined from all angles. For architecture is the manipulation of space. That the elevation should interest the eye is not enough; the organization of solids and voids must arouse one's visual and intellectual curiosity so that one is tempted to move further and further into the building to experience fresh arrangements of colour and texture, solid and void. The study of books must, then, be supplemented by as many visits to buildings as possible. The wider one's experience of buildings, the more understanding one can bring to the interpretation of illustrations of those it is impossible to visit.

At the present time, when so many new buildings are going up around us, and the architects and planners have so many new problems to face, it is especially important to have an informed and creatively critical public, both to safeguard our present heritage and to ensure that what we build in future is worthy of it. Thus if the book that follows can do anything to encourage the reader, of whatever age, to look at the buildings around him and to form his own critical judgements of them, it will not have been written in vain.

ACKNOWLEDGEMENTS

Many people have helped in the preparation of this book, but there are certain of them whom I should like to mention in particular. Firstly, I would like especially to thank Mr J. F. Symmons, Head of the History Department at Ashville College, and Mr D. L. Lockwood, an erstwhile colleague, for the help they have given on matters of historical fact and background. I am also indebted to Mr Lockwood for the many discussions we had on the method of presentation of the material, in the very early days, when the book was almost in draft form. Mr T. R. J. West, sometime member of the English Department at Ashville, also helped me read through the typescript at a much later date, and made many helpful suggestions as to English style.

I would also like to thank Mr D. J. Welsh for helping with the task of numbering the figures and plates in the text.

The discussions which I had with the School Chaplain at the time, the Rev. D. C. G. Whittle, were both stimulating and helpful in trying to distinguish and evaluate medieval and Renaissance attitudes towards religion and architecture.

I must also thank various members of the VIth Form Art set at Ashville, who have, on occasions, read the typescript and made suggestions either for clarifying the material or for expanding topics where they felt that more detailed information was necessary as a basis for their essays or notes.

I am also indebted to Mr Geoffrey Kirk for his work on the index.

The help given, on very many occasions, by members of the staffs of the Reference Department of the Harrogate Public Library and the Print Room and Art Library in the Leeds City Art Gallery must also be mentioned. In both cases they have devoted much invaluable time to tracking down odd items of information and generally easing the task of verification which a book of this nature presents.

Lastly, I must thank Miss Helen Foggitt and my wife, who also helped with reading the proofs, for undertaking the formidable amount of typing entailed; my daughter, who helped with organizing the material in the Glossary; and the Publishers for their constructive suggestions and their invaluable help in editing the whole into a clear and accessible shape.

J.B.N.

The publishers gratefully acknowledge the help given by the following in respect of the illustrations listed overleaf:

PLATES

Aerofilms 29, 30, 36, 60

T. & R. Annan, Glasgow 47

Architectural Review 59

Archives Photographiques, Paris 8

Stewart Bale 61

The British Museum 37, 38, 40

Photographie Bulloz 51, 52

Country Life 33

D. & W. Archiv-Photo, Berlin 57

Gabinetto Fotographico Nazionale, Rome 18

Giraudon 6

Lucien Hervé 55, 58

Martin Hürlimann, from *English Cathedrals* (Thames and Hudson) 25

J. Jeiter 15, 22

A. F. Kersting 2, 7, 12, 19, 24, 34a, 34b, 39, 44, 45, 62

The Mansell Collection 4, 14, 16, 17, 20, 21, 50

Foto Marburg 3, 5, 10, 11, 13

Eric de Maré 49

Foto Mas, Barcelona 54

Ministry of Public Buildings and Works 26

Soprintendenza ai Monumenti del Piemonte, Turin 23

National Buildings Record 35, 41, 42, 43, 48

Jean Roubier 9

The Royal Institute of British Architects 31

Edwin Smith, 27, 28, 32

G. E. Kidder Smith, New York 56

The Times 1

West Midland Photo Services, Shrewsbury 46

FIGURES

Gilyard Beer: *Abbeys* (H.M.S.O.) 106

Jacob Burckhardt: *Die Baukunst der Renaissance in Italien* (Schwabe, Basel) 97

K. J. Conant: *Carolingian and Romanesque Architecture* (Penguin) 167

Ampliaciones y Reproducciones Mas, Barcelona 252

G. H. Cook: *The English Mediaeval Parish Church* (Phoenix House, Ltd) 121, 123, 124

Banister Fletcher: *A History of Architecture* (Batsford) 2, 7, 17, 18, 19, 22, 23, 44, 56, 58, 90, 108, 109, 110, 111, 119, 155, 172b, 175, 189, 194

Ann Fokker: *Roman Baroque Art* (Oxford) 99

Jurgen Joedicke: *A History of Modern Architecture* (Architectural Press) 255, 272

Nikolaus Pevsner: *Outline of European Architecture* (Penguin) 80, 88, 93, 102

Società Piemontese di Archaeologica e Belle Arte 100

Heathcote Statham: *A History of Architecture* (Batsford) 29, 30, 31, 32

Sir John Summerson: *Architecture in Britain* (Penguin) 177, 202, 210

Sir John Summerson: *John Nash* (Allen and Unwin) 212

Sidney Toy: *The Castles of Great Britain* (Heinemann) 138, 140, 141, 143, 144, 146, 147, 149

Arnold Whittick: *European Architecture in the Twentieth Century* (Crosby Lockwood & Son) 265

Wittkower: *Art and Architecture in Italy, 1660–1750* (Penguin) 98

CONTENTS

Introduction   v

Acknowledgements   vii

List of Plates   xi

List of Figures   xii

Table 1—Chronological Chart   xvi

PART ONE: THE CLASSICAL AND EUROPEAN BACKGROUND   I

    1. The Architecture of Greece and Rome   3

    2. Gothic Architecture in Europe   30

    3. The Renaissance in Europe   52

    4. Baroque Architecture in Italy   86

PART TWO: ARCHITECTURE IN BRITAIN 1066–1800   101

    5. Gothic Ecclesiastical Architecture   103

        The Constitution of the English Church   103

        The Abbey-Cathedral Type of Church   106

        The Monastery   118

        The Medieval Parish Church   123

            The Timber Roof   129

            The Tower   132

        Recognition Points for the Styles   134

    6. The Castle   140

        Medieval Warfare and Weapons   141

        The Development of the Castle   144

        The Age of the Great Stone Keep   145

        The Castle Triumphant   151

        The Decline of the Castle   157

        The Fortified Manor House   159

        A Note on Scottish Castles   161

    7. The Medieval and Tudor House   163

        Medieval Domestic Architecture   165

        The Early Renaissance House   175

    8. The Age of Jones and Wren   184

    9. Interlude: English Baroque   209

    10. The Eighteenth Century   218

PART THREE: THE NINETEENTH AND TWENTIETH
CENTURIES   235

  11. The Nineteenth Century   237
        Architecture in Britain 1830–90   244
            The Greek Revival   244
            The Gothic Revival   249
            Domestic Architecture   262
            The use of Iron, and the Crystal Palace   266
        Developments in Europe   276
            The Greek Revival   276
            Rundbogenstik   277
            Architecture in France   277
            Architecture in Austria and Italy   280
        Developments in America   281
  12. The Modern Movement   293
        Europe and America   295
        Great Britain   320

    General Bibliography   331
    Glossary   335
    Index   347

LIST OF PLATES

Plate

1 The Stoa at Athens—reconstruction
2 The Colosseum, Rome
3 The Pantheon, Rome—exterior
4 The Pantheon—interior
5 The Baths of Caracalla, Rome
6 The Abbey Church of St-Denis, Paris—interior
7 The Abbey Church of La Trinité, Vendôme—façade
8 St-Maclou, Rouen—façade
9 Laon Cathedral—nave
10 Amiens Cathedral—nave
11 Beauvais Cathedral—exterior of choir
12 Chartres Cathedral—west front
13 Bourges Cathedral—exterior of choir
14 St Peter's, Rome—façade
15 The Church of the Gesù, Rome—interior
16 SS. Martina e Luca, Rome—exterior
17 S. Maria della Consolazione, Todi—interior
18 SS. Martina e Luca—interior
19 St Peter's, Rome—the colonnade
20 S. Teresa in Ecstasy by Bernini
21 S. Carlo alle Quattro Fontane, Rome—façade
22 S. Ivo, Rome—view into dome
23 S. Lorenzo, Turin—view into dome
24 Durham Cathedral—the nave
25 Wells Cathedral—interior
26 Hampton Court Palace—The Great Hall
27 Winchester Cathedral—nave vaulting
28 King's College Chapel, Cambridge—fan-vaulting
29 Caernarvon Castle, North Wales
30 Dover Castle, Kent—the keep
31 St Paul's Cathedral—Inigo Jones's drawing for west front
32 Wilton House, Wilts.
33 Coleshill House—the staircase hall

34a The Sheldonian Theatre, Oxford—façade
34b The Sheldonian Theatre—auditorium
35 St Paul's Cathedral, London—west front
36 The Royal Naval Hospital, Greenwich
37 Castle Howard, Yorks.
38 Blenheim Palace, Oxfordshire
39 Holkham Hall, Norfolk
40 The Adelphi, London
41 The Circus, Bath
42 The Royal Pavilion, Brighton
43 The Bank of England—Consols Office
44 The Reform Club
45 The Roman Catholic Cathedral, Westminster—interior
46 The Benyon, Bage & Marshall Mill, Ditherington
47 Warehouses, Jamaica Street, Glasgow
48 The Oriel Chambers, Liverpool
49 The Boat Store, Royal Naval Dockyard, Sheerness
46–9 Forward-looking British architecture
50 The Crystal Palace, London
51 The Opéra, Paris—the foyer
52 The Bibliothèque Sainte-Geneviève, Paris
53 The staircase at No. 6, rue Paul-Émile Janson, Brussels
54 The Cathedral of the Sagrada Familia, Barcelona—Nativity Transept
55 A house in rue Franklyn, Paris
56 S. C. Johnson & Son, Inc., Wisconsin—Administration Building
57 The Einstein Tower, Potsdam
58 Unité d'Habitation, Marseilles
59 The Boots Factory, Beeston, Nottingham
60 The Roehampton Estate, London
61 Liverpool Cathedral—interior
62 Guildford Cathedral—interior

LIST OF FIGURES

Figure

1 Various types of Greek temple in plan and elevation
2 Diagram of an order with the parts named
3 The Doric Order
4 The Ionic Order
5 The Corinthian Order
6 The Parthenon from the front
7 The Parthenon—plan
8 The Parthenon, seen from the most advantageous viewpoint
9 The Erechtheum—plan
10 The Erechtheum
11 The Erechtheum—eastern elevation
12 The Erechtheum—the famous caryatids
13 The Temple of Nikè Apteros, Athens
14 The Choragic Monument of Lysicrates, Athens
15 The Temple of Zeus, Athens
16 The function of the capital, column, and base
17 The Mausoleum at Halicarnassus
18 The theatre at Epidaurus
19 Sir William Chambers' 'Comparative Proportions of the Classical Orders'
20 The Temple of Fortuna Virilis, Rome
21 The Maison Carrée, Nîmes
22 The Maison Carrée—plan
23 The Basilica of Trajan, Rome—plan
24 The Arch of Constantine, Rome
25 The Arch of Trajan, Beneventum
26 The Temple of Portunus, Rome
27 The Pont du Gard, Nîmes
28 A typical Roman house plan
29 Plan of a dome on a square base
30 The simplest way of bridging corners
31 The squinch arch
32 Method of corbelling out successive courses
33–7 The construction of a dome on pendentives
38 An intersecting waggon vault, viewed from below
39 An intersecting waggon vault, viewed from above
40 Early rib-structure of intersecting waggon vaults

41 The arrangement of semicircular arches over an oblong bay
42 The rib-structure of pointed arches
43 The flying buttress
44 Salisbury Cathedral—plan
45 Amiens Cathedral—plan
46 St-Étienne, Caen
47 The Abbey Church of St-Denis, Paris
48 Notre-Dame, Laon
49 Notre-Dame, Paris
50 St-Firmin, Amiens
51 Notre-Dame, Reims
52 English rectangular voutains
53 French carved and shaped voutains
54 Soufflet
55 Mouchette
56 Notre-Dame, Paris—plan
57 Reims Cathedral—plan
58 Bourges Cathedral—plan
59 The Foundling Hospital, Florence
60 The golden section, method of construction
61 The dome, Florence Cathedral
62 The dome, St Peter's, Rome
63 The dome, St Paul's, London
64 S. Maria della Consolazione, Todi
65 The Palazzo Rucellai, Florence
66 S. Francesco, Rimini
67 S. Andrea, Mantua
68–70 Pier and column in relation to wall
71 The Palazzo Ducale, Urbino
72 The Palazzo Medici, Florence
73 The Cancelleria, Rome
74 The Tempietto of S. Pietro in Montorio, Rome
75 Niches in the Medici Mausoleum, Florence
76 The tomb in the Medici Mausoleum
77 The Biblioteca Laurenziana, Florence
78 The Palazzo Vidoni Caffarelli, Rome
79 The Palazzo Farnese, Rome
80 The Palazzo Farnese—plan
81 The Piccola Farnesina, Rome
82 The Palazzo del Tè, Mantua—the entrance façade
83 The Palazzo del Tè—the courtyard façade

Figure

84 The Palazzo del Tè—the garden façade
85 The Palazzo Massimi, Rome
86 The Palazzo Farnese, Rome
87 The Capitoline Palace, Rome
88 Bramante's first plan for St Peter's, Rome
89 The Villa Capra near Vicenza
90 The Villa Capra—plan
91 The Palazzo Chiericati, Vicenza
92 The Villa Maser, Asolo
93 The Villa Trissino, Meledo
94 S. Francesca della Vigna, Venice
95 S. Giorgio Maggiore, Venice
96 Il Redentore, Venice
97 S. Maria della Consolazione, Todi
98 SS. Martina e Luca, Rome
99 S. Carlo alle Quattro Fontane, Rome
100 The Church of the Immaculate Conception, Turin
101 S. Andrea al Quirinale, Rome
102 S. Andrea al Quirinale—plan
103 S. Lorenzo, Turin—plan
104 The Saxon tower, Sompting, Sussex
105 The Saxon Church, Bradford-on-Avon
106 St Albans Cathedral—eastern arm
107 La Trinité (Abbaye-aux-Dames), Caen—plan
108 St Étienne (Abbaye-aux-Hommes), Caen—plan
109 Norwich Cathedral—plan
110 Westminster Abbey—plan
111 Canterbury Cathedral—plan
112 Southwell Cathedral—west front
113 York Minster—west front
114 Ripon Cathedral—west front
115 Peterborough Cathedral—west front
116 Wells Cathedral—west front
117 Lichfield Cathedral—west front
118 Beverley Minster—west front
119 Fountains Abbey, Yorkshire—plan
120 Kirkham Priory, Yorkshire
121 St Mary Redcliffe, Bristol—plan
122 The parish church, Patrington, East Yorkshire
123 Abingdon Church, Berkshire—plan
124 Warmington Church, Northants—plan
125 Lavenham Church, Suffolk
126 The tie-beam
127 The trussed rafter
128 The arch brace
129 Hammer-beams
130 The tower of St John's, Glastonbury

131 Typical lancet tracery
132 Typical plate-tracery
133 Typical geometrical decorated tracery
134 Typical curvilinear decorated tracery
135 Typical perpendicular tracery
136 Rochester Castle—the square keep
137 Tower of London—The White Tower
138 The Tower of London—plan
139 Restormel Castle, Cornwall
140 Restormel Castle—plan
141 Conisborough Castle, Yorks.
142 Conisborough Castle, the keep
143 Caernarvon Castle—plan
144 Conway Castle—plan
145 Dover Castle, Kent—the gatehouse
146 Beaumaris Castle, Wales—plan
147 Harlech Castle, Wales—plan
148 Bodiam Castle, Sussex
149 Bodiam Castle—plan
150–1 Two types of cruck house
152 The Manor House, Boothby Pagnell
153 The Fish House, Meare, Somerset
154 Cothay Manor, Wellington, Somerset
155 Penshurst Place, Kent
156 The Jew's House, Lincoln
157 Little Wenham, Suffolk
158 The Grevel House, Chipping Campden, Glos.
159 Synyards, Otham, Kent
160 Blagroves, Barnard Castle, Co. Durham
161 Ockwells Manor, Bray, Berks.
162 Sutton Courtenay, Berks.
163 Knook Manor, Wilts.
164 Daneway House, Glos.
165 Ashleworth, Glos.
166 Cold Ashton Manor, Glos.
167 Yatton Keynell Manor, Wilts.
168 Nether Lypiat, Glos.
169 Hunt's Farm, Kent
170 Haddon Hall, Derbyshire—plan
171 Compton Wynyates, Warwickshire
172a Longleat House, Wilts.
172b Longleat House—plan
173 Wollaton Hall, Notts.
174 Hardwick Hall, Derbyshire—plan
175 Hardwick Hall—façade
176 The Queen's House, Greenwich
177 The Queen's House, Greenwich—plan
178 The Queen's House, Greenwich—façades
179 The Banqueting Hall, Whitehall, London
180 Chevening, Kent

Figure

181 Raynham Hall, Norfolk
182 Coleshill, Berks.
183 Thorpe Hall, Northants
184 Belton House, near Grantham, Lincs.
185 Wren's plan for rebuilding London after the Great Fire
186 St Mary-le-Bow, Cheapside
187 St Vedast, Foster Lane
188 St Bride, Fleet Street
189 St Stephen, Walbrook—plan
190 The proportions of a Classical door
191 Chelsea Hospital
192 Blenheim Palace, kitchen gateway
193 Castle Howard, Yorkshire
194 Castle Howard—plan
195 Castle Howard, The Temple of the Winds
196 Castle Howard, The Mausoleum
197 Blenheim—the quadrant colonnades
198 Seaton Delaval, Northumberland
199 St Anne's, Limehouse
200 St Mary Woolnoth
201 St Mary Woolnoth—plan
202 St Paul's, Deptford—plan
203 The Dowry House, Bristol
204 No. 32 St James's Square, London
205 No. 72 High Street, Marlow, Bucks.
206 Church Langton Rectory, Leics.
207 No. 20 St James's Square, London
208 Newby Hall, Yorks.
209 Chiswick House, London
210 St Martin-in-the-Fields, London—preliminary plan
211 The Radcliffe Camera, Oxford
212 Regent's Park and Regent Street—plan
213 Cumberland Terrace, London
214 Nineteenth-century housing at Leeds
215 Modern development at Leeds
216 A late-Victorian middle-class house in Harrogate
217 The British Museum, London
218 The Altes Museum, Berlin
219 St George's Hall, Liverpool
220 The Royal Scottish Academy, Edinburgh
221 Caledonia Road Free Church, Glasgow
222 The Houses of Parliament, London
223 St Pancras Hotel, London
224 St Mary's, Studley Royal
225 Swan House, Chelsea
226 No. 6 Ellerdale Road, Hampstead
227 No. 170 Queen's Gate, London

228 The Red House, Bexleyheath, Kent
229 Smeaton Manor, Yorkshire
230 Clouds House, East Knoyle, Wilts.
231 Moor Crag, near Windermere
232 The Pastures, North Luffenham, Rutland
233 Coalbrookdale Bridge, Shropshire
234 Craigellachie Bridge, Banff
235 The Menai Suspension Bridge, North Wales
236 The Clifton Suspension Bridge, Bristol
237 The Marshall Field Store, Chicago
238 The Allegheny Courthouse and Gaol, Pittsburgh
239 Stoughton House, Cambridge, Mass.
240 The Watts Sherman House, Newport, Rhode Island
241 The Monadnock Block, Chicago
242 The Home Insurance Building, Chicago
243 The Reliance Building, Chicago
244 The Auditorium Building, Chicago
245 The Walker Warehouse, Chicago
246 The Wainwright Building, St. Louis, Mo.
247 The Guaranty Building, Buffalo
248 The Carson, Pirie, Scott Store, Chicago
249 A small Mid-Western bank
250 Glasgow School of Art
251 The Park-keeper's House, Parque Güell, Barcelona
252 Casa Milá, Barcelona—plan
253 The James Charnley House, Chicago
254 Falling Water, Bear Run Park, Pa.
255 The Ward Willitt House, Highland Park, Illinois
256 The Robie House, Chicago
257 Taliesen West, Arizona
258 The Guggenheim Museum, New York
259 The A.E.G. Turbine Factory, Berlin
260 The Fagus Works, Alfeld a. d. Leine
261 The Werkbund Exhibition Building, Cologne
262 The Bauhaus, Dessau
263 The Bauhaus—plan
264 The Villa Savoye, Poissy
265 The Villa Savoye—side elevation
266 The Weissenhof Housing Scheme, Stuttgart
267 The Villa Garches, near Paris
268 The Swiss Students' Pavilion, Paris
269 Notre-Dame-du-Haut, Ronchamp
270 The Farnsworth House, Plano, Illinois
271 Tugendhat House, Brno
272 Project by Mies van der Rohe

Figure
273 The Seagram Building, New York
274 The Chapel for the Illinois Institute of
     Technology, Chicago
275 The National Theatre, Mannheim—project

276 The Deanery Gardens, Sonning, Berks.
277 New Ways, Northampton
278 The Peter Jones Store, London
279 The Royal Festival Hall, London

LIST OF TABLES

		page
1	Chronological Chart	xvi–xvii
2	Chart showing the three divisions of the English Cathedral	102
3	Some early structures which exploited the use of iron	267

TABLE 1—GENERAL CHRONOLOGY

MONARCH		PERIOD	ARCHITECTURAL DEVELOPMENT IN BRITAIN	CULTURAL AND SOCIAL EVENTS		DEVELOPMENTS OUTSIDE BRITAIN
WILLIAM I	1066	*Norman* / NORMAN / L	Introduction of Pointed Arch in South aisle of Choir, Durham—first example in Europe — 1095–8	Work started on a large number of Major Churches	Twelfth century	
WILLIAM II	1087					
HENRY I	1100		—1100—			Romanesque style in French cathedrals reaches its full development
			The century of the Square Keep—Colchester, The White Tower, Rochester, Hedingham, etc. Bastard Castles during Stephen's reign	The Crusades opened up trade routes with the East, gave an impetus to the study of warfare and the art of fortification, and led to an influx of Eastern scholars and thinkers to Europe		1137 St Denis, Paris by Abbot Suger
STEPHEN	1135					1163 Notre-Dame, Paris
HENRY II	1154		1175 Choir at Canterbury (William of Sens) Transitional Keeps—Orford, Conisborough			
RICHARD I	1189					
JOHN	1199		—1200—			
HENRY III	1216	*Early English* / P L A N T A G E N E T / A V E I	Cathedrals—Lincoln—Angel Choir (1192–1200) Salisbury, mostly Early English		Thirteenth century	The zenith of French Gothic (Rayonnant) reached in this century, in the cathedrals of the Île de France area: Amiens, Chartres, Reims, Beauvais, etc.
			1230–40 York—'Five Sisters' window			
EDWARD I	1272		Beaumaris, Conway, Caernarvon, Flint, etc. The Great Edwardian Castles of Wales	Medieval Wall Paintings		
EDWARD II	1307	*Decorated* / D	—1300— Exeter Cathedral—mostly 'Decorated'		Fourteenth century	Flamboyant style in France. This style persists into the sixteenth century, but no major cathedrals are built—only parish churches
EDWARD III	1327		Haddon Hall	1349 The Black Death		
RICHARD II	1377			Chaucer		Milan Cathedral
HENRY IV	1399	*Perpendicular* / LANCASTER / E	—1400— Growth of the Manor House	Owing to more settled conditions and to the need to use paid soldiers, the castle begins to decline during the first half of the century	Fifteenth century	The dome of Florence Cathedral
HENRY V	1413		1446–1515 King's College Chapel, Cambridge			1421 The Foundling Hospital, Florence
HENRY VI	1422		1450 Great Chalfield Manor, Wilts.	The Wars of the Roses Gunpowder Invented Caxton introduces printing to Britain		The Palazzo Rucellai, Florence
EDWARD IV	1461	YORK	1482 Oxburgh Hall, Norfolk			
EDWARD V	1483					
RICHARD III	1483					
HENRY VII	1485					

Vertical headings in the original: "MEDIÆVAL" (beside the PERIOD column) and "FEUDALISM" (beside the CULTURAL AND SOCIAL EVENTS column).

A chronological chart of English architecture and its historical and artistic context.

Royal Houses, Monarchs and Architectural Periods

House	Style Period	Sub-period	Monarch (accession)
TUDOR	M[edieval]	Early Tudor	HENRY VIII 1509
TUDOR	M / TRANSITION		EDWARD VI 1547; MARY I 1553
TUDOR	TRANSITION	Elizabethan	ELIZABETH I 1558
STUART	TRANSITION / RENAISSANCE	Jacobean	JAMES I 1603
STUART	RENAISSANCE		CHARLES I 1625
STUART	RENAISSANCE	Restoration	COMMONWEALTH 1649; CHARLES II 1660; JAMES II 1685
STUART	RENAISSANCE		WILLIAM & MARY 1689; ANNE 1702
HANOVER	GEORGIAN	Early	GEORGE I 1714; GEORGE II 1727
HANOVER	GEORGIAN	Late	GEORGE III 1760
HANOVER	GEORGIAN	Regency	REGENCY 1811; GEORGE IV 1820; WILLIAM IV 1830
HANOVER	REVIVALS		VICTORIA 1837
WINDSOR	MODERN		EDWARD VII 1901; GEORGE V 1910; EDWARD VIII 1936; GEORGE VI 1936; ELIZABETH II 1952

Sixteenth century

- **British Architecture:** 1520 COMPTON WYNYATES, Warwickshire; 1515–30 HAMPTON COURT PALACE; The Elizabethan Great House—ROBERT SMYTHSON; LONGLEAT, WOLLATON, HARDWICK; MONTACUTE
- **Arts & Literature:** REFORMATION; DISSOLUTION OF THE MONASTERIES; HOLBEIN, SPENSER, HILLIARD, TALLIS, SHAKESPEARE
- **History:** Rise of Puritanism; Rise of Capitalism; English colonization leads to greater wealth though Crown is poor
- **European & World Architecture:** St Peter's, Rome, begun; Palazzo Farnese; Palazzo Massimi; Council of Trent; Mannerism; St Peter's Dome

Seventeenth century (c. 1600–1700)

- **British Architecture:** INIGO JONES—The Queen's House, Greenwich (1635); CIVIL WAR; CHRISTOPHER WREN—St Paul's Cathedral, City of London Plan, City Churches (1675–1710); ENGLISH BAROQUE (1690–1715)
- **Arts & Literature:** BYRD; VAN DYCK; DRYDEN, PURCELL
- **History:** PLAGUE; FIRE OF LONDON; Foundation of BANK OF ENGLAND
- **European & World Architecture:** St Peter's Nave (Maderno); Rise of French Classicism; St Peter's Colonnade (Bernini); Versailles

Eighteenth century (c. 1700–1800)

- **British Architecture:** VANBRUGH and HAWKSMOOR; ST MARTIN-in-the-FIELDS, London; PALLADIANISM led by LORD BURLINGTON, KENT, CAMPBELL; RADCLIFFE CAMERA, Oxford; The ADAM BROTHERS; WILLIAM CHAMBERS; SOMERSET HOUSE
- **Arts & Literature:** HANDEL, POPE, HOGARTH; REYNOLDS; CONSTABLE, TURNER, COLERIDGE
- **History:** Rise of LONDON as an important centre of world trade; Industrial Revolution; Napoleonic Wars
- **European & World Architecture:** Church of Les Invalides, Paris; St Sulpice, Paris; The Panthéon, Paris; The French Revolution

Nineteenth century (c. 1800–1900)

- **British Architecture:** JOHN NASH; Beginnings of REVIVAL STYLES—Greek, Roman, Renaissance, etc.; PUGIN; PLAYFAIR's work in Edinburgh; ST GEORGE'S HALL, Liverpool; The CRYSTAL PALACE; The ENGINEER-ARCHITECTS; ART NOUVEAU; The DOMESTIC REVIVAL—SHAW, VOYSEY, WEBB
- **Arts & Literature:** WORDSWORTH, SCOTT, BROWNING, TENNYSON; PRE-RAPHAELITES; WILDE, ELGAR, WHISTLER, SHAW
- **History:** Railways; Early Socialism—Ruskin, William Morris
- **European & World Architecture:** Paris replanned by Haussmann; Influence of Ecole des Beaux Arts; Labrouste; J. L. C. Garnier; GALLERIA VITTORIO EMANUELE, Milan; OPÉRA, Paris; Chicago Fire and rise of Chicago School—Sullivan and multi-storey building; JUGENDSTIL, STYLE MODERNE, etc.; Gaudi

Twentieth century (1900–)

- **British Architecture:** 1903 LIVERPOOL CATHEDRAL begun (Scott); 1926 'NEW WAYS' (Behrens); MARS GROUP and Thomas Tait introduce modern architecture; TECTON makes important developments; 1945 New Towns and city development; 1951–62 COVENTRY CATHEDRAL (Spence)
- **Arts & Literature:** ELIOT, VAUGHAN WILLIAMS, CAMDEN TOWN GROUP; BRITTEN, SUTHERLAND, FESTIVAL OF BRITAIN
- **History:** The Welfare State
- **European & World Architecture:** FAGUS FACTORY, Germany; Werkbund Exhibition; Corbusier; The BAUHAUS; FRANK LLOYD WRIGHT; Buckmaster-Fuller; Brasília

PART ONE

The Classical and European Background

1

THE ARCHITECTURE OF GREECE AND ROME

The story of western European architecture began in Greece. The people of that Mediterranean archipelago must be credited with the creation of a style and a language of architectural form which were to prove of immense significance in the shaping of subsequent ideas. The Egyptians had evolved an architecture which was admirably suited to the type of society which prevailed throughout the long centuries of their civilization. However, the grand monumental forms which they created, though expressive of the might of priest and Pharaoh, have proved of only limited importance to subsequent developments. Though the Greeks took some of the Egyptian methods of stone construction, the form of the Greek temple comes more from the architecture of the Mycenaean megaron than from its infinitely more complicated Egyptian counterpart. The precise origins of Greek architecture are shrouded in conjecture and need more detailed examination than there is space for in the present book. The Greek style as we know it, however, began to emerge around the end of the eighth century B.C., after that period of retrogression which followed the abrupt termination of the Mycenaean civilization.

We are concerned here only with the period from the seventh century to the fourth century B.C., when Greek civilization reached its most sophisticated state and built a more developed architecture than Western Europe had seen before. Despite this sophistication and refinement it was a simple and limited architecture. The Greeks had no royalty to house, and because of the very favourable climate most of their activities took place out of doors, so that the people themselves paid little attention to their houses. Therefore, they were able to lavish their entire skill and attention on the perfection of their temples.

The temple was the principal building, and though the details of its plan varied, the form remained essentially the same. A temple was usually raised on a platform or stylobate; the principal room, known as the cella or naos, contained the statue of the deity to which the temple was dedicated, and there was occasionally a separate room for the treasury adjoining the cella. The whole was surrounded by a row of columns, or, in the case of the smaller examples, a row of columns was placed across the shorter end. There were variations on this basic arrangement (the Erechtheum has the most irregular plan of all Greek temples), but they were of only a minor character (Fig. 1). Even in its most complex form the plan retained the greatest simplicity, and the constructive principle on which the temples were built was also very elementary. The simplest way to erect a building is to put up two posts and then place a beam across the top, rather as at Stonehenge. This is known as the 'post-and-lintel' system of construction,

4

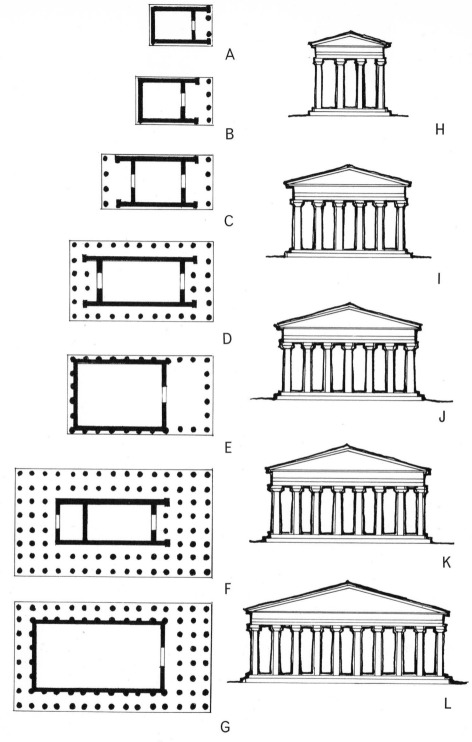

Fig. 1 *Various types of Greek temple in plan and elevation*

KEY TO FIG I

A *Distyle in antis:* having two columns in front between antennae or pilasters—the simplest form of temple

B *Prostyle:* having free-standing columns in front of the temple

C *Amphiprostyle:* having free-standing columns at both ends of the temple

D *Peripteral:* having columns all round the temple

E *Pseudo-peripteral:* having columns attached to the wall, and not free-standing as in a colonnade

F *Dipteral:* having a double row of columns all round the temple

G *Pseudo-dipteral:* appearing as dipteral from the front, but with the inner range of columns either attached to the wall or omitted altogether

H *Tetrastyle:* with four columns at the front

I *Hexastyle:* with six columns at the front

J *Heprastyle:* with seven columns at the front (very rare)

K *Octastyle:* with eight columns at the front

L *Decastyle:* with ten columns at the front

and was the method the Greeks used. This uniformity of construction is largely responsible for the unity which was one of the characteristics of Greek architecture. The marvel of it is that by subtlety of carving, decoration, and proportion, the Greeks were able to make these very elementary components so beautiful.

They made their buildings more aesthetically pleasing than Stonehenge by developing what is known as the order, a system of design which was the great feature of Greek architecture. The 'order' comprises the column, with its capital and base, and the entablature which the columns support. The Greeks developed three orders, the Doric, the Ionic and the Corinthian, to which the Romans added two more, of which we will have more to say later. Each of the orders had its own set of proportions, which evolved as the result of generations of trial and error. (Fig. 2 shows an order with the parts named.)

The origins of the orders are, like the origins of the architecture as a whole, open to conjecture. Many authorities claim that the Doric order evolved from wooden temple construction. Others trace its origin as far back as the tombs at Beni Hasan in Egypt (2500 B.C.–2200 B.C.). The Doric is the most characteristically Greek of the three orders, and it was the Greeks who imbued it with its most heroic form. The best examples of Doric temples are only to be found on Greek soil or in the territories colonized by the Greeks; some of the finest are in southern Italy and Sicily. The Ionic order was developed on the islands to the east of the mainland, and in Asia Minor. This was a more delicate order, and the most

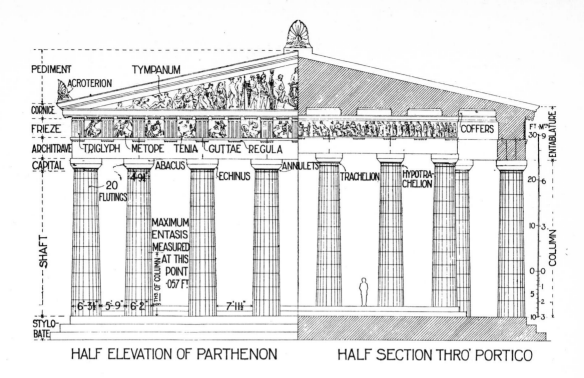

Fig. 2 *Diagram of an order with the parts named*

Fig. 3 *The Doric Order*   Fig. 4 *The Ionic Order*   Fig. 5 *The Corinthian Order*

Fig. 6 The Parthenon (477–432 B.C.) from the front

striking feature was the capital with its beautiful volutes. These two orders developed more or less contemporaneously; the more involved and decorative Corinthian order came later, and was little used by the Greeks. Its ornate character was more in keeping with the architecture of Rome, and it was the Romans who developed this order to its fullest extent (Figs. 3, 4, 5).

The characteristics of the three orders can be briefly summarized as follows:

The Doric Order

[Examples: three well-preserved temples at Paestum, and the Theseion and the Parthenon at Athens (Figs. 6, 7, 8).]

The COLUMN stood directly, without base, on the STYLOBATE, usually of three steps. The height of the column (including capital) was usually four to six and a half times the diameter at the base. The shaft of the column was usually divided into twenty flutes. (Other numbers were sometimes used, but twenty flutes ensured that a projection, or

arris, would come under each of the angles of the square abacus above, and at the same time allow a flute at each centre of the column when seen from front, back, and sides.) The capital consisted of annulets, echinus and abacus. The ECHINUS varied in

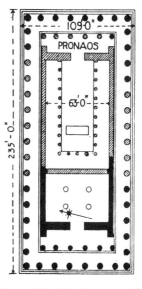

Fig. 7 The Parthenon—plan

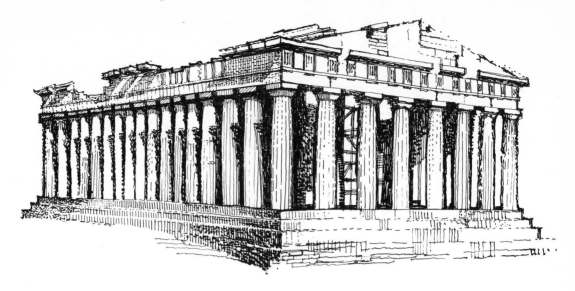

Fig. 8 The Parthenon, seen from the most advantageous viewpoint

the fullness of its curve according to the date of the building. The ABACUS was a square unmoulded slab, crowning the echinus.

The ENTABLATURE was usually about a quarter of the height of the 'order', and there were three main divisions:

(i) The ARCHITRAVE (or principal beam), usually of considerable depth, with a vertical face in one plane. (In the Ionic and Corinthian orders the architrave was usually divided into three horizontal bands, the upper ones each projecting slightly in front of the one below.) Separating the architrave from

(ii) The FRIEZE was a flat moulding called the TENIA, and under this, at intervals corresponding to the triglyphs, was a narrow band called the REGULA, with six small conical GUTTAE. The frieze was formed of TRIGLYPHS (which had three upright channels carved in them) alternating with METOPES; these rectangular panels were usually ornamented with relief sculpture, as at the Parthenon. The triglyphs came immediately over each column, and usually over each intercolumniation too.

(iii) The CORNICE. This was the crowning part of the order and consisted of a narrow moulding, beneath which was a corona or vertical face. The SOFFIT or underside was inclined to approximately the same angle as the rake of the roof and was decorated with flat blocks or MUTULES suggesting the ends of sloping rafters. The mutules occurred over each triglyph and metope.

The Ionic Order

[Examples: the Erechtheum (Plan, Fig. 9; Figs. 10, 11, 12), and the Temple of Nikè Apteros (Fig. 13).]

The Ionic order was developed in the islands and coastal cities of the Aegean in the first half of the fifth century B.C. The remarkable volute or scroll capital may have developed from the Egyptian lotus-motif, though the spiral has been found in Assyria and Asia Minor. Natural objects, such as the sea-shell or ram's horns, may also have suggested the idea to some observant architect. It remains almost impossible, however, to say with any certainty its exact origins. The column, including capital and base, was usually about nine diameters in height and had twenty-four flutes separated by fillets, not sharp edges as in the Doric. The moulded base had no square plinth. The capital was usually about two-thirds of the diameter of the column in height.

The entablature varied in height but was usually about one-fifth of the height of the whole order. It consisted of the usual three divisions:

(i) The ARCHITRAVE, which consisted of a triple fascia, reminiscent of superimposed beams.

(ii) The FRIEZE, sometimes plain, but usually ornamented by a band of continuous sculpture. It was not divided into triglyphs and metopes as the Doric, and in this way

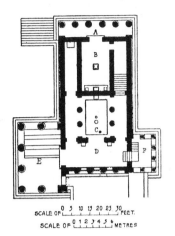

SCALE OF 0 5 10 15 20 25 30 FEET.
SCALE OF 0 1 2 3 4 5 6 METRES

Fig. 9 The Erechtheum—plan

it incorporated sculpture much more organically into the whole design. In a few Asiatic examples the frieze was omitted.

(iii) The cornice; here DENTIL BLOCKS were used in place of the mutules of the Doric order. These features are rather reminiscent of the square ends of rafter timbers.

Fig. 10 The Erechtheum (420–393 B.C.)
—a Greek temple with a most
irregular plan

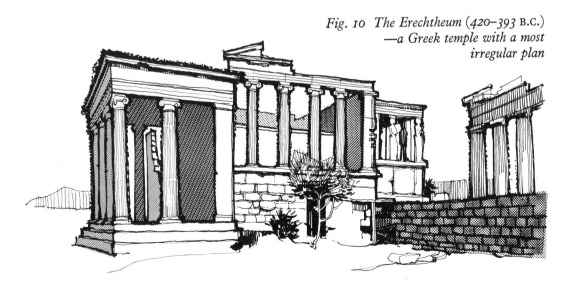

The Corinthian Order

[Examples: the Choragic Monument of Lysicrates and the very late Temple of Zeus at Athens, which was not completed by the Greeks (Figs. 14, 15).]

This was the least used of the orders. The base and shaft of the column resembled those of the Ionic, and it was generally about ten diameters in height. Like the other orders the column was usually placed on a stylobate. The distinctive capital, much deeper than the others, was usually about one and one-sixth diameters in height. The origin is uncertain, but it consisted of a deep inverted bell, the lower part of which was surrounded by two tiers of eight acanthus leaves. From between these leaves rose the CAULICOLI (stalks), which terminated in volutes supporting the abacus and central foliated ornament.

(The details of the three orders are illustrated in Figs. 3, 4, 5.)

All the orders conformed to a very carefully adjusted system of proportions which was based on the MODULE. The module corresponds to half the diameter of the column at the base, never at the top for this was always slightly less, as we shall see in due course. The module was then further split up into thirty smaller divisions known as PARTS. The module was thus not a fixed measure, but varied from building to building, depending on the size of the columns.

The orders provided the bare bones of the architect's language; in putting them together in the final building he observed even further refinements. Experience had made the Greek architects aware of certain distortions which were the result of optical illusion. In the correction of these distortions they evolved a number of very subtle modifications. These modifications are all to be found in the Parthenon, which is generally considered to be the culminating point of Greek architecture. If built perfectly straight, the long horizontal lines of stylobate and cornice appeared, when seen from a distance, to sag slightly towards the middle. To counteract this the architects gave these features a slight convex curve. The sagging effect may have been produced by the sloping lines of the pediment, for the shorter sides have a more pronounced curve than those on the long side, where this feature is absent. The columns themselves are all very slightly inclined inwards, and their axes, if produced, would meet at a point about a mile above the building. The pyramidal effect so produced is just enough to offset the known tendency of the parallel vertical sides of a building to look as if they are sloping outwards, making the building look wider at the top than at the base. The shafts of the columns are also given an 'entasis'. This is a slight convex curve, starting at the base of the shaft and continuing to the neck of the column where the diameter is usually about two-thirds of the width at the base. (This is why the module is always measured at the base diameter and not at the neck.) If the sides had been straight they would have appeared concave, which is a weak shape to support a roof. It was also common for the distance between the columns to be reduced from the centre of both façade and flank, and the corner columns were also rather thicker, because it was found that columns seen against the sky

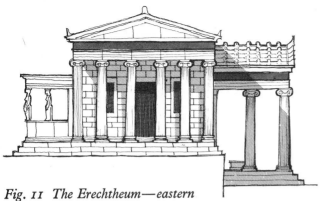

Fig. 11 *The Erechtheum—eastern elevation, showing the arrangement of the various levels of the temple*

Fig. 14 *The Choragic Monument of Lysicrates, Athens (353* B.C.*). A very early use of the Corinthian order*

Fig. 12 *The Erechtheum—the famous caryatids*

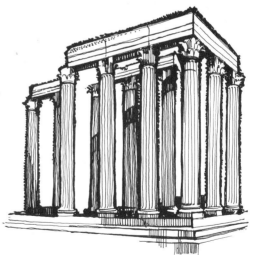

Fig. 13 *The Temple of Nikè Apteros, Athens (c. 426* B.C.*). One of the finest small Ionic temples, dedicated to the 'Wingless Victory'*

Fig. 15 *The Temple of Zeus, Athens (c. 147* B.C.*) A temple using the Corinthian order, which became increasingly popular in Hellenistic times*

looked thinner than those seen against the shaded wall of the cella behind.

The extraordinary lengths to which these optical corrections were carried produced buildings of great beauty and harmony. Some, indeed, would have us believe that Greek temples, and the Parthenon in particular, are the most beautiful architecture produced by the mind of man. If this assessment of the Greek achievement is accepted, one is bound to wonder what architects have been doing for the last two thousand years. The subject of the pre-eminence of Greek art in general is always fuel for debate. Greek architecture is great architecture, but it is a limited architecture. Perhaps the limiting factor of Greek building is the same as that of Greek sculpture, namely that the Greek artist set himself a goal which could be attained. The aim of the Greek sculptor was physical perfection, and this he achieved; but the greatest art is the outcome of the artist striving for the unattainable. The Gothic cathedral may be less 'perfect' than a Greek temple, but it is not therefore less great as a work of art. The temptation to regard Greek architecture as a world of its own must be resisted; their achievement must be looked at in the context of the whole development of western European architecture.

To return to a consideration of the development of this architecture as a whole, the Greek temple was, as we have said, built to house the cult statue or emblem of the deity to which it was dedicated, or more rarely to house an oracle. The statue was housed in a room which had a doorway facing the rising sun, whilst the altar was invariably placed out of doors on the east side of the temple. The temple itself usually stood in a sacred enclosure, often on a high rock called an acropolis. Entry to the enclosure was through a gateway or propylaeum; this was usually placed so that the temple was approached diagonally, as this was considered to give the best aspect.

The Egyptian temples had always had their columns inside the building; the Greeks on the other hand always placed their columns externally, thus giving them much greater importance. Where columns were used internally a different order was often employed. The Parthenon may well have had Ionic columns in the inner chamber, and the Propylaeum had both Ionic and Doric columns. The circular temple or Tholos at Epidaurus had Doric columns externally and Corinthian columns internally. Although it is reasonably certain that timber was used for the structure of the roof, it is by no means certain what method of construction was used, though it does seem safe to assume that the Greeks had no knowledge of the tie-beam. In all probability the roof-structure was covered with thin marble slabs, which, being translucent, would let in some light; otherwise the only source of daylight was the door.

By the middle of the fifth century stone construction had reached a very high state of development; no mortar was used in the building of walls, and the stones were accurately dressed and held in place by metal dowels—usually of iron or bronze— which were themselves set in molten lead. The columns were made up of separate drums, aligned by a central metal dowel set in wood. The final carving of the flutes on the columns was generally carried out when all the drums were in position. From about 480 B.C. onwards Pentelic marble replaced Parian marble as the most popular stone for building. The closer grain of this extremely beautiful stone made a much finer finish possible.

The exquisite detail of the mouldings is one of the most important facets of Greek architectural decoration. The contours of the mouldings themselves are of the greatest subtlety and are almost always made up of conic sections. Great emphasis was laid on the carving of these details, and the same rate of payment was made for carving the characteristic 'egg-and-dart' moulding as was made for the carving of the figure sculptures on metope or pediment. This meant that the best sculptors were not averse to this kind of work, though in later times such 'hack' decoration was handed on to apprentices just learning their trade.

The place of sculpture on these temples was considered of the first importance. The most common places to find this form of decoration were: on the top of the cella walls, where it was lit by reflected light from the marble floor of the portico; around the frieze, either in a continuous band in the Ionic order or in the metopes of the Doric order; and, lastly, in the pediments. Here the composition of the figures to fill the triangular space was both ingenious and aesthetically pleasing. The sculptures in the pediments were also of much deeper relief, and indeed often free-standing.

The carved decoration on cornice and entablature, and the volutes on Ionic columns and similar architectural features, were also freely coloured. The most popular colours were red and blue, with green, yellow, black, and gilding to give relief. The colour was often applied over a stucco base which, according to Vitruvius, was polished until it reflected like a mirror. To the eye of the northern European, used to a softer, more misty light, this must seem harsh, if not gaudy, colour, but in the hard brilliant light of the south such heraldic treatment would have been quite acceptable.

The consideration of the Ionic order poses the interesting problem of the treatment of the base of the column. Why did the Ionic column have a base, whilst the Doric did not? This can probably be explained on the grounds of either function or aesthetics, or a combination of the two. But first we must examine the purpose of these two additions to the vertical shaft. To place two members, one horizontal and one vertical, in direct contact must have been, to the Greek mind, too brutal a statement of function. Some intermediary must be interposed between the two members to make the transition from horizontal to vertical emphasis more smooth. Just as the capital, which can be any crude block (Fig. 16), is sufficient to carry out this transition at the top of the columns, and at the same time appears to gather the weight of the superimposed member on to its central axis so, at the bottom of the column, the base likewise softens the impact, and this time appears to spread the load over the ground.

The base of the Ionic column does just this, but the Doric is planted firmly without interruption on to the stylobate. This may be because the close spacing of the sturdy Doric columns made the architects feel that any protrusion around the base would cause

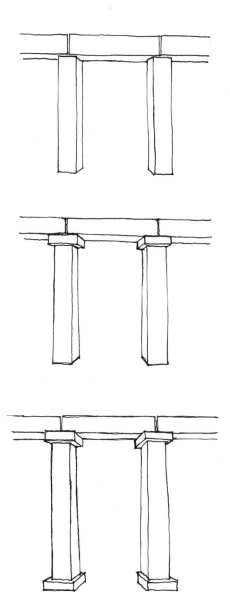

Fig. 16 The function of the capital, column, and base

Even this simple diagram shows how the insertion of capital and base gives a more 'finished' appearance to the whole

an unnecessary encumbrance and impede free passage to and from the temple. On the other hand the Doric is the most uncompromising, most intellectual, of the orders, and has little of the sensuous charm of the Ionic. On these grounds, therefore, it may be argued that the addition of a base was aesthetically superfluous. There can be little doubt that the sheer impact and strength of the Doric column would be dissipated by the addition of a base. There is only one example of Doric columns with bases, and that is the enormous temple of the Olympian Zeus at Agrigentum, in Sicily, but the structure here was so huge that the builders seem to have lacked the confidence to build in the genuine post-and-lintel style; the columns are attached to the walls, and the entablature is corbelled out over them. This example may give some confirmation to the idea that the bases were omitted to allow clear passage to the cella behind.

The more delicate proportions of the Ionic order, and the lighter entablature, made a wider intercolumniation possible, and so the question of free movement did not arise. The problem which faced the designers of the Ionic capital was that of the treatment of the volute when seen from the side. Undoubtedly the best view of the Ionic volute is from the front. From the side the semicircular form between the volutes is both heavy and cumbersome. Further, when the two volutes meet at right angles on the corner columns, the effect is most awkward. This problem was met by inclining these volutes at an angle of about 45 degrees, though even this was not altogether a satisfactory solution. This weakness in design seems to show fairly conclusively that the

Fig. 17

The Mausoleum at Halicarnassus (353 B.C.)

A restoration of the monument which introduced the word 'mausoleum' into the language

Ionic capital was intended to be used on columns between antae, and not on prostyle or peripteral temples (Fig. 1), where the columns are open to view from all sides.

The Ionic order was also used on the legendary Mausoleum at Halicarnassus (Fig. 17), and remains of this famous monument are now in the British Museum. From these remains, and Pliny's rather vague description, it is just possible to get some idea of what the building looked like, though there are still certain features which are difficult to explain.

As a focal point in the life of the community the acropolis was rivalled by the agora. As the course of the political system changed to its final democratic state, so the importance of the agora grew until finally it fulfilled a great number of functions. It was not only the market-place, but also the venue for public meetings and entertainments. In addition it was the scene of litigation and minor religious festivals. In many ways it foreshadowed the Roman forum, though architecturally it was less flamboyant in character. Around the open space of the agora were ranged the important civic buildings, and prominent among these was the *stoa*. This took the form of a long covered promenade or loggia. The roof was supported on one or (in the larger stoas) two rows of columns. Part of the space may well have been partitioned off to provide shops or stalls for the sale of merchandise. The Stoa of Attalus (Pl. 1) has recently been skilfully restored.

Some mention must be made of the Greek theatre, though remains are scanty and this makes reconstruction somewhat conjectural. In the first instance there seems little doubt that the stage was simply a circular earthen platform, so arranged that spectators could take advantage of the sloping side of a hill. Gradually the central stage, or orchestra, became an essential part of the arrangement, and by the middle of the fourth century theatrical conventions had become so advanced as to warrant the construction of a

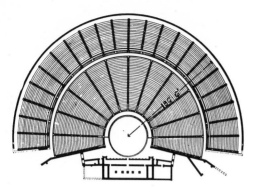

Fig. 18 The theatre at Epidaurus

long building which served as a changing-room for the actors, and whose façade, facing the audience, could be used for painted scenery. The theatre at Epidaurus is not only well preserved but also shows the way the architects took advantage of a fine natural setting (Fig. 18).

Although the architecture of Rome never reached the state of refined detail and subtle proportion achieved by the Greeks, it nevertheless had other qualities which were to prove of tremendous consequence in the development of European architecture. What Roman building lacked in elegance it made up for in imagination. Rome began to emerge as an important city around the year 500 B.C., and during the next century the Etruscan cities to the north were to fall under the rule of the rapidly expanding Republic. The influence of the art and architecture of these Etruscan cities made itself felt during this first century of domination. Greece herself and Asia Minor, however, remained faithful to Greek taste until the early years of Christianity. The tremendous differences between Greek and Roman civilization manifested themselves in the great

increase in the number of different types of buildings which were produced. Rome herself became both a mighty city and the centre of an empire which included most of the known world. A city of this magnitude needed an architecture which would impress, and give visible evidence of her power and wealth. To meet these demands not only were new types of buildings required, but also new methods of construction such as would provide open space within the buildings themselves.

The scope offered by the post-and-lintel system of building was no longer adequate. Because stone is strongest under pressure and weakest under tension it was necessary to place the columns very close in order to prevent the stone lintels cracking under the strain of the superstructure. Roman architects and engineers had therefore to find a new way of spanning the distance between columns so that they could be placed farther apart. The first of the structural advances that the Romans made was the development of the semicircular arch. This feature was not altogether new; it had been used by the Etruscans, and even in Hellenic times in Greece, but those builders had never exploited the advantages which this method of construction offered. The main advantage is that by spanning the gap between columns with an arch made up of small wedge-shaped stones (voussoirs), the architect ensures that the structure remains under pressure. The thrust of the superstructure is spread round the arch and on to the columns or piers supporting it. By this means the supports could be placed much farther apart, thus giving much greater flexibility of planning than was possible by the older method.

Plate 1 The Stoa at Athens, as reconstructed by the American School of Classical Studies

The logical development of the semi-circular arch is the barrel vault, which is simply made up of semicircular arches placed continuously one after another along the length of the building. Once the barrel vault became accepted the next step was the intersecting vault, where two barrel vaults meet at right angles. The mastery of this elementary form of vaulting was essential to the Roman architect, so that he could achieve the clear floor-spaces which were necessary for the conducting of the complicated public functions which the buildings had to house.

One of the most important materials in Roman construction was *pozzolana*. This was a variety of sandy earth which had the peculiar quality of making an exceedingly hard and cohesive concrete when mixed with lime. This material made possible some of the most daring feats of construction, for,

when set, domes and vaults made of this particular mixture were of rock-like solidity, and had little more lateral thrust than an inverted tea-cup. The lack of lateral thrust in the construction of domed structures made it possible to span enormous distances, and the dome of the Pantheon was of such magnitude that it remained unequalled until the introduction of steel construction in the nineteenth century.

The use of concrete led to a different method of wall-construction. Previously, where stone had been used as a building material, it had been customary to build the walls from solid blocks of stone throughout. The Romans, however, made extensive use of the composite wall, where a brick or rubble infilling was faced with a variety of substances such as marble, mosaic, alabaster, and so on. In this way decoration became

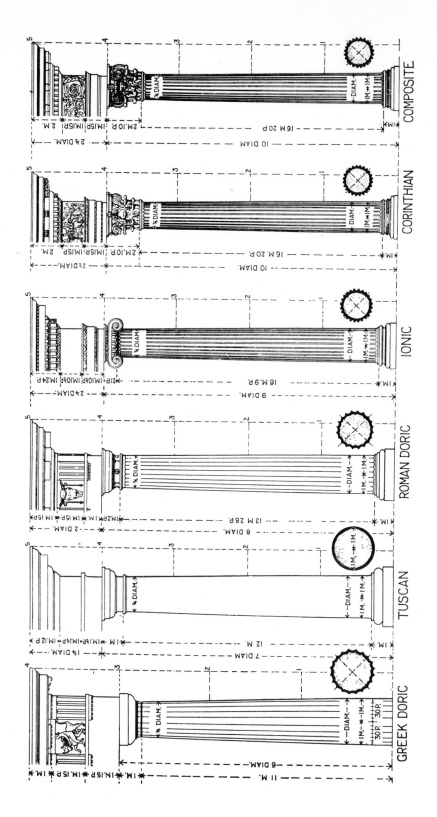

Fig. 19 Sir William Chambers's 'Comparative Proportions of the Classical Orders'

more lavish, and even the orders became decorative rather than structural features. This was a startling departure, for in Greek times the columns were always regarded as being structural and not decorative members. As we shall see, Alberti, following Roman precedent, regarded the orders as the principal feature of architectural decoration (see Chap. 3, p. 59 *et seq.*, for a discussion of this aspect of the use of the orders), and he was largely responsible for the Renaissance way of thinking about the orders.

Giving the orders a decorative, rather than a structural, role to play in a building led to a much greater freedom in the way they were used, and very frequently they were reduced to pilasters and half-columns attached to the walls. The Romans were also responsible for the introduction of two more orders, the Tuscan and the Composite. The Tuscan resembled the Greek Doric, but had none of the latter's strength and dignity and was only used in very early wooden temples built by the Etruscans. It was, however, taken up later by both Renaissance and nineteenth-century revivalist designers (see Sir William Chambers's comparison of the Greek and Roman orders, Fig. 19). The Composite was a combination of Corinthian and Ionic capitals. As the columns were now reduced to decorative elements and were no longer expected to carry any weight, their forms often became weaker and their shafts more elongated. The Corinthian was the most used of the five orders, for above all the others it typified Roman requirements —richness, costliness, and exuberance of ornament. The even more ornate Composite was usually confined to triumphal arches, of which the Arch of Titus is a good example.

Whereas the centre of Greek civic life had been the agora, the centre of Roman civic life was the forum. Originally it was the town market-place, lined with booths and shops. As town life became more attractive and the towns themselves became larger, the more important religious and public buildings soon came to be built round the forum, and the stalls and shops were pushed into the adjoining side streets. The forum at Rome was much more grandiose than the agora at Athens, and the many buildings gathered around it created a fine feeling of splendour.

Of the many types of buildings which the Romans erected, those which most concern us here are the temple, the basilica, and the triumphal arch, for these have the most direct effect on subsequent developments.

The Roman temple differed from its Grecian counterpart in several ways (Figs. 6, 7 and 20, 21). The internal arrangement was much simplified (Fig. 22), and the whole building was placed upon a podium. The treatment of the side walls was reminiscent of Etruscan models, though the continuation of the portico columns along the side wall in the form of half-columns (making the buildings pseudo-dipteral) was a Roman device. The whole building was clearly intended to be seen from the front, as the flight of steps suggests, and it was the custom to place the temple at the end of a vista, often backing on to an enclosing wall. Used in such a way the order demonstrated both its decorative and its structural aspects, as the columns round the portico were functional whilst those along the ·screen wall were decorative.

The basilica, that indispensable adjunct of Roman life and city planning, provided the

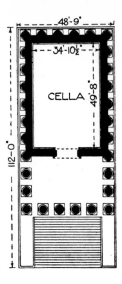

Fig. 20 *The Temple of Fortuna Virilis, Rome*
(C. 100 B.C.), showing the use of columns
as both decorative and structural members

Fig. 22 *The Maison Carrée—plan*

Fig. 21 *The Maison Carrée, Nîmes (C. A.D. 117–138)*
An excellently preserved example of a
Roman temple

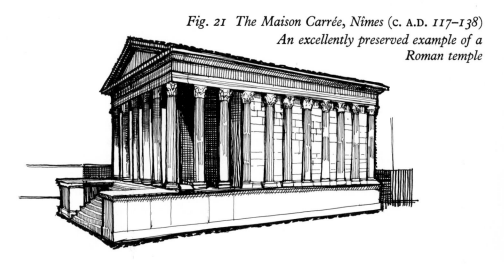

link between classical and Christian times. The Roman basilica was associated not only with the communal activities of social and political meetings, but also with the administration of justice, for it was the law court. The plan (Fig. 23) usually took the form of a rectangle twice as long as it was wide, the length being divided into either three or five aisles by two or four rows of columns, which supported galleries. From the gallery level further columns supported the roof. The construction of the roof was of timber, and though no actual roofs remain, it seems safe to assume that Roman engineers had

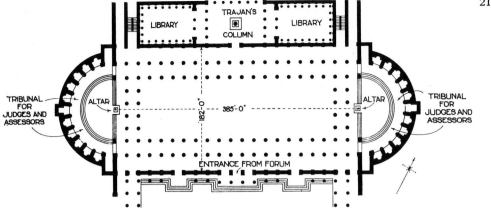

Fig. 23 The Basilica of Trajan, Rome—plan

mastered the use of the tie-beam. There were apsidal terminations at either or both ends, and entry was from the side or at one end. The tribunal was usually situated in the apsidal ends, usually on a raised dais, and often separated from the main body of the building by a row of columns or low balustrade. The form of the basilica is of importance because of the link with the form of the Early Christian church. Indeed, these early churches were often constructed from the remains of earlier basilicas.

The triumphal arch was another feature which was to prove of importance to the architecture of the Renaissance (Chap. 3) and that of subsequent periods. In Roman times these arches were put up for a variety of reasons, sometimes to commemorate a battle, sometimes in memory of some famous emperor or general. They appeared throughout the Roman Empire, and they were all similar in design (Figs. 24, 25). The larger ones consisted of a central round-arched opening, flanked on either side by smaller openings, whilst in the smaller ones the central arch was simply flanked by two massive piers. The orders, usually Corinthian or Composite, played an important part in the design, either as free-standing columns or as engaged half-columns. The massive attic storey was used as a place for further decoration, either a descriptive piece of relief sculpture or, another favourite Roman device, an inscription in the beautiful incised Roman alphabet. The order was usually carried through the attic in the form of pilasters. Sometimes these archways were placed across a main thoroughfare, or alternatively in the middle of an open space, as a piece of pure architectural decoration.

The need to accommodate enormous crowds of people in places of entertainment created the amphitheatre and the circus. The greatest of the amphitheatres was the Colosseum in Rome (Pl. 2). Architecturally, the merits of this building may be limited, though it did establish the sequence of superimposed orders which was to become universally accepted (i.e. the heavy Doric at the bottom, working through to the more delicate and decorative foliated orders at the top). As a piece of organization, however, its ingenuity cannot be denied. Structurally, it involved the building of a classical Greek theatre on a huge scale (it would hold about 50,000 people) and without the aid of a scooped-out hillside, which the Greeks had relied upon, to support the seats. The

Fig. 24 *The Arch of Constantine, Rome* (A.D. *312*)
An arch of fine proportions—compare
similar 'triumphal arches' by Alberti
and other Renaissance designers

Fig. 25 *The Arch of Trajan,*
Beneventum (A.D. *114*)
One of the best preserved
arches in south Italy

attached columns have no function, for the building is supported on the huge piers of the arcade which runs round the entire building. The skill of the Roman engineers is further demonstrated by the way the building material was varied according to the job it had to do in the structure as a whole. There were several different types of concrete, the heaviest being used near ground level, the lightest at the top of the building. Similarly the salient points of the stone structure were built with harder stone, forming a sort of skeleton holding the softer masonry together. When the building was in use, a silk awning was stretched across the galleries, leaving the central arena open to the sky. The footings for the posts which supported this great screen are still discernible in the building today.

The circular temples which the Romans built must be mentioned, for they are of importance in later church architecture, as we shall see in due course. One of the most beautiful of the smaller ones is the Temple of Portunus, in Rome (Fig. 26). Built in 31 B.C., probably by Greek craftsmen, this represents a delightful relief from the more full-blown and grandiose Roman buildings.

In complete contrast to the intimacy of this little temple is the Pantheon (Pl. 3). Though the form is essentially simple, the size is overwhelming and is a further testimony to the skill of the Roman engineers. The origins of the building are vague, though it is generally agreed that the greater part of the structure was put up by the Emperor

Fig. 26 *The Temple of Portunus, Rome* (*31* B.C.)
This most satisfying little temple should be compared with the Tempietto,
the dome of St Paul's, and the Hawksmoor mausoleum at Castle Howard

Plate 2 The Colosseum, Rome (A.D. 72–80). *As a piece of engineering this is a remarkable example of Roman skill, though architecturally it is comparatively uninteresting*

Hadrian between A.D. 120 and A.D. 124. It consists of a huge domed rotunda some 124 feet in diameter, with an impressive pedimented portico in front. Exactly how the dome was erected it is difficult to say, as there is so little visible evidence of any internal system of support, and it must be accepted as a *tour de force* of constructional technique. This is one of the most complete examples left to us of Roman architecture, though it has been much restored and the marble facing has been removed. The interior (Pl. 4) represents in its monumental simplicity one of the greatest achievements of the period. The modest size of the internal order, though criticized by some, gives the sense of immense space which the original architects must have intended. The deep coffers of the roof, which must substantially reduce the weight, were originally decorated with bronze ornaments. Though these have now disappeared, the stark angularity remains impressive. The interior is lit by a single oculus, 27 feet in diameter, in the crown of the roof.

Other examples of Roman engineering are the many aqueducts, of which the Pont du Gard near Nîmes, A.D. 14, is an excellent example (Fig. 27), and the many roads which they constructed throughout Europe for the speedy movement of troops and goods so necessary for the continuance of their huge empire.

The amphitheatres and circuses provided places of entertainment. The thermae, or bathing houses, provided the richer members of Roman society with the opportunity to while away their leisure hours. The plans of these buildings were complex and sophisticated, and represented the first attempt to

Plate 3 The Pantheon, Rome (A.D. *120–124*)—*exterior. Another example of Roman engineering ability and ingenuity*
From an engraving by Piranesi (*1720–78*), *whose work, though highly romanticized, was accurate and did much to influence the taste for Classical architecture in the eighteenth century*

Plate 4 The Pantheon—interior

design a whole scheme of rooms in conjunction with one another and at the same time make the shapes varied and pleasing. The Baths of Caracalla (Pl. 5) show the luxuriance of the interior decoration. Structurally, the complex heating arrangements provided problems which the engineers and architects must have enjoyed solving.

Water must have been a constant source of fascination to the Romans, for they scattered fountains over their cities, not only in Italy but throughout the empire. They took the form of either large basins of water, or spouting jets, or a combination of the two. These basic designs were enriched by bronze statuettes of figures or lions' heads, whilst coloured marbles made the designs more attractive.

The problem of accommodation in the towns was solved by building large tenement blocks. These must have served the great majority of the inhabitants, whilst the rich had their own private houses and sometimes a country villa as well. The main feature of the private house was the central open courtyard called the atrium, which acted as a waiting-room for retainers and clients. The rooms for guests and servants, and the semi-public rooms such as the library, were ranged round the four sides, and only received light from their doorways. Attached to the main body of the house was the peristyle, which often formed the garden, and was also the centre of the private part of the house.

The floors and walls were decorated with mosaics and fresco paintings, and the dining-room or triclinium was provided with couches for nine people—the recognized number for a Roman feast. The kitchen and pantry were situated at the side of the peristyle, farthest away from the entrance, but convenient for the side street (Fig. 28).

It is to the architecture of Greece and Rome that architects have turned again and again for inspiration. Of the two, perhaps

Fig. 27

The Pont du Gard, near Nîmes
(A.D. *14*)—*a fine example of*
Roman engineering

Plate 5 The Baths of Caracalla, Rome (A.D. 211–17)
*From a print of 1832, which gives a good idea of the splendour of
Roman interior decoration*

Fig. 28 A typical Roman house plan

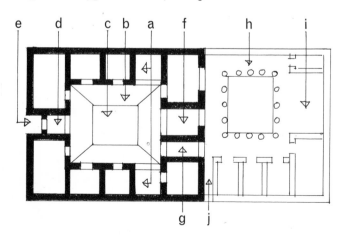

KEY
(a) *ala*
(b) *atrium*
(c) *impluvium*
(d) *fauces*
(e) *vestibulum*
(f) *tablinum*
(g) *passagio*
(h) *peristylum*
(i) *exedra*
(j) *posticum*

the Roman has proved the most potent source, for although Roman architecture is more brash, its architects were more fertile, their imagination more free ranging, in response to the more exacting demands made on their ingenuity. Whilst the orders placed rigid limitations on proportion, these very limitations seem to have formed their own strength and enigma. They were, and continued to be, both a unifying element and a vitalizing force, which acted as a spur and an inspiration to the best architects.

Early Christian, Byzantine and Romanesque

Of Early Christian, Byzantine, and Romanesque architecture there is not the space to say much here, but there are some developments which must be mentioned to maintain continuity. The most important structural developments were those made by the Byzantine architects in the development of the dome. Despite their mastery of engineering and dome construction the Romans had never managed to erect a dome over a square space. The difficulty is, of course, how to bridge the roughly triangular spaces which fall between the sides of the square and the perimeter of the circle which is contained in it (Fig. 29). There are several methods of making the conversion from square to circular shape. The simplest, but least effective, as it is only useful for very small structures, is simply to throw a large flat stone across the corner of the square (Fig. 30). A more successful one is to turn the square into an octagon by building diagonal arches (squinch arches as they are called) across the corner (Fig. 31). A further method is to corbel out a number of stone

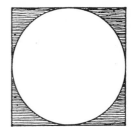

Fig. 29 *Plan of a dome on a square base, showing the roughly triangular segments between the circle and square*

Fig. 30 *The simplest way of bridging the corners, with triangular stone blocks*

Fig. 31 *The squinch arch. By placing one of these across each corner the square is converted into an octagon, which conforms much more closely to the circular base of the dome*

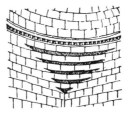

Fig. 32 *This method of corbelling out successive courses of stone makes a smoother transition, but is structurally weak*

Fig. 33

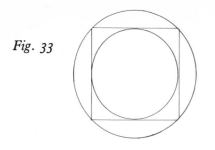

Fig. 34

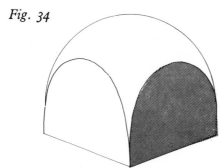

Fig. 35

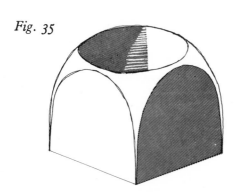

Fig. 36

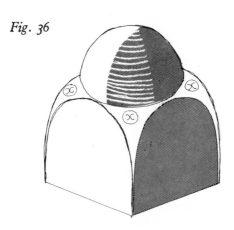

Fig. 37

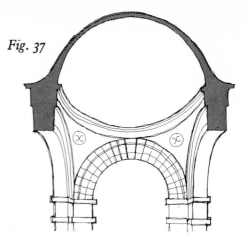

Figs. 33–7 Successive aspects of the construction of a dome on pendentives, marked 'x' in Figs. 36–7

courses which are concentric with the perimeter of the final dome (Fig. 32). These methods are effective but not suited to work on a large scale. The Byzantine builders managed to evolve the pendentive, which is more logical both in its transmission of thrust and in its continuity of line. The build-up of the dome on pendentives is shown in Figs. 33–37. By the use of these pendentives the outward thrust of the dome which they support is collected on the four points which form the corners of the square. One of the most striking examples of such construction is the great church of S. Sophia. The dome here is 107 feet in diameter and the four semicircular arches on which it immediately rests are supported on four massive piers some 25 feet wide and 60 feet deep.

The important contribution of the Early Christian architecture was the development of the basilican plan for the church. Based on the basilica of classical Rome, these churches, with their long colonnades of columns and rich mosaic decorations, set the pattern of church-planning which was to be adopted throughout the Romanesque and Gothic periods in the west and north of Europe.

Before we turn to a consideration of the Gothic period a brief reference to Romanesque architecture must be made. Too often this noble architecture is looked upon as a mere transition between two great styles. But the impressive cathedrals of France such as Vézelay and Toulouse, and the Norman cathedrals in England, such as Durham or St Albans, made up a style of monumental grandeur. This was a ponderous architecture but it can be considered as a fully developed style. Though lacking the brilliant daring of fully developed Gothic, it has other and equally satisfying aspects. A full consideration of the early Christian, Byzantine, and Romanesque styles falls outside the scope of this book, but they must not be overlooked in the development of European architecture, and the reading list gives suggestions for further study.

FURTHER READING

D. S. Robertson, *A Handbook of Greek and Roman Architecture*. C.U.P., 1954.

W. B. Dinsmore, *The Architecture of Ancient Greece*. 3rd ed., Batsford, 1950.

These two books are generally considered to be the standard works on the subject.

A. W. Lawrence, *Greek Architecture*. Penguin Books, 1957.
A very valuable work, containing a particularly interesting passage on the correction of optical illusion.

Gisela M. A. Richter, *A Handbook of Greek Art*. Phaidon Press, 1959.
A useful compendium with a good selection of illustrations.

Michael Grant (ed.), *The Birth of Western Civilization*. Thames & Hudson, 1964.
A series of chapters by various authorities on the life, culture and the visual arts of Greece and Rome. The illustrations are very lavish. The reader is also directed to the books by R. L. Scranton and F. E. Brown in the 'Great Ages of Architecture' Series mentioned in the general bibliography.

2

GOTHIC ARCHITECTURE IN EUROPE

It is paradoxical that one of the most fruitful and intensely creative periods in the whole history of architecture should be known by a term intended, when first used, to imply derision and scorn. The word Gothic implies a connection with the barbarous and warlike tribes who overran Europe in the fifth and sixth centuries; but in fact Gothic Architecture has no connection with these uncivilized hordes. Vasari (1511–71), the eminent Italian art-historian, coined the phrase to denote the 'crude barbaric' style which preceded the revival of the classic orders. The term stuck, and continued to be used as a term of abuse until the Gothic revival in the nineteenth century. The Gothic period covered the twelfth to the fifteenth centuries, and during this time an immense amount of building took place. Gimpel states that in France alone, during the three centuries 1050–1350, more stone was quarried than during the entire period of Egyptian architecture.*

Gothic art is a linear art. The tenacious line that bounds the figures in an illuminated manuscript, outlines the fantastic folds of the turban of Van Eyck's painting 'Portrait of a Man' in the National Gallery, or runs through the drapery folds of the carved figures on the front of Wells Cathedral or the porches at Chartres, is essentially the same. The vigorous angularity of a misericord or

roof-boss in some remote country church is fundamentally the same as that which gives such force and power to Grünewald's Isenheim altar-piece. These qualities, coupled with a love of the grotesque and a wry sense of humour, are universal elements of the Gothic spirit throughout Europe. They are unified by a sense of complete conviction in the value of the work undertaken and a simple faith in God, for whom many of the finest buildings were erected.

The fact that the style is associated with the pointed arch, and is sometimes referred to as the pointed style, should not mislead us into thinking that it was the Gothic builders who invented this feature. The principle had been known and used for some considerable time. The Assyrian palace of Khorsabad (c. 722 B.C.) uses the pointed arch in the drainage system, and in Romanesque work in both France and Italy it is used extensively. The church of Saint-Pierre-de-la-Tour (1119–35), at Aulnay, one of the most splendid Romanesque monuments, has pointed arches which form a fine porch-like arcade; and the south arm of the transept has a magnificent portal consisting of a pointed arch under the gable. There is also a pointed arch in the arcading over the door, in which is set a circular window. Internally, the naves of Autun and Paray-le-Monial use the pointed arch with grand effect. It was, however, the Gothic builders who realized the potential of the pointed arch and de-

* Jean Gimpel, *The Cathedral Builders* (Evergreen Profile Books, 1961).

veloped it in a much more adventurous way —exactly how and with what advantages will be considered later.

Although Gothic architecture is usually associated with sacred work, its achievements in the whole field of secular buildings must not be overlooked. They are as much a part of Gothic as the cathedrals themselves. Without doubt, however, it is the cathedral which is the summation of the medieval achievement. The Gothic cathedral is the outcome of a particular set of phenomena which produced some of the greatest buildings of all time. It was the combination of vision and the means to give visible expression to that vision that made possible the spire at Salisbury or the west front of Amiens. The vision was of God; for religion in medieval times was a much more integral part of life than it is today. It was the overwhelming desire to build to the glory of God, to send nave and tower soaring ever nearer to his domain that triggered off the astonishing feats of structural engineering which make up the simplest Gothic church.

The means to achieve these ends were the pointed arch and the flying buttress. By their use, the medieval mason was able to catch thrust and counter-thrust and direct them on to a point. Compare the plan of any typical Gothic cathedral with that of any Roman temple; Salisbury or Rouen are good Gothic examples, and the Pantheon at Rome or the Maison Carrée at Nîmes provide Roman models (Figs. 22 and 44). It will be seen at once that the first is a system of points, the other an arrangement of walls. Here then is the essence of Gothic planning. Without arch and buttress, crocket and finial, the rushing fugues of sculptured and

moulded form which make a Beauvais or an Amiens would have been impossible. Not that the mason's virtuosity came overnight. It was the result of many years' trial and error. So daring were the experiments made, that many a choir or nave collapsed during construction. Just as King's College Chapel at Cambridge is the culmination of work during the preceding centuries in England, so Beauvais is unthinkable without the experience of Amiens, Laon, and Notre-Dame de Paris.

It is this unity, this inevitability, which gives the architecture of these centuries their flavour. Once started, the progression from simple and direct statement to full orchestration of form follows with unerring logic. In France the massive boldness of Romanesque, as at Tournus or Nevers, gives way to the lighter forms of Amiens and finally to the flamboyance of Auxerre or Tours. In England this increasing richness can be seen in the window tracery, which from the simplicity of Early English plate-tracery develops into the more fanciful Decorated or the more intricate Perpendicular styles. English vaulting also shows this enhancement of a simple statement. For example, the simplicity of the nave at Durham grows to the more complex statement of vaulting by the introduction of tiercerons, as at Lichfield or Exeter. Further complexity is introduced by adding lierne ribs, which produce the more varied 'stellar' vaulting, as in the choir at Ely. Finally, English vaulting culminates in the fan-vault, as at King's College Chapel, Cambridge, or St George's Chapel, Windsor.

The habit of thinking in terms of watertight 'periods'—Early English, Decorated, and Perpendicular in English Gothic, and Rayonnant and Flamboyant in French work —though helpful as a guide, tends to lead to unnatural divisions. There are in fact certain points of similarity between French and English styles—for example, the Decorated reredos (c. 1335) at Beverley Minster, Yorkshire, would seem to be the forerunner of the French Flamboyant style, though it took almost forty years for the French to adopt a similar form of double-arched tracery. The sense of continuous development must not be lost, for the builders themselves did not think they were working in 'Early English' or 'Decorated' styles; they simply built as best they could. So, through the centuries, little pockets of work continued to be done in an earlier style outside the main stream. However, despite the fact that communications were slow and old traditions died hard, in the main, masons and patrons alike patronized the 'modern movement' with vigour and foresight.

The cathedral was the centre of life in the medieval town. To it, on religious festivals and saints' days, flocked the entire population. Amiens, covering 208,000 square feet, permitted the entire population of the city, just under 10,000, to attend the same service. The scale of the buildings was immense; today a 40-storey skyscraper would be required to reach the height to which the builders of Strasbourg pushed their spire of 466 feet.* These figures may further be compared with those of the new cathedral at Coventry. It was estimated that for a city of some 700,000, a cathedral to hold a con-

gregation of 2,000 would be adequate. As it stands at present, the building will hold 1,350 people in comfort and some 2,000 when filled to capacity. The building is some 270 feet long and 80 feet wide, which is only moderate in size when compared to Lincoln, which is over 450 feet, or Winchester, which is over 500 feet.

Around the walls of these cathedrals the illiterate peasants could see the stories of the scriptures set down in terms they could understand. The stained-glass windows set out in glowing colour the simple Bible stories. Carved on capitals and porches, choir stalls and bosses, incidents from the scriptures were protrayed in graphic form. Often walls were decorated both inside and out with paintings, and the cathedrals in their present state must only be a shadow of their former glory. The colour has been allowed to deteriorate, and in only a few places, such as York Minster, have attempts been made at restoration.

In work of extraordinary variety and vitality, these artists set down in wood, stone, glass, or paint their various subjects. Scenes of everyday life, often of almost Rabelaisian humour, jostled scenes of the Resurrection and Crucifixion, portrayed with moving simplicity and honesty of purpose. The grotesque rubs shoulders with the majestic in a rich, but never tawdry, welter of incident. Today we tend to look only at the surface of this decoration, missing its true significance, because the language these carvers and glaziers used was so full of symbolism which is no longer part of our experience.

What of the men who built these complex structures—the masons, carpenters, quarrymen and apprentices? Working days were

---

* For these and many other facts and comparisons the reader is referred to Jean Gimpel, op. cit.

long, usually from dawn to dusk, but with the large number of feast days—several monastic records catalogue as many as thirty in the course of the year—a five-day week was usual. In fact five days seems to have been the most common unit for payment.*

Unfortunately the Latin tongue does not permit of differentiation between the man who quarries the stone and the mason who does the final dressing and carving of mouldings or figures, and it was to be well into the fourteenth century before the mason had enough independence to call himself a sculptor in the modern sense of the word. However, despite the general anonymity, which would be well nigh intolerable to the modern 'artist', several of these masons are known to us. Their signs have been found on the doorways, roof bosses, and many other features which they carved so lovingly —often in the most inaccessible places— but visible to the eye of God if to no one else.

The title 'architect' is a product of the Renaissance concept of the arts. Such an intellectualization would have been impossible in the period under review. Nevertheless the design of each of the great cathedrals was conceived by a single man; or at least one man was in charge of each stage of the building programme. He was known as the master-mason and must be regarded as a trained architect, well versed in design, engineering, and geometry. Unlike his Renaissance and modern counterpart, however, he was not above turning to manual work on the site.

One of the most famous of these master-masons was Villard de Honnecourt, the thirteenth-century cathedral designer. His

notebook is still in existence and gives an invaluable picture of the insatiable curiosity of the minds of these men. This extraordinary document, consisting of thirty-three leaves of parchment, contains plans, elevations, and sketches of existing buildings. Besides these there are notes on figure drawing and design, mechanics, furniture design, and practical geometry, as well as drawings of wild and domestic animals, birds, and insects. This list shows the wide interest and the extent of the knowledge of these early architects. So wide were de Honnecourt's interests that architecture occupies the least space in his notebook. Like other master-masons of the time, he travelled extensively. Sometimes this travel was undertaken by the masons for study, sometimes in search of work, or better pay and conditions.

It is against this background that we must view the achievements of the Gothic period. It is this vital creative force, this urge to give vivid expression to a transcendental vision, that we must have in mind when next we stand in wonder in front of Wells or Beverley, Chartres or Reims (Pl. 25, Fig. 116; Fig. 118; Pl. 12; Fig. 51).

Before consideration of the stylistic development of Gothic in Europe can be undertaken it is essential that the principles of vaulting be thoroughly understood.

One of the cardinal problems in architectural design is the roof, i.e. how to spread a canopy over a given area, and support it without danger of collapse. The post-and-lintel method of Greek and Egyptian times was primitive, and allowed little freedom of design. The Roman engineers developed the semicircular arch and vault—a method which gave more flexibility but still had

* Jean Gimpel, op. cit.

serious limitations. Stone is strong under compression, but weak under tension; hence, it will be recalled, the close spacing of columns in Greek temples. The round arch with voussoirs means that the downward pressure is dispersed round the arch, each stone taking part of the strain.

The waggon (or barrel) vault—merely a continuation in depth of the round arch, i.e. in the form of a half-cylinder—was heavy and cumbersome, both to look at and to build. It was expensive too, as it needed extensive timber centering erected along its entire length to support the stones until the whole stone structure was complete. Moreover, as pressure was exerted not only downwards but also outwards, owing to the pressure of the arch voussoirs, the walls on which these pressures were exerted throughout their entire length had to be sufficiently thick to contain the thrust. Also, the intersection of two vaults had to be square on plan to provide uniform roof-height (Figs. 38, 39). Even so, the diagonal arches were flattened (Fig. 40), resulting both in a weakening of the structure and an increase in outward thrust. When semicircular arches were used on oblong bays, the arch on the shorter side had to be raised on stilts to keep the roof-line flat (Fig. 41).

The round arch and waggon-vault, though a step forward in constructive techniques, was, as we have shown, too cumbersome a tool to be the real solution to the problem. It was the pointed arch which gave the master-mason the freedom he required. It now became possible to achieve a flat roof-line simply by adjusting the degree of pointedness of the arch employed (Fig. 42), and the incorporation of oblong bays was no

longer a problem. (An oblong bay permits the use of more piers down the length of a nave or transept and this means that each pier has less weight to support.) Further advantages were that the extensive centering necessary for the waggon-vault was unnecessary. The ribs which replaced the groins of earlier work could be erected over light scaffolding, which could be removed after the plaster had set. The cells then could be filled in with lighter slabs, called voutains, using a circe or light movable centre. Not only was this method of roofing lighter in weight, providing an opportunity for enlarging clerestory windows, but it also *looked* lighter and suggested a less solemn rhythm than round arches; and, of course, the pointed arch carried the eye up to God far more satisfactorily than its more self-contained predecessor.

As the skill of the masons increased, the ribs became lighter, and in England at any rate, more numerous. With the development of fan-vaulting, ribs ceased to have a function and were often carved as decoration on the slabs of stone set in the vault. But this development must be studied further in the more detailed account of English Gothic.

To support the weight of their roofs, the French designers developed the flying buttress. The English, who did not build as high as the French, had no need of such extensive or deep buttressing systems. These flying buttresses give that peculiar flavour, rather like some fairy cascade, to the apsed east-end of so many French cathedrals. Again, with true Gothic ingenuity, the problem is solved with mastery. The function of each part of the flying buttress is shown in Fig. 43.

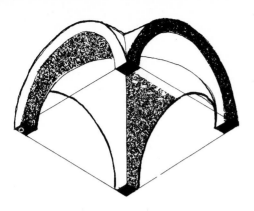

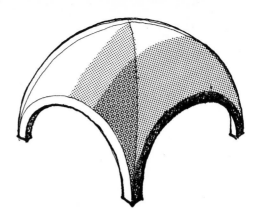

Fig. 38 An intersecting waggon vault, viewed from below

Fig. 39 An intersecting waggon vault, viewed from above, when the transverse arch is semicircular, giving a domical vault

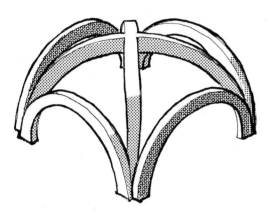

Fig. 40 Early rib-structure of intersecting waggon vaults

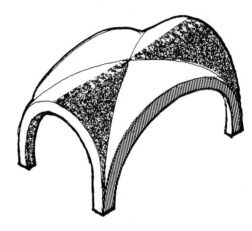

Fig. 41 The arrangement of semicircular arches over an oblong bay

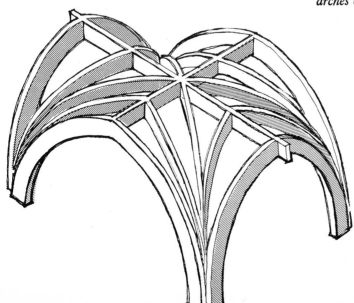

Fig. 42

This diagram shows the rib-structure where pointed arches are used. A flat roof-line is now easily achieved simply by adjusting the degree of pointedness of the arches

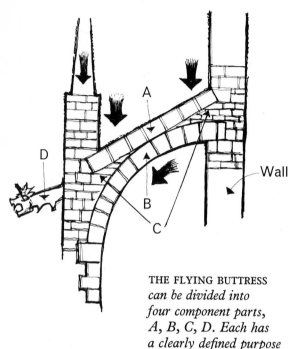

A

D

Wall

B

C

THE FLYING BUTTRESS
*can be divided into
four component parts,
A, B, C, D. Each has
a clearly defined purpose*

A THE PROP MEMBER *can resist the outward
pressure of the building up to breaking
point. It also provides load for:*

B THE ARCH COMPONENT, *which exerts
continuous pressure against the wall. It
also prevents buckling of A by means of*

C THE INFILLING, *which unites A and B,
giving each mutual strength*

D THE GARGOYLE, *which carries away rain-
water channelled across the top of A, and
by discharging well clear of the masonry
prevents excessive corrosion due to water
running down the face of it.*

Even the lofty and beautifully embellished
PINNACLE *gives extra stability by its weight*

Fig. 43 The flying buttress

Before embarking on a more detailed
study of national styles, a comparison of
typical French and English plans will
demonstrate the differences in approach to
the problem. For this purpose Salisbury and
Amiens may be taken as typical of English
and French design respectively (Figs. 44,
45). At first glance, there are radical differences of layout. The French plan looks more
unified, as the outline of the shape is not
interrupted by the protruding transepts.
Salisbury, like Lincoln and Wells among
others, employs double transepts. These
transepts are usually at least two bays deep,
whilst it will be noted that transepts on
French cathedrals generally protrude by
only one bay.

The French favour a double aisle whilst
the English use only one; this gives the
French cathedral a much greater width in
relation to length. The monastic origin of
many English cathedral foundations gave
rise to the need for a cloister, which is rare
on the Continent, and it also helps to account
for the fact that the English cathedral is often
sited away from the busy town centre, as at
Ely, where the church is set in a close, or
Durham, where few can fail to be moved by
the sight of the cathedral towering so majes-
tically over the town from its hill-top site.

The processional nature of the French
religious service calls for movement around
the altar. To facilitate this movement the
aisles are continued round the apse to form
an ambulatory. Where the ambulatory gives
on to small radial chapels, the arrangement
is known as a chevet, as at Amiens.

The square east-end is favoured by
English planners, and in most cases the
earlier apsidal form has been squared off, as

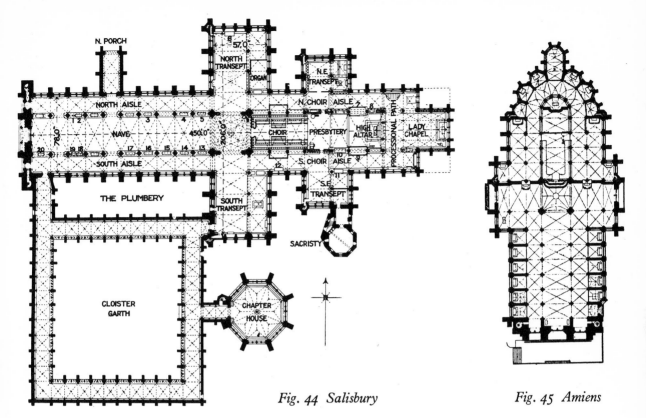

Fig. 44 Salisbury   *Fig. 45 Amiens*

*The plans of these two cathedrals clearly illustrate the
differences between typical English and French planning*

at Ely, St Albans, or Durham. Norwich, Lichfield, and Canterbury remain as three cathedral churches in England without square east-ends—Canterbury, with its almost circular corona, being unique.

In the case of chapter houses, too, the designs are different; the English used the polygonal form, as at Salisbury, York, or Lincoln, whilst the French favoured the rectangular form of plan. The English often chose to make a prominent feature of a central tower, as at Salisbury, Gloucester, or Hereford. Durham and York, however, provide an alternative arrangement, for here the central tower is combined with the two western towers. Lichfield, with its three towers and spires, remains unique. The

French tended to plan in groups of towers. Chartres was to have had nine and Laon seven, but otherwise two western towers are characteristic—as at Reims or Amiens. A *flèche* (slender wooden spire) often took the place of the central tower which English builders placed on the intersection of their transepts and naves.

These differences constitute the main points of contrast between French and English cathedral plans. The striving for height of the French Gothic designers has already been emphasized, but this was not so characteristic of English work. Westminster, with a height of 102 feet, is the highest vault in this country, whereas in France Beauvais rises to 157 feet. The height

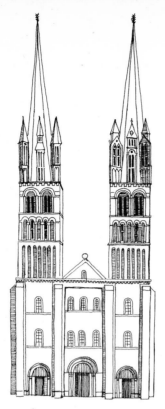

Fig. 46 St-Étienne, Caen (1066–77)—the Abbaye-aux-Hommes

Fig. 47 The Abbey Church of St-Denis, Paris (1132–44)

Fig. 48 Notre-Dame, Laon (1160–1225)

Fig. 49 Notre-Dame, Paris (1220–50). The west front was started in 1208.

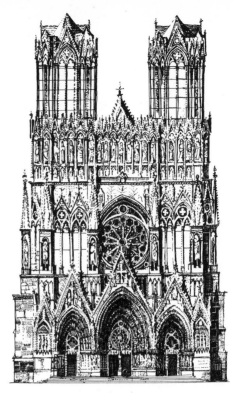

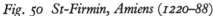

Fig. 50 St-Firmin, Amiens (1220–88)   *Fig. 51 Notre-Dame, Reims (1255–90)*

THE DEVELOPMENT OF THE WEST FRONT IN FRENCH CATHEDRAL DESIGN

The west fronts of the six cathedrals here illustrated show clearly the development of this feature in French design. To the medieval mind the cathedral was a symbol of heaven and the west front formed the gateway. As building technique improved and as the ability to express ideas in stone developed, so the western façade became at once more unified in design and structurally more adventurous.

The lower part of Caen Cathedral has that fortress-like quality which is so typical of Romanesque (the spires are later additions). The front of St-Denis has many features which form the basic elements of later designs and which became the lasting glories of medieval French design. Laon presents a dynamic design of tremendous power. The sense of movement created by the deep recesses of the porches and the rhythmic contrast between circle and pointed arch make a memorable composition. Notre-

Dame de Paris is a design of great subtlety, and here the line of the kings of France is introduced: all the ingredients of the west front are now present—triple doorway, arcade and line of kings, rose window and twin towers. At Amiens and Reims these features are used with increased virtuosity. The division of the façade of Amiens, where the line of kings is placed directly on top of the arcade, has been criticized; nevertheless, this is a design of great richness. Whilst at Reims, the elegance of the design and the unity of composition are incomparable, the relationship between architectural form and sculptural decoration here reaches a state of rare homogeneity. From the solidity of the buttressed doorways to the lightness of the towers the graduation of weight in each succeeding stage is perfectly judged, so that the eye moves easily and smoothly upwards. The result is architecture of the highest order.

of English cathedrals is apparent rather than real. The piers are placed much closer than in French examples and the repeated verticals down nave and choir help to give an illusion of height. Owing to a greater use of elaborate carving on mouldings, capitals, and tombs, English interiors are richer and more intimate. Though French cathedrals impress by their height and staggering sense of space, to some English tastes they appear rather cold and barren.

If a style can be said to have started in any one building, or to have been the product of any one man's imagination, then Gothic can be said to have started at the Abbey Church of St-Denis (Fig. 47) on the outskirts of Paris, and Abbot Suger was the man responsible. Abbot Suger must have been a man of extraordinary vision, foresight, and courage, for the design of St-Denis was well ahead of its time. Unfortunately the haste with which the building was erected (1137-44), led to disaster, for it collapsed and had to be rebuilt within a century of its construction. Parts of the original building still remain, and from reconstructions it can be seen to have possessed, in embryo, the essential features of the typical French Gothic west front. It is true that the rather unique square shape of the main body of St-Denis, with its twin towers of modest proportion, presents a rather unexciting comparison with the lofty spired Abbaye-aux-Hommes at Caen (Fig. 46). Nevertheless, the other features—triple doors, and the large circular window, destined to develop into the rose-window of Paris or Chartres—are clearly evident. The open gallery is missing, as well as the line of sculptured

kings, so much in evidence at Amiens and Reims; but it is not difficult to see how, from this rather pedestrian and unspectacular beginning, with its play of rhythm between round-headed and pointed arches, the west front of subsequent cathedrals grew.

Sens, almost contemporary with Suger's St-Denis, is better preserved and here the early use of the sexpartite vault can be seen. But it is in Notre-Dame de Paris that the culmination of twelfth-century building is apparent (Fig. 49). Begun in 1163 by the Bishop Maurice de Sully, it was almost complete, except for the west front, by the end of the century. It is this latter feature which sets the pattern for the typical French cathedral west-end, and here comparison with the west-ends of Laon, Amiens, and Reims is instructive. Each uses the same ingredients, but each has its own individuality. That of Laon (Fig. 48) is a magnificently bold conception, full of character and rugged strength. The one at Amiens (Fig. 50), arguably the most satisfactory west front of all, has tremendous virility and vitality compared to that of Reims (Fig. 51), which is lighter and perhaps more sophisticated in conception.

During the thirteenth century French Gothic reached its full maturity, and work in the Île-de-France district dominated the period. Three cathedrals, Chartres (1194), Rouen (1200), and Reims (1212), were rebuilt after extensive damage by fire; Amiens and Beauvais were begun in 1220 and 1225 respectively. Bourges and Coutances, and the choirs of Le Mans and Auxerre, all date from the thirteenth century also.

In all these structures, except Bourges, quadripartite vaulting replaces the sexpartite of the earlier century. The change is justifiable on structural grounds, as masons found that it was easier to contain the thrust of diagonal members in a narrow bay, where the angle between diagonal and transverse ribs was less than 45 degrees. This reversion to a simpler form of construction meant that the French never achieved the glorious complexities of rib arrangements common in England. True, the richly intricate English roofs were the result of a less systematic, more rough-and-ready method of dealing with the voutains (Figs. 52, 53), but this seems a case where a less methodical approach has produced more spectacular results (Pl. 6).

The fourteenth century was not a period of rapid progress in France. The energy expended in the preceding centuries seems to have sapped enthusiasm and inspiration. Internally, disastrous wars and the Black Death all but brought building to a standstill. New enterprises were rare, and indeed it was often difficult to raise enough money to complete existing schemes. The most common development was the addition of side chapels between existing buttresses. Generally, however, work carried out in this period had a dull, rather mechanical aspect, and lacked the power of invention and creative force of the preceding century. Auxerre is a good example of work of this period. The coldness of the vaulting shafts, which run in unbroken lines from floor to roof-ridge, is somewhat offset by the enormous clerestories, which provide a rich array of stained glass.

The fifteenth century saw a revival of inspiration, and the style known as Flamboyant remained in use until ousted by the

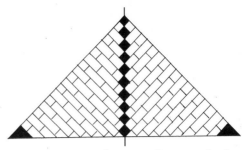

Fig. 52 The use of rectangular voutains by English masons required the use of a stout rib to cover the jagged edges left down the roof ridge

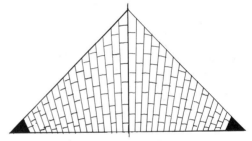

Fig. 53 The more carefully carved and shaped voutains used by the French made a neater joint, and ribs were not so necessary

Italian Renaissance style introduced by Queen Catherine de Médicis. There was little change in plan or elevation, but the method or ornamentation was revolutionized. To quote a phrase, 'decorated architecture took the place of architectural decoration'. The ogee, or reverse curve, was introduced, probably from England, and the tracery became a combination of soufflet and mouchette shapes (Figs. 54, 55). The interior stonework became more severe, but fittings and furniture were of extreme richness.

The façade of La Trinité at Vendôme is a fine example of the style (Pl. 7). Tracery replaces sculpture in the tympanum of the doorway, the line of figures has gone; so,

Plate 7 The Abbey Church of La Trinité, Vendôme (c. 1500)—façade

A fine example of the flamboyant style. Note the
profusion of 'soufflet' and 'mouchette' shapes

Plate 6 The Abbey Church of St-Denis, Paris (begun 1231)

This view of the nave and choir shows the great height of French
churches and the apsidal termination to the east-end. The careful
shaping of the voutains in the nave-vault is also clearly visible

Fig. 54 Soufflet   Fig. 55 Mouchette

too, has the rose-window; but the design is unified, though a little restless. The elaborate tracery is almost entirely composed of mouchette shapes, which show clearly how the style got its name. Cusping is carried on round the arches, even those of the flying buttresses, giving the whole a most sumptuous effect. St-Maclou is a magnificent parish church in the same style, with a façade of five open porches, the two outer ones being bent back. Again the carving is rich with false gables, so popular with French designers (Pl. 8).

With this final flurry of activity the Gothic style in France came to an end. Suger's St-Denis had provided the flash of inspiration which, complete in one building, had presented a new style. The Gothic builders had tried to provide in their cathedrals something more than a house of God. They had attempted to create a gateway into heaven. The more one becomes familiar with their achievements, the more one believes that in many buildings they all but succeeded. Certainly their piety and conviction can never be doubted, for the building of a cathedral was a corporate act of worship, a task in which the whole town joined, often

at great personal loss. Even in times of great hardship, money and labour must have been forthcoming for the town's cathedral or church.

The age of the cathedral closed, and with it went a way of life. A new culture grew up, with other interests, and the architect had to serve these new ideologies. The cathedral ceased to play such a vital part in society. Each of us must evaluate the success subsequent designers have had in their solutions to the problems of cathedral-building in a different ideological environment.

Notre-Dame de Paris

As we have already noted, this façade (Fig. 49) set the pattern for the typical French west-end. The main body of the church, begun in 1163 from the designs of Eudes de Montreul, was complete before work on the west front was started. Commenced about 1200, work was not finished on the towers until fifty years later.

The composition of this bold façade is one of those instances of inspiration which abound in French Gothic. The transition from the almost Romanesque solidity of the first stage to the lightness of the towers is a masterly conception.

The triple doorways, deeply recessed between the heavy buttresses necessary to support the twin towers, are topped by the massive row of twenty-eight kings. By some miracle this line of sculptured figures does not cut the composition completely in half, and the next stage, containing the rose-window, flanked by bluntly pointed arches, passes smoothly into the final lightness of

Plate 9 Laon Cathedral (begun c. 1160)—interior of nave
This shows how the boldness of the exterior is carried into the interior treatment. Note also the square east-end and sexpartite vaulting

Plate 8 St-Maclou, Rouen (begun c. 1500–14)—façade
It is interesting to compare the façades of Vendôme and Rouen with those of Amiens and Paris

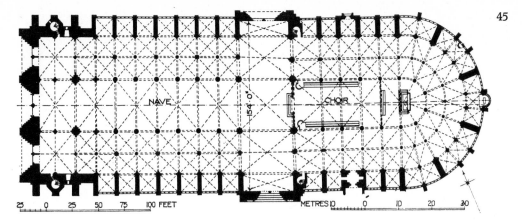

Fig. 56 Notre-Dame, Paris—plan. Note the bent axis and the very simple system of vaulting in the chevet

the upper gallery from which the towers flow.

The plan, either by accident or design, is on a bent axis, but is otherwise typical of its kind. The chevet, the earliest of its type, is notable for the vaulting scheme, which is simple yet ingenious in concept (Fig. 56). The glass in the three rose-windows, west-end, and north and south transepts, though much restored, is particularly rich.

This majestic building may be taken as a typical example of twelfth-century design, or, as it is sometimes called, 'Gothique à Lancettes'. There is much fine sculpture on the west front, though it suffered a great deal during the Revolution. This great church was extensively restored in the second half of the nineteenth century, when the central flèche was added.

Laon, Notre-Dame

A noble western façade of great boldness (Fig. 48) is the most striking feature of this splendid cathedral. Sited on the summit of a hill, the building dominates the landscape much as Durham does. The dynamic rhythm between rose-window and flanking bays and their relationship to their supporting arches, make a most vital impression. The tremendous depth of the doorways, created by the heavy buttresses which carry the two towers, is a memorable piece of three-dimensional design. It is almost as if some superhuman being had pushed and pulled the stones until finally his purpose was achieved. If the more intellectual poise of, say, Amiens or Reims may be likened to a Bach fugue, then surely this structure may be likened to the titanic struggles of Beethoven or Brahms.

The towers were notable from their inception. Villard de Honnecourt made drawings of them in his sketch-book. Again that tremendous flow, created by almost semi-circular arches, is maintained. An interesting feature of the towers is the statues of bulls which adorn the corners; they are set there to commemorate the noble animals who dragged the stones up the hill to build this mighty edifice. Note that here the gallery is broken, thus avoiding the strong horizontal emphasis of Paris. As at Paris, however, a sexpartite vault is used in the nave (Pl. 9). Laon is almost alone in that it has a square east-end.

Plate 11   Beauvais Cathedral (begun c. 1235)—exterior of choir
This shows the complex system of flying buttresses required
to contain the outward thrust of roof and walls

Plate 10   Amiens Cathedral (begun 1220)—interior of nave
Note the tremendous impression of height and the way the
whole is held together by the strong horizontal band of

Amiens, St-Firmin

The western façade here, along with that at Reims, constitutes the apogee of the Geometric or Rayonnant style of the thirteenth century. Amiens is perhaps the more impressive of the two; more solid in impact and some 220 feet high, it creates an overwhelming impression of grandeur (Pl. 10). It will be noted that quadripartite vaulting is reverted to in the nave, and here the designer, Robert de Luzarches, has shown such mastery of the engineering problems, that the simplicity achieved is almost cheeky. Yet few structures have realized their aims with less fuss or more grace. Few decorative features have been so cunningly placed as the band of exquisite foliage which runs round the entire building just below the triforium. It is this feature which contributes the necessary horizontal to hold the parts together, and is the foil to the otherwise unbroken rush upwards from floor to crown of vault.

Reims, Notre-Dame

This fine cathedral (Fig. 51) has suffered greatly at various times throughout its history, and is now much restored. There was a severe fire in 1481, and much exterior damage was inflicted during German bombardments in the First World War. It is as well that the fabric was constructed so solidly, better probably than that of Amiens, for at this time the vaulting had great holes knocked through it and many buttresses were smashed. However, restoration has been loving and skilful.

The present building was begun in 1212,

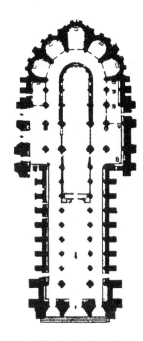

Fig. 57 Reims Cathedral—plan

from the designs of Jean d'Orbais. The building was carried through with great speed, as the west front was started about the middle of the century and the rose-window opened before 1290.

The west front, whilst not possessing the cliff-like strength of Amiens, is a composition of great beauty—one might almost say sophistication, but perhaps 'subtle unity' is a more fitting expression. The gallery of kings is here raised to the top of the main body, immediately under the very fine towers. It is in one continuous band, but avoids the dangers inherent in the arrangement used at Notre-Dame de Paris, for now the pointed niches lead naturally into the open-work of the towers.

The great rose-window is echoed in the smaller rose-windows which take the place of the more usual carved tympana over each of the doors. The three gables are filled with a sumptuous array of carving, by various hands and of various standards. Nevertheless it is generally held to be the consummation of the work of the period. Whilst the carving is very rich, it is never allowed to obliterate or detract from the essential form of the building. The buttressing, with its magnificent decoration of the heavy pinnacles, attains, with the great angels with outstretched wings, one of the most superbly imaginative touches in the whole of the French achievement.

This is, of course, the coronation cathedral of France—hence the broadening of the eastern arm to include transepts into the chevet. In this way the necessary space is achieved for the coronation ceremonies. Because of this close relationship with French royalty, Reims is a treasure house of works of art and stained glass.

Beauvais, St-Pierre

This building (Pl. 11) is chiefly notable for its great height, which on first acquaintance is almost terrifying. The whole conception has proved to be a debating-point for pedants. Opinions range from active dislike to adulation.

The height to the crown of the vault is 157 feet, and for many generations it was the highest building in the world. Unfortunately it was never finished, and in its present state it looks an ill-proportioned lump. None can deny, however, that it is the product of an imaginative genius that has hardly been surpassed. The point has already been made in this survey of the Gothic movement that, once started on its course, the style went from experiment to experiment. Vaults were pushed higher, walls became thinner and lighter. The whole structural problem was brought down to increasingly daring arrangements of thrust and counter-thrust, until finally the whole building became poised at a point of equilibrium.

Each building was an adventure into the unknown. Certain rule-of-thumb principles could be applied, but in each major work attempted, the designer tried to improve on, or go one better than, the last that was built. If this method of building is practised for long enough, at some point a building like Beauvais must be attempted. Here imagination and vision just overstepped the bounds of possibility. The end had been reached; stone construction with the knowledge and techniques available would not stand this daring enterprise, even with the help of iron bars and chains.

The roof fell in 1284. The reconstruction of the choir and the introduction of intermediate piers was completed in 1347. This task of interposing new piers between those already in existence, and the rearrangement of the vaulting into a sexpartite form, was one requiring no small amount of technical skill. Until 1573 there was an open-work spire rising to a height of 500 feet, but this collapsed, partly because there was no nave to buttress it on the west. The history of Beauvais reads like a chapter of accidents, but in spite of this, there can be no doubt of its importance, or the magnificence of its aspirations. Its place in Gothic architecture is assured.

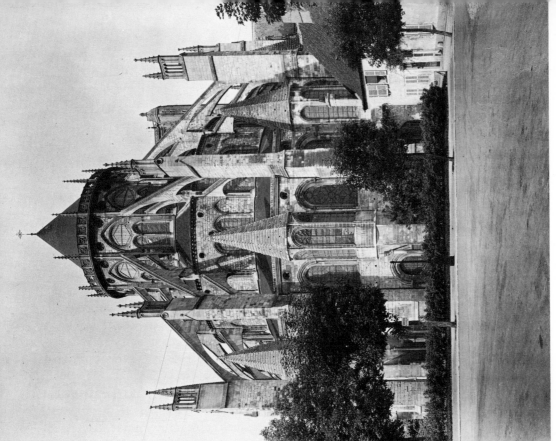

Plate 13 Bourges Cathedral (begun c. 1200)—exterior of choir
Note the complex flying buttresses

Plate 12 Chartres Cathedral—west front
North tower 1134 (spire 1507); south tower 1142; portal c. 1145;
rose window designed c. 1196, executed 1216. At first sight this
appears a rather unbalanced and casual composition, but closer
inspection reveals its subtle rhythms and harmonies

Chartres, Notre-Dame

This massive structure has a long and rich history. The building has suffered greatly at the hands of the restorers, particularly those of the eighteenth century.

The nave is the widest in France or Germany and the massive, almost Romanesque, proportions give it power rather than grace. The most notable features are the twin western towers, the sculpture, and the glass.

The western façade is not so immediately breath-taking as those of other cathedrals, but the towers are both of great beauty (Pl. 12). The southern one, of simple solemnity, relies for its effect on architectural proportion and the fine way the transition from square to octagonal shape is handled. Built between 1145 and 1170, it is one of the finest of its type in Europe. The northern one, though the older of the two up to roof level, had a splendid spire added to it, designed by Jean Texier. This is a fine example of Flamboyant design and may be considered to be one of the most beautiful spires in Europe.

The sculpture, comprising some 2,200 figures, cannot be overlooked. The symbolism of the subjects depicted is too involved to be fully covered here, and really needs specialized study. The porches on north and south transepts are perhaps those with the best sculpture.

The thirteenth-century glass is generally held to be the finest in France. In all, some 124 great windows (including 3 great rose-windows, 35 lesser roses and 12 smaller ones) provide an incomparable collection of historical and legendary incident. Some 3,889 figures have been counted, and verbal description is a poor substitute for such colourful splendour.

Bourges, St-Étienne (Pl. 13)

Work was started on the building in 1190, but the name of the designer is unrecorded. The plan (Fig. 58) is typical: double aisles are used, and there are no transepts. The interior of this great hall, unbroken by transepts, gives a tremendous sense of space.

The western façade is impressive and has the unique feature of five porches, giving access to each part of the interior. It should be compared with the west front of Reims, for the small gables at Reims are reminiscent of the arrangement here. Sexpartite vaulting is used in the nave.

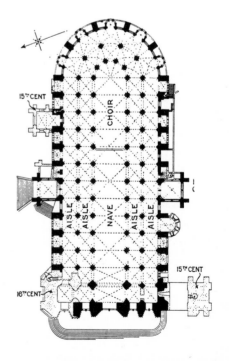

Fig. 58 Bourges Cathedral—plan

FURTHER READING

K. J. Conant, *Carolingian and Romanesque Architecture, 800–1200*. Pelican History of Art, Penguin Books, 1959.
>A marvellous book, with well-chosen illustrations and a most authoritative text.

Joseph Gantner and Marcel Pobé, *Romanesque Art in France*. Thames & Hudson, 1956.
>Particularly valuable for the photographs.
>These two books conveniently supplement the present volume.

Arthur Gardner, *An Introduction to French Church Architecture*. C.U.P., 1938.
>A valuable introduction to the subject.

Joan Evans, *Art in Mediaeval France*. C.U.P., 1948.
>A monumental tome.

Henri Focillon, *The Art of the West*, vol. i; *Romanesque Art*, vol. ii; *Gothic Art*. Phaidon Press, 1963.
>These two volumes are a brilliant and stimulating contribution to the literature of the period.

Emile Mâle, *The Gothic Image*. Fontana Library, 1961.
>This is obviously the result of a lifetime's work—it is particularly important if we are to begin to understand the symbolism behind the Gothic cathedral.

Hans Jantzen, *High Gothic*. Constable, 1962.
>A very enlightening book. For an understanding of the great cathedrals of France this is essential reading.

P. Frankl, *Gothic Architecture*. Pelican History of Art, Pelican Books, 1963.
>As important as all the other books in the series. Contains a great deal of information on Gothic vaulting.

Otto van Simson, *The Gothic Cathedral*. Routledge & Kegan Paul, 1956.
>A scholarly study of the theory and intentions of the Gothic builders.

W. R. Lethaby, *Mediaeval Art*, revised by D. Talbot Rice. Thomas Nelson, 1949.
>A fine book on the principles of Gothic art and architecture.

Jean Gimpel, *The Cathedral Builders*. Evergreen Profile Books, 1961.
>A book which gives a fascinating account of the background of the people who built the great cathedrals.

Jean Bony, *French Cathedrals*. Thames & Hudson, 1951.
>Contains valuable photographs.

The reader is also directed to William MacDonald's book in the 'Great Ages of World Architecture' Series, which is a good introduction to the subject, and to John Beckwith's *Early Mediaeval Art*, published by Thames & Hudson. The latter, like other books in the 'World of Art Library', has many illustrations in colour. J. G. Davies's *The Origins and Development of Early Christian Church Architecture* (S.C.M. Press, 1952) is another interesting book on the subject.

3

THE RENAISSANCE IN EUROPE

When we think or speak of 'the Renaissance' we usually have a mental picture of a body of work, painting, architecture, sculpture, and literature which was produced in Italy from about the middle of the fifteenth century to the end of the sixteenth century. The influence of this movement spread throughout Europe like the ripples on a lake when a stone is thrown in, but in the first place, the Renaissance was confined to one particular area, namely Tuscany, and was essentially the product of one town, namely Florence.

The exact moment of birth is hard to define, but there can be little doubt that the Renaissance spirit was afoot earlier in painting and literature than it was in architecture, and that the leading figures were all either Tuscans or Florentines. Giotto was painting his great series of frescoes in the early 1300s. The poet Dante died in 1321 and Petrarch and Boccaccio died within a year of one another in the mid-seventies of the same century. The work of these writers helped rekindle an interest in classical literature, and this in its turn fostered an interest in the classical world as a whole, which was, of course, the prime force behind the whole movement.

After this early stirring, however, it is not until the early fifteenth century that the full outpouring of creative activity bursts. Masaccio, Donatello, and Ghiberti were all Florentines; so, too, was the architect Brunelleschi, whose Foundling Hospital in Florence (Fig. 59) was the first Renaissance building.

Florence was also fortunate at this time in having two chancellors, Coluccio Salutati and Leonardo Bruni (the office corresponded to that of a modern secretary of state), who were also literary figures of originality. And there were other men of both artistic and literary ability who would have to be mentioned in order to give a comprehensive picture of the intellectual and cultural atmosphere in the city from the last two decades of the fourteenth century until the middle of the fifteenth century. In the first instance, then, the Renaissance really means the Renaissance in Florence.

The peculiar social and political circumstances in Italy also had an effect on the arts. The fact that the country was divided up into a number of separate states, each of which was completely autonomous, led to the formation of a number of different schools, each with its own particular flavour. The painting and architecture of the Florentines is quite different from that of the Romans or the Venetians.

The intellectual atmosphere of Florence was such that she seemed to draw to herself the best minds of the period. This magnetism can well be illustrated by a remark of Donatello, who said that he had to leave Padua, where he was praised, yet did nothing well for Florence, where he was endlessly

*Fig. 59   The Foundling Hospital, Florence (1420), by Brunelleschi.
The first true Renaissance building*

criticized, but was stimulated and able to do better work. The importance of the artist in the life of the city is again reflected in the choice of Giotto as city architect, as the city council decided that the training of the artist was the best possible recommendation for such a post.

The remark of Donatello just noted also shows the importance which artists placed on the criticism of their patrons. Seldom had the opinion of the layman been so informed or enlightened, and it was hardly ever to reach such a state again. The great patrons of the Italian Renaissance—the Church, the various city states, and the great number of rich and influential nobles —played an important part in determining the quantity, quality and kind of work produced. In Gothic times the Church had been the prime force behind the great architectural achievements, in the Renaissance it was the rich nobles and business families which dictated the demand. If the cathedral was the product of medieval society, then the palazzo is the typical product of the Renaissance society. This change in emphasis shows the change which came over men's thinking and philosophy.

We have already seen that the Renaissance was a rebirth of classical knowledge. But that was not all, for man was beginning to look at himself, not only in relation to God, but in relation to his environment, in an entirely different way. The humanistic preachings of St Francis had not gone unheeded, and many would claim that he was the instigator of the new humanistic philosophies which began to take hold of the minds of the people of Quattrocento Florence.* The growth of man's interest in himself is reflected in his study of anatomy. Artists of the calibre of Pollaiuolo, Leonardo da Vinci and Michelangelo were all vitally interested in this subject, and dissection formed a vital part of the artist's training.

Leonardo's work in this field has been of lasting importance, and modern X-ray techniques have only confirmed the accuracy of many of his observations. Leonardo practised dissection in the hospital of S. Maria Nuovo in Florence, where it seems possible that Pollaiuolo had directed his studies. Leonardo may have helped him

* Generally the evolution of the Italian Renaissance is divided into centuries and each century is given its Italian name:

Thirteenth century—Dugento
Fourteenth century—Trecento
Fifteenth century—Quattrocento
Sixteenth century—Cinquecento

54

whilst still a young man, but in order to be able to draw figures with greater expression and verisimilitude Leonardo took his studies much further than his master, and was indeed on the brink of discovering the circulation of the blood.

The other important field of research was, of course, perspective, and again the great artists of the period have left many drawings and paintings which bear witness to their interest. Paolo Uccello, with his battle scenes, and the theorizing of Alberti, are of great importance in this respect. The science of representing the third dimension on a flat surface and the methods of drawing correctly reflections, cast shadows, and inclined planes were in many ways to determine the way painters and architects saw things until the end of the nineteenth century. The long horizontal lines of Renaissance buildings and the lines of buildings around a square or along a street suggest the carefully prepared perspective drawing. It may be argued that this is too much the painter's way of looking at architecture, but it must be borne in mind that the great architects of the Renaissance, especially the the Florentines, were not usually architects by training. They were all either trained as painters or by painters, and the 'pictorial' quality of Renaissance architecture represents the close alliance between the two branches of the arts. It is only natural that the rather mathematical nature of perspective should lead to an interest in proportion and an attempt to devise some ideal proportion which would enable the artist or architect to design beautiful paintings or buildings. The 'golden section' had been known for centuries, certainly since Greek

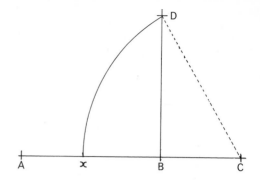

Fig. 60 Method of obtaining the golden section

To find the G.S. of AB, produce AB to C so that $BC=\frac{1}{2}AB$.
Draw BD perpendicular to AC so that $AB=BD$.
With centre C and radius CD, draw an arc to cut AB at X.
Then X is the G.S., for $AX:BX$ as $BX:AB$.

times, and artists turned once more to this division in an attempt to find some means of achieving perfection. The usual method of stating the 'golden section' is to cut a finite line so that the shorter part is to the greater part as the greater part is to the whole (see Fig. 60). The resulting division is roughly in the proportion of 8 to 5 (or 8 to 13, 13 to 21, etc.), but never exactly so. To mathematicians this proportion is known as an irrational, and it is this quality that has given to the section a great deal of its mystical significance. Of the more complicated systems of proportion we shall have more to say later when we deal with the work of Palladio, for in his work the mathematical content becomes of paramount importance.

This preoccupation with number and mathematical proportion is given further weight by the architect's preference for certain geometrical shapes, particularly the square and the circle. These two shapes had for the Renaissance architect divine qualities. For him the circle represented the completeness of God's universe, endless and perfect in every way; and the problem of working out human proportion from various combinations of a square and its related circle had fascinated artists and architects from Vitruvius onwards. In Renaissance times Leonardo and Dürer were only two of the great masters who attempted solutions to the problem.

As the square and circle were of such significance to these artists, it is not surprising that the shape of the church began to change. The Gothic cruciform plan was replaced by the centrally planned church, which consisted of a dome covering a square area under it, with apsidal additions to the four sides of the square. This is beautifully illustrated in the Umbrian church of S. Maria della Consolazione at Todi, of 1520 (Fig. 64). This new shape for the church was developed to express the new concept of beauty and religious truth. For it must now be clear that the Renaissance saw a fundamental change in the attitude to both beauty and religion. If the cruciform church can be taken as a symbol of Christ suffering on the cross, then the centrally planned church, with its overtones of geometric and mathematical perfection, can well be looked on as the symbol of a triumphant Christ, risen and perfect.

The Gothic movement had never taken such a firm hold in Italy as it had in the northern European countries. Even Milan cathedral, a building of staggering beauty and the most Gothic in feeling of all Italian buildings, has a quality of composure that sets it rather apart from the great cathedrals of the north. It lacks the sheer vitality of a northern church, that quality of pulsating life—the urge to create—which makes a Gothic cathedral such a unique and unforgettable experience. A Gothic building seems to lay bare the nerves of creation; a classic building clothes them in a mantle of discipline and mathematical theorizing. It is not surprising, therefore, that the new movement should have arisen in Italy. Moreover, reminders of the past splendours of Rome were too close and too plentiful to let the calm order of classicism be forgotten. These constant reminders of past glories, in the shape of Roman remains, were to provide the paradigms and textbooks on which Renaissance architects based their researches and their scholarship. In Gothic times the apprentice learned his trade by working alongside the master-mason, who, with the other masons, was actively engaged in the erection of the building. The Renaissance mind, however, was more interested in the problems of theory and proportion, than with the practical aspects of construction, and so the old methods of training began to die. The student now turned his attention to the active study of antiquity, not only because the subject was of consuming interest, but also because of the social distinction which it brought.

Just as the Romans had taken the basic elements of Greek architecture, namely the 'orders', and given them new life and vigour by a more imaginative treatment, so the great masters of the Renaissance took Roman architecture and brought to it a new vision and freedom. As Sir John Summerson pointed out in a notable series of broadcast talks* the 'order' is the Latin of architecture,

* Sir John Summerson, *The Classical Language of Architecture* (six talks broadcast between 29 May and 3 July 1963). Methuen, 1964.

Fig. 61   The dome, Florence Cathedral
(c. 1420), by Brunelleschi

Fig. 62   The dome, St Peter's, Rome
(c. 1546–90), by Michelangelo

it is a language and a discipline. The marvel of the Renaissance architects' achievements is the freedom which they developed in the handling of these elements.

As we have already seen, the rules governing the orders are precise and strictly defined; each part, down to the finest moulding, must be exactly related to the 'module' for that particular order. It is to the Renaissance architect's credit that he could take these apparently intractable elements and out of them fashion buildings which were at once individual and the product of his own inspiration and personality.

It is true that the buildings were not the outcome of a logical constructive principle,

in the way Gothic architecture had been. From a strictly structural point of view Renaissance architecture was regressive rather than progressive. Painters and sculptors were commissioned to design buildings because of their understanding of the universal formal problems of artistic creation. Today this practice may be hard to swallow by architects who tend to think of the problem of building in strictly technical terms, yet the Renaissance approach can be vindicated on the ground that it was the artists who made the technical advances, whilst the technician merely interpreted traditional practices. The Renaissance architect found the solution of the problems of proportion

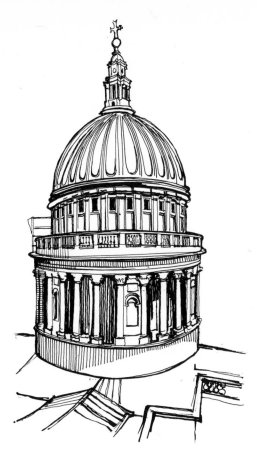

*Fig. 63 The dome, St Paul's, London
(c. 1697–1709), by Wren*

and composition, the control of the movement of space within a building, and the
added force and emphasis that lighting
could give, more important than structural
principles. For this reason, contrary to
Gothic or nineteenth- and twentieth-century
practice, technology was forced into the
background. It must be admitted that, in
the hands of lesser men, this method of
working leads to much architectural hum-
bug; but on the other hand it can be argued
that in similar hands the strictly 'functional'
school can produce work which is as arid
and comfortless as the other is bombastic
and meaningless. So strong was the Renaissance architect's conviction, so powerful his

inspiration and power of invention, that we
are unaware of how the building was put up,
and indeed the method often seems un-
important. Whether it be the calm assured-
ness of the Foundling Hospital, or the
sublime sculptural rhetoric of Michelangelo's
Medici Tomb, we are faced with an architecture which we can only accept and enjoy.

Brunelleschi

Some twenty-five years before King's College Chapel was started, and almost a century before the King Henry VII Chapel at
Westminster was completed, Brunelleschi's
Foundling Hospital in Florence (Fig. 59)
ushered in the Renaissance style in Italy.
Brunelleschi had already been at work on
the magnificent dome of the Cathedral in
Florence (Fig. 61), but whether this should
be called a Renaissance or a Gothic monument is a matter for debate. Undoubtedly
the 'dome' is a Renaissance concept, but
Brunelleschi had used Gothic methods of
construction, and by comparison with St
Peter's or St Paul's, there is undoubtedly a
Gothic 'feel' about the shape of his dome at
Florence (Figs. 61, 62, 63). With the Foundling Hospital, however, there can be no mistaking the calm unruffled composure of this
long horizontal façade. No trace of the surg-
ing verticality of the Gothic style is found
here; instead, in the measured intervals of
the delicate columns supporting their wide
semicircular arches, we find the urbanity
which is so typical of the new style.

Even when he takes a plan which is basically Romanesque, as he does at S. Spirito in
Florence, Brunelleschi manages to breathe
into it something of the new concept of

space and the delight in antiquity. The new concept of space is evident in two aspects. Firstly, when looking down the nave the eye begins to wander out to the sides; and secondly, in his use of the dome over the crossing, he foreshadows the development of the centrally planned church, which was to become the favourite layout for succeeding generations. To show his interest in antiquity, he constructed the nave arcade of columns with correct Corinthian capitals and bases, and above them the suggestion of an entablature, which afforded a break between the circular column and the semicircular arch which it supports. This point is worth noting, for we shall have more to say about this matter when we come to deal with the

work of Alberti, who was very conscious of the awkward transition from column to wall.

Whilst he was still engaged on S. Spirito, Brunelleschi designed what must be considered the earliest centrally planned church, namely S. Maria degli Angeli. He may well have formed his ideas for this church during a visit to Rome which it seems certain he made in 1433, the year he designed S. Maria degli Angeli. Unfortunately the church was never completed, but from the plan and other remaining evidence it was to have been much heavier in character than any of the work we have so far considered. It was to have consisted of a centrally domed space with eight side chapels opening out from the central space. Whether or not Brunelleschi actually copied an existing Roman temple it is difficult to say; but one such copy, by a contemporary of his, does exist, the SS. Annunziata, Florence, by Michelozzo, a direct copy of the Roman temple of Minerva Medica.

Amongst the many centrally planned churches that were built around 1500 can be mentioned S. Maria della Consolazione at Todi (Fig. 64). This beautiful church shows the utmost simplicity of design and planning. The predilection for simple geometric shapes is evidenced in the drawings not only of Alberti, but also of Leonardo and many others. In the present instance the solution could hardly be more elementary, for we are presented with a square plan with apsidal additions to the four sides. The dome, topped by an unobtrusive lantern, is almost completely unadorned and relies for

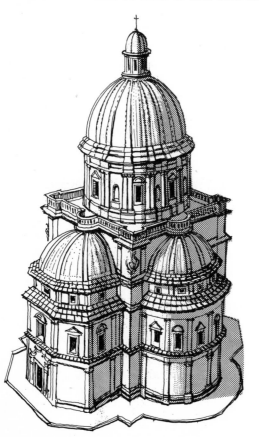

Fig. 64 S. Maria della Consolazione, Todi (1508). Probably designed by students of Bramante

its effect on the elegance of the outline. The apsidal projections, with their semi-domes, continue the flow of line created by the silhouette of the main dome, into a shape which is at once satisfying aesthetically, and sound structurally. There are few churches to compare with this, apart from Bramante's Tempietto in Rome, and this we shall discuss later (Fig. 74).

Alberti

If Brunelleschi was the first important Renaissance architect, Alberti was the first great Renaissance theorist. Leon Battista Alberti (1404–72) exerted a profound influence on succeeding generations of architects, both through his buildings and also through his writings. His most important and influential writing is contained in the three books which were published during his lifetime. The first of these *Della pittura*, was concerned with painting. It was the first book which expounded the new Renaissance spirit, and was particularly concerned with the new naturalism, as opposed to the mysticism of the medieval period. The Renaissance artist was, of course, primarily concerned with this problem of 'appearance' —hence his interest in anatomy and perspective. From his observation and knowledge of the visible world he tried to create 'ideal types'. This is almost the exact opposite of the way his medieval forebears looked at the world. They had been interested in representing only the mystery of creation and the universe.

Of the other two books which Alberti published, *De re aedificatoria* and *De statua*, a work on sculpture, only the former will interest us here. The ten volumes of *De re aedificatoria*, which he began about 1450 and continued writing and revising until his death in 1472, contain his theoretical ideas on architecture and are of great importance in the understanding of the way the Quattrocento architect thought about his subject.

Alberti was a man of wide learning and interests, and besides the three books just mentioned he wrote pamphlets on philosophy and the natural sciences among many other subjects. He was very conscious of man's civic rights and responsibilities and his philosophy was basically rationalist. These views, widely held at the time, were paramount in shaping his concept of architecture, and this outlook is reflected in his writing.

His sense of civic pride led him to devote one volume of his work to the subject of town planning, which he thought of vital importance. He felt strongly that individual buildings should be subservient to the idea of the 'town' as an organic whole, and that standard designs should be imposed on the whole street. He disliked intensely the medieval way of letting a town grow, each building being an expression of its own individuality, and he saw architecture as an entirely civic activity.

When his work is compared with that of Brunelleschi it soon becomes evident that his scholarship was more profound and his application of archaeological knowledge more scientific. But he always managed to reinterpret classical models, never simply to copy them. In the Palazzo Rucellai in Florence (Fig. 65), he introduced into Renaissance architecture the idea of using superimposed pilasters. By taking the

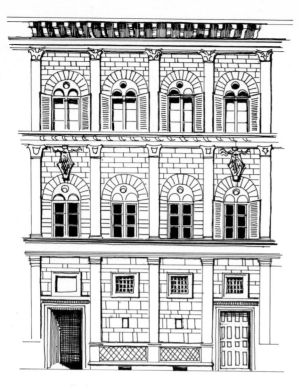

Fig. 65

The Palazzo Rucellai, Florence (1446–51), by Alberti

sequence used on the Colosseum (i.e. Doric at ground-floor, Ionic at first-floor and Corinthian at top-floor level), he showed his indebtedness to classical Rome, and this treatment was to become general practice. Similarly his definition of the ideal church puts the Renaissance view with admirable clarity, and was to prove equally influential to the course of subsequent building. In his view, the church should be the noblest building in the city and its beauty should surpass imagination. His definition of beauty was based on Vitruvius, and, simply stated, was that all parts should be integrated with the whole, and that it should not be possible to add or take away anything without detracting from the whole. From this it is not difficult to understand Alberti's liking for the circle or some closely related shape for the plan of a church. Of the figures related to the circle he lists the square, the hexagon, the octagon, the decagon and the

dodecagon as being particularly pleasing. He goes so far as to claim that, without this organic geometrical equilibrium divinity cannot reveal itself.

The design of the entrance façade occupied his thoughts, and was one of his main concerns in the design of churches—or temples, as he called them. He chose as the model on which he was to base his designs the Roman triumphal arch. A comparison of the fronts of S. Francesco at Rimini (Fig. 66), S. Sebastiano at Mantua, and S. Andrea also at Mantua (Fig. 67), shows his increasing mastery over the problem. The similarity of the façade of the latter church with the Arch of Trajan (Fig. 25) is particularly striking. The different solutions to the problem which Alberti offered were to set the standard for subsequent generations.

Not only were Alberti's developments in the design of the façade important; he was also conscious of the importance of the column. He emphasized the idea that 'the principal ornament in all architecture is the column', and here he touches on one of the basic problems of the Renaissance architect. Aware as he was only of Roman models, he was ignorant of the fact that the column had in Greek times been a strictly structural member. The Romans had used the column in both capacities, but largely as ornament, for theirs was essentially a wall architecture, and the Renaissance architects followed them in this.

Alberti was sufficiently acute in his reasoning to see that a wall pierced by semi-circular arches was but a solid wall discontinued in several places, and that the most suitable support for a semicircular arch was not a column, which is a three-dimensional unity in itself, but a pillar, which continues the face of the wall to the ground (Figs. 68, 69, 70). He also saw that there was a contradiction between the flat surface of the wall and the curved surface of a half-column. A comparison here of the façades of S. Francesco at Rimini and S. Andrea at Mantua (Figs. 66, 67) shows that, at least in church design, he finally abandoned the half-column in favour of the more logical pilaster. He was equally wary of placing a semicircular arch on columns or pilasters and preferred to top his vertical members with a straight architrave and entablature.*

It will be seen from the foregoing that Alberti's writings were both far-reaching in their scope and searching in their inquiries. For although he has been called the first dilettante architect, his knowledge and scholarship cannot be doubted.

Equally interesting were his theories on proportion, particularly those concerning

* For a further discussion of this problem, see R. Wittkower, *Architectural Principles in the Age of Humanism* (Alec Tiranti, 1962), originally published as vol. 19 of the Studies of the Warburg Institute, 1949.

Fig. 66 S. Francesco, Rimini (1446), by Alberti

Fig. 67 (right) S. Andrea, Mantua (c. 1470), by Alberti. This façade and that of S. Francesco show Alberti's debt to the Roman triumphal arch

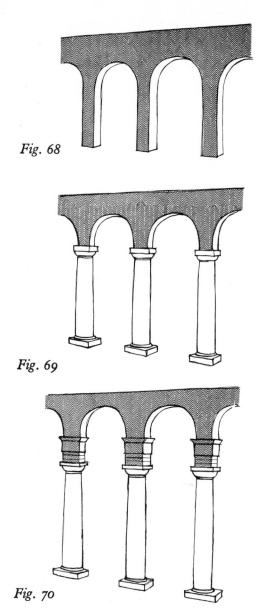

Fig. 68

Fig. 69

Fig. 70

Figs. 68, 69, 70 These three diagrams show that a pier continues the face of the wall to the ground, whilst a column interrupts the wall at the height of the capital. The inclusion of an 'entablature' between column and wall was an attempt to make the transition easier, but was not very successful in practice

number and ratio. For these he went back to Pythagoras's theories of proportions, which were closely based on musical harmonies. From a study of musical theory Alberti proposed using three types of mean on which to base a mathematical system of good proportion. The three methods involved calculating one of the following means: (i) the arithmetic mean; (ii) the geometric mean; (iii) the harmonic mean. The arithmetic mean is the intermediary produced by halving the sum of the other two terms—i.e. 2 3 4. The geometric mean is found by calculating the square root of the product of the other two—i.e. 4 6 9. The harmonic mean is calculated by dividing twice the product of the other two by their sum—i.e. 3 4 6. These means can be more simply remembered by the equations:

$$I = \frac{a+c}{2}, \; I = \sqrt{ac}, \; I = \frac{2ac}{a+c}$$

respectively, where $I=$ intermediary and a and c represent the other two terms.

This passionate belief in number and ratio can be traced back to the writings of Plato as well as Pythagoras. In *Timaeus* Plato had tried to explain not only the rhythm of the universe but the structure of the human soul in the two geometrical progressions 1, 2, 4, 8, and 1, 3, 9, 27— often expressed in the shape of a 'lambda':

$$
\begin{array}{ccc}
& 1 & \\
2 & & 3 \\
4 & & 9 \\
8 & & 27 \\
\end{array}
$$

The significance of these sequences is that they both start with unity and end with a cube, which again is important for one cannot proceed beyond the third dimension. (The number three is, in any case, rather special; not only is it the number of the Trinity, but it is also the first number to have a beginning, a middle and an end, so that any number connected with three had special significance.)

To make this last series of progressions workable Francesco Zorzi (or Giorgi), a neo-platonic friar deeply interested in archi-tecture, suggested that 6 be used as the lowest term. In this way we get 6, 12, 24, 48, and 6, 18, 54, 162, and into these geometric progressions the harmonic and arithmetic means can be inserted without recourse to fractions.

We may seem to have spent a long time in the discussion of these problems of pro-portion, but if we are to understand the way in which the Renaissance mind worked we must have at least a smattering of know-ledge of them. This brief skirmish is only by

Fig. 71 The Palazzo Ducale, Urbino (c. 1470–5). By Luciano Laurana?
A typical fifteenth-century Italian palace courtyard

Fig. 72 The Palazzo Medici, Florence (1444), by Michelozzo
A typical Florentine palace façade

way of an introduction to an absorbing subject, and the inquiring reader cannot be better advised than to continue his studies with the aid of Wittkower's admirable examination of the whole field. Of Palladio's contribution to proportion we shall have more to say later.

The new movement made itself felt not only in church-architecture but in the design of private residences. The important and imposing palazzi built in the fifteenth century were the outcome of the desire of the rich families to build themselves fitting homes. These buildings had much in common; the warm climate favoured the open *cortile* and sheltering colonnade, and this central courtyard is a common feature (Fig. 71). Lack of snow made low-pitched roofs possible, and this forced into prominence the cornice and balustrade. Bright sunlight

made large windows unnecessary, and the comparatively small ratio of window to wall helps to impart to these buildings a massive monumental character, whilst the quarries of Tuscany supplied the large blocks of marble and stone which were necessary to give them their imposing character. A useful comparison here is between a typical Italian palazzo, say the Medici or Strozzi, and a typical early Renaissance house in England, say Longleat or Hardwick (Figs. 172, 175). The Palazzo Medici (Fig. 72) was designed by Michelozzo, *c.* 1444, and has all the typical recognition points—heavy rustication, prominent cornice, clear horizontal division and sparing use of detail—combined in an effect of simplicity and boldness.

If most of the Florentine palaces run roughly true to type there is one notable exception, and that is the Palazzo Rucellai

(1446–51), by Alberti (Fig. 65). Alberti's ascending arrangement of the orders has already been mentioned, and though the treatment of the detail is very free the orders are clearly recognizable. The proportions of the façade and the vertical and horizontal divisions are worked out with his usual thoroughness, and each part is carefully calculated in relation to the whole. In this respect this façade approaches what Alberti considered to be the ideal, namely that it should not be possible for any part to be altered or taken away without detracting from the whole.

By the end of the Quattrocento, Florence was on the decline both as a power and as an artistic centre. Nor was she alone in this, for Milan and Urbino were suffering the same fate. So far Rome has not entered into our study, but it was at this moment that she began to dominate the scene with profound effects on all that followed. That she should have done so was due to a multiplicity of reasons, but important amongst them was the influence of Pope Julius II, who managed to attract into the city the best artists of the period. Rome had not previously produced any outstanding native talent, so all the architects and painters had to be imported. In consequence of this, whilst the Quattrocento had tended to produce schools of a strictly regional character Rome was to produce an international style.

The building of the Cancelleria (Fig. 73) signals the swing away from Tuscany, and the arrival of Rome as an international centre for architecture. This was the city's first important Renaissance building, and the unknown designer gave the city a façade

of distinction. The proportion of the windows is carefully related to the rectangle in which they are placed, and further architectural emphasis is given to the composition as a whole by projecting bays at either end.

That moment between the early Renaissance and Mannerism known as the High Renaissance was but short-lived. Born in

Fig. 73 The Cancelleria, Rome (1486–98) Architect unknown

*Fig. 74   The Tempietto of S. Pietro in
Montorio, Rome (1502), by
Bramante*

*This little building should be compared with
the dome of St Paul's, the Roman Temple of
Portunus, and the mausoleum at Castle
Howard*

full flower in Bramante's Tempietto, 1502
(Fig. 74), it was dead by the time Michelangelo designed the Medici Mausoleum and
the Laurenziana Library, 1526 (Figs. 75, 76,
77). However, in the brief span of rather
less than three decades, the High Renaissance produced a series of buildings of such
beauty and harmony of proportion that they
have hardly been equalled since.

Bramante

The period was dominated by the work of
one man, and that was Bramante (1444–
1514). There can be little doubt that
Bramante owed a great deal to the theories
of Alberti, not only in respect of his attention to proportion but also in the care which

he took over the detail of his buildings. He
had already done some work on the eastern
portion of the Gothic church S. Maria delle
Grazie in Milan, but in 1499, along with
other leading artists of the day, he left Milan
as the invading French troops entered and
made his way to Rome at the invitation of
the Pope.

Bramante had been trained as a painter
before taking to architecture, but his first
important building in Rome, the Tempietto,
shows his marvellous grasp of sculptural
form. In all great building the exact division
between architecture and sculpture becomes
exceedingly hard to define; there is a fundamental grasp of three-dimensional thinking
that is common to both arts. This peculiar

*Fig. 75 (above) and Fig. 76 (opposite) show details of the niches and the
tomb in the Medici Mausoleum in the Medici Chapel, Florence (1521–34),
by Michelangelo. These two illustrations show the first breathings of the
unrest that was to lead to Mannerism and the Baroque*

synthesis is to be found in the best buildings regardless of country or period, and when it happens we are faced with a building that enlarges our experience and knowledge of both architecture and sculpture.

The Tempietto is a supreme example. This tiny building, sheltering in the cloisters of S. Pietro in Montorio, is based on the circular pagan temples of ancient Rome. The circular form is, of course, the 'ideal' of Alberti, and the proportion between circular base, drum, and dome is completely satisfying. So beautiful is the proportion that Bramante does not feel the necessity for any further ornamentation, except for classical triglyphs and metopes on the entablature above the Tuscan Doric columns of the circular colonnade. In most photographs the surrounding buildings can be clearly seen and if it were not for this fact we should have little idea of the size of the temple, for so complete is the realization of volume and scale within the parts that whether the building were 50 feet or 500 feet high the effect would be as satisfying. It is, in fact, only 15 feet in diameter.

The Pope was impressed with the Tempietto, and gave Bramante the task of designing a new façade for the Vatican Palace and the new plan for St Peter's to replace the old fourth-century basilica. Bramante's original plan for the new church dates from 1506, and was to have been based on a massive Greek cross with a domed

Fig. 77 The Biblioteca Laurenziana, Florence (1542), by Michelangelo
Note that by placing the columns in niches their function is totally negated

Fig. 78 The Palazzo Vidoni Caffarelli, Rome (1515–20), by Raphael

central area. The plan shows a new concept of space, for in it the wall is no longer a device to divide and separate spaces but is used, in a much more fluid way, to mould volumes. Despite the apparent rigidity of the shape—basically a square with protruding apsidal terminations to the four arms of the cross—the arrangement of the inside walls which support the main dome and the four smaller domes produces a feeling of great fluidity of movement around the central space. If Bramante's plan had been carried out, St Peter's would have been the greatest monument to the High Renaissance in existence, but the architect was over sixty before the foundation stone was laid and his original intention was not adhered to. In fact the church was not completed until 1667, when Bernini built his impressive entrance piazza.

Bramante had been trained as a painter,

and it was Raphael (1483–1520), one of the most eminent painters of the period, who became his successor at St Peter's. In his painting of 'The Marriage of the Virgin', Raphael had paid homage to Bramante's Tempietto by painting a very similar and very beautiful little circular temple in the background. Of the buildings for which Raphael was responsible, only the Palazzo Vidoni Caffarelli in Rome need detain us here (Fig. 78). The difference between a Roman and a Florentine palazzo is already becoming evident, for here the wall is seen as something much more plastic. The ground floor has still something of the Florentine heaviness, but the first floor shows much more movement in the treatment of surface modelling. The double semicircular half-columns impart not only a lightness, but also a sort of wave-like movement across the area which makes the limit of the wall less precise. The first floor is an example of the piano-nobile, a feature which Raphael took from the house Bramante designed for him, and which was to become such an attractive feature of the later Palladian houses. In the Palazzo Pandolfini in Florence and the Villa Madama in Rome, Raphael continued to develop his master's principles, into a much more personal and sophisticated style of great elegance.

Sangallo

The finest of Roman palazzi was the work of Antonio da Sangallo the younger (1485–1546). The calm order and symmetry, combined with the rich texture which the window detail imposed on the façade, make the Palazzo Farnese in Rome the outstanding secular building of the High Renaissance (Fig. 79). The confidence of the design makes the Florentine palazzi look rather parochial by comparison. The building is strongly axial, and the apartments are arranged around an internal courtyard 81 feet square (Fig. 80). The triple division of the façade provides for a fine piano-nobile, and relief is provided by a fine entrance designed, like the top storey, by Michelangelo. This façade was to provide the model for many London clubs and banks in the nineteenth-century revivals. Sangallo was also responsible for one of the most delightful smaller Roman

Fig. 79 The Palazzo Farnese, Rome (1534–45), by Antonio da Sangallo. The dignity and richness of this façade became the accepted style for many European clubs and banks

town houses, La Piccola Farnesina (Fig. 81).
This dates from 1523, and again there is the
same feeling for proportion, and the relationship between solid and void makes a rich
pattern of the façade. Yet despite the success
of these two buildings his ideas for the continuation of the work at St Peter's display a
certain inability to think on a really monumental scale. The plans and models which
he prepared for this subject show too great
a liking for rather fussy detail, which could
only have detracted from the grandeur of
conception which was required. As a technician and as a master of construction he
was Bramante's superior and had, in fact,
to correct major weaknesses in some of the
earlier master's work. However, despite his
scholarship—and he was the first of the

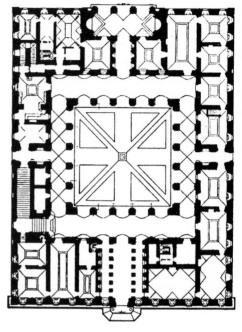

Fig. 80 The Palazzo Farnese—plan

Renaissance architects to be actually trained
as an architect—he was never given the
universal recognition that Bramante had
received.

The period of the High Renaissance was,
as we have seen, of only a short duration,
but during that period architecture underwent a transformation. The form of Gothic
architecture had been determined by technique and structure; the Renaissance architects discovered new values which were not
so much dependent on the mechanics of
building as on the aesthetic appeal of mass
against mass, solid against void. The control of space became more deliberate, and it
now needed some mighty mind to crystal-
lize all that had gone before and open the
way for the next phase in architectural
development.

Fig. 81 The Piccola Farnesina, Rome (1523), by Antonio da Sangallo

Michelangelo

The turbulent spirit which was to perform this transformation was found in the person of Michelangelo, and it is to a consideration of his work that we must now turn. To deal adequately with the achievements of Michelangelo Buonarroti (1475–1564) really needs three volumes, one for his painting, one for his sculpture, and another for his architecture. In each field he takes up the art at a certain point in the High Renaissance and leaves it facing in quite another direction. Whatever he touched became an entirely personal utterance, which in some way reflected his personality and his most deeply held beliefs. Of his painting and sculpture we will have little to say here, and then only insofar as they shed further light on his achievements in architecture.

His architecture falls into two groups: the early work done between the years 1516 and 1526, and the later and more important work done between his seventy-second year and his death. Between these groups come a series of influential buildings by other architects, which must be considered in chronological order. Michelangelo gave birth to the style which has been called by modern scholars 'Mannerism', and it will be as well to try to define exactly what this style means before actual buildings are considered. The fundamental qualities of the early and high Renaissance styles can best be summarized as order and balance. The forms are clear-cut and the articulation and relationship of parts stated in a clear and unequivocal manner. The lean athleticism of the figures of such painters as Botticelli or Fra Angelico is clearly reflected in the youthful lines of the Foundling Hospital and other buildings. In the High Renaissance the form becomes more mature. Youthful elegance gives way to the strength of manhood, and the maiden becomes the developed woman, conscious of her sensuous charms. This change is reflected in the buildings by the increased richness of the forms of the façade. Compare here the paintings of early Renaissance painters with those of Raphael, and the architecture of a similar period with, say, the Palazzo Vidoni Caffarelli (Figs. 59, 78). Mannerism throws the equilibrium of earlier work out of joint and introduces a feeling of unbalance, awkwardness and unrest. Yet, and this is the crux of the matter, no new elements have been introduced. The classical order, the acme of controlled regularity and discipline, now becomes the vehicle for expressing tension and discord. 'Classicism' as it had been understood from Greek and Roman times was stood on its head and a new and vital architecture emerged triumphant.

In his first important building Michelangelo expressed this new spirit. The first major commission came to him when he was already forty-two years old, and that was to design the façade of the church of S. Lorenzo in Florence, which had already been begun to the design of Brunelleschi. However, in 1520 the contract was cancelled and in the following year he started work on the Medici Chapel (Fig. 76). It is easy in the case of the Medici Tomb to dismiss the work as simply a setting for sculpture, but this is to do it less than justice. Already the signs of Mannerism are there. The architectural background is handled with that air of plasticity and massing that could come only from a sculptor; the juxtaposition of mass against mass, solid plane against recessed niche, gives evidence that the whole thing was seen 'in the round', not thought up on the flat plane of the drawing-board. There is something unbearably 'tight' about the whole concept, almost like a cocked gun waiting for somebody to press the trigger. The part which the sculpture plays in this scheme must not be overlooked or underestimated, for there have been few occasions when architecture and sculpture have been so dependent one upon the other. The tension created between the figure of Lorenzo and the surrounding niche is so great that he is almost bending the straight sides which hold him captive. He is the nodal point of an action which starts in mid-air at the feet of the reclining figures of Evening and Dawn at either side. These two figures seem to catch the upward surge of the architectural setting and bend it into an almost Gothic 'ogee' arch. Yet with all their apparent languor their position on the sarcophagus itself is far from easy. They keep their place by the titanic will of the sculptor, for perched as they are on the smooth curve of the scroll, they would surely fall off if not kept there by some external force. Muscular as they are, their strength is self-contained; though we are aware of their power we observe it without being part of it.

After this early experiment Michelangelo then tackled, in 1524, the design of the Biblioteca Laurenziana (Fig. 77). Again he creates a new sensation of space not only in his sense of detail, but in the very contrast between the shapes of the rooms. The ante-room is tall and narrow, whilst the library itself is long and low, and this sets up an immediate tension between the two rooms. In the ante-room all is discord, and the concept of strict functionalism is turned upside down. The idea of a pillar is that it should carry a weight, yet by placing the columns in a recess in the wall Michelangelo makes it appear that the walls are supporting the columns, an impression further enhanced by the fact that the columns are placed directly above scroll-like corbels, which are obviously incapable of carrying the weight on top of them, and in fact carry no weight at all. The whole impression left by this room is one of discomfort, even though this unease is rendered with the materials of the architecture of the High Renaissance. Again, as with all Michelangelo's work, we are confronted with sublime unrest. The artist seems out of tune with society and his times.

After this first essay in architecture, Michelangelo turned again to painting and sculpture, and except for the fortifications for Florence which occupied him in 1529 he built no more until the last twenty years of his life.

Giulio Romano

During the time Michelangelo was working on the Laurenziana, Giulio Romano (1492–1546) was at work on the Palazzo del Tè at Mantua (Figs. 82–84), and Peruzzi designed the Palazzo Massimi at Rome (Fig. 85). Both these buildings were important landmarks in the development of Mannerism.

Sir John Summerson refers to the Palazzo del Tè as 'the world's most perverse and extravagant adventure in rustication'.* Rus-

* Sir John Summerson, *The Classical Language of Architecture* (broadcast talks).

Fig. 82 The Palazzo del Tè, Mantua (1526–31), by Giulio Romano—the entrance façade

tication was not a new or unknown form of building. It had been used in the past to give an added sense of strength to the lower parts of classical buildings. Employed systematically in this way it is a useful method of giving weight and substance to a wall surface. In the hands of Giulio Romano, however, it becomes a means of giving added emotion to a façade. Today we have been sated with rustication, and we can no longer see it with a fresh eye. But to the sixteenth-century eye it must have been a revelation, as indeed must the whole of the Palazzo del Tè, which is not empty bombast but the expression of a genuine spirit. Not only does Giulio

Romano manage a contrast between the members of the separate façades, but he manages to contrast one façade with another. If we take the courtyard façade (Fig. 83), we can see at once that this is no rehash of arid classicism. We are now presented with a very complicated set of rhythms and counter-rhythms. There seems here to be a strong element of the accidental. We could well imagine that a severely classical scholar, such as Alberti, would dismiss this as the work of a bungler, the detail being too clumsy and 'incorrect'.

Nevertheless Giulio Romano created a new way of looking at a wall, for this is a

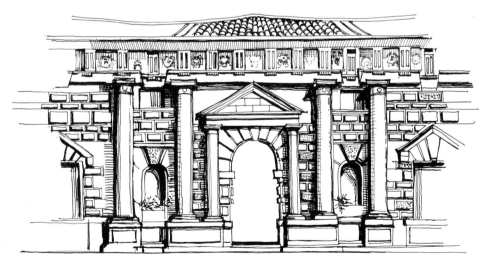

Fig. 83 The Palazzo del Tè—the courtyard façade

Fig. 84 The Palazzo del Tè—the garden façade

wall full of movement. The considered awkwardness of the whole wall is built up by a series of departures from the classical norm. Note how the entablature is poised so uncomfortably on the sharp edge of the pediment over the central arch, but without causing any irregularity in the architrave, which instead appears to slip out of joint between the double half-columns on either side. This breaking of the entablature is done again over the pediments of the blind windows, which themselves appear to be pushed out of place by the massive keystones which are trying to break through the apex. Even the rustication is not systematically applied, for apparently random spaces are left without any rustication, whilst in others the stones are given an extra roughness. Another feature of Mannerist work is the use of two orders, one within the other. Here Tuscan Doric is used in both cases, though elsewhere different orders, one within the other, give an even richer effect.

Another building which is of importance is the Palazzo Massimi, by Peruzzi (Fig. 85). A comparison of the two buildings is interest-

Fig. 85 The Palazzo Massimi, Rome (1535), by Peruzzi

ing, for both are Mannerist yet very different. Like Giulio Romano's building this is the architecture of sophistication, and both architects achieve this sophistication by an outrage on classical concepts. Peruzzi achieves this quality by elegance, Giulio Romano by carrying excess to extremes—one is tempted to say to the limit of endurance.

The most striking feature of the Massimi building is the taut, springlike curve of the façade. This curve is more like a sheet of tempered metal than a building of stone. The second- and third-storey windows, with their curious scroll-like surrounds, seem to lie on the wall rather than pierce it.

But perhaps the most striking feature of the whole design is the almost brutal way in which the entrance interrupts the flow of the wall around it. There is no build-up either at the sides or at the top, for the heavy cornice makes an almost knife-like cut between ground and first floor. This cornice is not echoed elsewhere, for the roof is crowned by deeply overhanging eaves, without the heavy cornice or balustrade one might well expect; nor indeed are the pilasters carried through as unifying elements in the design as they had been so often before.

The curving façade is also noteworthy in that it was to become an important feature in subsequent design. It is the beginning of the new concept of space which, starting at this period, reaches its fullest expression in the full-blown Baroque movement which was to follow.

Apart from the last work of Michelangelo, Giulio Romano was the most important and influential architect of Mannerism. Besides

the Palazzo del Tè, he designed a house for himself in Mantua which, although not so exotic, still manages to use classical motifs in a rather surprisingly un-classical way.

Another important figure was Sebastiano Serlio, a pupil of Peruzzi. He spent most of his career in France, but his writings, which he began to publish in 1537, were to provide subsequent architects with ideas and inspiration for generations to come.

St Peter's, Rome

In the year 1534 Michelangelo left Florence for good, and moved to Rome. His first work there seems to have been the addition of top storey to the Palazzo Farnese, which had been started by Sangallo the younger (Fig. 86). In 1535 he was appointed Superintendent

Fig. 86 The Palazzo Farnese, Rome—courtyard. The top storey was added by Michelangelo in 1548

Fig. 87 The Capitoline Palace, Rome (1540–1644), by Michelangelo. One of the twin palaces which Michelangelo designed for this early example of town planning

of the Vatican Buildings by Pope Paul III, and on his death in 1546 Michelangelo took over work on St Peter's. The building of St Peter's is, however, a long story, and there is one scheme of Michelangelo's which must be mentioned before it, namely the design of the Capitoline Hill. The twin palaces which he designed for this project, one of which is illustrated (Fig. 87), show developments which are important. For the first time we see the use of the 'colossal' order, that is, an order in which the column embraces more than one storey. This device certainly gives the façade a great deal of unity, and here Michelangelo plays off the colossal Corinthian pilasters against the smaller inset Ionic columns which huddle against them at ground-floor level. The ground-floor openings are square and un-compromising, and Michelangelo introduces the wanted richness by giving the first storey windows curved pediments standing on yet a third and small order. Then follows

the typically heavy cornice, topped by balustrade and sculptured figures. At ground-floor level the central entrance is unaccented, but at first-floor level the central bay is marked by a larger window with a triangular pediment. This is un-deniably grand architecture, mature and rich in all its aspects. Despite certain awk-wardnesses, such as the close spacing of the massive pilasters and the brusqueness of the ground floor openings, this remains one of Michelangelo's happiest designs. There seems to be less struggle with intractable elements here than we have seen before, and certainly less than occurs in his greatest work, the dome of St Peter's.

The history of the building of this great Christian monument is long and com-plicated. If Bramante's plan (Fig. 88) had been carried out it would have epitomized the ideas of High Renaissance church plan-ning—a central space covered by a dome—which Bramante had based on that of the

Pantheon. Briefly, the chronology of the building can be summarized as follows:

1506 Work begun on Bramante's design, which was based on a Greek cross.

1513 Death of Julius II. Bramante superseded by Giuliano da Sangallo, Fra Giocondo (who both died in 1515), and Raphael. Raphael proposed substituting the Latin cross.

1520 Death of Raphael; Peruzzi takes over. He reverts to the Greek cross.

1527 Work held up owing to lack of money; the sack of Rome disorganizes all artistic production in the city.

1536 Death of Peruzzi. Antonio da Sangallo takes over. He proposes a plan with a sort of prolonged porch or vestibule.

1546 On the death of Sangallo Michelangelo takes over, and reverts to the Greek cross.

1564 Death of Michelangelo. Vignola adds side cupolas.

1585-90 Work on Michelangelo's dome completed by Giacomo della Porta and Domenico Fontana, from working drawings and models left by the master.

1606-12 Maderna adds nave and gigantic façade. This long nave detracts from Michelangelo's dome and the side cupolas.

1626 Work on the main church completed.

1655-67 Bernini adds the piazza.

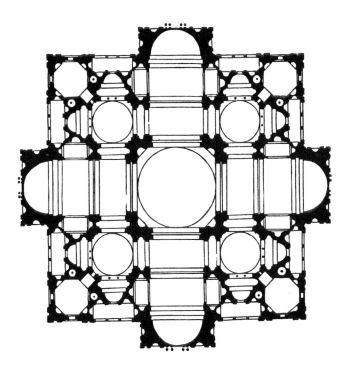

Fig. 88 Bramante's first plan for St Peter's, Rome

Plate 14 St Peter's Rome (1506–1626). A view showing Maderna's façade (1606–12)
The long horizontal on top of the façade tends to cut off the dome and diminish its importance

The dome is, of course, very much a Renaissance concept, and a comparison of the dome of St Peter's with those of the Tempietto and of St Paul's is always fascinating (Figs. 62, 74, 63). Of the three, St Peter's is probably the most exciting, but the other two are probably more satisfying. No piece of architecture shows so clearly Michelangelo's struggle with himself and his God. The form of the dome is powerful in its weight and majesty, every line speaking of latent strength. Many speak of its upward thrusting appearance, yet one cannot but be conscious of its material weight bearing down on the great internal piers which support it.

These great piers had been in existence from Bramante's time and for many years had stood alone because nobody had felt capable of the gigantic structural problems involved in the erection of a dome to crown them. Bramante himself had died too early, and Raphael must have been acutely em-

barrassed by the problems. So, through succeeding generations, the task was shelved until someone with enough courage would undertake it. If Michelangelo's plan had been carried through in its entirety the final effect would have been magnificent, but this was not to be. The best expression of his ideas can be seen at the 'eastern' end (N.B. to avoid confusion the normal designation of east and west ends is used though it must be remembered that, in fact, the orientation is reversed) where something of the fluidity of the design can be appreciated. Round this apsidal end he uses the colossal order, this time 100 feet high, surmounted by a low attic storey. The whole concept has that suppleness and sculptural quality that we have already noted in the Medici Tomb. Although he had intended the church to follow the Greek cross, he had marked the 'western' front by another of his innovations, namely two rows of colossal columns, ten in the back row and four free-standing columns

in front. However, this idea was never carried out and was finally replaced by
Maderna's nave and rather uncomfortable
western façade. Internally, the nave may be
of some advantage because of the additional
spaciousness which it lends to the building,
but externally it detracts from the importance
of the dome, which is soon hidden as the
building is approached.

The composition of the façade is far from
happy (Pl. 14). The pediment tends to be
dwarfed and squashed by the heavy attic,
and the figures tend to destroy the sense of
scale; but despite the many incongruities
and changes of architect and plan, the
church as a whole remains one of the greatest
creations of the human mind. Much of its
size and magnificence must be the result of
Michelangelo's inspiration; his vision was so
big that it could not be destroyed by the
work of lesser men.

Michelangelo came to architecture when
the High Renaissance was in full flower; he
left it on the threshold of an entirely new
style. He had little use for rustication; the
wall to him was too important a medium for
the expression of a tense and sculptural
form. He took the rigid discipline of High
Renaissance classicism and forced out of it
a new means of expression. Subsequent
architects went on to explore space with even
greater freedom in the Baroque style of the
seventeenth and eighteenth centuries.

Palladio

There is one more architect who is important to developments in Europe, and particularly England, namely Andrea Palladio
(1508–80). His work is important from two
aspects, firstly for the buildings he put up,
and secondly for his writings and theories.
His *I Quattro libri dell' architettura* show not
only buildings now lost to us but also the
pains he went to in the measurement and
study of the antique buildings of Rome. The
writings and drawings show that he was the
most learned and understanding of the
architects working at this time and for many
years afterwards.

The plans of his villas and palazzi were
worked out with great care, and usually conformed to a set pattern which he managed
to vary with great ingenuity to meet the
individual needs of his patrons. This scheme
consisted of a centrally placed hall or loggia,
surrounded by smaller rooms. The stair-
cases were generally placed at the sides of
the hall, but occasionally he used a circular
form opening off the hall.

He proposed seven ideal shapes for rooms,
and these can be summarized as follows:

(i) Circular
(ii) Square. Ratio 1:1
(iii) Diagonal of Square = length of room.
Ratio $\sqrt{2}$:1. (Being an irrational this
proportion is hardly ever used.)
(iv) Square and a third. Ratio 3:4
(v) Square and a half. Ratio 2:3
(vi) Square and two-thirds. Ratio 3:5.
(He was himself particularly fond of
this proportion, and rooms $18' \times 30'$
or $12' \times 20'$ are scattered throughout
his buildings.)
(vii) A double square. Ratio 1:2

It will be appreciated that these only give
the proportions for the length and breadth
of the rooms, and give no idea of the height.

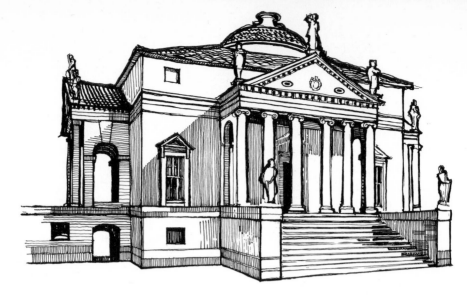

Fig. 89 The Villa Capra (or Rotonda) near Vicenza (built 1567), by Palladio. This fine house was to prove a model for many eighteenth-century houses in England. Compare it with Chiswick House (Fig. 209)

This was arrived at by calculating one of the 'means' which have already been described. Palladio also related the dimensions of one room to another by either geometric or harmonic means. He was also equally exact in calculating the proportions of the façades of his buildings, though it must be admitted that the careful arrangements and dimensions which he worked out on the plans of his buildings had on occasion to be altered in the actual building, because of difficulties or peculiarities of the site.

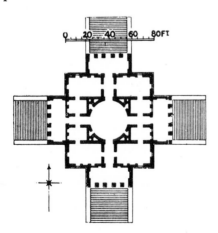

Fig. 90 The Villa Capra—plan

It is perhaps this strongly mathematical basis that gives such nobility and repose to his buildings. For although his treatment of detail and his use of orders is Mannerist, his buildings show little of the awkwardness and unbalance which is so typical of the Mannerist movement. His work as a whole is characterized by an urbanity and ease which was to prove so attractive a quality to Inigo Jones and to many of the English architects working in the eighteenth century.

The most perfect example of the centrally planned house is the Villa Capra, or Rotonda as it is sometimes known, at Vicenza (Figs. 89, 90). The façade is strikingly simple, with a well-proportioned portico and broad flight of stairs. As in most Italian villas, the proportion of window to wall is small, but the large unbroken flat surfaces give a sense of great dignity and repose. The composition rises easily to the dome, and the transition from one floor to the next is achieved with effortless ease.

The plans of the villas show the complete symmetry which Palladio insisted on. True,

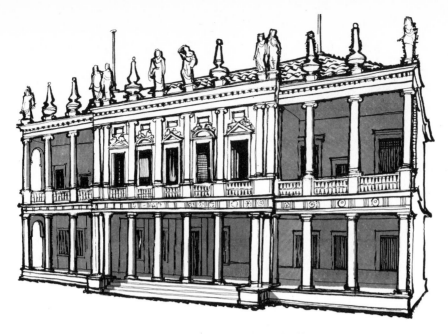

Fig. 91 The Palazzo Chiericati, Vicenza (1550), by Palladio
This shows the introduction of the colonnaded loggia into palazzo
design, and should be compared with the Queen's House, Greenwich (Fig. 167)

the Renaissance as a whole had paid lip-service to the idea of symmetry, and this was observed in the design of façades, but more often than not the disposition of the rooms behind the façade broke away from the ideal. In the majority of Palladio's plans, however, symmetry is internal as well as external.

At about the same time (*c.* 1550) as he designed the Villa Rotonda, he also designed the Palazzo Chiericati at Vicenza (Fig. 91). This was a town house and therefore had to be looked at from the street, not from the open countryside, as was the case with the Rotonda. This situation calls for a different treatment of the façade. Palladio solves the problem not by a central cube, of which we are very conscious in the Rotonda, but by two classical colonnades, one on top of the other. As usual, he chooses to put the Ionic order on top of the Tuscan Doric and then he proceeds to make a magnificent arrangement of solids and voids to form the whole composition. The entrance on this

occasion is unemphasized; the central section of the façade is marked on the ground floor by double columns and the emphasis repeated at first-floor level by double pilasters. At this level, however, he brings the wall forward, piercing each bay with two windows, the lower and larger enriched with alternate arched and pointed pediments, supporting reclining figures. The movement created by the play of light and shade across the front makes this one of his most visually exciting façades. The whole composition has about it an air of poised and expectant calm, of action caught at that moment of inertia which can be found in the sculptures of athletes in Greek art of the best period.

The Palazzo Chiericati dates from about 1550, and some sixteen years later came the Villa Maser near Asolo, a design of rare beauty and refinement. The façade (Fig. 92) is a design of distinction, and shows Palladio's command of classical form and

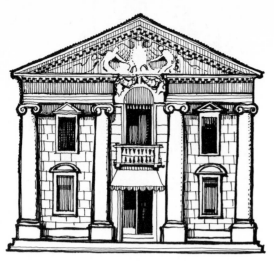

Fig. 92

*The Villa Maser, Asolo (1566?),
by Palladio*

The plan of the Villa Maser will serve to show the method Palladio employed in the interrelation of rooms. The plan is of the central block and outlying wing type of which he was so fond. The long wing which lies behind the main block consists of three groups or blocks of buildings, each with three rooms. The widths of the rooms as laid out on Palladio's plan are 16 feet, 12 feet, 16 feet; 20 feet, 10 feet, 20 feet; 9 feet, 18 feet, 9 feet; which can be expressed in the following ratios, 4:3:4, 2:1:2, 1:2:1. The central block itself is divided into three rooms, each 12 feet across, making a total of 36 feet in all. At the rear this block is again divided into three rooms, this time the 36 feet being split up into 9 feet, 18 feet, 9 feet. It will be noted that 12 is the harmonic mean between 9 and 18. From this basis he then proceeds to build up the whole plan in a similar manner, each part having some form of mathematical relationship with its neighbour and with the whole.

detail. In contrast to many of his other houses, the Villa Rotonda or the Villa Malcontenta for example, which have freestanding porticos, in the Villa Maser the four columns are moved back and become engaged with the wall. The Villa Thiene at Quinto, of the same period as the Chiericati, also uses this device, but there is none of the rich decoration of the Villa Maser. The inspiration of these houses is the ancient temple-front, which Palladio had wrongly assumed to have been used in both religious and secular buildings alike. How he arrived at this conclusion need not concern us here, for without doubt he managed to create with this formula a number of splendid designs.

These villas with their low, outlying wings were a favourite type of building with Palladio (Fig. 93). It is obvious from his writings that he gave careful consideration to the problem of their design. They gave fine expression to the idea of richness, spaciousness and importance which the Italian nobles of the period so ardently required. The outlying wings also estab-

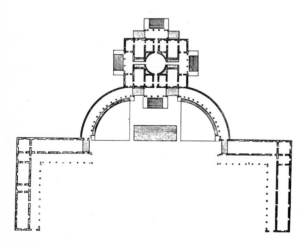

*Fig. 93 The Villa Trissino, Meledo (c. 1552),
by Palladio—plan*

lished a much more intimate link with the landscape around the building, and so for the first time it became necessary to consider the arrangement of the garden and environs of the house in much greater detail. It also created a new group of spatial relationships between the building and the landscape in which it is set, for the division between building and environment becomes much more ambiguous. Between the inside and the outside of a typical Renaissance palazzo of the Florentine type there is a clearly stated wall, and there can be no doubt as to whether one is inside or outside the building. The sweeping wings of the Palladio-type dwelling establish a slightly more subtle relationship, for with the spreading of the wings of the building, like arms, a person standing within the reach of those arms is in a much more intimate relationship with the structure of the building than when standing before the flat

screenlike wall of a Florentine mansion. Though he is not physically 'inside' the building he is much more part of it. Palladio may well have taken this idea from the work of Trissino, who had been his early master in classical studies.

Although his domestic buildings generally overshadowed his churches, this side of his architecture was no less important, especially to later architects of Venice. His main achievements in this field were the façade of S. Francesco della Vigna at Venice (Fig. 94), designed in the first place by Sansovino, and two churches designed completely by himself—S. Giorgio Maggiore (begun in 1566, façade 1597–1610) and Il Redentore (1576–92), both in Venice (Figs. 95, 96).

The façades of the three buildings all show a logical development of one idea: the adaptation of a Roman device consisting of the interpenetration of two or more orders and pediments. This means in effect that

Fig. 94 S. Francesco della Vigna, Venice, by Palladio

Fig. 95 S. Giorgio Maggiore, Venice (begun 1566), by Palladio

Fig. 96

*Il Redentore, Venice (1576–92),
by Palladio*

the façade is really made up of two temple façades, a complete front for the nave and a second interrupted one above and behind for the aisles. The idea had already been attempted by both Bramante and Peruzzi, and there can be little doubt that Palladio was conscious of these earlier attempts when he made his designs. Of the three, the front of Il Redentore is the most integrated and powerful as a piece of design.

The designs of S. Francesco della Vigna and S. Giorgio Maggiore, are both similar, but tend to be rather fussy and over-crowded with details when compared with the Redentore front. From drawings that Palladio made of the Pantheon it is clear that he found justification there for his treatment of the façades of his churches. The façade of the Il Redentore has something of the classical calm which we have become accustomed to expect from his treatment of the fronts of his best villas and palazzi. Use is made of the integration of orders of different sizes, and the architrave of the smaller order is carried right across the façade to draw the broken side pediments into the composition. The smaller pediment contained within the central bay appears to support the entablature perched upon it, and reminds one of the awkward feeling that has already been seen in the Palazzo del Tè half a century before.

Just as Alberti had achieved a solution to the problem of the church façade in the Quattrocento, so Palladio had provided a solution in the Cinquecento. And influential as Palladio's buildings were, his writings and drawings were even more important, providing inspiration for generations of architects to come. Moreover, the careful record drawings which he made of various antiquities are now invaluable, because many of the buildings which he drew are no longer in existence.

FURTHER READING

Peter Murray, *The Architecture of the Italian Renaissance*. Batsford, 1963.

An excellently written and well-illustrated account of the period.

R. Wittkower, *Architectural Principles in the Age of Humanism*. Tiranti, 1962.

This is a fascinating book—especially for those who are interested in mathematics and music. Particularly valuable are the passages on Alberti and Palladio.

Heinrich Wölfflin, *Renaissance and Baroque*. Fontana Library, 1961.

Though what Wölfflin calls Baroque we would now call Mannerism, this remains an excellent and perceptive study.

J. S. Ackerman, *The Architecture of Michelangelo*. Zwemmer, 1961.

A most authoritative text on the great Italian master; the introduction is very valuable for a concise summary of the architectural scene into which Michelangelo came.

Jacob Burckhardt, *The Civilization of the Renaissance in Italy*. Phaidon, 1937.

One of the great books on art history and criticism. However, modern scholarship repudiates many of Burckhardt's opinions, and the book should be read with a critical attitude.

4

BAROQUE ARCHITECTURE IN ITALY

The transition from Renaissance to Baroque was not so much a change in style as a change in the conception of space. Scholars of the past have looked upon Baroque as a period of decay, during which the vital creative forces of the Renaissance were spent and the impetus was running out. To the modern student, however, the period represents the emergence of a new and revitalizing force, whereby the familiar classical details are given a new, and to the purist sometimes a fantastic, lease of life.

The decline of Mannerism coincided with the Council of Trent, which sat periodically between 1545 and 1563. The edicts of the council had widespread effects on all the visual arts. Not only was the fig-leaf the direct outcome of their deliberations; they were also responsible for the architect's and painter's attempts to represent the glorification and transcendence of the divine mysteries. There was a new religious fervour abroad, and architecturally this manifested itself in a spate of new churches which were as ornate as they were complex. On a more secular level the trend was towards an architecture which not only reflected the wealth of the patron, but, in the royal palaces, something of the divine right of kings.

The Council of Trent had called in question the whole purpose and function of the arts and had directed that the artist should concern himself with the representation of all aspects of Christian belief. The result

may seem far removed from the severity of the Council's doctrines, but only a few will deny that Baroque painting, sculpture, and architecture does make the church's teachings abundantly clear and actual. Indeed, it may well be argued that the images the Baroque created were so real, so much of this world, that their spirituality is lost. Many people find the ostentation of High Baroque churches so distracting that worship becomes all but impossible. We are then faced with the intriguing question as to whether these are churches at all, or simply monuments to a taste—less discerning than our own. However, we must concern ourselves here with the development of architecture; and though the products may be in question, the method by which they came about is more straightforward.

It is the Baroque architect's handling of space which is of importance to the present study. To the Renaissance architect the practice of architecture had been largely an intellectual pursuit; the Mannerist had shown that the classical language of Rome could be made to yield effects of intense emotion; the Baroque architect wielded the same components to produce effects which were at once more plastic and more theatrical. It is possible to suppose that the architect of the early or High Renaissance would have found the forms of the Baroque architect both vulgar and ostentatious. In

Plate 15   The Church of the Gesù (begun 1568), by Vignola
The decoration is later, but it is interesting to compare this interior with
a Gothic one, such as that of Amiens. Note the dramatic effect achieved
by lighting in the present example

fact it is doubtful whether the earlier architect could have conceived such forms as the
Baroque architect included in his vocabulary. Nevertheless these new forms came
into existence, and architecture was enriched by their invention.

The earliest Baroque church is that of the
Church of the Gesù, Rome, begun in 1568
by Vignola (Pl. 15). This was designed as
the mother church for the powerful Society
of Jesus. The plan was prepared by Michelangelo and based on Alberti's design for

Plate 16 SS. Martina e Luca, Rome (1635–50), by Pietro da Cortona—exterior
The comparison of this 'façade' with the exterior of the little church at Todi (Fig. 64) shows clearly the change in attitude between Renaissance and Baroque concepts

S. Andrea in Mantua. The façade was altered by other artists but became the standard type for the whole European Baroque. The powerful two-storey design of the Gesù was to form the basis of the form of church façades throughout the Baroque period. The immediate effect was to be seen on the Roman churches of S. Andrea della Valle and S. Ignazio, though both these churches had certain elements of Mannerism still in their design.

There are, however, two churches of

similar plan which illustrate the essential difference between Renaissance and Baroque concepts of space and the handling of mass. One church has already been referred to, the S. Maria della Consolazione at Todi (Fig. 64); the other is the SS. Martina e Luca (1635–50) at Rome by Pietro da Cortona (1596–1669, Pl. 16). The church at Todi shows Renaissance church design at its most concentrated. From the elevations it would be quite easy to reconstruct the plan, for the exterior is the logical outcome of the interior. The simple square shape of the central block is given the most direct expression, and it is perfectly clear that the apses are simple additions to the four sides. It is almost as if the architect had drawn a tight skin over his idea. The result is completely satisfying, nothing could be added, nothing taken away, without serious detriment to the whole. A comparison of the plan of this church with that of the one by Pietro (Figs. 97, 98) shows that in essence they are very similar indeed. Both have a square central space with dome and apsidal additions. In the Pietro plan, however, the apses are more extended, whilst the façade is made into a full-scale architectural composition of its own. Further, this façade bears little relation to the building behind. This is not a tight skin, but the orchestration of an idea. Whilst the church at Todi had no particular viewpoint, the Pietro design now has front, back, and sides, which are clearly demonstrated in the plan. The high viewpoint used in the drawing of the Todi church (Fig. 64) makes it possible to admire the concept of the church as a whole; such a viewpoint for the Pietro-designed church might well be a disadvantage.

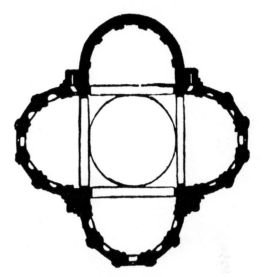

Fig. 97 S. Maria della Consolazione, Todi (1508)—plan

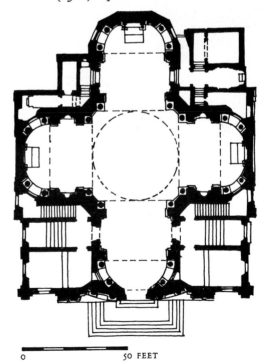

0   50 FEET

Fig. 98 SS. Martina e Luca, Rome (1635), by Pietro da Cortona—plan

Plate 17 S. Maria della Consolazione, Todi—interior

If we now turn to a consideration of the interiors we shall find that again the solutions to the problem are very different (Pls. 17, 18). The interior of the S. Maria della Consolazione is as clear-cut and logical as the exterior. The expression of the central square is pointed by the angle pilasters, the division of the wall gives scale to the interior, and the pilasters and entablatures divide the wall-space into intellectually satisfying proportions. These are again subdivided by the windows, which are cut quite deliberately into the walls, filling the interior with a clear, almost clinical light

*Plate 18 SS. Martina e Luca—interior. Plates 17 and 18 must be looked at with Plate 16
and Fig. 64 to clarify the different conceptions behind the two styles*

revealing the simple geometry on which the whole idea is based.

The interior of the Baroque church, SS. Martina e Luca, is a very different matter. Though the central space is marked by columns and pilasters, the sharp definition of the square is blunted by the bevelled plane set between them. The effect produced by this interior is much more busy than that of the S. Maria; the walls are set in motion by columns and the sharply projecting entablatures. The effect is that of a wall made up of advancing and receding planes. The obvious sources of light which impartially revealed the interior of S. Maria are now transformed into concealed sources of light—the only window to be seen is that in the far apse, which picks out certain features and throws others into shadow. The result of this method of handling space is that we can infer no idea of the exterior from the interior, whereas in the earlier building the two are linked by a logic which cannot be escaped. In the Pietro church the only point where any reference to the exterior is made, is where the window pierces the dome. At S. Maria, on the other hand, we sense that the exterior fits the interior like a cap. The church of SS. Martina e Luca points to the direction architecture was to take; for the ambiguity and lack of definition between surface and surface, wall and ceiling, solid and void, were to be the characteristics of Baroque architecture.

*Fig. 99 S. Carlo alle Quattro Fontane, Rome (1638–41),
by Francesco Borromini—plan*

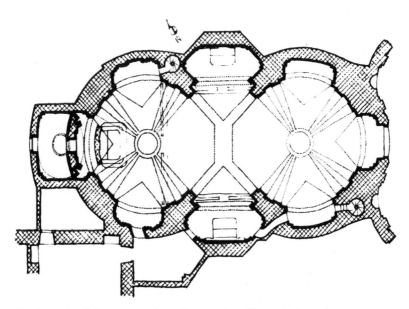

*Fig. 100 The Church of the Immaculate Conception, Turin (1672–9),
by Guarino Guarini—plan*

Plate 19 The colonnade in St Peter's Square, Rome, by Gian Lorenzo Bernini
This gives a good idea of the power and magnificence of Bernini's conception

To further this new conception, sculptors and painters co-operated with the architect —if he were not already an able practitioner in the various arts himself—to produce buildings which give an astonishing illusion of space and movement. By the use of painting and modelling the exact point of change between ceiling and wall became all but impossible to define. Very often the top of the building was burst open by painting the dome with figures in violent perspective and foreshortening, rushing upwards into a limitless sky. This feeling of movement was further enhanced by the adoption of the circle and the ellipse, replacing the right angle and the rectangle of the Renaissance. The interplay of curved surfaces is a vital factor in the development of the Baroque plan (Figs. 99, 100), giving the buildings a dynamic movement of space in contrast to the static self-sufficient space of the century before.

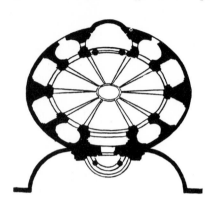

Fig. 101 *S. Andrea al Quirinale, Rome (1658–70), by Bernini—façade*

Fig. 102 *S. Andrea al Quirinale—plan*

The work of Pietro da Cortona, Gian Lorenzo Bernini, and Francesco Borromini dominated the period of the High Baroque in Italy, which lasted from about 1625 to 1675. Maderna's work at St Peter's has already been mentioned, but the area in front of the great church still remained unfinished. Maderna had finished his work by 1612, and for nearly forty-five years work on the cathedral was at a standstill. In 1656, Bernini was asked to complete the design of the piazza in front of the church, and the result was one of the grandest conceptions of the Baroque period (Pl. 19). Maderna had already designed a fountain in front of the cathedral, and there was an obelisk in the square, placed there by Sixtus V. Bernini's scheme left these two features intact, and organized the space around them into the awe-inspiring colonnade (Pl. 14) with which we are familiar. So sweeping was Bernini's conception that Maderna's façade is almost dwarfed, and yet the result is a unified whole.

Bernini

Bernini (1598–1680) has been called the Michelangelo of the seventeenth century, and not without some cause, for the breadth of his knowledge and the scope of his achievement were immense. The most striking of his churches is the S. Andrea al Quirinale, 1658–70. The entrance is less complex than in many of his churches, but none the less theatrical for that (Fig. 101). The plan is a simple oval, with the long axis at right-angles to the entrance (Fig. 102). The Baroque combination of painting and sculpture is well illustrated in the altarpiece, where the theme of the martyrdom of St Andrew is painted over the altar and his body is shown rising to heaven in a piece of sculpture striking through the heavy broken pediment above. In S. Andrea Bernini used his talents as architect, sculptor and dramatist to produce an interior designed to transport the beholder to a state of exaltation. He also achieved similar apocalyptic effects in his sculpture, imbuing it with a lightness and complexity of movement that belied the intractable materials from which it was made. The 'St Teresa in Ecstasy' (Pl. 20) in the S. Maria della Vittoria in Rome is one of the finest High Baroque sculptures, and has a flexibility which one would usually associate with the painter rather than the sculptor.

In the façade of the Palazzo Chigi-Odescalchi at Rome, Bernini harked back both to Bramante's House of Raphael and to Michelangelo's Capitoline Palace, the result was so dignified and gracious that it became the standard pattern for the European palace for the next century and a half.

Plate 20 S. Teresa in Ecstasy (1645–52), by Bernini
  This shows Bernini's power as a sculptor, as well as the way in which Baroque artists used light as an important element in design. The strong top light makes this group appear to materialize out of the surrounding gloom

Borromini

Scarcely less impressive are the achievements of Francesco Borromini (1599–1666). More of a perfectionist than Bernini, his first work, S. Carlo alle Quattro Fontane at Rome, shows his command of Baroque form.

Borromini had worked with his uncle, Maderna, at St Peter's but his first work shows both his originality and his independence of thought. The façade of this beautiful little church (Pl. 21) shows the Baroque

Plate 21

S. Carlo alle Quattro Fontane, Rome (1638–41)— façade (1665–7), by Francesco Borromini

The wave-like formation of this façade is a thrilling architectural conception; the care with which it was built can be seen in the deliberate juxtaposition of concave and convex curves

Plate 22 S. Ivo, Rome (1642–50), by Borromini—view into dome

architect's preoccupation with the circle and the ellipse. The two storeys are an object lesson in the management of curve and counter-curve. The total effect is at once both tense and monumental. The church is so small that the story goes that it could have been built in one of the piers of St Peter's, but the façade gives no suggestion of this minute scale. The interior is further proof of the architect's ability to use the ellipse. The elliptical dome gives more flow and movement to the interior than could be achieved by the conventional type, and is more suited to the space-concept which the architect wished to create.

Using a somewhat similar plan in the church of S. Ivo della Sapienza, in Rome he manages to effect a dome of even greater freedom and lightness of design (Pl. 22). This splendidly sprung dome (he dispensed with a drum) is a fitting point of climax to an exceedingly unified space-conception. The dome as used by the Renaissance designers suggested a much more finite shape than the elliptical domes the Baroque designers favoured. Indeed, this new sense

Plate 23 S. Lorenzo, Turin (1666–79), by Guarino Guarini—view into dome
Both Plates 22 and 23 are examples of fine domes, the latter showing how, by the
use of light, Baroque artists managed to give the impression of dissolving space

of freedom was so great that Guarini, in the church of S. Lorenzo in Turin (Pl. 23), almost managed to dissolve the dome altogether.

Guarini

In many ways Guarino Guarini (1624–83) was the most daring and original innovator of the Italian Baroque movement. His plan for S. Lorenzo is a miracle of complexity (Fig. 103). Within a roughly square shape he manages to create a feeling of great fluidity and movement of mass against mass. This can well be considered as the first Late Baroque church. Though the plan is square at ground level, this shape is transformed half-way up the building into an octagon with alternate concave and convex sides. In

this way the rigidity of the ground plan is broken and the way is prepared for the final effect of the dome, where space appears to dissolve into a delicate filigree of light and shadow.

Guarini's Palazzo Carignano in Turin with its bold movement across the façade, is a most arresting composition; but the Church of the Immaculate Conception in the same town proved to be his most influential building. The plan of this church (Fig. 100) is formed of two circles on the long axis which do not quite intersect. There is neither domed crossing, nor central area, and Guarini uses his knowledge of vaulting—which was both extensive and original—to produce an effect of continuous movement throughout the interior.

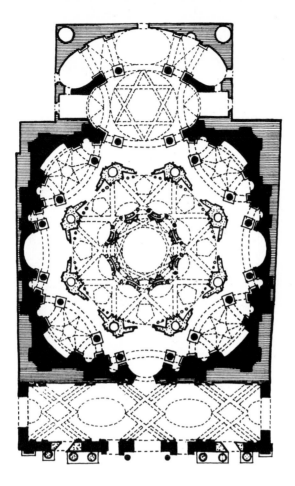

Fig. 103 S. Lorenzo, Turin—plan

By the beginning of the eighteenth century Baroque was ready to move into a further stage of development. The forms became lighter and more assured, *trompe-l'œil* painting brought about the complete fusion of surfaces, and decoration became lighter and more restrained. Striking developments were to be made in France, and in Austria the work of Balthasar Neumann, especially the Pilgrimage church at Vierzehnheiligen, was to bring European Baroque to its conclusion. These developments, however, are outside the scope of this book.

Baroque architecture is far removed from the style of building with which this study of Italian architecture began. As we have seen, the early architects might well have frowned upon the free use made of the elements which they would have considered sacrosanct. It is possible that the Gothic masons would have had more sympathy and understanding, for in many ways the Baroque and the Gothic were like kindred spirits.

FURTHER READING

R. Wittkower, *Art and Architecture in Italy, 1600–1750*. Pelican History of Art, Pelican Books, 1958.

A very valuable book.

Germain Bazin, *Baroque and Rococo*. Thames & Hudson, 1964.

A valuable guide to the seventeenth and eighteenth centuries. The two centuries are covered country by country, and the illustrations are well chosen, many of them being in colour.

Victor-L. Tapié, *The Age of Grandeur*. Weidenfeld & Nicolson, 1960.

An excellent book; it gives a very full account of the birth of the movement and then deals in detail with the various European countries. 'Baroque Europe' in the 'Building of Europe' series referred to in the main bibliography, is valuable for the excellence of the photographs, and Henry A. Millon's book in the 'Great Ages of World Architecture' series is one of the best in the series; the illustrations are very good and the text is very informative.

PART TWO

Architecture in Britain 1066–1800

TABLE 2

CHART SHOWING THE THREE DIVISIONS OF THE ENGLISH CATHEDRAL

Cathedrals of old foundation	*Cathedrals of monastic foundation*	*Cathedrals to which bishops have been appointed since 1836*
These were served by secular clergy and not affected by the reforms of Henry VIII after the Dissolution.	These were served by monks or regular canons and were totally reconstituted in 1539.	

Chichester	Bath*		Ripon 1836‡ ⎰ old collegiate
Hereford	Canterbury*		Southwell 1884‡ ⎱ churches
Exeter	Carlisle†		
Lincoln	Durham*	In these the	
Lichfield	Ely*	Bishop acted	St Albans 1877* ⎰ abbey
London (Old St Paul's)	Norwich*	simultaneously	Bury St Edmunds 1914* ⎱ churches
Salisbury	Rochester*	as Abbot	
Wells	Winchester*		
York	Worcester*		Newcastle 1882
			Wakefield 1888
			Manchester 1847
Bangor ⎰	Bristol†	Abbey churches	Birmingham 1871 ⎰ Parochial
Llandaff ⎱ Welsh	Chester*	made cathedrals	Truro 1880 ⎱ churches
St David's	Gloucester*	at Dissolution	Chelmsford 1914
St Asaph	Oxford†	by Henry VIII	Southwark 1905
	Peterborough*		Coventry 1918
	Westminster (can be included in this latter group, but only retained cathedral status for a few years)		Liverpool, etc
			Dates in this column refer to elevation to cathedral status.

Coventry and Lichfield shared a diocese until 1918 as Bath and Wells still do.

Key: * Benedictine Order   † Augustinian Regular Canons   ‡ Secular Canons

5

GOTHIC ECCLESIASTICAL ARCHITECTURE

Dating the period of Gothic architecture in England presents several problems, though the most generally accepted divisions are:

1066–1189 — Norman — 12th century
1189–1307 — Early English — 13th century
1307–1377 — Decorated — 14th century
1377–1485 — Perpendicular — 15th century
1485–1558 — Tudor — 16th century

The Norman Conquest may be taken as an easy date to mark the beginning of the Gothic period, though it must be remembered that Norman architecture is really a branch of Romanesque, rather than true Gothic, which is characterized by the pointed arch. The Normans did not normally use this feature, though at Durham, one of the supreme examples of Romanesque architecture, the pointed arch does appear in the south aisle of the choir. This is generally accepted as the first instance of the use of the pointed arch in a high vault in Europe, and the date, somewhere between 1093 and 1098, places it some years before Suger's church at Saint Denis (begun 1137); there had, however, been isolated instances of the use of the pointed arch before this.

It is almost equally difficult to say when the period ended. The historian would give 1485, with the accession of the first Tudor monarchs, as the generally accepted date. Architecturally, Henry VIII is usually credited with the introduction of the Renaissance style to England, after he had been to the Continent for the Field of the Cloth of Gold in 1520. Although he imported foreign craftsmen to carry out designs in the new Italian style, many of the buildings of this period retain an essentially Gothic framework, with classical detail and ornament stuck on. Therefore, to try to maintain a sense of continuity it is helpful to think of the Gothic period as one lasting from the Conquest to the end of the Tudor monarchy—though the last fifty years show increasing signs of Renaissance influence.

The Constitution of the English Church

The division of the Greater English Church into cathedrals, abbeys, minsters and priories is architecturally somewhat misleading. The monastic churches—abbeys and priories—are distinguished from the others only by having additional buildings. The plan of the church itself remains fundamentally the same for all four types. To clear the ground, a definition of these terms will be helpful:

CATHEDRAL The principal church of a diocese. It contains the bishop's throne (*kathedra*—Greek).

ABBEY A monastery for persons of either sex, presided over by an abbot or an abbess. The clergy may be monks or canons regular.*

MINSTER The church of an abbey or priory, but the term is often applied (particularly in the north of England) to a cathedral church without monastic connections (e.g. York).

PRIORY This is a convent for either sex ruled over by a prior or prioress. To this group can be added CHARTER HOUSES, Carthusian foundations, which are of little importance architecturally because remains are so slight.

It will be seen from the chart on page 102 that some of our present cathedrals were built as monastic churches, whilst many were simply parish churches which were later raised to cathedral status for political, economic, or ecclesiastical reasons—sometimes without regard to architectural design or significance. Architecturally, then, it is clear that English churches fall into two groups, each having quite distinct qualities and characteristics; these are the greater

* There are two types of canons—canons regular and secular canons. Canons regular have taken religious vows and live under a monastic rule (*regula*). The term applies particularly to the rule of St Augustine, and the members were known as Augustinian Canons. Secular canons lived as ordinary ecclesiastics in the world, were allowed to own property, and owed canonical obedience to their bishop.

church or the abbey-cathedral type, and the parochial or parish church type.

Very early in ecclesiastical history it was decided that the bishop's cathedra could only be placed in the church of a town, not that of a village. This caused no difficulty on the Continent, where towns were numerous and were natural centres for trade and the dissemination of culture and religion. In Saxon England, however, where towns were few and far between, the bishop was quite often the head of a tribe (e.g. the Bishop of South Saxons, the Bishop of West Saxons, and others), and as the tribes tended to move about, the bishop's throne was much more migratory and was often set up in a village church. In 1075 a council held in London under Archbishop Lanfranc took steps to regularize and make more permanent the towns where the various bishops' dioceses were to be centred. Although the bishop was nominally the head of the cathedral church, the actual running and administration was left in the hands of the dean and chapter. The bishop was very often engaged in political service, administrative work—or even warlike pursuits—and was often absent from the diocese for long periods.

During the first half of the thirteenth century, as a result of the work of the Lateran Council, there was a general stocktaking of parishes and a re-defining of parish boundaries. This move, together with the growing prosperity of agriculture and commerce helped in turn by Henry III's granting of markets and fairs to many market towns, resulted in the rapid growth of parish churches. Many new churches were founded, and existing churches were enlarged or remodelled.

Though it is possible to argue that by the time of the Dissolution the monasteries had served their purpose, during their years of ascendancy they had played an important part in the economic and cultural growth of the country. Monasteries were the storehouses of knowledge and learning, and were also important trading centres (see p. 118 et seq.). Again, abbots and the clergy frequently served as ambassadors and envoys of state, and played an important part in the affairs of the day.

At the time of the Dissolution the whole monastic system had fallen from public and royal favour, and the monastic way of life had become a target for satirists and critics. Many of the lusty tales collected by the troubadours contain bawdy references to monks and friars. There can be no doubt that some houses were guilty of vicious and carnal behaviour, but on the whole the main cause of dislike was probably more the laxity and laziness in the observation of the rules of their orders than actual vicious living. Henry VIII embarked on the Dissolution for a number of reasons, though the most important were doubtless connected with finance, for he was in urgent need of money. The operation was completed in two stages. The greater monasteries were dissolved in 1539, but the smaller houses with incomes of less than £200 per annum had fallen three years earlier. Having completed the work of dissolution Henry set about an entire reconstruction of the church. The thirteen cathedrals of the old foundation, served by secular clergy, were not affected by his reforms. The nine monastic cathedrals, where the bishop was also an abbot, were reconstituted; and the five abbey churches (six if we count Westminster, which did not continue for long as a cathedral) were promoted to the status of cathedrals (in strictly ecclesiastical terms, cathedrals of the new foundation) and put under the rule of a dean and chapter (see centre column of chart on page 102). This number remained constant until 1836, when the creation of new dioceses and cathedrals took place. After the Dissolution still further complications arose because in many cases abbeys were bought at the Reformation by the local parishioners to serve as parish churches. Examples of this sort are Tewkesbury, Glos., where the whole church was acquired; the nave of Bolton Abbey, Yorks.; the choir and transepts at Pershore, Worcs.; and the abbey church of St Albans, which served as a parish church until created a cathedral in 1877. This briefly outlines the constitution of the greater churches in England.

Because of the complicated nature of the early history and constitution of the church administration it has been necessary to outline the development in some detail. In this way a starting point is given to the present history, and the background knowledge and definitions assumed by most other books on the subject are provided. Once it is understood that the terminology is ecclesiastical rather than architectural, many of the apparent contradictions disappear.

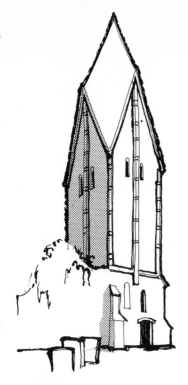

Fig. 104 The Saxon tower, Sompting, Sussex (Early eleventh century)

Fig. 105 The Saxon Church, Bradford-on-Avon

The Abbey-Cathedral Type of Church

The remains of pre-Conquest churches, though plentiful, are fragmentary and scattered. There are, of course, the magnificent towers at Earls Barton, Northants., and Sompting, Sussex (Fig. 104), and churches at Bradford-on-Avon, Wilts. (Fig. 105), Escomb, County Durham, and Barton-on-Humber, Lincs. These examples show the skill of the Anglo-Saxon masons. By comparison, the Normans were clumsy and inept in their handling of stone, relying on mass rather than fine masonry for strength. Presumably the Saxons used timber extensively, though because of its perishable nature little evidence exists to show the way in which it was employed. From about 1090 onwards an intense outburst of building activity took place. Many churches which must have been in a perfectly good state of repair were pulled down, the Saxon prelates deposed and replaced by Norman ones, and a church of much greater magnificence erected on the old site. These vast churches were embarked upon to implement William's general policy, which was to overawe and impress the conquered people. In plan the Norman churches closely resembled their counterparts in France, but in size and scale they were much more vast, and were with few exceptions unequalled for size throughout Europe. Within half a century of the conquest the rebuilding of at least seventeen of the major churches, including Canterbury, Durham, Lincoln, London (Old St Paul's), Norwich, York, St Albans, Ely, Gloucester and Peterborough, was begun. This spate of building was not matched on the Continent at the time.

As we shall see, the French characteristics in the plans of these early churches became

Plate 24

Durham Cathedral
(c. 1098)—the nave,
looking east

One of the
grandest pieces
of Romanesque
architecture in
Europe

almost totally obliterated through succeeding centuries. Owing to the very English custom of almost constant rebuilding, there are hardly any major churches which do not present a complete history of stylistic development—Norman, Early English, Decorated, Perpendicular—in their fabric. The characteristic Norman plan was of the cruciform type, the most striking peculiarity being the extreme length of the nave. Peterborough and Fountains Abbey, York-shire, were eleven bays in length, and Byland Abbey, also in Yorkshire, had twelve bays. St Albans had thirteen bays and Norwich had fourteen bays, while Winchester had the same number when first laid out, but only twelve remain. Even Durham, with only eight bays, runs to 200 feet, whilst Norwich is 260 feet, and the nave at Winchester is over 300 feet long. The naves of Durham (Pl. 24), Ely and Peterborough show English Romanesque at its finest. At

Gloucester, however, the relationship between nave arcade, triforium, and clerestory is uncomfortable. The massive unbroken cylinders of the nave-columns dwarf the arches on top of them, so that in no sense do these arches grow from the columns; and there seems hardly to have been room to squash the triforium in under the clerestory.

At the crossing of nave and transepts it was usual to put a low tower, and twin towers at the west, as at Canterbury and Durham, were not uncommon. The Cistercian orders forbade the use of central towers, though some of the richer houses indulged in them none the less, as at Kirkstall Abbey in Yorkshire and also at Fountains, where a splendid tower was erected at the end of the north transept. The transepts made bold projections on these early plans, and had apsidal chapels to the east, which were sometimes squared off externally as at Hereford.

As for the east-end or choir arm, in the case of most English cathedrals this feature has been so remodelled that all the character of the Norman building has been lost. The apsidal termination, almost universal in France, soon lost favour in this country and was replaced by the characteristic square form. It is possible, however, from Norman remains and plans, to discern two methods of planning: firstly, the parallel-apsed plan and secondly (mainly confined to monastic houses—Old St Paul's and Lichfield being the only secular examples), the peri-apsidal type.

Of the parallel-apse type (Fig. 106) there are now no examples extant in this country, as all have been replaced by later remodelling. The central apse still remains at Peterborough, though it was pierced with arches

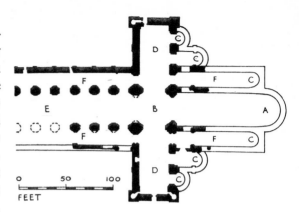

Fig. 106 St Albans Cathedral—eastern arm
An example of a parallel-apsed plan

when the retrochoir was added in the fifteenth century. This form was used in the Conqueror's two churches at Caen (Figs. 107, 108), and was introduced into England in the Confessor's abbey at Westminster. The main objection to this arrangement was that, at times of pilgrimage and festival, those paying homage at the shrine found movement to and from the altars difficult and congested. In the cathedrals known to have possessed such a feature, it has been replaced—at Canterbury by the unique *corona* (or 'Becket's crown'), a circular addition to the apsidal Trinity Chapel; at Bath by the Lady-chapel; at Durham by the Chapel of Nine Altars; at Ely by the presbytery and retrochoir; at Exeter by the Lady-chapel; at Lincoln by the presbytery; at Peterborough by the retrochoir; and at St Albans by the Lady-chapel.

To facilitate this movement a more complex form of eastern termination was evolved. This was the peri-apsidal type (Fig. 109), where the sanctuary terminated in an eastern apse, around which the aisles continued as an ambulatory. The chapels were

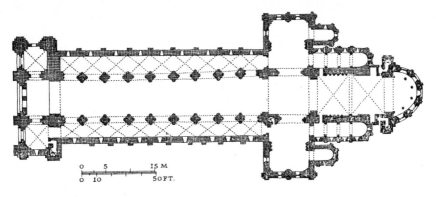

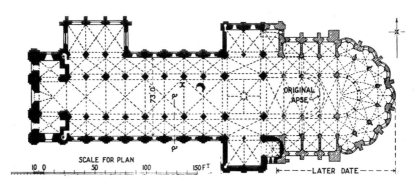

Fig. 107 La Trinité (Abbaye-aux-Dames), Caen—plan

Fig. 108 St Étienne (Abbaye-aux-Hommes),
Caen—plan

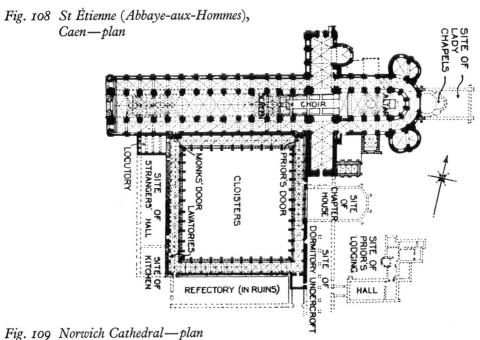

Fig. 109 Norwich Cathedral—plan
An example of the peri-apsidal
type of eastern arm

then set out in a radial fashion at north-east, east, and south-east points. It will be seen at once that the flow around this passage-way is much smoother here than in the previous style. Both Gloucester and Nor-wich are fine examples of this type of layout and fortunately neither has been so altered that the original intention is obscured. Except at Westminster Abbey (Fig. 110) this form never developed into the chevet, as was common in France. Canterbury, with its unique complexity of plan, is without equal in the land (Fig. 111). By the end of the twelfth century the apsidal east-end had been abandoned. New buildings used the square termination, and in most cases exist-ing apses were replaced by the new form, which lasted until the end of the Middle Ages. At Durham, for example, the old apsidal end is marked on the floor quite clearly, but, of course, the eastern end is now the famous 'Chapel of Nine Altars', which was erected between 1242 and 1280.

Characteristic of English cathedrals is their extreme length, which is due not only to the length of nave already mentioned, but also to the length of the choir. There can be no doubt that the great length of the eastern arm is due to the example of Canterbury, where rebuilding took place in 1174 after a disastrous fire had gutted the existing choir. The Frenchman William of Sens was given the task of reconstruction, using the existing outer walls and entirely rebuilding the central part, the piers, the arches and walls above, etc. Unfortunately William suffered a bad fall from the building and returned to France a cripple. However, his successor, William the Englishman, pre-sumably the Frenchman's chief assistant,

took over the work, and carried out his master's design with little variation. The French master-mason was doubtless well acquainted with the design of the French cathedrals at Sens and Noyon, and this influence is evident in his designs for Can-terbury. At this time, too, an important factor in the extension of the choir was the increasing importance attached to the wor-ship of the Virgin Mary. From the thirteenth century onwards any major church, whether secular or monastic, would have been con-sidered incomplete without a chapel dedi-cated to Our Lady. Generally the Lady-chapel is an unaisled hall placed, wherever the site permitted, as an eastern annexe of the retrochoir, as at Salisbury, Exeter, or Chichester.

At Durham, Bishop Pudsey started to build a Lady-chapel beyond the shrine of St Cuthbert. However, cracks and settle-ments began to appear, and these were attributed to St Cuthbert's well-known dis-like of women or anything feminine. The chapel was moved to the other end of the building, and the beautiful little 'Galilee'* was built on to the west front, on a very cramped site bounded by an almost precipi-tous descent to the river below.

The thirteenth century saw drastic changes in the development of the eastern arm, but generally few alterations were made in the planning of the nave. In a few cases western transepts were thrown out to provide more altar space, but altars so far removed from the choir were found to be impractical, and

---

* The name Galilee was the name given to the last place in the church visited by the Sunday procession, and was so called from the disciples having being told that the master would go before them into Galilee.

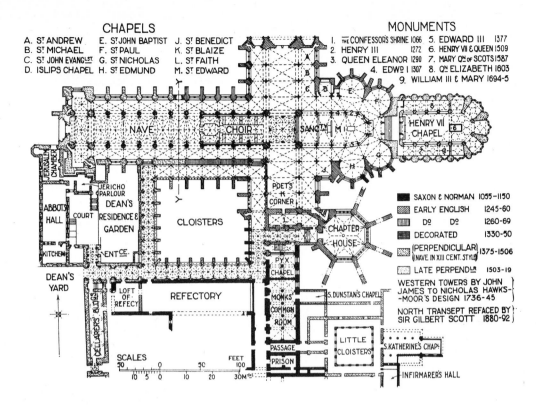

CHAPELS

A. ST ANDREW   E. ST JOHN BAPTIST   J. ST BENEDICT
B. ST MICHAEL   F. ST PAUL   K. ST BLAIZE
C. ST JOHN EVANG LST   G. ST NICHOLAS   L. ST FAITH
D. ISLIPS CHAPEL   H. ST EDMUND   M. ST EDWARD

MONUMENTS

1. THE CONFESSORS SHRINE 1066   5. EDWARD III 1377
2. HENRY III 1272   6. HENRY VII & QUEEN 1509
3. QUEEN ELEANOR 1290   7. MARY QN OF SCOTS 1587
4. EDWD I 1307   8. QN ELIZABETH 1603
9. WILLIAM III & MARY 1694-5

JERUSALEM CHAMBER

NAVE   CHOIR   SANCTY M

JERICHO PARLOUR

ABBOTS HALL   COURT   DEAN'S RESIDENCE & GARDEN

KITCHEN   ENTCE

CLOISTERS

HENRY VII CHAPEL

POETS CORNER

CHAPTER HOUSE

SAXON & NORMAN 1055-1150
EARLY ENGLISH 1245-60
DO DO 1260-69
DECORATED 1330-50
(PERPENDICULAR) 1375-1506 (NAVE IN XIII CENT. STYLE)
LATE PERPENDLR 1503-19

WESTERN TOWERS BY JOHN JAMES TO NICHOLAS HAWKS-MOOR'S DESIGN 1736-45
NORTH TRANSEPT REFACED BY SIR GILBERT SCOTT 1880-92

DEAN'S YARD

CELLARERS BLDGS

LOFT OF REFECY   REFECTORY

PYX CHAPEL

MONKS COMMON ROOM

PASSAGE   PRISON

S. DUNSTAN'S CHAPEL

LITTLE CLOISTERS

S. KATHERINES CHAPL

INFIRMARER'S HALL

SCALES
50   50   FEET 100
10 5 0   10   20   30 MTRS

Fig. 110 Westminster Abbey—plan
This is the closest that English planning comes to the French 'chevet' type of eastern arm

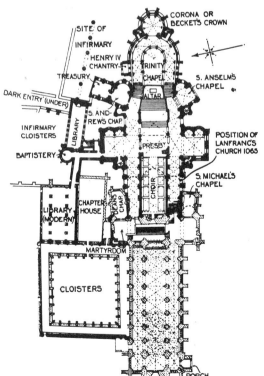

SITE OF INFIRMARY
CORONA OR BECKET'S CROWN
HENRY IV CHANTRY
TREASURY
TRINITY CHAPEL
S. ANSELM'S CHAPEL
DARK ENTRY (UNDER)
ALTAR
S. AND-REW'S CHAP
INFIRMARY CLOISTERS
LIBRARY
PRESBY
POSITION OF LANFRANC'S CHURCH 1065
BAPTISTERY
CHOIR
S. MICHAEL'S CHAPEL
LIBRARY (MODERN)
CHAPTER HOUSE
DEANS CHAP
MARTYRDOM
CLOISTERS
PORCH

Fig. 111 Canterbury Cathedral—plan
There is no other eastern termination like this one

so this type of transept never became popular. Ely and Peterborough are examples of this form of design.

Ely and Durham, which have already been mentioned, are peculiar in that they both have Galilees tacked onto the west front. The Galilee porch at Ely, 1198–1215, is architectually one of the finest in Europe, showing as it does great beauty of proportion and refinement of detail. There is another notable Galilee porch at Lincoln, on the western corner of the south transept.

The central tower is one of the splendours of the English medieval greater church. If the French tried to make the whole building lead up to God, then the Englishmen pointed the finger of the central tower to the same goal with equal force. Yet these vast structures were a constant source of worry and anxiety. Very often their construction was weak, and it was only by trial and error that success was achieved. Frequently the towers collapsed without warning, and sometimes, as at Wells for example, extensive alterations and the strengthening of the existing structure had to be undertaken. The scissor-crossing at Wells was made necessary in order to withstand the weight of the additions to the central tower started in the first quarter of the fourteenth century (Pl. 25).

Salisbury employed a similar method in the eastern transepts, but with a much less dramatic effect. There are many criticisms levelled at the treatment of these added arches at Wells, yet the great staring eyes and cavernous mouth formed by the arrangement of the arches reflects the love of the grotesque element which is so characteristic of the period. In addition, it seems a brilliant solution to an extremely difficult problem.

As a matter of architectural composition these vast central towers were necessary, otherwise the long low silhouette of the building would have been unbearably monotonous. Exeter is the only cathedral not to have a central tower, whilst Ely owes its glorious octagon to the collapse of the Norman tower in 1322.

When they were first built the central towers were intended to contain bells, but in some later rebuildings the bells were removed and the towers converted into lanterns. Partly because of the height of the tower, and partly because of the smallness of the windows, this was not always successful, though York and Ely provide fine examples of this use of the central tower. It was usual to plan the central tower in conjunction with twin western towers, as at Durham and Lichfield for example, and it was often the intention to crown these towers with spires. Lichfield is unique in that it retains its full complement of three spires (the Three Ladies, as they are known locally), whilst the beautiful spire at Salisbury is so well known that we almost tend to be indifferent to its quality. The importance of the central tower and spire can be realized more fully if they are momentarily obliterated on photographs by putting a piece of paper over them. By a similar method taller towers and spires can be given to others, with striking improvement in design and balance. The point is too often overlooked that, when we consider the greater churches of the Gothic period in England, and on the Continent too, we are often looking at buildings which, for one reason or another, are unfinished. It speaks well of their basic conception that they can give so much pleasure.

In spite of the long and continuous ties with France, typified by the union of the throne of England and the duchy of Normandy, the Hundred Years War, and the actual coronation of Henry VI as king of France, French influence on English architecture was not so profound as one might expect. Such influence as there was on Norman church-building, for instance, was soon lost in later rebuildings. Westminster Abbey and Canterbury Cathedral are the only two great churches which possess French characteristics. The differences between French and English cathedral design have already been mentioned (see Chap. 2). They were many and fundamental: the English

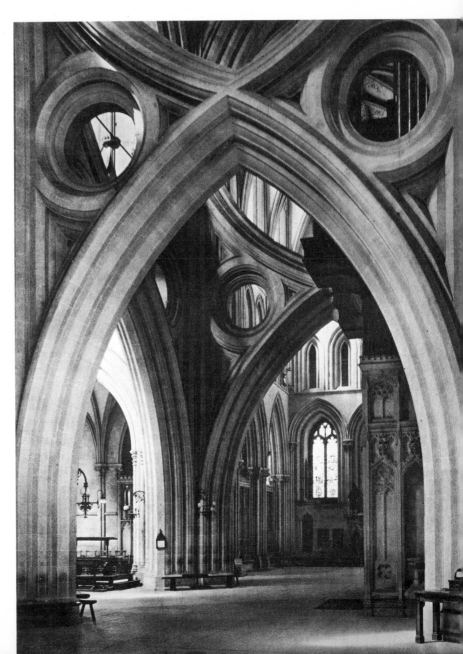

Plate 25

Wells Cathedral —'St Andrew's Arches', inserted 1338

These inverted arches were added to support the weight of the newly erected tower

builder lacked the Frenchman's love of logic, and he never stormed the heights as the French did at Reims or Beauvais. Nevertheless the greater churches of England offer other and no less rewarding achievements. The west front, one of the glories of French Gothic, assumes nothing of the same grandeur in England. Quite often it is of little architectural significance, as at Winchester or Worcester. There is no really fine example of a Norman west front now in existence; even that at Tewkesbury, though magnificent with its massive round arched portal, has suffered a great deal by the inclusion of a huge window, a seventeenth-century copy of a fifteenth-century original. In the same way at Southwell it has been spoiled by the addition of a large fifteenth-century window; however, it probably gives a fair idea of an English Romanesque western front, and a comparison with the Abbaye-aux-Hommes at Caen is inescapable (Figs. 112, 46). The west front of Durham, of course, suffered when Archbishop Pudsey built his famous Galilee on to it.

The French regarded the west front of the cathedral as the main access to the church which lay behind. It had to provide a fitting entrance for the bishop, who was regarded as the spiritual father of the townspeople, to enter his domain. English greater churches were usually placed well away from the busy centres of towns, and often in walled precincts (there are many such examples: Fountains Abbey, Lichfield in the cathedral close, Durham on its rocky crag, etc.), and consequently the same importance was not attached to the west front either of cathedrals or of abbey churches. The twin-towered façades of York

and Ripon (Figs. 113, 114), though they lack the deep, richly sculptured porches and mighty rose-windows, are the nearest approach, together with the west front of Peterborough (Fig. 115) with its tremendously forceful arrangement of triple arches. The west fronts of monastic houses were generally of a nondescript character and of little architectural significance—those at Winchester, Norwich, and Gloucester are typical.

In secular cathedrals the west front was occasionally conceived as a screen for the display of sculptured figures. Wells is perhaps the finest example of this type (Fig. 116). Erected between 1225 and 1275 it creates a tremendous impression. The six deep buttresses not only add richness and depth of light and shade, but also divide the façade into its component parts of nave and towers. Neither windows nor doorways are allowed to interfere with this division. Indeed the doorways are so small that they have often been likened to mouseholes in a wainscot, but it must be remembered that originally they looked on to a lay cemetery. The main entrance for canons and clergy was the north-west porch.

This idea of masking the western end of the church by a screen wall is fraught with danger, for so often it tends to obscure the internal divisions of the building. Somewhat later than Wells is the west front of Salisbury which, whilst fulfilling the dual purpose of providing a screen for figures and a buttressed façade, does tend to be rather clumsy and muddled. This may well be because the horizontal divisions are both too numerous and too insistent, and at odds with the verticality of windows and arcading. The

Fig. 112 *Southwell Minster—west front
Early thirteenth century*

Fig. 113 *York Minster—west front
(1291–1345)*

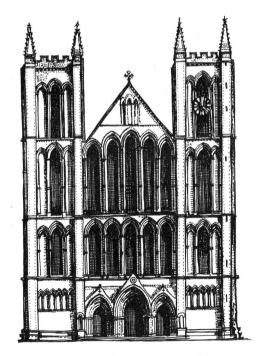

Fig. 114 *Ripon Cathedral—west front
(c. 1230–40)*

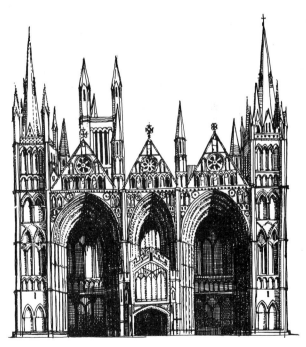

Fig. 115 *Peterborough Cathedral—west
front (1193–1230)*

*The seven west fronts illustrated in Figs. 112–18 show something of the variety
of English design. Though lacking the singleness of purpose which imbues their
French counterparts, they have other qualities that make them memorable*

doorways too, whilst of some importance, just fail to assert their position in the whole conception. The 120 niches now have only a few statues remaining in them, and indeed it is doubtful if they were ever filled.

The gigantic screen-front at Lincoln, erected in front of the massive earlier Norman work, provides a fine example of the Lancet style. Yet because of the great width of this later addition, the towers behind it now appear too closely set and give a rather cramped feeling. Lichfield (c. 1275; Fig. 117), provides a combination of a twin-towered façade and a screen, with rows of statues standing on brackets, not in niches, within simple wall arcading. But this treatment is not really satisfactory, as the effect tends to be too flat and monotonous. Niches would have provided the necessary contrast of light and shade, and variety of texture, needed to make the façade interesting. On first acquaintance the sight of Lichfield, with its complete complement of three spires is very exciting, and the naturally warm colour of the stone adds to one's enjoyment, but because there is so little variety in light and shade, one soon tends to lose interest.

At Exeter the screen (c. 1370), is kept purposely low so as not to interfere with the great west window. But whilst this treatment is interesting it tends to lack unity.

Remarkable amongst western façades of the Abbey-Cathedral type church in England, is Beverley (Fig. 118), which is of the twin-towered type, and few can fail to be moved by its exquisite proportion. Erected between 1380 and 1420 it is a unique example of the Perpendicular style. The design is far superior in conception to that of its neighbour at York, yet because this splendid church has had the misfortune to remain a minster, the west front, along with many other felicities of design, is generally overlooked. Placed amongst its richer and more complex French counterparts Beverley would hold its own by virtue of its purity of line and beauty of proportion. Seldom in England has such a gracious relationship between towers been established; even as one approaches the town from the high ground to north-west their character is apparent. Hardly a church in England produces such an impression of soaring height as these tapering towers manage to effect.

To say that any one façade of a greater English church is typical would be misleading, as each has its own peculiar quality. Probably the safest method is to mention three: that at Peterborough, with its powerful arrangement of triple arches, spoiled alas by the intrusion of the porch in the central one; that at Wells, as the finest example of the screen type front; and the one at Beverley, for the most exhilarating use of the twin towers.

The long period of time during which these buildings were under construction meant that only a few churches were finished as originally planned. It is a tribute to the courage and skill of the designers that we are so seldom worried by the change in style which takes place throughout a single building. Today we are so intent upon putting up buildings which 'fit in' or 'blend with' or 'do not detract from' their surroundings that one often wishes that something of the fearless courage of these medieval masons could be given to some of our contemporary city-fathers and corporations.

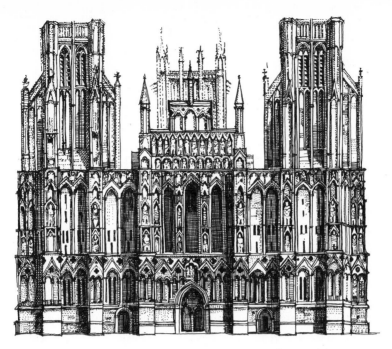

Fig. 116 Wells Cathedral—west front (1230–60)

Fig. 117 Lichfield Cathedral—west front
(1265–1327)

Fig. 118 Beverley Minster—west front
(1380–1420)

The Monastery

The origins of monasticism can be traced far back to Egyptian times, when the custom of giving up the material things of life and retiring into the wilderness to lead the life of a hermit first developed. From there this habit of self-imposed withdrawal spread throughout Europe and the Near East. Indeed, in England the earliest monasteries, dating from Celtic times, are more like groups of hermits' cells than a unified community.

Monasticism as we understand it, however, dates from the founding of an order by St Benedict in Italy in the year A.D. 529. The Benedictine rule became the basis for the whole of monasticism throughout Europe. St Augustine was responsible for the introduction of the order into this country when he founded the convent at Canterbury in the year 598. This foundation was to have a continuous history for over a thousand years, for along with a few of the Celtic monasteries in Wales and the West country, Canterbury was the only monastic foundation to survive the ravages of the Danish invasion.

The monastic revival in England was headed by the Archbishops Dunstan of Canterbury and Oswald of York and Bishop Ethelwold of Winchester in the second half of the tenth century. Earlier, the foundation of the great reforming order with its headquarters at Cluny in Burgundy had given a new impetus to monasticism on the Continent.

Cluniac influence came to this country through William the Conqueror; and Norman reorganization not only coloured monasticism throughout the rest of the medieval period, but also perpetuated certain Celtic features, because the seats of bishops were founded in the more important houses, making the monastic church serve as cathedral as well.

Whilst this was happening in England, on the Continent growing dissatisfaction with the Cluniac order—monasticism always tends to fall away from its original fervour—led to the foundation of a number of more severe orders during the late eleventh century and early twelfth century. The strongest of these was the Cistercian order founded at Cîteaux in 1098, and it quickly spread through Europe and England. The followers of this order expended their energies on large-scale agricultural developments, and the sites they chose were usually in remote country, well away from towns.

Monasticism reached its peak in this country in the twelfth century. During the thirteenth century there was a slackening of impetus, due in no small measure to the arrival of the friars in the first half of the thirteenth century. The first of these to arrive were the Dominicans and Franciscans, and they were followed by the Augustinians and Carmelites. They had a radically different view of the conduct of the religious life and they drew much support away from the monks. After the middle of the fourteenth century monasticism almost petered out.

Little is known about the arrangement of pre-Conquest monasteries in England, and the first signs of coherent arrangement do not appear until the tenth century. It was at this time that the cloister made its appearance, the first examples in this country being at Canterbury and Glastonbury. At the same time the numerous small churches of the earlier monasteries were replaced by fewer, but more imposing, structures. The essential constituents of monastic layout can be summarized as follows:

(i) The church

(ii) The buildings in which the monks lived

(iii) The buildings in which they cared for the sick and dispensed hospitality

(iv) The buildings which served the day-to-day maintenance and administration of the estate.

As in the medieval house, the arrangement of the buildings was both simple and practical. The church itself generally occupied the highest part of the site and formed one side of the cloister; the other three sides were made up of the buildings in which the monks lived. To the west of the cloister it was usual to place the outer court and its associated buildings. This was the place where such contacts with the outside world as were necessary took place. On the opposite side of the cloister, and away from the noise and bustle of the outer court, were placed the quarters for the sick. The whole was surrounded by an outer wall, with one or more gate houses.

The very earliest monastic churches were simply aisleless rectangular buildings, narrow in proportion to their length and without internal structural division between nave, choir and presbytery. The Normans replaced these with the type of church already discussed, and in due course, alterations to the eastern arm were undertaken. These rebuildings usually took one of three forms. The first type, usually restricted to the larger houses of the south and west, took the form of a square east end with an aisle continued all round, giving on to a Lady-chapel; St Albans is a good example of this type. The second type, favoured by the more moderate-sized houses, such as Lanercost, was a square-ended presbytery, flanked by short aisles. The third method, which did not find general support in this country, consisted of the apsidal end with ambulatory, after the French method; Westminster is an outstanding example of this type, and it was also used at Battle and Tewkesbury. In Cistercian houses, owing to a general relaxing of austerity during the twelfth century, and a pressing need for more altars, the presbytery was aisled and the eastern aisle gave directly onto a row of altars, as at Jervaulx and Byland. The great eastern transept that was added to the existing presbytery of five bays at Fountains Abbey has already been mentioned (Fig. 119).

The choir occupied the crossing and eastern bays of the nave and was open to the presbytery, although closed by screens on the other three sides. The screen at the west-end, known as the 'pulpitum', often held the organ loft, but changes in the ritual at the Reformation have left few of these intact. There was another screen further to the west of the 'pulpitum' and this was the rood screen. The one at St Albans is still in existence, and traces of others still remain in many churches.

The position of the cloister was determined by the lie of the ground and the needs of the drainage scheme. Whenever possible,

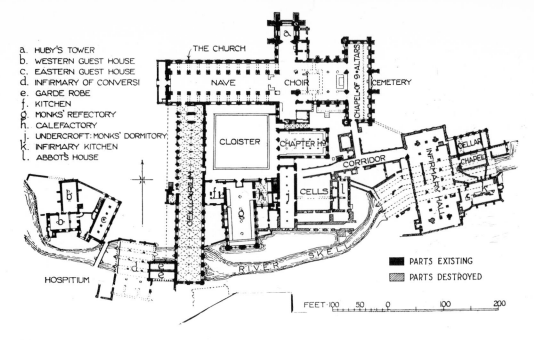

a. HUBY'S TOWER
b. WESTERN GUEST HOUSE
c. EASTERN GUEST HOUSE
d. INFIRMARY OF CONVERSI
e. GARDE ROBE
f. KITCHEN
g. MONKS' REFECTORY
h. CALEFACTORY
j. UNDERCROFT: MONKS' DORMITORY
k. INFIRMARY KITCHEN
l. ABBOT'S HOUSE

Fig. 119 Fountains Abbey, Yorkshire—plan. This shows the typical layout of a large monastery

however, it was placed on the south side of the church, west of the crossing. The covered way round the cloister was usually of one storey, though some of the later ones had two. The twelfth-century and early thirteenth-century cloisters had open arcading on low walls, supporting a lean-to roof. The capitals on the columns of the arcade afforded the masons an opportunity to show their skill in carving, and there are fine examples of conventional leaf-form capitals at Byland. Even though the cloisters were situated on the south side of the church, so as to make the most of the sunshine, they must have been cold, draughty, and cheerless in the long winter months. As a good deal of work and study was done there, an attempt was made to make some of them more comfortable by fitting wooden frames filled with glass between the columns of the arcade. It is still possible to discern the grooves for these frames in some columns.

The arrangements of accommodation around the cloister usually followed the same sequence; to the east was situated the dorter range, to the south (opposite the church), the frater range, and to the west, the cellarer's range.

The dorter, or monk's dormitory block, was usually of two storeys, and gave direct access to the church through the south transept by a flight of stairs. These were known as the night stairs, and very few of them remain intact—though there is a fine example at Hexham. Direct access between dormitory and church was essential, for the monks began their arduous day early in the morning. Each order varied their daily timetable according to their rules, and very often the different houses of the same rule made their own local variations. However, this brief summary of the 'horarium' of Canterbury will serve as a guide to what went on in other establishments:

'The day began at 2.30 a.m. with psalms and prayers, followed by Nocturns, the first service of the day. This was followed by Matins and at dawn, Prime. After Prime there was reading in the cloister until about 8 o'clock when the monks assembled once again for Terce and the Morrow Mass. This was followed by the daily meeting of the chapter, in the chapter house, at which day-to-day matters of administration of the estate were dealt with, duties allocated, faults confessed, and any punishments given. There then followed a long period of work until noon, when the brethren returned to church for Sext, High Mass and None. At about 2.00 p.m. the monks assembled in the frater for the only substantial meal of the day and then returned to their labours for the afternoon until Vespers, at about 5 o'clock in the evening. After Vespers the monks went to the frater to take a drink before returning to the church for a short reading and Compline, the last service of the day. That concluded the daily routine and they then made their way to the dorter to sleep until roused by a bell at 2.30 a.m. for the beginning of another day.'

The dorter block also had direct communication with the reredorter, or latrine block. The reredorter had to be sited over the main drain, which was usually beautifully constructed. Generally speaking the drainage system in monastic houses was of a far superior standard to that of secular buildings, and monasteries were always carefully sited to ensure an adequate supply of water. There was usually a 'slype' or passage-way between dorter and transept, leading to the cemetery.

The chapter house was second only in importance to the church. The polygonal form was popular, though the more austere Cistercians preferred the rectangular type. Rievaulx contains one of the most lavish chapter houses in the country, as it has both apse and ambulatory.

The frater was the monk's dining hall, and might be either on the ground floor or on an undercroft, as at Rievaulx. The general arrangement resembled that of the secular great hall, with the addition of a pulpit near the high table so that readings from the scriptures could be made during the meal. In the cloister, close to the frater, there was a lavatory for washing hands. This usually took the form of a long trough in an arcaded

Fig. 120

Kirkham Priory, Yorkshire— the lavatory in the cloister

recess; there is a very fine one at Kirkham (Fig. 120). The kitchen was usually on the side of the frater away from the cloister. As in secular examples, it was usually free standing and generally rectangular in shape, though polygonal examples are known; the famous one at Glastonbury is square.

The fourth side of the cloister was occupied by the great storehouse or cellar; in this position direct contact with the outside world was possible, without disturbing the rest of the community. The cellarer was the most important of the obedientiaries not connected with the service of the church, and it was his responsibility to supervise the provisioning of the monastery. The vaulted cellar range at Fountains is one of the finest in Europe. Between the cellar and the main entrance was the outer court. In the greater houses this must have been the scene of constant activity and bustle, for the monasteries were trading communities as well as religious foundations. Durham had coal mines, Byland mined for iron, and Bolton had lead mines. Many foundations had salt pits, and some had iron forges. Their commonest asset, however, was wool, and this commodity of theirs was famous throughout Europe.

The buildings of the outer court might well comprise barns, malthouse, mill, slaughter-house, pigsty, cattle sheds, stables, smithy, henhouse, bakehouses, brewhouses, and so on. Few of these apartments remain, for most of them were timber-framed. The larger monasteries may well have had a permanent lodge for the mason, as well as a carpenter's shop and often an almonery for the dispensing of alms to the poor of the district.

On the far side of the cloister would be the infirmary. This group of buildings was sometimes so complex as almost to comprise a separate community within the greater one. The essentials of the hospital or infirmary group were:

(i) Hall and chapel
(ii) Kitchen
(iii) A special frater, or misericord, where it was permitted to eat meat
(iv) One or two rooms for the infirmarer in charge.

The monks' infirmary took much the same form as the medieval hospital, and often resembled the church in plan. The nave, which was often aisled, had the beds ranged in the side aisles, leaving the central space clear to act as a hall; the chancel acted as the chapel. In the largest houses the infirmary was correctly orientated.

The accommodation for the abbot (or president, as the person in charge of the foundation was sometimes called) was, in its most developed form, very similar to that of a secular manor. At first it was expected that the abbot should eat at the common table and sleep in the dorter, but as his responsibilities and duties increased he became more and more detached from the monastery, so it became customary to provide him with separate accommodation. The more important abbots were influential patrons of architecture, and their apartments played an important part in the development of the secular house. The smaller convents provided abbot's lodgings on the first floor of the cellarer's range; in that case the accommodation consisted of hall, chamber and chapel. Finchale had a separate block for the president's lodgings, consisting of hall, chapel, and chamber at first-storey level, whilst at Gloucester there were particularly princely apartments for the abbot.

The gatehouse was usually of two storeys, and provided entrance for both wheeled and foot traffic. The prison was often placed here; this was for the lay folk who came within the jurisdiction of the abbot, or even perhaps for recalcitrant monks.

Extensive parts of the monastery were often outside the main precinct. These included farms, fishing rights on rivers, and often large fish hatcheries. It will be seen from this account that monasticism played a vital part in medieval life and economy. The exception to this was the Carthusian order, which made little material impact on the community. The extreme austerity of the order severely curtailed the number of their followers, but their withdrawn life, which resembled that of a collection of hermits living in one building, meant that, unlike the other orders, they played little active part in bettering the community as a whole. The effect on the plan is best illustrated by Mount Grace Priory, which is little more than a collection of individual cells ranged around the cloister, which was also the cemetery. The architecture of these charterhouses is so austere that it is of little importance or interest.

Austerity, coupled with a desire for a building as simple as possible yet compatible with ritual needs, meant that there was a certain similarity between monastic plans, irrespective of date. At their finest and most developed, as at Fountains Abbey for instance, monastic buildings were a remarkably efficient solution to the problem of providing for a living and working community. Their abrupt end in 1539 meant that, architecturally speaking, the full impact of the Renaissance was never felt by them in either plan or elevation.

The Medieval Parish Church

So far, the development of Gothic church architecture has been traced through its most spectacular examples. The parish church is more modest in intention, and is not the place to look for developments either in structural technique or in architectural style. The highly skilled masons and craftsmen were too busily employed in the service of the crown, ecclesiastical authority, or nobility to spend their time on the smaller, less important, projects. The master-mason from the cathedral or abbey may have acted, on occasion, as consultant to a neighbouring parish church, or the stone-carvers from a major church may have done some of the carving in a near-by parish church if work on the cathedral was held up for some reason or another; but, generally speaking, parish church architecture followed the fashion, rather than set it.

The countryside was dotted with churches, and of all European countries

England was the most remarkable for the number and beauty of her parish churches. Each village had its own church, and sometimes, as at Magdalen Laver, in Essex, the village has disappeared, leaving the church still standing. On the Continent the church was built to accommodate a much larger number of people, as the villages were much further apart and for the sake of safety the bulk of the population lived in walled cities. The reason for the remarkable number of these churches in England was partly the influx of the preaching friars, who needed a suitable place in which to preach, and partly also the custom of rich burghers and landowners of setting up a church for their own private use.

In Saxon times the parish church was a simple two-celled building, consisting of nave and chancel (Fig. 105). Aisles were not used, and these early buildings were high and narrow. Windows were small and placed high in the wall, so that the interior was very dark. These churches were orientated correctly, though this was not enforced by ecclesiastical authority, but had become established through tradition. By the eleventh century a western tower had become popular, the ground stage acting as the main porch. The cruciform plan was uncommon in pre-Conquest churches, and it was not until after the Norman invasion that it made its appearance, though it never became very popular, because the heavy piers necessary to support the central tower proved too much of an obstruction to both sight and hearing.

In the century after the conquest, part of a monastic church was often shared by the local parishioners, though this arrangement presented difficulties, as the lay services tended to interfere with those of the monastery. The nave was the most usual place for this type of service, or occasionally a transept, though in this case it was always the one furthest away from the cloister. Sometimes an aisle was used, though this was rare. Some of the monastic houses built a parish church within the precinct, but as the presence of another church near the conventual one was unpopular, a parish church was usually sited outside the walls.

Although the two-cell plan continued in use, the increasingly complex ritual of the twelfth century demanded more space, and so the three-cell division was introduced. This consisted of a rectangular nave, a central quire (approximately square), and the sanctuary, the internal divisions being made clear by arches. By the end of the century the development of the church became one of piecemeal expansion. This could be achieved lengthways by the additions to the chancel (or, more rarely, by extensions to the nave) or—and this was the most popular method—laterally, by the addition of aisles and chapels. This constant expansion was brought about mainly by two forces; firstly the steadily increasing population, the bishop being keen to see that the churches within his jurisdiction kept pace with this rise, even to the extent of enforcing re-building if he thought necessary; and secondly the custom of giving chantries* to the church. This was done either by private benefactors or, later, by the various trade

* A chantry foundation is an endowment for a mass to be celebrated at an altar for the well-being of the benefactor during his lifetime, and the repose of his soul after death.

and guild associations. Although the main altar might well serve for these chantries, it was usual to endow separate chapels as well.

The result of this constant rebuilding was, in many cases, an apparently irregular and haphazard layout, which obliterated all trace of the original plan; further additions, such as towers, vestries, and porches, added to this effect. It is this casual shape of the plan which constitutes one of the main differences between the greater and the parochial churches. In this respect the smaller churches differed from their counterparts in France which, from the point of view of design, had little to differentiate them from the great cathedrals. One of the most striking exceptions to this general rule in England is St Mary Redcliffe, Bristol (Fig. 121). The greater part of this church was built after the Black Death, and the plan is remarkably similar to that of many of the greater churches, though of course it is not so large. The magnificent church of St Patrick at Patrington, East Yorkshire, is similarly cathedral-like in form (Fig. 122). This may well have been due to the munificence of the archbishops of York, who took an active interest in the building. This church is also remarkable for the unity of its design. The building was in an advanced state when operations were interrupted in 1349; the chancel was finished in 1360, and the entire building was complete by 1410.

When additions and extensions to the existing fabric were to be made, the greatest care was taken to ensure that the day-to-day cycle of ceremonies was interfered with as little as possible. When an aisle or chapel was to be added, the new walls were built up outside the existing ones. Spaces were

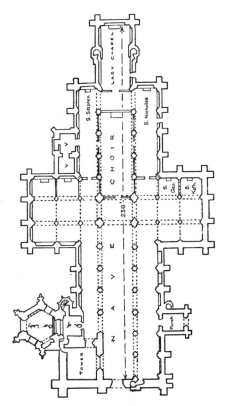

Fig. 121 St Mary Redcliffe, Bristol—plan
A parish church with a cathedral-type plan

then cut in the old wall to take the new columns or piers, which were then carefully built up in the spaces, the arches spanning the new supports being added in the same way. When this operation was completed the rest of the old wall was removed, and the new accommodation brought into service. In this way the routine of the church suffered the minimum of inconvenience. This reluctance to disrupt the working of the church explains why the lengthening of the nave was so unpopular, for this would have meant almost the entire rebuilding of the church, during which time the services would have had to be suspended. When only one aisle was added it was usually on the

Fig. 122 The parish church, Patrington, East Yorkshire

north side; in this way the building would not encroach on the cemetery, which was usually to the south, or cut off light from the nave.

The grafting-on of aisles resulted in the churches becoming an aisled rectangle in plan. If two aisles were added on each side of the nave the result was a rectangle only slightly less wide than it was long. At St John's, Cirencester, the width of 104 feet is only 6 feet less than the length, whilst the chancel is nearly twice as wide as it is long. At St Helen's Church, Abingdon, which has no less than five aisles, the width exceeds the length by some 17 feet (Fig. 123). During the thirteenth century further developments in the ritual and ceremonial aspects of the service resulted in the need to enlarge the chancels. This generally took the form of a lengthening to the east. The growing veneration of the Virgin Mary, which produced the Lady-chapels of the greater churches, had a similar effect upon the lesser churches as well. If possible the Lady-chapel in the smaller churches was usually placed as near to the main altar as possible, and so an aisle flanking the altar was a favourite position. Generally the chancel was aisled later than the nave, the sole purpose being to provide extra altar space.

The plan of the parish church takes so many forms that it is almost impossible to name any one as a standard pattern. However, one form is quite common, though by no means universal. This consists of an aisled nave with western tower, north and south

Fig. 123 Abingdon Church, Berkshire—plan. This shows extreme width, due to the addition of side aisles

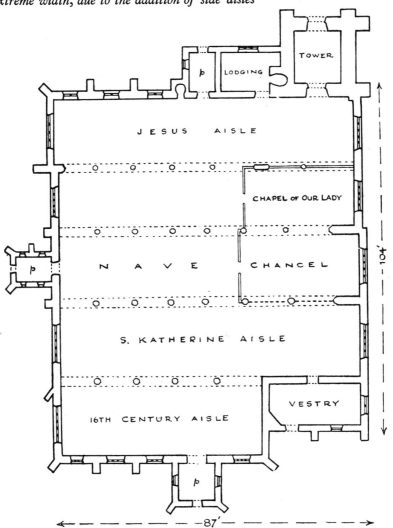

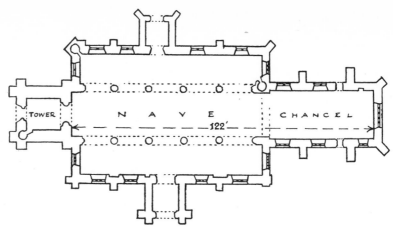

Fig. 124 Warmington Church, Northants—plan. A typical parish church consisting of aisled nave, western tower, north and south porches, and an unaisled chancel

porches, and chancel, often unaisled. The church at Warmington, Northants. (Fig. 124), is a good example, and St Botolph, at Boston, is equally fine as an example of this type of plan. Developments in planning did not even take place at a uniform rate throughout the country. As the expansion of the church depended in so many cases upon patronage of one kind or another, the prosperity of the district often decided the size of the church. Similarly the size of the many chantry chapels was dependent not only on the piety of the donor, but on the amount of money the particular benefactor could afford at that time. At the time of the development of the wool trade, for instance, the churches of Norfolk, Suffolk (Fig. 125), and Somerset underwent most extensive and elaborate improvements.

English parish churches suffered severely at the time of the Reformation. Subsequently chantry endowments were plundered for the Privy Purse, and in the late 1540s all images, ornaments and treasures were removed. The stone altars were replaced by wooden ones, and paintings were either destroyed or covered with whitewash. Stained glass suffered a similar fate and the windows were filled with clear glass,

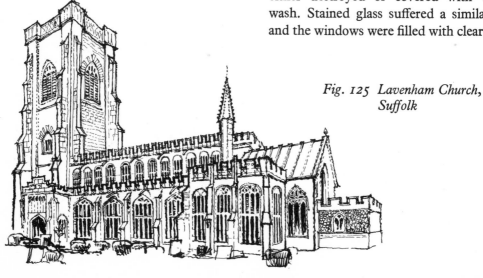

Fig. 125 Lavenham Church, Suffolk

with unfortunate effect, for though coloured glass may have made the churches dark, it must also have imparted a sense of unity to the architecture, which sometimes appears stark and harsh in the cold light of clear glass.

The parish church may not have the breathtaking splendours of the greater churches, but despite the wanton destruction they underwent at the Reformation and again during the Cromwellian era, they present a rich and rewarding heritage. The reign of Mary Tudor was too short to replace the riches which had been plundered. In any case the new style in architecture was at hand, for Henry VIII had already introduced the foreign craftsmen who were to spread the Renaissance style.

THE TIMBER ROOF

A common and very distinctive feature of the parish church is the timber roof. The intricate design of such roofs satisfies not only the sense of structure, but also that of beauty. Unlike the stone vaulting of the greater churches, the timber roof follows no distinct evolution, and all the forms, with the exception of the hammer beam, which developed in the late fourteenth century, were used indiscriminately throughout the centuries. The chief change which took place was in the gradual flattening of the external pitch of the roof.

The chief types of open timber roofs (Figs. 126–129) were:

> (i) the tie-beam
> (ii) the trussed rafter
> (iii) the hammer beam
> (iv) the collar braced.

Because of the perishable nature of the material, few of the very earliest roofs survive, but it seems reasonable to assume that the complex structures of the fifteenth and sixteenth centuries were the result of the experiments of the preceding centuries. It seems likely that the early timber roofs were imitations of stone construction; at the cathedrals of York and St Albans and the abbey at Selby there are vaults of timber which are ribbed in the manner of stone vaulting.

The perishable character of wood is not the only factor which has robbed us of many of these early roofs. The churches of the twelfth, thirteenth, and fourteenth centuries were both low and dark. The passion for light in the fifteenth century resulted in the introduction of clerestory windows, and many original roofs must have been destroyed to make way for this new feature. The new roofs were flatter in pitch, and were designed to ensure that the outward thrust was not too much for the lighter clerestory walls.

The craftsmanship of these roofs is always admirable. The timbers are usually large in section, 6 inches by 4 inches being the standard size for the rafters, which were left undecorated. The other members were often elaborately moulded and expertly framed and pinned. Oak was the wood universally used, and no metal ties or nails were used in the construction. The following points of construction may be noted.

Tie-Beam (Fig. 126)

This type of roof was used throughout the Gothic period, but was most common in the early centuries. The weakness of this type of construction is that, since the ridge rib is

Plate 26

*Hampton Court Palace,
Middlesex—
The Great Hall
(1531–6)*

*The roof designed
by James Nedham—
a fine example of the
hammer-beam roof*

supported by a king post, placed in the middle of the tie-beam, the weight of the roof falls on the lateral member where it is weakest and most likely to warp and sag. The idea of the lateral member was to contain the outward thrust of the rafters, and from this aspect the structure was successful over a narrow span. To prevent the tendency to sag, the transverse member was often curved slightly upwards, or two queen posts replaced the central king post. If the end of the principal rafters became damp and rotten, they were often taken down, the ends sawn off and the roof re-erected with a flatter pitch. During the fifteenth century, when the pitch was exceedingly flat, the space between tie-beam and principal rafter was so small that it was often filled with pierced and carved panelling. In cases where the tie-beam rose slightly towards the centre

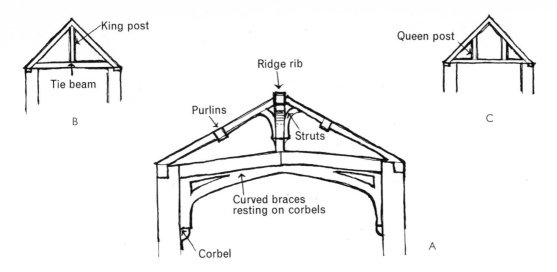

Fig. 126 The tie-beam

and was further supported by curved brackets underneath, it formed, in effect, a four-centred arch.

Trussed Rafter (Fig. 127)

The disadvantage of this type of roof was that it lacked adequate longitudinal ties, as the pairs of rafters were unconnected except at the wall-plate. This weakness was offset to some extent by the addition of interior boarding, which made a polygonal or waggon-shaped roof, as at Wimbotsham,

Norfolk. The shorter length of timbers required did, however, mean that larger spans could be undertaken than were possible with the tie-beam roof. The arched braced roof (Fig. 128) is very similar to the trussed rafter type.

Hammer-Beam (Plate 26; Fig. 129)

This form of roof-construction was introduced in the late fourteenth century and is the noblest and most ingenious of all. It may have originated in France, and there is an

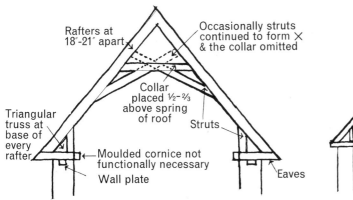

Fig. 127 The trussed rafter

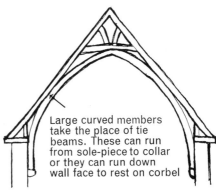

Fig. 128 The arch brace

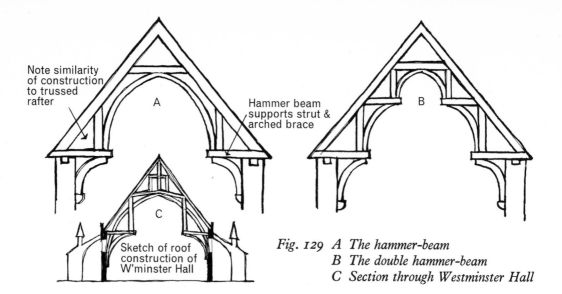

Note similarity of construction to trussed rafter

A

Hammer beam supports strut & arched brace

B

C

Sketch of roof construction of W'minster Hall

Fig. 129 A The hammer-beam
B The double hammer-beam
C Section through Westminster Hall

example in Villard's sketch book, but it never reached the same popularity in that country as it did in this. It incorporated the experience gained from all the other forms, and is particularly suitable for wide spans. The roof in the Great Hall at Westminster is the finest in Europe, with a span of almost 70 feet (Fig. 129c). This form of roofing is very common in East Anglian churches.

Carpenters of the fifteenth century were not afraid to mix types of construction in the same roof. The church at Leighton Buzzard, Beds., for example, alternates tie-beams with hammer-beams. Originally all these splendid roofs were richly painted and gilded, and few of them were without carving, so that they often impart distinction to an otherwise nondescript building. It is fortunate that these timber roofs did not suffer in the ravages which were perpetrated after the Reformation.

THE TOWER

Towers and spires provide a subject scarcely less fascinating than the timber roofs. Their original purpose was to house the bells, which served so many purposes in medieval times. Bells were rung on a variety of occasions, not only for services, church festivals, saints' days, baptisms, and funerals, but also to warn of impending danger and disaster. The most striking feature of these towers is their variety of shape, and the number of different materials with which they were constructed. On plan they may be square, oblong, round or polygonal; the earliest ones were often made of wood, whilst later ones were constructed of stone, flint, brick, or chalk, depending on the district. Work on them sometimes continued over a number of centuries, so that whilst the base might be Saxon or Norman, the final stage might well be Decorated or Perpendicular. They were usually built with a slight batter to avoid any feeling of top-heaviness. Saxon towers tended to be of slender proportion (Fig. 104) whilst Norman ones were much more solid and massive. One particular aspect of twelfth-century design is manifested in the round towers of the flint areas around Norwich, Lowestoft and Yarmouth. The majority of the round towers of Norfolk are of the twelfth century, though some go back to pre-Conquest times. There is some evidence to suggest that they may well have served as defensive strong-holds, somewhat comparable to the shell keep. Towers which may also have been designed with a similar purpose in view are to be found in the border counties of Wales and Hereford and in Northumberland and Cumberland.

The thirteenth century saw striking advances in tower-design, especially in districts where good building stone was ready to hand. These towers were usually topped with a spire which became an integral part of the design. The first spires were of wood construction, but gradually these were replaced by more permanent ones in stone. The octagonal spire was almost universal, and the broach spire was popular because it was a very effective way of converting the square of the tower into the octagon of the spire. These spires were not without certain disadvantages, however, for they were both inaccessible and difficult to repair because the oversailing walls of the spire made the erection of ladders and scaffolding difficult. The solution to this problem was to set the spire back, so as to leave a platform round the top of the tower, from which to erect ladders and so on. A similar effect was achieved on some towers by building a projecting parapet.

Further advances made during the thirteenth century were in the development of decoration. Generally speaking the top of the tower had richer decoration than the base. The practice of using wall-arcading as a feature of surface decoration split the height of the tower into a number of stages, usually beautifully proportioned. Buttresses

also received their share of attention; these developed from the early pilaster strips to bold projections which gave to the building a great feeling of stability.

By the middle of the fourteenth century the broach was abandoned for a spire of more slender proportions which sprang from within the parapet. This meant that the buttresses, which in the case of the broach spire had had to stop short at the top of the tower, could now continue and be finished off with pinnacles which were in keeping with the lofty spire rising above them. Further aids to repair were provided by the crockets which adorned the arrises or ridges of the spire. Although these are extremely decorative they have the purpose of providing support for the ladders, or even a useful foothold.

Fig. 130 The tower of St John's, Glastonbury— one of the finest in the west country

To prevent outward thrust, the joints of a spire were always horizontal. By corbelling the structure in this way there was only vertical pressure on the tower below. At the base, the sides of a spire would be some 6 inches to 9 inches thick; near the top this would be reduced to between 4 inches and 5 inches, whilst the last few feet would be solid.

The Perpendicular period is especially noted for the number of towers that were built. The spire was abandoned and the tower was made to terminate in battlements, which were carved, pierced, and enriched with pinnacles into a silhouette of great fascination. The beautiful towers of Somerset (Fig. 130) stand out, and are in a quite separate class from those in the rest of the country. Even the most modest Somerset church rears a proud and magnificently proportioned tower to the sky. The intricacy and beauty of the stone carving is due to the fine quality of the local stone, which also weathers to a wonderfully rich colour.

Recognition Points for the Styles

Anglo-Saxon or Pre-conquest

Plans were very simple. Walls were made up of rubble or ashlar masonry. The Anglo-Saxons were good masons and they possessed a mortar which was much superior to the Normans'. It may well have been this very hard-setting mortar which encouraged them to build walls that were thin in relation to their height.

Long and short work on corners (Earls Barton) and pilaster strips were very characteristic. Arches were semicircular or triangular-headed. Columns tended to be short and stumpy, with square blocks of stone in place of capitals. Stone vaulting was very elementary in construction, and was based on Roman methods; presumably timber was also used, though as there are no remains of these roofs, methods of construction can only be conjectured.

Norman 1066–1189

The chief characteristic of Norman work is its massive, fortress-like character. Walls were immensely thick, 10 feet or more being common, and buttresses very flat. Plans were simple, and in major churches the extreme length of the nave was characteristic. Columns were massive cylinders, topped with simple cushion or cubiform caps. Arches were semicircular. (Durham is the supreme example of all the foregoing points.) Windows tended to be small, so emphasizing the fortress-like character of the style. Stone vaulting began to be introduced during this period in an attempt to reduce the danger of fire, which was a constant source of worry with the timber roofing. The introduction of stone construction led to the development of the rib-vault, which gradually replaced the earlier groin-vault because it was easier to build. Colour also began to play an important part in church-decoration, and stained glass began to make its appearance towards the end of the period. Typical features are the deeply recessed doorways, which were richly decorated. Chevron, zig-zag, billet, beak-head, and nail-head were all types of decoration popular at this time. Though the workmanship was often crude, it had great vigour and naïve charm.

Early English 1189–1307

The thirteenth century saw a great lightening of the framework of the building, as a result of the general improvement in building techniques, whilst in the technique of stone-carving there was a better understanding of constructional methods and a more widespread use of the pointed arch, which was much less cumbersome than its semicircular predecessor. Oblong vaulting bays replaced square ones as a consequence of the adoption of the pointed arch. (This has already been discussed in the section on Gothic in Europe.) The concentration of weight and thrust on buttresses, rather than on solid walls, became more pronounced. Tall, narrow (lancet) windows (Fig. 131), usually set in groups of three, five, or seven, began to give that feeling of lightness and grace so typical of Gothic work (e.g. the Five Sisters at York, and the west front at Ripon). Columns and piers became lighter, and plate-tracery was introduced in window heads (Fig. 132). Roofs became much steeper in pitch, and owing to the introduction of ridge ribs, and later of tiercerons, vaulting became more complex. The use of the chisel in place of the earlier axe resulted

in finer detail and more deeply-cut mouldings. Foliage was introduced as a decorative motif, though it was stiff and conventional in treatment. The most popular ornament was 'dogtooth' and this abounds on all buildings of the period (e.g. Lincoln). Stained glass became more plentiful, and sculptured figures in niches made their appearance.

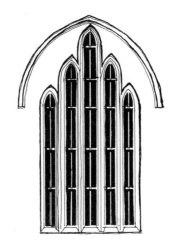

Fig. 131 Typical lancet tracery

Fig. 132 Typical plate-tracery

*Fig. 133 Typical geometrical decorated
tracery*

*Fig. 134 Typical curvilinear decorated
tracery*

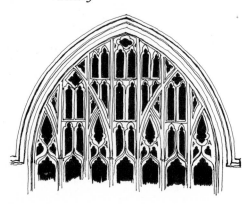

Fig. 135 Typical perpendicular tracery

Decorated 1307–77

The fourteenth century saw further development in the technique of stone-carving, resulting in a further enrichment of ornament and decoration. The carving of foliage reached its highest degree of naturalism, with splendid control of surface modelling. The further reduction in the weight of piers and columns gave an increased sense of interior spaciousness. Windows achieved a magnitude undreamed of previously and walls became little more than a framework to hold the vast windows of glowing glass.

To support thrust, buttresses became very deep, richly decorated with crockets, and finials, etc. Tracery became increasingly rich and flowing (Figs. 133, 134). The 'ogee' arch was introduced, and is a characteristic feature of the period. The roof became less steep in pitch externally, whilst internally the vast increase in the number of ribs in the vault, by the addition of lierne ribs, led to 'stellar' vaulting (Pl. 27).

'Ball flower' is the most typical form of decoration. The interiors of many churches were enriched by the erection of tombs and shrines.

Perpendicular 1377–1485

Owing to the intense activity of earlier periods, which left little need for new churches, and also to the shortage of labour after the Black Death in 1349–50, the only work undertaken at this time was the enlargement and modification of existing buildings. The predominant feature is verticality, the flowing tracery of the previous period giving way to rigid rectilinearity (Fig. 135). The mullions pushed relentlessly up-

Plate 27

*Winchester Cathedral
—nave vaulting
(1394–1450)*

*A good example of
'lierne' and 'tierceron'
rib-vaulting*

ward from sill to arched window-head. The 'ogee' arch was still used, but the complicated and involved detail of the decorated period gave way to a more stringent control of ornament. The four-centred arch was introduced and is characteristic of the Perpen-dicular and Tudor periods. There was a passion for well-lighted interiors, and new larger windows appeared in many buildings. (At Peterborough more than 70 Norman windows were replaced during the fifteenth century.)

Plate 28

*King's College Chapel,
Cambridge—
fan-vaulted roof
(1446–1515)*

Externally, roofs became almost flat, with high pierced parapets to relieve the monotony. Internally, beautiful timbered roofs of the hammer-beam type became popular, especially in East Anglia. In stone, 'fan' vaulting evolved from 'stellar' vaulting, and the English roof reached its highest levels of excellence (Pl. 28). Later, pendant vaulting was introduced, as in Oxford Cathedral choir or Henry VII's Chapel, Westminster.

The central tower became an important feature of the greater church—those at York, Gloucester, and Canterbury being particularly fine examples.

FURTHER READING

Francis Bond, *Gothic Architecture in England.* Batsford, 1906.

This is an old book, but none the less valuable for that; it contains a mine of information.

G. H. Cook, *The English Medieval Parish Church.* Phoenix House, 1954.

A very thorough survey with plenty of illustrations and plans.

F. H. Crossley, *The English Abbey.* Batsford, 1935.

J. C. Cox and C. B. Ford, *Parish Churches.* Batsford, 1934.

These are now available in paperbacks, and are good value. The volume on churches is particularly valuable for the diagrams showing the typical development of a church through the centuries.

C. W. Budden, *English Gothic Churches.* Batsford, 1927.

A useful little book containing a lot of detailed information.

R. Gilyard Beer, *Abbeys.* H.M.S.O., 1958.

Very good value, with concise introduction, plenty of plans, and well-chosen illustrations.

English Cathedrals, with a foreword by Geoffrey Grigson. Thames & Hudson, 1950.

Olive Cook, *English Abbeys and Priories.* Thames & Hudson, 1960.

Both these books are valuable for their photographs.

The reader is also directed to two King Penguin volumes: *Unknown Westminster Abbey* (1948) and *Medieval Carvings in Exeter Cathedral* (1953). These little books contain many photographs of details that are easily missed or are almost invisible.

6

THE CASTLE

The study of ancient fortifications is always fascinating. In the scattered remains dotted about the countryside it is possible to reconstruct some of the most vital pages of this country's history. From the splendours of such magnificent structures as Stirling or the great castles of Wales, to the more humble remains at Knaresborough or the small 'peel' towers along the Northumbrian border, man's attempt at self-preservation can be studied. His habits and mode of living can be vividly experienced, for in whatever state of preservation the building may be, something of its spirit comes across to us. The style of architecture in such buildings is so elemental, so reduced to the bare necessities, that their purpose is more forcibly conveyed than in the more bland and urbane styles of later generations, when the urgent task of self-preservation was no longer present. For this reason each visit to a castle becomes not just another excursion to a place of interest, but an exciting adventure into the past.

The word castle (coming from the Latin *castellum*, which is the diminutive of *castrum*: a fortified town), is now much misused, and is often applied rather indiscriminately, not only to pre-historic earthworks, but also to buildings which were purely residential, or even to Gothic Revival shams.

Strictly the term should not be used for any structure in the British Isles erected before the Norman Conquest. In addition it should be applied only to structures of primarily military intention. This rule is not easy to maintain in relation to some of the later work of the fourteenth and fifteenth centuries, as it is often difficult to determine the difference between a castle and a fortified manor house—a problem which will be discussed in due course.

Just as the cathedral was the product of medieval religion, so the castle was the product of the feudal system. Most of these castles (the exact number is almost impossible to estimate, but perhaps 400–450 in the middle of the twelfth century is a safe working figure) were built by the Normans to protect the king, to maintain control over hard-won conquests, or to defend a powerful lord or baron and his retainers. A glance at a map of their distribution shows that castles were erected not only along the border counties of Wales and Scotland and along the east coast to repel invasion, but also fairly evenly over the whole country. The sites were usually chosen with considerable skill—to guard a road, command a valley, protect an important ford or town, or simply to police an area. The study of the medieval period is usually dominated, architecturally speaking, by the splendours of the great churches and cathedrals, and secular building tends to be overlooked. Yet the castle is just as representative of the period which produced it as the cathedral. Each castle sheds a different light on the society of the time. Just as large sums were spent on making cathedrals and churches more elaborate and complete, so large sums were spent on fortifications too.

From the royal records it is possible to discover the proportion of the king's income spent on castle-building. Sums in excess of £1,000 a year are often recorded— occasionally as high as £4,000. This may seem a small figure today, but it must be remembered that the entire annual income of the crown was only in the region of £20,000. In this period a knight or country gentleman could live comfortably on £10– £20 per year.

The account of expenses at Orford castle, which was of some importance to the king, and of advanced design, shows a cost of about £1,400 spread over a period of eight years. Dover, on the other hand, which was entirely rebuilt between 1179 and 1191,

cost almost £7,000. These figures are easily surpassed, however, by the great castles of Wales. Conway alone cost £19,000 and it has been estimated that Edward I spent over £80,000 in twenty-five years to build his eight Welsh castles.*

From the point of view of the planning and organization of labour on the site, the building of these castles serves as a model of the thoroughness and capability of medieval administration. The master-mason received a comfortable payment and there can be no doubt that he was a thoroughly experienced and competent organizer of the large labour forces, sometimes 1,000 or more men, which were often engaged in transporting building materials for great distances over difficult country.

As we shall see, the castle progressed from simple earthwork beginnings to the complex impregnability of the concentric castles.

Medieval Warfare and Weapons

Broadly speaking, medieval warfare was of two kinds, though inevitably they were interwoven in the overall progress of the battle. These two types were long-range bombardment and close hand-to-hand fighting. The weapons for the latter were of course swords, lances, axes, etc., but the long-range weapons were basically the great siege-engines, known since classical times.

Siege-engines

Of these the 'mangon' or 'mangonel' and the larger and more powerful 'trebouchet'

were the most important. The exact difference between these machines is often confused, and the names sometimes are interchanged. Generally, however, the mangon works on the principle of torsion created by twisted ropes, whereas the trebouchet works on the principle of the pivot and counterweight. The fact that this counter-weight was often in the region of eight or nine tons gives some idea of the size of this type of

* These figures are summarized from J. G. Edwards' *Edward I's Castle Building in Wales* (Sir John Rhys Memorial Lecture, British Academy; O.U.P., 1944).

structure. The trebouchet was in commission for many years and was used as late as the eighteenth century in the siege of Gibraltar. The usual missiles for these machines were large lumps of rock or stone, which they were capable of hurling great distances—a quarter of a mile or more. As the trajectory was very high, the splintering of the stone on the castle walls must have proved a very effective anti-personnel weapon.

Another favourite and dreaded projectile was an inflammable liquid known as 'Greek fire', the secret of which was brought back by the returning crusaders. There are also a number of contemporary illustrations showing siege-engines loaded with the putrid carcasses of animals and humans. This seems to be an early attempt at bacteriological warfare, though one might assume that it was a more effective weapon in the warmer climates of the crusades than in the more temperate zones of northern Europe.

The 'ballista' or 'springal' was another of the great siege-engines. This took the form of a huge crossbow, and indeed the crossbow was developed from it. Like its smaller counterparts, the ballista fired a metal bolt, and as the trajectory of the missile was flatter than in the case of the trebouchet the ballista was noted for its accuracy.

Gunpowder did not, as some would have us believe, make much impression on warfare during the medieval period. The early cannon were heavy and very expensive, and indeed were probably as dangerous to the users as to the enemy. The actual damage inflicted by this early ordnance was probably slight, but the noise would have terrified the horses. It was not until the fifteenth century

was well advanced that rapid developments were made in the design of fire-arms. Even so, many medieval fortresses, refurbished in the Cromwellian period, held out stoutly against heavy pounding by Roundhead troops.

Close-range Weapons

Of the close-range weapons the battering ram was a crude but effective device. This was simply the largest and heaviest tree to be found, hoisted on ropes so that the iron-capped end could be swung against a door or gateway. The bore was a similar device— not so large, but used effectively against sharp angles and corners in the huge pile of masonry. The 'escalade' was simply the use of scaling ladders, an exposed and hazardous method of gaining the walls, but the 'belfry', or movable tower, was a more formidable structure. This provided a lofty firing platform which often commanded the interior of the castle itself. The 'penthouse', a low wooden structure covered with raw hides or sheets of metal, provided cover for those working at the ram or bore, and also for those engaged on what was probably the most deadly and effective method of attack against the square keep, namely the mine.

The Mine

The mine was most effective when excavated across a corner of the keep, and was in fact the main reason for abandoning this feature in favour of round or polygonal towers.

As the square keep was usually sited on high ground, the attacker would set out to dig a mine across one of the corners. As the mine progressed, the roof was supported with timbers, and when operations were complete the mine would be filled with brushwood and then set on fire. As the timbers burned away, the mine would collapse, bringing with it the whole corner of the keep above.

Defence against the mine was difficult, and occasionally the attackers would invite the besieged to inspect the mine in an attempt to reach a settlement and so save extensive damage to the castle above. One answer to the mine was the counter-mine, sunk from inside the fortifications, but this was not very successful, as fighting in the cramped, dark space was difficult. The only real answer was a deep and wide moat well filled with water, and, as we shall see, the moat became more and more important in castle-planning.

Ultimately the castle's greatest defence was its own immense strength, but it was supplemented by the skilful design of features such as battlements, firing apertures, machicolations, hoardings and flanking towers. The whole development of the castle shows increasing mastery in the placing of these features for the repelling of attacks.

The exact number of men manning the towers is almost impossible to estimate, but it is safe to say that it was generally quite small. There were seldom over one hundred and fifty knights and men-at-arms, and often as few as ten or twenty. Important amongst these were the crossbow-men, for the crossbow was generally held to be the most accurate hand-weapon of the period.

The castle was primarily designed for military or police duties, though as much care as possible was paid to its domestic appointments. Once the primary needs of defence were accounted for, and as money and power increased, so the domestic arrangements became more lavish. Royal castles, particularly Winchester and Windsor, had large amounts spent on their domestic arrangements. The king was then much more mobile, and had to spend a good deal of his time moving about the country. With him went a large section of the court for he not only ruled but actively governed the country. For this reason the larger castles had to be provided with more than average comfort. The richer barons, too, spent large sums on living quarters, for the splendour in which they lived sometimes rivalled that of the king. This type of development became typical from the fourteenth century onwards, when the military importance of the castle began to decline.

As we have already pointed out, the castle was the particular product of the feudal system, and consequently became the normal type of residence of the great ones of the land. Many castles were the centre of local government, and the castle hall became the local county court or administrative centre of a shire. Often the castle was the local treasury, sometimes the armoury, and inevitably the local prison. This function has led to the derivation of our word 'dungeon' from the Norman 'donjon'.

The causes of the decline of the castle were many, and were not connected only with the decline of the feudal system— though this was, of course, a major factor. The growth of towns and the rise of the middle class were also important. This development called for the fortified town, as the towns themselves became desirable prizes of war. Many towns—York and Caernarvon, to mention but two—still retain considerable sections of their medieval fortifications. To a certain extent the castles, due to their sheer impregnability, were the cause of their own downfall. Because they became so difficult to overthrow, wars came to be waged in the open field, with larger armies than the castles could easily accommodate.

By the end of the fourteenth century castle-building had almost ceased. Henry VIII built extensive coastal defences—for there were signs that invasion was imminent in 1540—and further defences were provided about 1588, at the time of the Armada. A whole chain of castles, stretching from Hull to Milford Haven, was envisaged. Walmer castle is a good example of this later type, but the most impressive were those built in the Thames, of which unfortunately none remain.

The Development of the Castle

The earliest fortifications in England which concern us were simply earthworks. The Romans, masters of masonry construction, had built a number of substantial defence works. When they left these shores the use of fortifications lapsed until the tenth century, when it was revived by the Saxons in their attempts to repel the Danes. Although many remains of these early fortifications are dotted about the countryside, and some of them—Berkhamsted, Pleshy or York, for example—have become castles through later additions, none of the original superstructures exist today.

The Saxon works are known as 'motte and bailey' castles, the name being derived from the division of the layout into two parts, the 'motte' and the 'bailey'.

Although the lay-out took many forms, depending upon the site and the exact requirements of the builders, the most popular shape was roughly that of a figure 8.

The smaller loop became the motte and the larger the bailey, and the whole was surrounded by a ditch, which is fundamentally the simplest defensive position possible. The earth thrown up from the ditch was used to form embankments on both sides, and also to make a hill, rather like a huge sand-pie, for the motte.

The larger open space at the foot of the motte was the bailey. This was usually surrounded by a wooden palisade, though in the very earliest examples a thick hedge of thorn and briar bushes may have had to suffice. Entry was through a narrow gateway with a primitive drawbridge. Barns and lean-to sheds were built to provide shelter for men and beasts. The motte was separated from the bailey by a ditch, and crude steps up the side of the mound were made so that the flat top could be reached. This was again surrounded by a timber palisade, and in the centre there was a wooden tower or house which served as an apartment for the chief and his closest retainers—and as a look-out post as well. The reasons for separating the motte from the bailey were two-fold. Firstly, although the bailey might be captured, the motte as a self-contained unit could still offer resistance; and secondly, should the retainers in the bailey turn traitor, the lord or chief still had his own separate stronghold from which to defend himself if the occasion should arise.

Naturally, since the principal material was wood, fire was the principal method of attack. To prevent the walls catching fire the defender usually soaked them with water, or threw wet raw-hides over them. For this reason a well was a vital part of the bailey, though as water was often scarce and the greatest economies had to be observed, early forts must have fallen victim to the flames.

When and where this type of fortification developed is unknown. There is a reference to a castle of this type in A.D. 1010 on the river Loire in France, and several are shown on the Bayeux tapestry. Their chief advantage seems to have been that they could be thrown up with great haste, and many of them, now no more than grassy mounds, may well have been rushed up in the course of some campaign or other. Hence they remained in use in this country for over a century after the Conquest, even though building with stone was by then a common practice. These 'adulterine' or 'ephemeral' castles were built without licence, and indeed so many were constructed during the reign of Stephen (1135–54) that Henry II (1154–89) had a great number of them destroyed and thereafter enforced a licensing system with some success. Anyone could apply for a licence to crenellate, and the majority of later castles were built upon private estates for the protection of the lord and his descendants.

The Age of the Great Stone Keep

The primitive motte and bailey soon proved inadequate, and the Norman conquerors, those great builders in stone, introduced into England the square keeps so typical of twelfth-century castle design. These were better suited to become the permanent fortifications which the Normans needed in order to impose their rule on the conquered people. Because of their great weight, these huge structures were seldom erected on the man-made mottes of earlier fortifications. A new site was chosen—on a natural mound if possible, where there would be no problems of settlement of earth—although England is not particularly rich in sites which offer naturally defensive positions from all sides. Bamburgh in Northumberland and Peak castle in Derbyshire are about the only castles to enjoy such advantages, though Durham castle, situated on a neck of land, is a good example of a castle taking advantage of a site needing defence from one direction only.

As a rule the larger castles use the lunate

Fig. 136 The square keep—
Rochester Castle (c. 1130)

Fig. 137 The White Tower, Tower of London

plan. In this type the castle backs on to some natural obstruction, such as a gorge, ravine, river, or steep cliff face, and then spreads curtain walls in a half circle in front. Kidwelly, in Carmarthen, is a good example of this type of plan.

The keep is in the heart of these early castles, and is usually sited at the highest point of the terrain, with curtain walls around to provide a bailey or ward. It was primarily a military structure and took the form of a lofty stone tower with unusually thick walls. Rochester castle (*c.* 1130; Fig. 136), was one of the first to be constructed in this country, and is a fine example of its type. Both the famous White Tower of the Tower of London (Fig. 137), and the keep at Colchester were, indeed, begun at the instigation of the Conqueror himself. But these are exceptional, for stone fortification was almost unknown in this country in the eleventh century.

Castle Hedingham in Essex, *c.* 1140, which is almost contemporary with Rochester and was probably by the same designer, will serve very well as a typical example of the Norman keep; for although there were differences in the layout from keep to keep, all had a number of characteristics in common. These can be summarized as follows:

(1) A vast plain mass of masonry, usually devoid of decoration (the decoration found at Castle Rising and Norwich is quite exceptional)

(2) Long vertical lines of the shallow buttresses

(3) Angle turrets

(4) The structure pierced at each floor by narrow windows, the smallest nearest the ground

(5) Entrance some feet above ground, at first-floor level, below which is the—

(6) Cellar or storeroom

(7) The hall. At Hedingham this occupies two floors, and the provision of a mural gallery gives extra firing openings

(8) A room above the hall similar in plan to the entrance floor. This may have been partitioned off to provide private chambers. Most keeps had two storeys over the entrance floor, though some had three and a few of the smaller ones only one

(9) The roof, with a rampart walk, protected by battlements around it

(10) A spiral staircase, giving access to all floors

(11) The forebuilding, an external feature which housed the staircase to the entrance

(12) Immense walls, in excess of 13 feet thick in some places, and well provided with mural chambers, some to provide garderobes, others no doubt to provide private sleeping quarters.

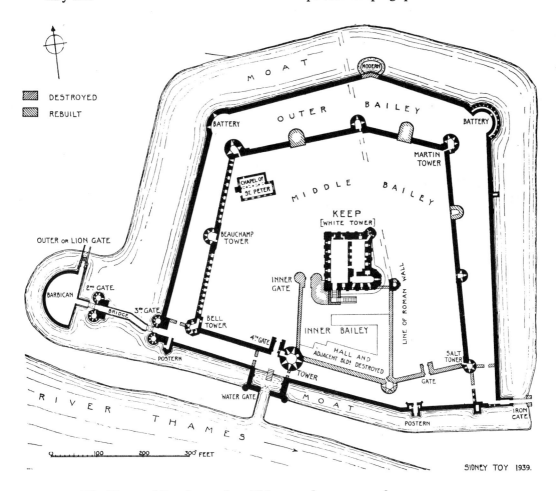

Fig. 138 The Tower of London—plan. This started as a square keep and ended as a concentric plan

Fig. 139 Restormel Castle, Cornwall (twelfth century)

Those were the regular points of the twelfth-century keep. There are deviations: the larger keeps, as at Rochester, Dover, or the 'White Tower' of London, were often divided laterally by an internal wall (Fig. 138). This not only strengthened the structure but also made it possible for stubborn defenders to withdraw from one half of the keep to the other so as to continue the fight if the attackers should gain access.

In some keeps the forebuilding also contained the chapel, an important feature of medieval planning. It must not be imagined, however, that the chapel was kept for strictly religious purposes. Space was too precious a commodity for such a luxury, and the chapel was frequently in use—perhaps as the castellan's private chamber, or as a room for the women. In contrast to the almost brutal simplicity of the rest of the keep, some simple but well-executed decoration is often found here.

The use of fireplaces was common, but it is not possible to say when they came into general use; many early castles were planned with wall fireplaces, just as some late ones had provision only for a central hearth or brazier. Fireplaces were very simple, and remained almost without alteration through-

out the twelfth century. A simple arched opening, with occasional decoration on the jambs as at Hedingham or Rochester, was typical. Flues were carried up at an angle through the wall, and the smoke passed out through one of two loopholes, which were generally tucked away behind the angle of a buttress. Only in shell keeps were short chimneys employed.

As glass was so expensive, windows were generally left unglazed; shutters or wooden frames covered with hides kept out most of the draughts. Windows such as these could have given little light to the halls within, but on the other hand they could be quickly and securely closed.

Although the rectangular keep is considered characteristic of Norman castle-building in the twelfth century, in some cases the old motte-and-bailey castles had their wooden palisades replaced by stone walls. These became known as 'shell keeps'. Restormel (Figs. 139, 140) and Trematon in Cornwall are fine examples of this type. In this kind of castle the apartments are ranged around the inside of the wall rather than one on top of another, as in the square keep (Fig. 138).

We have already seen that the square keep

was very vulnerable to the mine. In fact the round turret at Rochester was built to replace the corner destroyed by the ravages of this method of attack. Another problem was the difficulty of providing covering fire for the dead space at the foot of the walls. Generally the lower part of the walls was given a pronounced batter, to make the task of those engaged in mining and boring more difficult, but this was not altogether effective.

The real answer was the provision of curved surfaces, and, of course, the moat. So towards the end of the twelfth century we find that castles tend to be sited on low-lying ground so that water could be provided, either naturally or by diverting an existing water-course. This procedure often entailed the provision of a dam, which in turn needed protection. Caerphilly Castle, in Wales, has such a fortified dam.

The provision of extra flanking towers went on apace, either on the curtain wall or the keep itself. These towers were either round or polygonal. The early ones were built solid at the base with a firing platform on the top. Gradually they were made open all the way down to provide extra accommodation. Towers on the curtain walls were usually left open at the rear so that they could not be used as a strong point against the defenders in the centre.

Further offensive devices were provided in the form of either wooden hoardings or stone machicolations. These were overhanging structures, with openings along the floor, placed round the tops of walls and over gatehouses, so that the defenders could drop missiles onto the heads of the enemy beneath. Stories of pouring boiling lead onto the attackers should be treated with a certain amount of scepticism; lead was as expensive then as it is now, and stone, quick-lime, and boiling pitch were just as effective as deterrents.

Fig. 140

*Restormel Castle—plan
This shows a fine example
of a 'shell' keep*

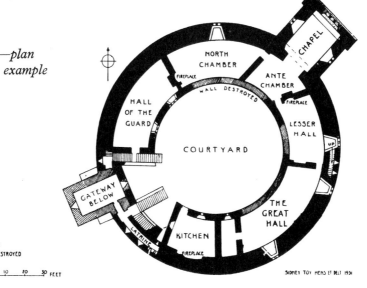

Before we leave the keep, one last development must be noted. This was the building in the last decade or two of the twelfth century of the round or multi-angular keep. There are two fine examples of the transitional multi-angular keep, one at Orford in Suffolk, the other at Conisborough in Yorkshire. The former of these was built between 1165 and 1173, and has a circular core even though the external walls are polygonal. To give extra strength there are three great tower buttresses. This remarkable piece of architecture is still in almost perfect condition. Conisborough, c. 1190, has an almost perfect cylindrical plan (Fig. 141), and again

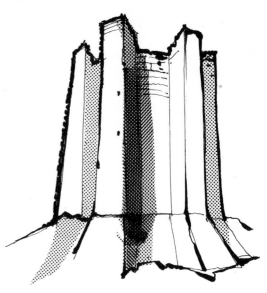

Fig. 142　Conisborough Castle, the keep

six huge buttresses give added strength (Fig. 142).

Cylindrical keeps proper, however, were confined to the first years of the thirteenth century and, except for the splendid isolation of Launceston in Cornwall, to Wales or the Welsh borders. Pembroke supplies the finest example, and its height makes a majestic feature of the whole layout. The cylindrical tower keep, even in its most interesting development at Clifford's Tower, York, where it becomes a quatrefoil shape, is not a major aspect of British castle design. It appeared at a time when, although its advantages were realized, new thoughts on the whole organization of fortifications were being brought back by the returning crusaders. Many of them must have seen or heard tales of such powerful strongholds as the 'Krak of the Knights', in the mountainous district of Syria. In the opinion of T. E.

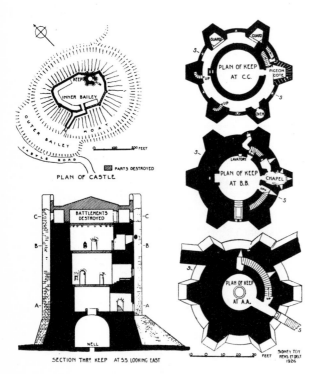

Fig. 141　Conisborough Castle, Yorkshire (1190). An example of a multi-angular keep

Lawrence this splendid fort was 'perhaps the best preserved and most wholly admirable castle in the world'. Even from photographs it is possible to appreciate its squat power.

English castles cannot match the might of these eastern bastions, with their impressive natural and man-made defences and extensive provision against siege. The cellars at Margat, for example, were constructed to hold provision for 1,000 men against a five-year siege. Nevertheless, the great castles of Wales pay tribute to their eastern counterparts in their well-planned efficiency.

The Castle Triumphant

As we have seen, by the middle of the thirteenth century the square keep was no longer considered to be the most effective system of fortification. The idea of keeping the plan in two separate parts, i.e. keep and bailey, with the keep providing a strong defensive position as a last stand should the bailey be taken, was falling out of favour. New ideas brought back from the east favoured a compact, unified design where an even concentration of fire-power around the entire building was possible. Not that some of the *ad hoc* additions to existing buildings had been made without a great deal of skill and imagination; the tower of London and Dover castle are but two examples. But the advantages of a thoroughly integrated system of towers and firing points, giving each other mutual support and cover, were obvious. The role of the castle was changing, too, from that of a purely defensive position to one of a much more aggressive character. The strength of the keep-and-bailey type of castle should not be underestimated, however, for such castles were built throughout the thirteenth and fourteenth centuries, even after the advantages of the more unified design were known. It is interesting to note that even in the midst of the great castles which Edward I built in Wales, Flint retains very clearly this keep-and-bailey division.

Now let us turn to those great Welsh castles built in the century 1272–1377 during the reigns of the first three Edwards. The eight castles which Edward I ordered to be built in Wales were Aberystwyth and Builth in mid-Wales, and Beaumaris, Caernarvon, Conway, Flint, Harlech, and Rhuddlan in the north. Of these, Beaumaris, Harlech, and Rhuddlan are splendid examples of the concentric castle, as were the nobles' castles of Caerphilly and Kidwelly. The concentric castle is the most typical and important development that Wales had to make to the history of fortification. However, before the principle of the concentric castle is discussed, two magnificent castles, Caernarvon and Conway (Figs. 143, 144) must be mentioned. Both of these were built with the intention of protecting a town, and both employed an irregular plan which was closely allied to the site. In addition, they depended for their strength on the skilful juxtaposition of mural towers which

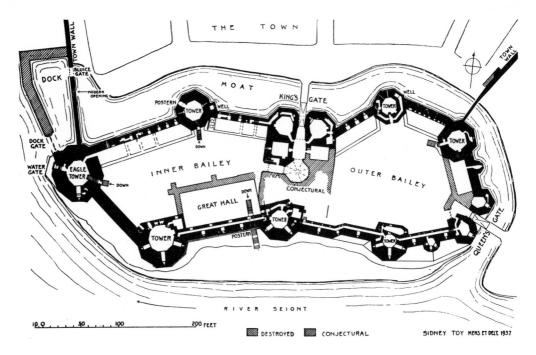

Fig. 143 Caernarvon Castle (1283–1323)—plan

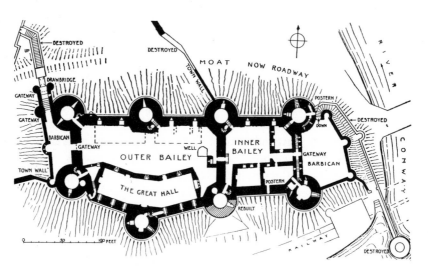

Fig. 144 Conway Castle (1283–1287)—plan

Plate 29 Caernarvon Castle, North Wales (1283–1323)

provided a deadly screen of cross-fire from all points of approach (Pl. 29). They also illustrate very well a further development in design, affecting the number and arrangement of gateways. Experience had taught that the weakest point in the link of defences was the gate; the thirteenth century therefore saw a great deal of attention paid to strengthening this weakness. Massive gatehouses appeared (Fig. 145), and in some cases they rivalled the keep in importance. They usually took the form of twin towers, with a bridging span to take the portcullis and drawbridge mechanisms. The arrangement of the various defences within the gatehouse varies slightly, but generally the portcullis stands in front of the door which it protects, with machicolations between, or sometimes in front. Further protection was often provided by a barbican.

Fig. 145

*Dover Castle, Kent—
the gatehouse*

posterns, and Caernarvon no less than three.

Both castles were originally divided by a cross-wall, though their inherent strength was so great that this would seem to have been an unnecessary precaution. They also contained a rich and well-appointed series of domestic apartments, though at Caernarvon these were never completed. These two great castles can be placed high in the order of medieval design and building, being surpassed only by the concentric castle.

The Edwardian castles of Wales are the finest examples of the concentric castle to be found. Of these, Beaumaris is undoubtedly the most magnificent and, to quote Hamilton-Thompson on this point, '. . . no other Edwardian castle presents so perfectly scientific a system of defence'.*

The basic principle of the concentric castle was a central block which replaced the earlier idea of a tall keep. This block was usually quadrangular in plan; it contained all the domestic apartments, and was in effect a complete fortification in itself. This stronghold was then further protected by a curtain wall, at a lower level, with well-placed flanking towers, the whole being surrounded by a wet moat and often by barbicans. Caerphilly has one of the most perfectly planned barbicans in Britain. Indeed, some hold that as a piece of military architecture it surpasses even Beaumaris.

The gatehouse being the centre of attack, the opposing forces were immediately concentrated at this point. A glance at the plans of Conway and Caernarvon shows, however, two main entrances. This arrangement means that the attacker must watch both gateways at once, thereby dividing his forces. If one gate were left unguarded it would be an easy matter to mount a counter-attack in the open field from this second gate. At Caernarvon both gates are protected by substantial gatehouses, but at Conway, where both gates lie between closely placed flanking towers and are protected by a large barbican, further protection must have seemed unnecessary.

Earlier castles had usually been provided with a postern-gate, normally situated well away from the main gate and at the most difficult point of access, perhaps opening on to a steep cliff leading down from the castle site to a river or lake. Conway offers two

* A. Hamilton-Thompson, *Military Architecture in England During the Middle Ages* (O.U.P., 1912, p. 279).

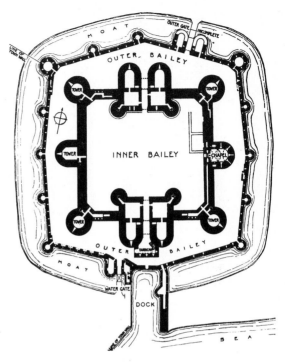

Fig. 146

Beaumaris Castle, Wales (1295–1323)
A perfect example of a concentric
castle

Examining the plan of Beaumaris (Fig. 146), we see at once the substantial walls of the central block, with the prominent towers at the four corners. Centrally placed on northern and southern walls are the formidable twin-towered gatehouses, the southern one further protected by a barbican. Midway along the eastern and western walls is placed another flanking tower, the one to the east containing the chapel—ten towers in all. Closely hugging the outline of the central block is an eight-sided curtain wall, strengthened by a further thirteen towers, making a total of twenty-three towers in all—a formidable array!

The area between the outer wall and main block is known as the 'lists', and is usually very narrow. The wisdom of this is apparent if the situation in actual combat is imagined. Having negotiated the moat and the stiff climb of the outer wall, the bowman is then faced with the problem of having to make an almost vertical shot with his cross-bow or long-bow at the defenders above. This would be difficult enough if done at leisure, but in the heat and jostle of battle—for if one man could gain the lists, then it is safe to assume that the way must have been open for a considerable number to follow—the task would be immeasurably harder. From the defenders' position, however, it is simply a matter of discharging as many arrows as possible into the mass of struggling humans beneath.

It will be noticed that at Beaumaris the outer gateways are not in line with the gatehouse of the central block; in this way the enemy, making his way to the gatehouse, is forced to expose his flank to the raking fire from the defenders in the centre.

In this detailed description of the layout of defences at Beaumaris the system employed in all concentric castles has been described. The plans of Harlech (Fig. 147) and Rhuddlan, for example, show exactly the same basic plan. Douglas Simpson described Rhuddlan as '. . . a simple but perfect concentric plan'. Caerphilly, though not a royal castle, rivals Beaumaris in the completeness of its fortifications, for not only is it a perfect example of concentric planning but it also contains one of the most elaborately defended approaches in Britain.

Before we leave the concentric castle, mention must be made of Dover and the Tower of London. The examples in Wales

Plate 30 Dover Castle, Kent—the keep (c. *1179–94*). *This shows clearly how later additions have transformed the building into a concentric castle*

were, from their inception, concentric in plan; that is, they were the product of a unified scheme, carried out according to a predetermined design. In some cases, however, castles became concentric as a result of alterations and improvements carried out over a number of centuries.

The early work on the White Tower of London has already been mentioned. Subsequent work, largely in the thirteenth and early fourteenth centuries, made the Tower one of the largest concentric castles in the land. From a distance, the old keep seems to dominate the scheme, yet on closer inspection it is apparent that its military importance is comparatively insignificant. The strength of the castle lies in its inner and outer walls with their flanking towers and moat. As usual, the lists are narrow, and the main entrance, to the south-west, is provided with a barbican.

Dover is another example of a concentric

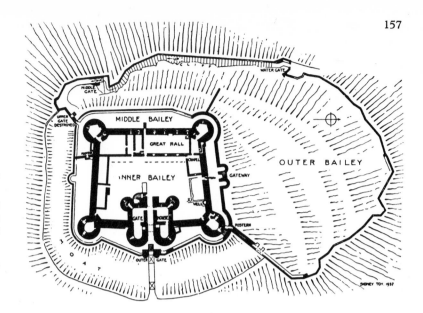

Fig. 147

*Harlech Castle, Wales (1283–90)
An example of extensive barbicans and outer defences*

castle developing over the centuries rather than being planned as such from the outset (Pl. 30). Henry II's splendid keep and inner bailey walls are encompassed by the outer curtain, which contains an impressive gatehouse. Points to notice are that the inner bailey employs square flanking towers and that the gateways are well off-set.

Of the smaller castles, Goodrich provides a typical example of late thirteenth- and early fourteenth-century developments. The twelfth-century keep still stands but, as at London and Dover, is rendered almost superfluous from a military point of view by later additions. These take the form of a quadrangular arrangement of walls, with a drum tower at three of the corners and a substantial gatehouse and barbican at the fourth. Goodrich also provides a fine example of the spurred drum tower. These weighty projections to the towers were a further defence against the mine and bore, and also helped to give the castle that more aggressive appearance typical of the period.

The Decline of the Castle

By the middle of the fourteenth century, the hundred years which span what has been justly called 'the golden age' of castle-building was drawing to a close. From then on few, if any, real developments were to be made in planning, and apart from the few genuine castles still to be built during the second half of the fourteenth century, mostly of the type known as 'castles of livery and maintenance', we must concern ourselves with that elusive affair, the fortified manor house.

The castles of livery and maintenance were the product of the period known as

Fig. 148

Bodiam Castle, Sussex (1386–90). A castle of livery and maintenance

'bastard feudalism', to differentiate it from the genuine feudalism which preceded it. As far back as Henry II's reign, barons and knights had been allowed to pay 'scutage' or 'shield-money' in lieu of their forty days' military service due under the original feudal terms. This new method of payment had two by-products. On the one hand, it meant that an English knight, though trained in the sports of jousting and the tournament, might never have seen a battlefield: he was on the way to becoming the English country gentleman, for agriculture and the care of his lands became daily more important to him. On the other hand, it produced a large number of mercenaries and soldiers of fortune who hired out their services to the highest bidder. The richer and more powerful barons collecting their rents in money instead of kind, as under the original feudal system, could afford to pay large private bodies of retainers. This system produced at various times, especially when there was a weak king on the throne, periods almost amounting to anarchy, as the barons fought amongst themselves. This state of affairs culminated in the Wars of the Roses and the barons were not brought under control until the strong hand of the Tudor monarchy seized power.

The effect of this period on castle design is perhaps best illustrated by Bodiam castle in Sussex (Figs. 148, 149), built in 1386, as part of the coastal defences. Its founder, Sir Edward Dalyngrigge, received licence to crenellate—'to make a castle . . . in defence of the adjacent country against the king's enemies'. The plan is at once simple yet very cunning. Superficially it is a simple rectangle, with stout drum towers at the four

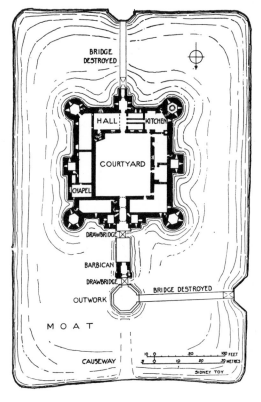

Fig. 149 Bodiam Castle—plan

corners and smaller square towers on east and west walls. To the north is a massive twin-towered gatehouse and to the south a postern.

The domestic quarters are ranged about the four sides, leaving a central open court. Closer examination, however, shows that these domestic apartments are duplicated and that there is no means of access between the two suites. The owner had his apartments along the south and east walls and also had access to, but no accommodation in, the gatehouse. And he had, of course, complete control of the postern. The remaining accommodation was for the retainers and was, like the owner's quarters, completely self-contained, with hall, kitchen, sleeping-space, etc. The reason for providing the two sets of apartments was that, should the paid retainers become dissatisfied and contemplate mutiny, the owner had a complete fortress within a fortress. These paid troops had not the same sense of loyalty to their overlord as the earlier dependants had had, and the fear of mutiny must have been very real.

Amongst castles which can be classified as castles of livery and maintenance are Harlech and Dunstanburgh; whilst the towers built at Raglan and Tattershall must have been built to provide similar protection. It is interesting to notice that these castles closely resemble in intention, if not in plan, the dual protection offered by the earlier motte-and-bailey castles. These late castles bring the development almost full circle, and except for the castles built for coastal defence in the reign of Henry VIII, such as Walmer and Deal, we can now turn our attention to the fortified manor house.

The Fortified Manor House

If we asked the question, 'When is a castle not a castle?' it would be easy if we could answer, 'When it is a fortified manor house', but unfortunately the same answer could be given to the question 'When is a house not a house?' This duality of purpose makes the definition of a fortified manor house difficult if not impossible. Fundamentally it represents a change of emphasis: the castle was primarily a military structure which could be lived in, whilst a fortified manor was a domestic structure which could be defended if necessary.

The fortified manor house is a kind of half-way stage between the castle proper and the great Elizabethan mansions, but—and this is important—it was not a new type of building. The sequence of development that we have traced over the past pages was not without its exceptions. Flint Castle (1277–81) has already been mentioned as an example of a castle apparently out of its period. At the other extreme, in the troubled border county of Northumberland, Aydon castle remained completely undefended in the late thirteenth century, and there must have been many others like it.

There are many buildings which it is

almost impossible to fit comfortably into one category or the other. Bolton castle, in Yorkshire, is an excellent example of this ambiguity for it is defined by some as a castle, by others as a fortified house. Built in 1379 by a noted master-mason, John Lewyn, it is in many ways similar to Bodiam in plan. The apartments are ranged around the four sides of an open courtyard. The four corners are marked by strong square towers—in contrast to the drum towers at Bodiam—with smaller flanking towers on the longer sides. By making the domestic apartments an integral part of the structure of the building, greater strength was achieved, and also a perfect blend of castle and house. For whilst these quadrangular castles present a stern exterior to the world, the comfort and convenience of the living provided is clearly evident from an internal view. As we shall see later, the scheme of ranging the living quarters around a central open court bears a strong resemblance to the idea behind the plans of typical manor houses of the fourteenth century.

Without doubt, the most commonly quoted example of a fortified manor is Stokesay castle. Here there can be no doubt that the original intention was to build a dwelling-house, and in fact the owner was not given a licence to crenellate until the end of the thirteenth century. The granting of a licence meant that he was permitted to put battlements round the top of the walls. The only real strong-point is the tower, and if this is taken away we are left with a typical manor house of the period. The hall, since rebuilt, was already in existence before the tower (a well-designed and carefully appointed multi-angular keep) was erected.

By this time, improvements in technique encouraged many prosperous owners to add some form of fortification to their houses. Stokesay is only one example of this kind of addition.

Another fine example of the fortified house from the middle of the fifteenth century is South Wingfield, Derbyshire, c. 1440. The buildings are arranged around two courtyards, which lie on a north-south axis. The southern or outer court has a large gateway to the south-east, and corresponds to the bailey of the motte-and-bailey castle, being intended to provide shelter for tenants and their flocks. Along the north side of the smaller quadrangle is a suite of domestic apartments of great richness and splendour. This was the principal living-space and has the usual attributes of hall, kitchen, and state apartments. What is most immediately striking, however, is the unusual arrangement of the latter. The hall lies at the extreme east-end of the range and is the full height of the block. The porch, at the west-end of the hall, leads into the screens, and there was probably a minstrels' gallery above. So far the arrangement is perfectly normal; but instead of a direct entry into the kitchens from the screens we find a building at right-angles to the axis of the main hall, with the great chamber on the first floor, the ground floor being occupied by store room. The kitchen lies beyond this block. This unorthodox placing of the great chamber close to the entrance, at the opposite end to the dais, is difficult to explain, but may have been due to the rather awkward site.

Little Wenham (Fig. 157) in Suffolk is another fine example of an early defended house; built in the last quarter of the thirteenth century, it is still in perfect preservation. In contrast to this modest example, Herstmonceux castle, *c.* 1440, is superficially imposing and, to quote Hamilton-Thompson, '. . . perhaps the best example in England of a castle which is one only in name is the brick house of Hurstmonceaux in Sussex'.* The gatehouse does offer some fortification and, as at many Tudor houses —Oxburgh or Kirby Muxloe for example— there was a wet moat.

The choice of which fortified houses to study must always be a personal one, however, and the student will have his own favourites. There is plenty of room for speculation, and much enjoyment can be obtained from the study of plans, buildings, and guide-books in an attempt to decide if a particular example is a castle or fortified house. This brings our survey of the major castles in England to an end. By 1500,

* Op. cit., p. 358.

England was entering an era of more settled conditions at home, and the castles had served their purpose. Before we close this section, however, mention should be made of fortification-building in the border counties. The unsettled conditions and intermittent raids along the borders of England and Scotland meant that some kind of fortification was necessary. To satisfy this demand many 'peel' towers were erected in the northern counties of Durham and Northumberland. These were often simply stone towers of three storeys surrounded by a stone wall which enclosed the 'barmkin', where cattle and stock could be sheltered. They comprise various degrees of complexity—from the extreme simplicity of the one at Corbridge to the more elaborate examples at Chipchase and Belsay. They were mainly the product of the fourteenth and fifteenth centuries, and might well be called the poor man's keep.

A Note on Scottish Castles

The castles of Scotland really form a subject for an entirely separate study, for developments there do not mirror those in England. There was no Norman invasion and conquest in Scotland; rather, Norman influences had gradually penetrated there under royal patronage. Motte-and-bailey castles were certainly known, but there are now only two or three castles, in the remoter parts of the country, which can be said with any degree of certainty to have stonework dating from the twelfth century. The castles of Scotland

had to stand up to rough usage, and rebuildings and alterations were common.

The thirteenth century can be said to be the 'golden age', and the finest castles of this period—Dirleton, Kildrummy, and Bothwell—for example—bear witness to the skill of mason and designer alike. These castles are known as 'castles of enceinte', the enceinte being the walls and towers which together enclose the courtyard.

During the wars of independence in the first half of the fourteenth century many more castles were damaged and destroyed than were built. The few that *were* built were mainly the simple rectangular tower-houses, similar in design to the Norman keep. Of these fourteenth-century tower-houses, Lochleven Castle, Kinross-shire, and Dundonald Castle, Ayrshire, are two fine examples.

Bastard feudalism had much the same effect on castle design in Scotland as in England. A magnificent Scottish example of the type of castle associated with it, is Tantallon, East Lothian, one of the mightiest fortifications of the country. Doune castle, Menteith, is later, and here the lord's apartments, in the forefront of the building, control the gateway and form a completely self-contained unit, inaccessible from another suite of domestic buildings clearly intended for the general garrison. In England, fortification of the home ended in the fifteenth century, but in Scotland, with its constant unrest and periodic fighting, every laird, great or small, had to maintain his 'house of fence' for at least two centuries longer. These 'houses of fence' were designed for the effective use of firearms. The use of flanking fire from firearms at a low level resulted in the spreading-out of the plan, with the blocks arranged to provide jambs or wings well pierced with gun-loops, so that covering fire could be given to two sides of the main building. Scalloway, Glenbuchat, and Claypotts give some idea of the development of this type of 'three-stepped' or Z plan, which became popular during the sixteenth century.

The great castellated houses of the sixteenth and early seventeenth centuries, which form the Scottish baronial style—such as Glamis, Craigievar and Caerlaverock castles—show in some of their detail the gradual adoption of the Renaissance style.

To summarize Scottish castle buildings—and there are almost a thousand of them—at this length is to do the subject less than justice. If what has been said is enough to whet the appetite, then it will serve its purpose. Such commanding examples as Stirling and Dirleton will, by their setting, fire the explorer's interest and imagination.

FURTHER READING

A. Hamilton-Thompson, *Military Architecture in England During the Middle Ages*. O.U.P., 1912.

Sidney Toy, *The Castles of Great Britain*, 2nd ed. Heinemann, 1953.

B. H. St-J. O'Neil, *Castles*. H.M.S.O., 1954.

Douglas Simpson, *Scottish Castles*. H.M.S.O., 1959.

Douglas Simpson, *Exploring Castles*. Routledge & Kegan Paul, 1957.

R. A. Brown, *English Medieval Castles*. Batsford, 1954.

The books by Hamilton-Thompson and Toy are generally considered to be the standard works on the subject, but all the others are well written and interesting. The H.M.S.O. books are particularly good value, as they have well-chosen illustrations, concise texts, and an abundance of simple plans.

7

THE MEDIEVAL AND TUDOR HOUSE

Our study of medieval architecture so far may have given the impression that the only interests of the people were battle or church. But life still had to go on, food had to be grown, cloth spun, and the business of the world transacted. These activities were carried out by the merchants from their houses. The splendour of the great cathedrals and castles tends to push the smaller less monumental buildings from our minds.

Examples of twelfth-century or thirteenth-century houses are few, for the peasants lived in huts of wattle and daub, or simple timber sheds, and these have perished, not having either the protection of sanctity, as the churches did, or the sheer mass of the castles. The basic unit of feudal society was the manor, which consisted of a house and a cluster of cottages around it. The lord of the manor often owned several estates, and would spend his time between them or in going away to do battle for his baron or king. In his absence, sometimes for quite long periods, the estate would be in the care of his bailiff, or sometimes his wife. The administration was no light task, as most things were made in the manor itself—cloth was woven and spun, corn harvested and ground into flour. The manor was, in fact, an efficiently organized living community.

Contact with the outside world was difficult; roads were poor and often impassable after heavy rain, and many of them were infested with robbers and bandits. Despite

these difficulties, people did manage to make surprisingly frequent journeys over long distances. It would appear that the most common mode of transport was by horse or foot, as gateways to manor houses were so narrow it would have been difficult to get a cart through.

To these people, the highlight of their lives must have been the local fair. Fairs were important features of medieval commerce, for they brought money and trade into the towns that were granted permission to hold them, and they enabled the inhabitants of the outlying districts to trade and barter their wares. The largest of these fairs also provided outlets for foreign merchandise imported from the Continent. In this way goods from France, the Netherlands, and as far away as the Mediterranean and Near East, found their way into the houses or on to the tables of English families. A popular import from the East was spices, for meals were often elaborate and highly seasoned. Food was served on wooden platters, two people usually sharing the same dish. Utensils were scarce; men used their own knives to cut their food and they ate with their fingers. A thick slice of bread or 'trencher' helped to mop up the gravy. There may well have been silver or pewter serving-dishes on the high table, which was probably covered with white table-linen.

Furniture was roughly made and not very plentiful. A rough table or two, probably supported on trestles so that they could easily be stored when not in use, perhaps a more elaborate 'refectory' type table for the lord and his family and guests, and a few stools and benches, completed the furniture of the hall. Chests were a necessity in bedroom and solar for the storage of clothing, arms, and personal belongings. It was not until Tudor times that more elaborate furniture was introduced. Comfort is a very relative thing, and compared with modern homes these early manors seem bleak.

Eleanor of Castile, wife of Edward I, introduced wall-hangings and carpets, which must have added greatly to the warmth and comfort of the home. In the richer homes there were tapestries imported from France, but in the less wealthy, imitation tapestries of worsted cloth, or coarse woven cloth, painted in the manner of their more expensive counterparts, were used. Previously, walls had been painted with simple diaper patterns, floral motifs or simple religious themes in bright colours. This love of colour must never be overlooked. Today we see only dull stone walls in cathedrals and houses, but in their day they must have presented a very different picture; it is unlikely that people who dressed so colourfully would have been content with plain stone walls. From the fifteenth century onwards, however, wainscoting became very popular as a wall finish, not only for its decorative qualities but also for its warmer effect.

It is difficult to give a precise date for the general introduction of glazing, but the middle of the fourteenth century, when the size of windows began to increase, provides a rough date. Some of the windows in Stokesay (second half of the thirteenth century) were glazed, but many buildings still had unglazed windows almost two centuries later.

Whilst on the one hand small windows admitted little light—and these early houses must have been gloomy places by present-day standards—on the other hand they did minimize draughts and give a sense of security. The openings may have been closed by wooden shutters, or by linen stretched over wooden frames and then dipped in oil or wax to give translucency. Those families rich enough to afford glazed windows had them made in movable frames, and carried them with them when they visited their other estates. It seems unlikely that they would fit perfectly into their new homes, and a certain amount of hasty carpentry must have been necessary when the family arrived for their stay. In some cases windows were divided into two halves, the bottom half closed by wooden shutters and the top half glazed.

Because root crops were unknown, most of the livestock had to be killed off in the autumn. The meat was salted down and stored for food during the winter months. This meant that a large amount of storage space had to be provided. Turner's *Domestic Architecture* lists the contents of a larder in 1311 as follows: The carcases of 20 oxen, 15 pigs, of herrings 8,000, of dograves (a sea fish) seven score, 20 pounds of almonds, 30 pounds of rice, 6 barrels of lard, enough oatmeal to last till Easter, 2 quarts of salt. This list makes the provision of adequate storage space obvious, and it must not be imagined that although the family lived in one or two rooms there were not other huts clustered around the main building.

Medieval Domestic Architecture

The history of the castle demonstrates man's developing ability to protect himself, whilst the growth of the house shows his increasing desire to provide himself with privacy and comfort. The house has been in existence since man began to settle into communities and to till the land. It is even possible to claim that the nomadic Arabian tribesmen with their tents clustered round the larger tent of the chief had, in effect, their own private houses; in some ways this arrangement is similar to the clusters of houses round the Norman castle or the feudal manor house. But however humble these structures may have been, were they merely of canvas, mud or timber, they still meant that man had his own private dwelling.

In Britain, the Romans had brought their larger houses to quite a high state of development, based, of course, on the classical plan. But when they left these shores domestic building declined and was not restored to a more permanent basis until after the Conquest. The Roman type of house, based on a large uncovered atrium, was unsuitable for the damp, dull climate of this country, and later builders made a covered central living space the hub of their house.

The Anglo-Saxons developed the 'cruck' house (Figs. 150, 151), which provided

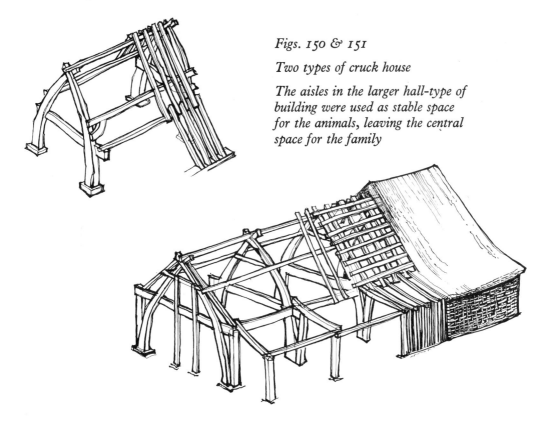

Figs. 150 & 151

Two types of cruck house

The aisles in the larger hall-type of building were used as stable space for the animals, leaving the central space for the family

accommodation for family, servants, and livestock under the same roof. These houses had grown from the prehistoric pole hut, covered by turf and bracken. The earth which had been dug out of the inside of the hut to give extra head-room was piled around the side, and this must have suggested the idea of making walls. Gradually the idea of supporting a ridge-pole with vertical poles along the length of the hut gave way in Saxon times to the idea of supporting the rafters by crucks. The sides were then built out to provide extra space.

It is still possible to find examples of these early cruck houses in villages in country districts today. There is one example in Lacock, in Wiltshire. Crucks were then replaced by vertical supports, which gave the central nave-and-aisle type of plan that was to become the standard method of constructing barns for centuries to come. These simple beginnings were to provide the foundation of fine craftsmanship in wood which was to make the timber frame house such a notable feature of the English architectural scene.

The Normans, with their passion for building in stone, began to introduce this more permanent material into the building of smaller houses, although remains of this type are rare indeed. In fact, remains of any domestic buildings before the fifteenth century are few. There are, however, enough for us to form a fair idea of what sort of house our ancestors lived in.

The smaller house, such as the manor house at Boothby Pagnell, near Grantham, Lincs., or the Fish House at Meare, Somerset (Figs. 152, 153), provided living accommodation at first-floor level. In this way some measure of protection was afforded to the occupants, and a safe store-room in the undercroft was also provided, as there was no doorway at this level.

The other type of house was that in which the hall was the nucleus; this was usually a single-storey building of the full height of the two-storey apartments which were tacked on at one end as private accommodation for the family. At the opposite end was the domestic range, comprising pantry, buttery, and kitchen. This layout is so

Fig. 152 The Manor House, Boothby Pagnell, near Grantham (c. 1180)

Fig. 153 The Fish House, Meare, Somerset (c. 1350)

Fig. 154

*Cothay Manor,
Wellington, Somerset
(1480)*

common that it formed the basis not only of such magnificent houses as Haddon Hall and Penshurst Place but also of the more modest Cothay Manor in Somerset (Fig. 154) and Knook Manor in Wiltshire (Fig. 163).

The Great Hall

The great hall is such an important feature of domestic architecture that a detailed description is essential (Fig. 155). Throughout the period, the basic design remained remarkably unchanged and only underwent refinements of layout, furnishing, and decoration. The main points of the typical layout can be summarized as follows:

(i) The entrance was always at one end, with the dais at the other. In the larger and more important houses the dais was generally built at the same time as the main structure, but in some of the smaller ones it may well have been a later addition.

(ii) The family quarters were situated behind the dais, in a two-storey block usually running at right angles to the long axis of the hall. This was known as the solar.

(iii) Since two doors directly facing each other at the far ends of the hall caused excessive draughts, spurs were thrown out at each side. By the fourteenth century these spurs had developed into full screens, 8 feet to 10 feet high and roofed over to provide a minstrels' gallery. (This gallery was important, as music and entertainment at meal times was popular. Travelling troupes of singers and strolling players went from manor to manor; whilst the

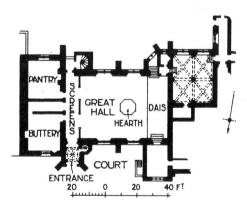

*Fig. 155 Penshurst Place, Kent (1341)
This plan shows the typical layout of a great hall, with solar at one end and domestic apartments at the other*

richer families often employed fools, jesters and tumblers to enliven the banquet with their capers from the floor of the hall.)

(iv) The wall behind the screens usually had three doorways, the outer ones for pantry and buttery, the middle one leading through a passage to the kitchen.

(v) The hearth was often placed in the centre of the hall, towards the dais end, either on stone slabs or in a brazier. The smoke found its way out through louvres in the open-timbered roof. The fourteenth century saw the introduction of a wall fireplace as standard practice.

If the floor was unpaved, the beaten earth may have been treated with ox-blood to give it a hard surface and then strewn with straw and rushes. Here, amongst the refuse of the meal, bones, discarded gristle, and unwanted scrapings from the table, slept the retainers. There is in existence a royal order to widen the door at Westminster Hall so that a cart could be brought in to clear the refuse from the 'marsh', as the lower part of the hall was known. How often this clearing took place in the average manor it is impossible to say.

As we have already noted, windows were small. If, however, the hall formed one side of a courtyard, then those facing inward were usually larger. The general gloom must have made the open fires doubly welcome, as a source of light as well as heat.

There is no real parallel to the great hall in modern times, and it is difficult for us to imagine living under such conditions. The growing desire for privacy and comfort during the centuries resulted in the break-up of this strong community life, and today such an existence would be distasteful if not intolerable. Yet in these early times when the great hall flourished, life must have been a constant struggle against the elements, famine, and disease. It is not difficult to see that the lusty camaraderie must have given some sense of comfort and safety to those engaged in the grim realities of existence.

Apart from being the central point of the medieval manor, the great hall was also important as a separate building in its own right. The guilds and societies began to build their own halls, of great magnificence, for their councils and banquets. The Guildhall in London has suffered many vicissitudes, including damage in the Great Fire of London (after which it was altered by Wren), restoration in the nineteenth century, and bomb-damage in the Second World War. The cities of Exeter and York both possess fine examples of this kind of hall, but the finest of all medieval halls is that of Westminster Palace. It was remodelled in the reign of Richard II, between 1394 and 1402. The mason was Henry Yevele and the carpenter Hugh Harland. The timber roof is the finest in Europe and spans almost 70 feet. The hammer posts which rise from the hammer beams of this magnificent structure are 39 feet by 25 inches and 21 feet long.

The universities also built magnificent halls, and there are fine examples at New College (1386) and Christ Church, Oxford (1525), and at Trinity College, Cambridge (1604). Collegiate halls were usually found in conjunction with a complete courtyard.

with student accommodation placed around.

Other examples of the hall are to be found in the monasteries of the period. The refectory was in effect the great hall of the monks, and the 'infirmaries' were in effect aisled halls. Unfortunately, owing to the damage done during the Dissolution and after, in many cases only the outline of these buildings can still be seen. There are substantial remains of a twelfth-century infirmary at Canterbury, and Rievaulx has, in common with many other Cistercian houses, the remains of a fine refectory.

Craft Houses

Before dealing with the larger and more important houses of the period there are a number of craft or vernacular houses which repay study. These are not only important in their own right but also help us to understand the work of certain of the nineteenth-century architects who revived this particular style of building with such striking success. The two pages of illustrations (Figs. 156–169) give some idea of the richness and charm of these dwellings. They are not the work of trained architects working to some preconceived style, but the outcome of local craftsmen using local material. The arrangement of the buildings arose from the requirements of the owner, and although some of them show signs of symmetry this is the outcome of an instinctive feeling for design rather than the striving after symmetry at all costs which was to be the ideal of the Renaissance architect. Some of these buildings show a natural feeling for local material and an instinctive and unforced feeling for texture. They were erected in an honest attempt to satisfy a demand, and as the general design lasted for so many centuries with only slight modification they must have served their purpose well. This was the architecture of necessity, designed without heed to style or effect, simply to be used.

Smaller Town House

In the latter part of the twelfth century and during the thirteenth century the smaller town houses began to be built of a more permanent material. This was due not only to the growing desire of the middle-class merchant to provide a more permanent abode, but also the need to cut down the risk of fire. This was a constant source of worry, and although by-laws were passed to compel the use of stone party-walls, they were not always enforced or heeded. The famous Jew's House at Lincoln and the Grevel House, Chipping Campden (Figs. 156, 158), give some idea of what these buildings were like. Because of the lack of space in towns, an outside staircase could not be provided, and consequently the living space in town houses tended to be on the ground floor rather than on the first floor, as in more rural buildings. Stylistically the smaller house remained relatively untouched by the dictates of style and fashion until almost the end of the seventeenth century.

Larger Town House

In the larger houses of the fourteenth century there was a growing concern for architectural effect. The change was slow but steady, and the hall still remained the nucleus around which improvements were

Figs. 156–169 are intended to illustrate the development of the smaller English house from the Conquest to the end of the seventeenth century ▶

Fig. 156 *The Jew's House, Lincoln* (c. *1150*)

Fig. 157
Little Wenham,
Suffolk (*1260–80*)

Fig. 158 *The Grevel House,*
Chipping Campden,
Glos. (c. *1400*)

Fig. 159 *Synyards, Otham, Kent*
(*Fifteenth century, altered mid-seventeenth century*)
A typical fifteenth-century yeoman's house

Fig. 161 *Ockwells Manor, Bray, Berkshire* (c. *1465*)

Fig. 160

Blagroves,
Barnard Castle,
Co. Durham
(*late fifteenth century*)

Fig. 162 *Sutton Courtenay, Berkshire—*
a typical manor house of the
sixteenth century

Fig. 163 Knook Manor, Wiltshire

Fig. 164 Daneway House, Gloucestershire
(mainly mid-seventeenth
century)

Fig. 165

Ashleworth, Gloucestershire—
an example of a symmetrical
façade in half-timbering

Fig. 166 Cold Ashton Manor, Glos. (c. 1570)
A small Elizabethan manor house

Fig. 167 Yatton Keynell Manor, Wilts.
(first half of seventeenth century)
An early Renaissance manor house
of the west country

Fig. 169 Hunt's Farm, Kent
(late sixteenth century)

Fig. 168 Nether Lypiat, Glos. A typical
classical house of the late seventeenth
and early eighteenth centuries

made. The typical larger house of the period was quadrangular in plan; this gave some measure of defence, and wherever possible a moat was a further safeguard. External walls tended to lack decoration—except, sometimes, on the façades in the courtyard. Windows on the external walls were small, and gatehouses became increasingly important—often becoming distinct architectural features in themselves, as at Oxburgh.

.The expansion of the house, due to the addition of rooms for specialized purposes, was general throughout the century. This was true even in the older castles, many of which saw the provision of more commodious apartments. At the castles of Alnwick in the north, and Kenilworth and Warwick in the Midlands, extensive alterations and additions took place. Kenilworth still retained its early keep, but late in the fourteenth century John of Gaunt embarked on an extensive rebuilding programme, including a great hall 90 feet by 45 feet in the Perpendicular style; this must have been one of the finest halls in the country at the time.

In the vast majority of cases the hall still retained its traditional form and arrangement. The one striking development which took place was the provision of a bay-window to the dais. This not only gave more light at that point but also gave greater importance to the area. In some cases, as at Great Chalfield, the window was so large as to be able to accommodate the staircase which led to the private quarters of the family, situated behind the dais.

Window openings, doorways, and so on followed the prevailing style of church architecture. The oriel window was one feature which gained prominence during the early part of the period. It is difficult to say exactly how the oriel developed. It may well have been a recessed opening in the hall, either for a chapel or for the reader's pulpit, but during the fifteenth century it became a window. The frequency with which it is found over gateways has led to the belief that it may well be a development of machicolations. However, it became one of the most striking features of the domestic design and is still to be found in use to this day.

The kitchen also became more substantial, though still frequently detached from the main part of the house. The very earliest examples were of such combustible material that none remain, and the finest surviving example of one of these early kitchens is at Glastonbury, dating from c. 1400. This is square on plan with fireplaces across each corner. These are arched over to produce an octagon, vaulted with eight stone ribs supporting a ventilating shaft, which appears to have carried the flues for the fireplaces below.

Haddon Hall

The finest of the fourteenth-century houses still remaining is Haddon Hall, in Derbyshire (Fig. 170). This magnificent house, nestling against a hillside, has been sufficiently well preserved for us to get a good idea of what it must have been like in its original state. The house is arranged around a double courtyard, with the entrance in the lower one. The position of the hall, lying between the two yards, afforded greater safety, and so permitted larger windows than

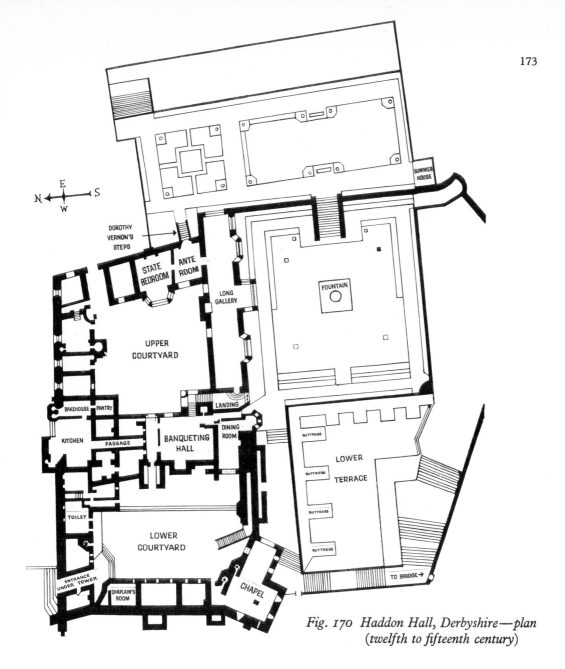

Fig. 170 Haddon Hall, Derbyshire—plan
(twelfth to fifteenth century)

might otherwise have been possible. The main fabric of the hall is late fourteenth century and originally there was a central hearth, the fireplace being added a century later. As was usual, the hall divided the house in two, and in the sixteenth century a gallery, running the length of the hall, was added to provide easier communication between the upper floors to the north and south of the house.

The private apartments, situated behind the dais of the main hall, consist of a dining room and great chamber. There are excellent decorations in the dining room, giving a vivid idea of what the original atmosphere of the room must have been. It seems probable that this room was originally a lofty solar, and that the great chamber above was formed, about 1500, in the upper part of it. At the other end of the hall are the usual three doorways—one to the pantry, one to the buttery, and one opening on to a central passage leading to the well-equipped kitchen.

The long gallery, 110 feet long and 17 feet broad, has a wonderfully light and airy aspect, the spacious windows revealing the delicate Renaissance detail in the panelling in a crisp, silvery light. So keen were these builders to give the maximum possible length to the long gallery that in this particular case the wing has been extended, and now protrudes beyond the original corner of the block.

The chapel contains a series of fine mural paintings on a variety of subjects. Today they present a series of harmonious greys, blacks, and muted colours, but it is not difficult to imagine that in their original condition they presented a colour scheme of greater intensity.

Despite its many defensive features, including a 12-foot-high wall, it is difficult to decide whether Haddon Hall can be classed as a fortified manor house. From the approaches it certainly gives the impression that it could be defended, though the battlements are decorative rather than military in intention. The banks of the river are steep and the river itself wide. Although it never became necessary, one feels that stout resistance could have been offered had the need arisen.

During the fifteenth century there was a further advance in the general provision of rooms for private use and in the increasing desire for comfort. In the larger houses there was a growing tendency to build with greater regard for symmetry, though the smaller traditional buildings continued in the style of picturesque irregularity. The gaunt character of the earlier buildings was softened by a little more decoration and a more fanciful and imaginative treatment of ornament. This was due not only to a growing prosperity throughout the country, but also to the fact that more settled conditions removed the fear of damage by violence.

Great Chalfield

An example of mid-fifteenth-century design is Great Chalfield, Wiltshire, *c.* 1450. This house is unfortified but is almost completely surrounded by a moat. The general layout is most picturesque, and the general character of the decoration shows work of good Perpendicular character. The hall follows the usual arrangement, and there is a large bay-window at the dais end.

Oxburgh Hall

Of the single quadrangular plan Oxburgh Hall, Norfolk, 1482, is a fine example. This is a moated house and has a most impressive brick gatehouse. The arrangement of the house shows the growing consciousness of a more 'architectural' effect, insofar as there is a feeling for balance in the façades and the arrangement of the plan, though not a strictly enforced symmetry.

The Early Renaissance House

The period known as the Early Renaissance in England can be subdivided into three stages: firstly, 'Tudor'—the transitional stage which saw the last of Gothic and ended with the death of Henry VIII in 1547; secondly, 'Elizabethan'—from 1547 until roughly 1600; and thirdly, 'Stuart' or 'Jacobean'—from 1600 to the Civil War in 1642.

The spread of the Renaissance was retarded in this country—on the one hand by Henry's quarrel with the Pope over his marriage to Anne Boleyn, and on the other by the orientation of English trade towards the countries of northern Europe. Early in his reign Henry had invited many Italian craftsmen to his court, but after the Dissolution he preferred to employ craftsmen from the Netherlands and North European countries. Merchants with strong trading connections also preferred to employ northern craftsmen, and so Italy herself was bypassed and the Renaissance came to these shores at second-hand rather than direct.

There was also an economic factor which retarded building, especially of smaller houses, during the fifteenth century and the early part of the sixteenth. This was the distinct threat to arable farming, particularly in the midlands, caused by the enclosure of large tracts of land for sheep-farming. This made the wool-lords rich, but caused great hardship, through unemployment, to the peasant farm-workers, because one man could look after many sheep. After the enquiry of 1517 the Crown took action against many enclosures, but with little effect. Such legislation would in any case receive little sympathy or support, as such a large number of the governing class were interested parties. It would seem that any attempts to check enclosures were bound to be fruitless and that any drastic remedy was politically impracticable. However, in the closing years of Elizabeth's reign there was a reversal of this trend, and the enclosure of land for sheep-farming began to abate. Arable farming began to prosper through the money invested by the wealthy, and so the demand for the smaller house for the yeoman farmer, such as Synyards (Fig. 159), began to increase.

The demand for food was also stimulated by the growing population and this fact, too, may have had some bearing on the change of emphasis in farming.

The growing importance of the cloth-making industry led not only to the construction of large houses for the clothiers themselves, but also to the building of many villages where the spinning was done. These villages, such as Bibury in Gloucestershire and Burford in Oxfordshire, contained well-built cottages of great charm. Further north, in South Yorkshire and around Bradford and Halifax, the manufacture of woollen goods provided the wealth for house and village architecture, which remained outside the fashionable influences found further south.

The dispersal of aristocratic and ecclesiastical lands also provided an opportunity for the middle class, which had grown richer by the profits of increased trade during the fifteenth and sixteenth centuries. This period saw the beginning of the growth of 'gentle' families by landlordship, which has continued until the present day. The sixteenth century also saw the break-up of the decaying manorial system. The resident squire became the focus of rural life, and as a Justice of the Peace he gradually took over the duties and powers of the medieval Lord of the Manor.

Other influences on architecture came from the books which began to circulate as a result of the spread of printing. One of the most important of these was that published by John Shute, which had the impressive title, 'The Firste & Chief Groundes of Architecture used in all the Auncient and Famous Monymenes: with a farther and more ample Discourse upon the same, than hitherto hath been set out by any other. Published by Jhon Shute, Paynter and Archytecte. Imprinted at London in Fletestrete near to Sainct Dunstans Churche by Thomas Marshe, 1563'. This book was by an Englishman who had toured Italy and met Vignola, Palladio and Michelangelo. Although Shute cannot be credited with any actual building, the influence of his book was widespread, and Shute himself was closely connected with a number of influential figures of the time. There were also a number of pattern books in circulation by Flemish, Dutch, and German authors who were all giving their version of Italian models.

The spread of the Renaissance style to the smaller houses was still slow, and the further north and west the houses were situated, the longer the traditional craft buildings continued to be built. It was only in the larger houses that the change took place—the houses of men who could afford either to travel themselves and copy what they saw or to employ those who had some knowledge of the new style. Cold Ashton in Gloucestershire is a good example of a smaller Elizabethan manor. The tidying up of plan and façade which took place is well illustrated, and the symmetry of the plan is natural and unforced (Fig. 166).

Compton Wynyates in Warwickshire (Fig. 171) and Layer Marney, Essex, provide two of the best examples of the larger house. The first of these was built around 1520, probably on the site of an earlier house. There have been many additions to the house over the centuries, including the bay-window and roof of the hall, which both came from Fulbroke Castle. The layout of the hall is traditional, except that it is now backed by a range of rooms added in Georgian times and that the spiral staircase from the hall has been replaced by one of more formal design. The courtyard is entered through a gateway which is almost opposite the screens entrance to the hall itself. The grouping of the building is as romantic and picturesque as one can imagine, with little of the regularity and symmetry which was to become the ideal of Renaissance designers. Unfortunately all the contents were sold in the eighteenth century and none of the original fittings remain. There is little left of the plan at Layer Marney, but the entrance gateway has something of the symmetry of a Renaissance building. Despite this, however, there is something undeniably Gothic about the verticality of the projecting towers with their four-centred arched

Fig. 171 Compton Wynyates, Warwickshire (1450–1523)—south front

windows. Terra-cotta panelling gives added richness to this impressive brick-built structure.

One of the most remarkable buildings of the Tudor Period must have been the mysterious 'Nonesuch Palace' in Surrey, built by Henry VIII in the later part of the fifteen-thirties with money from the dissolution of the monasteries. Like many other houses of the period, it was built around a double courtyard and the whole scheme must have been one of unparalleled magnificence. Unfortunately nothing remains of the actual fabric of the building, and it is only possible to get an idea of the scheme through looking at the few prints and paintings which still exist. Particularly important were the plaster decorations and statues that Henry commissioned, and it is only due to recent excavations on the site that we have had more than written descriptions of their novelty and splendour.

There are some who would criticize this period as being guilty of over-ornamentation, and to a certain extent this view may be justified in the case of some of the later buildings. But on the whole the elaboration of the numerous gables with balls, vases, heraldic animals and such, and the increased importance paid to the staircase with its carved newels, give the period a richness that fits well with the energy and virility of the time.

The more settled conditions and the general prosperity of Elizabeth's reign resulted in still further building activity. The rise of the new nobility led to the construction of many great houses of a size and scale not seen before. Changes in traditional design began to appear with increasing frequency and the Italian influence now came to these shores either direct from native craftsmen or through the interest created by visits to Italy itself.

The courtyard plan sank from favour, and in its place came the E- and H-shaped plans which were so typical of Elizabethan architecture. Cornices and pediments began to appear, and the pointed arch was replaced by the semicircular. Windows became square-headed and classic pilasters were introduced. The grand staircase with richly carved newels and pierced balustrades made a strong contrast to the cramped spiral of earlier times. The solar was replaced by the withdrawing-room, and there was a real striving for symmetry of layout and design. This growing formality was doubtless a reflection of the growing formality of manners and dress, and of a general desire of the wealthy to display their finery.

The most striking feature of the Elizabethan mansion was, however, the long gallery, which reached unmatched length and splendour. The exact origin and function of the long gallery is vague and difficult to determine. The most probable explanation is that it was simply a show-place for the treasures of the family—portraits, sculptures and so on—which it was becoming fashionable to collect. Some claims that it was a place of exercise for the women folk in the winter months, when outside exercise in their heavy elaborate dress would have been impracticable. Others think that it was a development of the minstrels' gallery of the great hall. Whatever its origin, however, its importance cannot be denied, and we have already seen that at Haddon the block was extended to accommodate an even longer gallery than would have otherwise been possible.

The most striking examples of Elizabethan great houses are Longleat, Wiltshire, 1567–80; Wollaton, Notts., 1580–8; and Hardwick Hall, Derbyshire, 1590–7; (Figs. 172–175). Despite their many differences, these three houses have a certain similarity, a fact which is easily explained if, as seems probable, Robert Smythson was connected in some way with all three.

Longleat

The earliest of them, Longleat (Fig. 172a), is certainly the most Renaissance in feeling. The courtyard plan is still retained (Fig. 172b) but there can be no doubt that with its great square-headed windows and clear definition of storeys this house deserves the tag which is so often quoted: 'the momentary High Renaissance of English architecture'. The present building—the result of reconstruction after a fire in 1567—is approached through a long drive through parkland, and there can be little doubt that the house fits well with its surroundings. Sir John Thynne, the owner, was an extremely active builder, and it is reasonable to assume that he was largely responsible for the design of Longleat. He did at that time employ the young Robert Smythson, then about thirty years old, as mason. This association seems to have had a profound effect on the development of the younger man, and much of his later work—and he was a man of outstanding talents—stems from what he must have learnt from Thynne.

This is the first of the outward-looking courtyard houses, and all façades are rigidly symmetrical. The front elevation presents to the world a calm ordered face which is quite new in English architecture. The flat bays are just enough to break the monotony of the façade without destroying the unity, and even the doorway, which was later to become such an important feature, is not allowed to obtrude. Gables and steep-pitched roofs are banished and their place taken by a classical balustrade, making the roofline flat and unworried. The interior was extensively restored early in the second half of the nineteenth century by Italian crafts-

Fig. 172a Longleat House, Wilts. (1567–80). This beautiful house is often referred to as the 'momentary High Renaissance of English architecture'

men. The heavy colour and detailing are out of character with the pristine beauty of the external elevations, and as far as internal decoration goes Hardwick is to be preferred.

Wollaton Hall

Longleat was the result of many years' effort, probably about twenty; Wollaton Hall (Fig. 173), usually called Smythson's masterpiece, was the work of about eight. Like Longleat, this is a most strikingly individual house and in their different ways each house

is unique in English architecture. In this house Smythson dispenses with the central court altogether, and it is replaced by the hall, lit entirely from the top windows in the great tower. This, then, is an almost aggressively outward-looking house. The plan is rigidly symmetrical externally, and the long gallery runs the entire length of one side at the upper end of the hall. The massing of the blocks of the building shows that daring and sculptural quality which seems to have been one of Smythson's great gifts, if we are to judge from his work at Hardwick.

Fig. 172b

Longleat House—plan

Though this house is a double courtyard house it is 'outward-looking', which is typical of Renaissance design

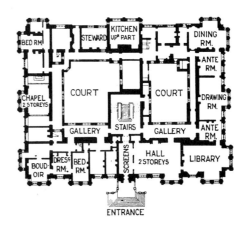

Fig. 173 Wollaton Hall, Notts. (1580–88)

Many would disparage Wollaton as being grandiose and lacking in taste, but this is revealed as a bold house—big in conception and flamboyant in execution. As one looks at it and moves around it, one feels that perhaps Smythson and Vanburgh were kindred spirits.

Hardwick Hall

What Hardwick (Fig. 175) lacks in flamboyance it makes up for in refinement. Here, that remarkable woman 'Bess of Hardwick', four times married, probably second in wealth only to the Queen, and an insatiable builder, is reputed to have taken a keen interest in the work. The story goes that Bess believed that she would never die so long as she kept building; she lived till she was ninety and was at that time engaged on building the old Chatsworth. During a very severe frost the builders were thrown out of

work, and during this stoppage Bess died.

Today Hardwick remains one of the finest examples of the period. Seen on top of its hill, through a slight haze, there is still something remarkably Gothic in the silhouette, yet as one draws closer, and the detail becomes clearer, the Renaissance ancestry becomes more apparent. One of the most striking features of Hardwick is the compression of the plan. While both Longleat and Wollaton were constructed around a central nucleus, Hardwick is compressed into a single block, vaguely reminiscent of the letter H (Fig. 174). The hall is placed on the axis of the entrance—thus solving the difficulty of the unsymmetrical placing of the door in the traditional layout—and the pantry and buttery are then placed on either side. The long gallery, a room of splendour and great length, runs the entire length of the east front, some 166 feet in all.

Fig. 174

Hardwick Hall, Derbyshire
(1590–7)—plan

An unusual plan, of which
the 'long gallery' is a
notable feature

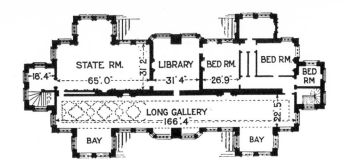

The interior of the house is spacious and airy, and the decorations, whether tapestries or painted and moulded friezes, are full of incident and interest. Especially noteworthy is the Great High Chamber, with its most beautiful plaster frieze and delicately coloured tapestries. The deep frieze, modelled in high relief, shows scenes of hunting, and must have been richly coloured; now it glows with a delicate iridescence in the light from the large windows. But the great fireplace (there are two more in the long gallery) shows not only the awkward transition from Gothic to classic, but also something of the ungainliness that suggests Vanbrugh.

Despite the many internal beauties, it is perhaps the outside which is the more impressive and memorable. The architect has managed to construct from his compact plan an elevation of striking success. The old tag 'Hardwick Hall more glass than wall' is understandable—though not literally true. The great rectangles of the windows impart to the façade a dignity unmatched in English architecture, whilst the square towers constantly present new arrangements and combinations of solids and voids as the house is viewed from fresh angles. From the entrance gate the house presents an aspect of dynamic repose but when seen somewhat from the side the sharp perspectives of towers, with their forthright angles and uncompromising rectilinearity, throw the façade into violent action, and we become conscious of tower and sky,

Fig. 175 Hardwick Hall—façade. The work of the outstanding architect Robert Smithson
is well illustrated in the bold massing of Wollaton and Hardwick

between and behind, solid and void—the basic elements of architectural composition.

Returning to the front elevation, the increasing size of the windows as they progress upwards should be noticed, but the clear horizontal divisions of the façade do not express the internal structure for at one level the floors correspond to the transoms of the windows, not to the external mouldings, as one would expect. Interesting, too, is the little entrance colonnade which stretches from tower to tower. The columns—one hesitates to say order—are Tuscan Doric, but the shafts are interrupted by little bands of rustication which give them a late Elizabethan flavour.

From documentary evidence, Smythson must also be credited with the design of Worksop Manor, Notts., which was burnt down in 1761, and he may well have been associated with a number of smaller houses, judging from the number of drawings in the collection of the Royal Institute of British Architects. On the evidence of Wollaton and Hardwick alone, however, Smythson must be regarded as one of the most dynamic and original designers England has produced.

During the last quarter of the sixteenth century and the first quarter of the seventeenth century there was a gradual change in the type of material used for house building. The once plentiful supply of wood was being seriously depleted by the constant demands of building, iron smelting, and heating. The land had been systematically denuded of forests, without any thought of replacement. Consequently the price of wood was forced up, and it no longer offered a cheap alternative to stone or brick. During this period the size of the brick was standardized at 9 inches by $4\frac{1}{2}$ inches by 3 inches, and the result was that in many parts of the country building passed out of the hands of carpenters and into the hands of the mason and bricklayer. James I issued an order forbidding the unlimited use of wood in buildings, and one has only to look at the amount of wood in such buildings as Ashleworth, Gloucester (Fig. 165), and compare it with such a building as Hunt's Farm in Kent (Fig. 169), to see what economies were made in the spacing of the timbers in the smaller house.

In keeping with the general air of pure extravagance, which amounts at times to what could be termed architectural hyperbole, is a small group of houses in which the plan was intended to express some form of symbolism. John Thorpe made several such plans—one quite impracticable, based on his own initials, and several others based on the triangle, symbol of the trinity. Sir Thomas Tresham, who, though of a Catholic family, had been brought up as a Protestant, but who reverted to the faith, was also responsible for several plans which had marked and often involved symbolic meaning.

FURTHER READING

S. O. Addy, *The Evolution of the English House*, rev. ed. Allen & Unwin, 1933.

This is an early work on the subject and full of interest.

J. A. Gotch, *Old English Houses*. Methuen, 1925.
— *Early Renaissance Architecture 1500–1625*. Batsford, 1901.

Gotch was a copious writer on the history of the English House. These books are of his usual standard. They all contain a great amount of detail and many useful illustrations, plans and diagrams, but the texts must be used with care as they are now rather dated.

H. and R. Leacroft, *Early Architecture in Britain*. Methuen, 1960.

A useful little book, well illustrated.

F. H. Crossley, *Timber Building in England*. Batsford, 1951.

The volume covers both religious and secular building from the earliest times to the end of the seventeenth century. It contains many photographs, drawings, and diagrams.

The reader is also directed to the main bibliography for further reading.

8

THE AGE OF JONES AND WREN

Inigo Jones

Now we must turn to the consideration of that somewhat enigmatic character, Inigo Jones (1573–1652). Jones is so much a man of the Renaissance style that it may be helpful to place him amongst his contemporaries before we begin to look at his work and achievement. An exact contemporary of Donne and Ben Jonson—with Heywood, Dekker, Webster, and Middleton all born within half a decade of him—he was nine years younger than Shakespeare and had reached the age of thirty before Elizabeth died. In view of this, it would not be surprising to find more than a trace of the Gothic inheritance in his work, but none is, in fact, discernible.

Of his early life we know little. He visited Italy before 1603, and whilst he was there he learned to draw in the free natural manner of the Renaissance masters, as opposed to the stilted, though beautiful, calligraphic manner of the Elizabethan draughtsmen. There can be little doubt that this ability to draw and give free expression to his ideas must have had a profound effect on his method of thinking. It is this ability, too, which marks the transition from the medieval to modern, for he found architectural draughtsmanship in one state and left it in another. It was as a stage- and costume-designer that he first came to the notice of the court. James and Anne held a much more lavish court than that of the thrifty Elizabeth, and with the ideas of Inigo the court masques were transformed from an elaborate charade into a dramatic performance. He must have studied the Italian theatre with care and attention on his first visit to Italy, and between 1605 and 1611 he produced a number of these masques of increasing lavishness and complexity.

In the year 1611, however, Jones was appointed Surveyor to Prince Henry. The young Prince, who was a person of outstanding intelligence, collected about him a number of cultured men, and his entourage had become the centre of artistic activity. It is one of the misfortunes which seem to have dogged Jones's career that this appointment was brought to an abrupt termination, after only two years, on the sudden death of the Prince. However, he was then given the office of Surveyor of the King's Works, to which he was appointed purely on the strength of his stage and costume designs, for there seems to be scant record of any building activity.

Jones then undertook his second visit to Italy, this time in the company of the Earl of Arundel, a most important patron of the arts in England, and the two of them made an extensive tour beyond the Alps, even going to Rome—a dangerous step for which Arundel at least must have had royal permission. Whilst in Rome, Jones carried out the excavation of certain Roman ruins and

Fig. 176

The Queen's House,
Greenwich,
by Inigo Jones
(designed 1616,
completed 1635)

probably paid a further visit to Vicenza and Venice to study Palladio's work again at first hand. He returned to England in 1614 and resumed the office of the King's Surveyor, and it is from this date that his architectural career began. For the next twenty-seven years, until the Civil War in 1642, Jones was constantly engaged on work in the royal residences. It was during this period that he designed most of his important buildings—which are, in fact, few in number, for Jones seems to have personally supervised all the work which came out of his office, however trivial.

The design for the Queen's House at Greenwich, which he started in 1617, was his first major undertaking in his own right. In this very first building we see both the thoroughness with which Jones must have studied his Italian master Palladio and also the completeness with which he had digested and understood the other's intentions. As in all his later work, this is no slavish rehash of his chosen master's work, but a re-

interpretation which is entirely personal.

In its present state (Fig. 176) the house appears to be a solid block approximately square on plan. But in its original form it was designed as a double house, divided by the public road running between Deptford and Woolwich, the two halves being joined by an overhead bridge (Fig. 177). When, in 1661, two further bridges were added, flush with

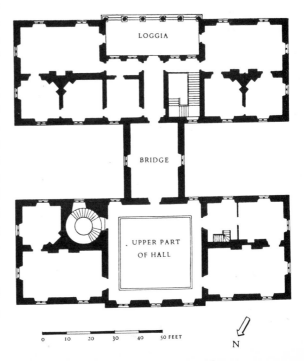

Fig. 177 The Queen's House, Greenwich—plan
This shows Jones's original plan, which has now been transformed into a solid block

the outer walls, the division in the plan was
no longer apparent from the outside and the
house presented its familiar aspect to the
world. In fact so successful was the transformation that it is scarcely credible that
such a curious duality ever existed.

Building was started between 1616 and
1618, but work was not completed until 1635,
doubtless owing to the state of the Stuart
finances. The façades (Fig. 178), show not
only Jones's command of classical form, but
that feeling for dignity and repose which
was his own personal quality. A comparison
with Palladio's Palazzo Chiericati (Fig. 91)
shows how Jones built on his master's ideas.
There are certain similarities in the two
concepts, but by changing the emphasis of
solid and void, and by using a generally
broader and more spacious sense of massing
and distribution of detail, Jones created a
new set of harmonies and relationships. The
Queen's House may not be as elaborate as
Palladio's palazzo but it has a classical
serenity which is deeply satisfying.

Between 1619 and 1622 Jones embarked
upon his most ambitious project to date, and
one that was to prove to be his masterpiece,
namely the Banqueting Hall in Whitehall
(Fig. 179). The building seems to have been
designed in the space of about three months,
and to have gone through several versions.
The original idea was to base the plan on the
Roman basilica, but the idea of nave and
aisles proved too constricting and this plan
was abandoned in favour of an uninterrupted
floor-space. The growth of the idea for the
long façade is interesting. As the building
was to flank the street, the first plan was to
use a similar scheme to that which Palladio
used in his town houses, complete with
advancing centre bays and crowning pediment. As Jones must have realized, this
implies a contradiction in axes, for in the
Palladio scheme the implication is that the
main axis of the building runs at right angles
to the façade, whilst in the Banqueting Hall
the main axis would run parallel with the
façade. To reduce the central emphasis,
Jones omitted the pediment, but realized
that by replacing the pilasters of the outer
bays by free-standing columns in the central
bays he achieved just that emphasis and

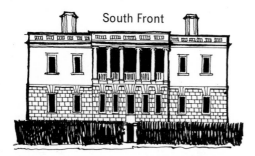 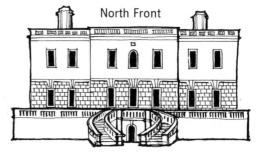

Fig. 178 The Queen's House, Greenwich

*These two views, with Fig. 176, give some idea of the majesty of Jones's design which, though
it owes much to Palladio, achieves a composure foreign to the Italian master's work*

Fig. 179 The Banqueting Hall, Whitehall, London (1619–22), by Inigo Jones

*This building is further proof of Jones's grasp of the Renaissance style;
it is not a Gothic framework decorated with Italian ornament*

interest that he needed to bring his design to life and prevent it looking flat and monotonous. So once again he started off with Palladio and finished with Jones, and provided London with a building the like of which it had not seen before.

The cleaning and restoration, completed in 1965, has made it possible to see this building afresh. It is now almost exactly as Jones intended it to look; modern window-sashes replace the earlier stone casements and the exterior has been completely refaced in Portland stone. As in the Queen's House, Jones used a rather broader and more spacious placing of detail and decoration than Palladio. The intercolumniation of the Banqueting Hall is wider than that of a typical Palladio façade, and this more generous spacing gives to the building a greater feeling of dignity and repose than the rather tense, closely spaced columns of the Italian master.

Before we leave the Banqueting Hall it should be noted that Jones used another Palladian device, namely the double cube, a proportion he was to use again with such striking success at Wilton House after the interruption of the Civil War.

During the years he was employed on the Banqueting Hall, Jones produced little other work of importance. In 1620 he was one of a commission set up to advise on the restoration of Old St Paul's, but because of lack of funds nothing came of this project until 1631, when another commission (without Jones this time) was set up through the efforts of Bishop Laud. In 1634 Jones was appointed surveyor to the commission, and work on the restoration of the cathedral began at once. The fabric of the cathedral was in a deplorable state, as it had been damaged by fire in Elizabeth's reign. The most striking feature of Jones's scheme was a great Roman portico in the Corinthian

Plate 31

St Paul's Cathedral—Inigo Jones's drawing of his own design for an addition to the west front of the original Gothic cathedral. (Work begun 1633)

order, but without a pediment. The portico must have been an impressive thing in itself, but no one can pretend that it was successful, for like oil and water the two styles, Classic and Gothic, will not mix, and any attempt to effect a combination is doomed to failure. However, the building was destroyed in the Great Fire of 1666 and we only have Jones's drawing of the scheme as he envisaged it (Pl. 31).

Jones was also concerned with the planning and layout of Covent Garden, though he seems to have had extensive aid from Isaac de Caus, who had worked with him on the Banqueting Hall. Jones was certainly responsible for the design of the church, though the present building is only a copy of the original, which was burnt down in the last years of the eighteenth century. But the most important scheme with which Jones was connected was the project for Whitehall Palace. The exact authorship of these plans has been the subject of some considerable confusion. In 1912, J. A. Gotch attributed

the whole scheme to Jones's assistant and amanuensis Webb, but in 1946, after further study and re-examination of the drawings, Margaret Whinney proved beyond reasonable doubt that Jones was in fact the true author.

The commission for the palace was first issued in the late 1630s, and would have provided the capital with a palace unmatched in size throughout Europe. Jones approached the task in a thoroughly Renaissance spirit, starting with a square central court and developing ten other courts around it.* The scheme, however, reveals Jones's weakness. He was a master in the organization of detail, and could manage a façade with subtle mastery—one only has to look at the Queen's House and the Banqueting Hall to realize this—but the palace required something more. In a building of such grandeur and complexity the ability to control a

* The plan often reproduced consisting of a large oblong court with three smaller courts on either side is a later design.

façade is not enough, for now the façades must be seen in conjunction and juxtaposition. Though the façades Jones designed are beautiful in themselves, they lack that sense of drama and impact necessary to carry off a conception of such magnitude. There is about these designs too much of the feeling of an elegant repeating pattern, which, because it lacks tension and variety, becomes monotonous. They have the subtle modulations of the Banqueting Hall but nothing more; in the last resort he seems to have been unable to think further than his previous effort.

During his period of surveyorship he was not restricted to royal commissions, and did in fact carry out several projects for private patrons. From 1629 to 1635 he was at work with Sir Francis Crane on the design of Stoke Bruerne Park, Northants. Sir Francis had brought the design from Italy, and the influence of Palladio is obvious. It was the first house in England of this type, and was to play an important part in the Palladio revival in the eighteenth century. He may well have had some part in the design of Castle Ashby and also—though here the origins of the design are doubtful in the extreme—the remarkable house known as Chevening, in Kent (Fig. 180). This was a revolutionary design and there was no other house like it in England until Pratt began Coleshill some twenty years later, in 1650. The features which point most to Jones as architect are the bold massing and the careful relationship of proportions between window and wall.

Early in his career, during the period he was engaged on work at the Queen's House, he also designed a number of charming ornamental gateways. There is one in Chiswick Park, which was moved there in 1740 from its original site at Beaufort House, Chelsea, and he also designed one for Lord Arundel at Arundel House, whilst there are designs for several others in his drawings. These charming fancies were fashionable at the time, and although they had no purpose they can be looked on as examples of the taste of the period.

Just before the Civil War broke out there had been a period of Dutch influence. Anglo-Dutch relations were very close at this period, and during the decade from

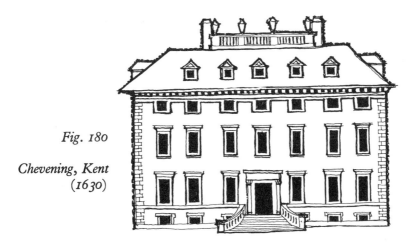

Fig. 180

Chevening, Kent
(1630)

Fig. 181

Raynham Hall, Norfolk (1635)

This is one of the best examples of the Dutch influence which showed itself for a short period in the first half of the seventeenth century

roughly 1625 to 1635 a number of houses were built with 'Dutch Gables'. This style particularly affected the smaller house, the usual plan being H-shaped. These houses were generally brick-built, with stone quoins and dressings. Raynham Hall, 1635 (Fig. 181), is a particularly fine example, and there are others at Kew Palace and Swakeleys. All these houses have the characteristic curved gables and either segmental or triangular pediments.

The Civil War not only put an end to the court life with which Jones was so familiar; it also interrupted building activity throughout the country. Supporters for both parties found that building was a hazardous venture, and between 1642 and 1660 there was little building carried out anywhere—indeed many houses were denuded of their treasures, either to pay for the war, or as a result of Puritan influence.

During the Civil War Jones left London and his estates were confiscated, but he managed to get a pardon and his estates were restored in 1646. In 1649 he was assisting the fourth Earl of Pembroke with the rebuilding of his house at Wilton, near Salisbury. Originally this was a Tudor building (reputedly by Holbein, though there

is much ground for speculation here), but a fire in 1647 provided the opportunity for Jones to carry out extensive remodelling and restoration. Exactly how much of the fabric of the building is by Jones it is hard to say, but he designed the whole of the garden front, along with the splendid suite of state rooms on the first floor. The most striking of these rooms are the double cube room (Pl. 32) and the single cube room adjoining it.

Jones had already used what was virtually a double cube in the Banqueting Hall, as we have previously noted. The room at Wilton is 30 feet high, 30 feet wide and 60 feet long, the height being broken by a heavy and deep moulding from which a vast cove sweeps the walls into the ceiling. The inspiration for the decoration is obviously French, as is much of the other decoration in the house. The room was designed to display the Van Dyck portraits which had already been painted, and seldom can a series of paintings have had such a splendid setting. The pine-wood walls are painted white, which is relieved with the most sumptuous carving of fruit and foliage, richly gilded. The ceiling itself is painted with a number of allegorical subjects, but more interesting, probably because of the tech-

Plate 32

Wilton House, Wiltshire,
by Inigo Jones
The Double Cube Room

nical difficulties, is the curved surface between wall and ceiling. This was painted by
the elder Edward Pierce and is a superb
piece of decoration.

The impressive doorway at the east end of
the room, with its broken pediment supporting larger than life-size figures, suggests that
Jones intended the double cube to be entered
from the single cube, for the doorway from
the smaller room is by no means so impressive, and the smaller room must have been
intended as a preface for the splendour to
come. On more human scale is the charming
'colonnade room'; here, despite the fact that
the colonnade across one end would appear
to split the room in two parts, there is a much
greater feeling of intimacy, and the decoration lacks the quality of heaviness that one
begins to feel in the more famous apartments
of the suite.

More perhaps than that of any other
architect, Jones's career is a succession of

Fig. 182

*Coleshill, Berks. (1650),
by Sir Roger Pratt*

*This fine house was one
of the most influential
to be built in the
seventeenth century*

'if's': *if* the young Henry had not died, *if* the Stuarts had had more money to finance his schemes, *if* the Civil War had not intervened, things might have been so very different. There can be no doubt, for instance, that if the Crown had been more affluent the Italianization of English architecture would have gone ahead at a much faster rate than it actually did. Jones certainly introduced the most pure and deeply felt and understood form of Italian architecture that England had seen up to that time. But his influence during his lifetime and for some years after

his death was restricted to a small number of nobles closely connected with court circles.

His output was not large, though in the past zeal, rather than scholarship, resulted in his name being attached to something in the region of 120 buildings. Prominent amongst these false attributions is the beautiful house 'Coleshill', Berkshire (Fig. 182), which is now definitely acknowledged as being the work of Sir Roger Pratt, though it is known that Jones knew Pratt, visited Coleshill, and advised on the design (Pl. 33).

Plate 33

*Coleshill House—
the staircase hall
(1662)*

*A splendidly
proportioned design
of considerable
dignity*

Fig. 183

Thorpe Hall, Northants
(1656)

Figs. 180-184 give a clear impression of
the course of building during the
seventeenth century
These are the houses which
set the style; the others tended
to follow their lead

This splendidly simple house, unfortunately burned down in 1952, set the pattern for many succeeding houses, such as Thorpe Hall, Northants (Fig. 183). Pratt was also responsible for the design of Clarendon House, which again provided a model for many others, Belton House being one of the most notable (Fig. 184).

Before we leave the subject of Jones, some mention must be made of his assistant John Webb. We have already mentioned his name in connection with the Whitehall scheme, and he was closely connected with Jones throughout his career. He came to Jones as a young man and underwent a thorough training in classical architecture from his master. He is also certainly responsible for a very large number of 'Jones's' drawings. In the late 1640s he was asked by Charles I to prepare plans for a new palace at Whitehall, and about this time he began to assert his own personality—though he was not a very original architect. Amongst his works can be listed Durham House in the Strand; Amesbury, Wilts.; Gunnersbury, Middlesex; and the King Charles block at Greenwich.

Fig. 184

Belton House,
near Grantham,
Lincs. (1689)

Sir Christopher Wren

The career of Sir Christopher Wren (1632–1723) did not suffer the same interruptions and delays that had so bedevilled the career of his predecessor, Inigo Jones. Wren was fortunate enough to see most of his schemes come to fruition. Son of a Dean of Windsor, and a scholar of Westminster College, the young Wren, after a period as assistant demonstrator in anatomy at the College of Surgeons, went up to Oxford to study science. At the university 'that miracle of youth', as John Evelyn called him, had a distinguished career and was responsible for many inventions, some concerned with cardinal problems of astronomy, physics and engineering.

In 1657 he was made professor of astronomy at London, and in 1661 moved to a similar post at Oxford. At this time experimental science was coming to the forefront throughout Europe. In Paris the Academy of Science was established, and Wren was one of the founder members of the Royal Society in London. His inaugural lecture to this society contained references to nebulae as the firmaments of other worlds like our own.

His earliest works were the Sheldonian Theatre, Oxford, and the Chapel for Pembroke College, Cambridge. He was at work on both these buildings in 1663; the chapel was completed in 1665 and the theatre in 1669. Of the two buildings, the theatre is the more important. Though the façade is rather flat and heavy (Pl. 34a), the structure of the roof is ingenious and allows the auditorium to be left free of supporting columns. The plan is similar to the plan of a Roman theatre as found in Serlio's edition of Vitruvius. After this early manifestation of an interest in architecture Wren made his only known visit abroad, and that was to France. The visit must have lasted about eight or nine months, and during that time he must have seen a great deal. The only documentary evidence known of this visit is a letter to friends in England. The letter contains reference to many buildings which he had seen during his stay, and also mentions his meeting with the aged Bernini, who allowed Wren a brief glance at his designs for the Louvre. During this visit there can be little doubt that Wren filled his mind with ideas and his luggage with books and engravings. From this storehouse of material he drew freely in later years, and indeed the whole trip was one of the most important influences on his later development.

As soon as he returned to this country he became involved in plans and discussions about the reconstruction of Old St Paul's. He made several suggestions as to the best method of restoration and went so far as to make a drawing of a dome which he proposed to erect over the crossing. However, on 2 September 1666 at ten o'clock in the evening all plans were cut short by the Great Fire.

It is difficult to say with any certainty exactly how much Wren was influenced in his decision to turn exclusively to architecture by the opportunity afforded by the Great Fire. However, the opening presented itself, and Wren grasped it boldly. At the time of the fire, London was a city of some 400,000 inhabitants—smaller than Paris, but growing rapidly. From contemporary

Plate 34a

*The Sheldonian Theatre,
Oxford (1669),
by Sir Christopher Wren
—façade*

Plate 34b

*The Sheldonian Theatre—
auditorium*

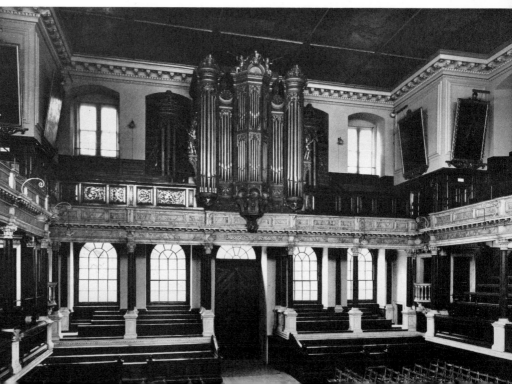

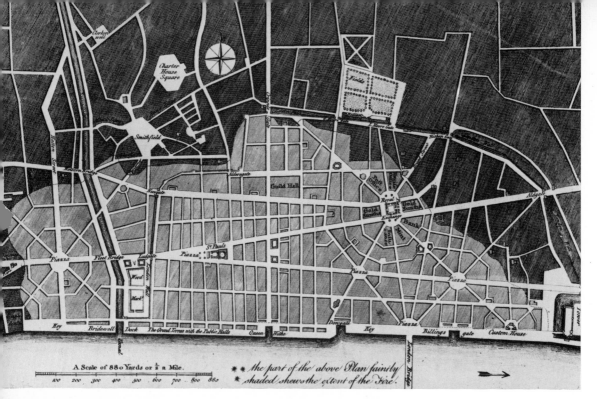

Fig. 185 Wren's plan for rebuilding London after the Great Fire (dark areas unaffected by fire)

accounts it must have been a wealthy town, crowded, and still medieval in character. Streets were still narrow and flanked by wooden frame houses jutting out for several storeys. Within the city walls attempts to prevent overcrowding had been unsuccessful, and the poor must have lived in grim conditions. Outside the walls things were better, and more commodious houses, frequently of brick, lined the wider streets.

On the eleventh of September Wren presented the King with his plan. This must have necessitated some rapid work on Wren's part, but he himself realized the importance of being first on the scene. Three days later his friend John Evelyn presented a plan to the King, and on the twentieth and twenty-first Captain Valentine Knight and Professor Hooke respectively offered theirs. It is interesting to note that all these plans — and there may have been more — were the work of amateurs.

Wren's plan (Fig. 185) was an example of the imposing monumental layout, and has been much admired by succeeding generations. Doubtless Charles would have liked to see his capital city laid out on the same monumental lines as Paris, but this was not to be. Attractive as Wren's plan may appear, and ideal as the solutions it offers may seem, the fact remains that at the time it would have been completely impossible to carry out. The principal weakness was that no attention had been paid to existing streets or the boundaries of private properties. Wren simply created his beautiful design as if for a virgin site. There was no system of valuation, nor could the Crown afford to pay the compensation which would have been equitable either to private individuals or to business men. Furthermore, a modern system of banking would have been necessary to provide the money that would have had to be found in order

to put into operation any building programme on the scale which Wren proposed.
It is not surprising, therefore, that his plan
was passed over. The fact that it was not
developed has been a constant source of
controversy ever since, for many have seen
in it the solution of many of the problems
which now beset London, but Rasmussen
in *London, the Unique City* is more sceptical
of its value.*

Whatever the shortcomings of the plan,
however, it must be considered a genuine
attempt on Wren's part to solve the traffic
congestion already hampering movement in
the city. The narrow crooked medieval
streets were already a cause of concern and
irritation, and Wren tried to alleviate matters
by running straight streets along the main
traffic routes, from north to south and from
east to west. Until the early eighteenth
century, London Bridge was the only point at
which the lower reaches of the Thames could
be crossed, and it thus provided the main
link from the midlands and the north to the
Continent and the south. This bridge therefore became the focus of four roads radiating
from its northern end. The east-to-west
flow of traffic was provided for by a new
avenue running diagonally between two
other east–west roads, which ran roughly
parallel with the river, to make a rather
flattened Z shape. At the north-eastern and
south-western apexes of this figure were
situated the Stock Exchange and St Paul's,
for it had always been Wren's intention that
these two buildings, symbols of commerce
and religion, should have dominating posi-

tions. Wren filled in the remaining area
between the two parallel arms of his Z shape
with a criss-cross pattern of minor roads,
running, as far as possible, at right angles to
one another. It was also intended to have a
broad quay along the river bank. To east and
west of his central figure Wren planned a
rather different arrangement, consisting of
nets of radiating and concentric streets
around large open spaces. The plan was a
typically Baroque conception and had its
roots in Rome and contemporary French
garden-planning. Modern critics would hold
that the attempt to impose a final and predetermined shape on a city stifles growth,
and that in this respect the fact that Wren's
plan was not carried out was no great loss.

Owing to internal pressure from the Lord
Mayor and city merchants, Charles was
forced to issue proclamations authorizing
the immediate commencement of building
more or less on the old sites, with only a few
alterations and improvements. Chief among
the new regulations were that streets should
be wider and that buildings should now be
built exclusively of brick and stone, and not
of wood. The idea of a broad quay which
Wren specified and about which he was so
enthusiastic was passed into law, but unfortunately never into practice. Not only
would this have provided an attractive feature in the capital city, but it would also have
made available the water from the river
itself, in case of further conflagrations. Work
on the embankment was begun in places,
but gradually the banks of the river became
more and more cluttered and the idea was
finally abandoned.

The other plans need not detain us long
because with the exception of that by Knight

* Cf. S. E. Rasmussen, *London, the Unique City.*
Pelican Books, 1960.

they are of little consequence. Evelyn's plan was clumsy, even though he tried to improve it by two revisions, and Hooke's plan has been lost, though it is known to have been of the grid-iron type. Knight's plan, however, is of more interest; it consists of a description only, and proposed the parcelling out of land in a series of units in a most economical manner. He proposed a grid made up of two main roads 60 feet wide running roughly parallel with the river, these being intersected at right angles by six similar roads. Each of the large blocks so formed was then further divided by secondary streets 30 feet wide, so arranged as to produce blocks of 500 feet by 70 feet, just wide enough to allow two rows of houses with a narrow yard between. However, all these schemes, like Wren's, came to naught, and the city was rebuilt slowly and laboriously from the proceeds of private enterprise.

Despite the fact that Wren's plan was passed over, his association with the city did not come to an end, for not only was he Surveyor-General, but he also served on a commission of six members who were to advise on the rebuilding which was taking place. In 1670 he embarked on what was to be his greatest undertaking, apart from St Paul's, namely the rebuilding of the City churches. These buildings are a reflection of the range of his creative ability and imagination. The spires alone show not only the freedom with which he could manipulate classical forms, but also the incomparable fecundity of his ideas (Figs. 186, 187, 188). Moreover, the best of the plans show his ability to organize space with mastery, and often the most successful are those on cramped and difficult sites.

Over eighty parish churches had been destroyed by the flames, and these were replaced by fifty-one, the Act of 1670 having united many parishes. This same Act had also raised the coal tax, to finance the rebuilding.

The liturgy of the post-Reformation church differed greatly from medieval practice, and Wren was actively concerned in devising a church plan which would express the new requirements. One of the most striking features of the post-Reformation service was that the congregation should take an active part, whereas in the medieval service the congregation had merely watched the clergy taking part in the religious mysteries beyond the rood-screen. In the new churches the rood-screen therefore disappeared, thereby bringing the congregation much closer into contact with the clergy. Further developments took place in the design and placing of the pulpit; never a prominent feature previously, it assumed a new importance as the significance of the sermon increased, until finally it became the 'three-decker' type with ornate sounding boards and an elegantly carved flight of steps. To support the congregation's singing an organ was often introduced—usually at the opposite end of the church, facing the altar. As many of the churches were on cramped sites the introduction of a gallery became a necessity.

To accommodate these radical changes Wren used several types of plan, including the Greek cross and the classical basilica, with or without aisles. His main aim was to achieve visibility and audibility, and to this end he contrived to give his churches the maximum spaciousness that the site would

Fig. 186 St Mary-le-Bow,
Cheapside (1611–83)

Fig. 187 St Vedast,
Foster Lane (1670–3)

Fig. 188 St Bride,
Fleet Street (1670–84)

These examples of the spires of Wren's city churches show his powers of invention
in transforming what is, in effect, a Gothic feature into a Classical one

permit. The effect of spaciousness was further enhanced by introducing as many
windows as possible in clerestories, in east
and west walls if possible, and under galleries—in addition to those along the nave
walls. The scheme of colour was generally
as simple as possible—rich brown wood
set against white painted walls decorated
with gilding. Unfortunately many of the
best churches were destroyed in the raids
on London in the Second World War,

though some have been successfully restored.

Undoubtedly Wren's most successful
City church is that of St Stephen, Walbrook.
This splendid building, his greatest achievement after St Paul's, seems to sum up his
ideas on the planning of the smaller church,
at the same time introducing new qualities
which were not present in his earlier efforts.
The frivolity of the little spire does, however contrast oddly with the serious beauty
of the interior, and in fact the external

appearance gives little idea of the masterly moulding of space within.

The plan (Fig. 189) is deceptively simple at first glance, but it becomes clear that Wren is grappling with the problem of the central dome over a crossing. The dome itself is supported on eight columns joined by semicircular arches. The four arches to north, south, east, and west give directly onto the nave, transepts, and chancel compartments, all of which are vaulted. The feeling of internal spaciousness is enhanced by the fact that the dome does not rest on external walls at any point. This creates a free passage all round the dome inside the church, and the freedom of movement so created is exhilarating. Viewed from the chancel, the perspective down the columns which form the short nave also helps to create a feeling of added depth.

Wren, as we have seen, gave his churches as much light as possible, and in some cases his effects have been spoiled by the addition of stained glass in the windows. Although the east window of St Stephen's has some stained glass of modern design, by Keith New, the restrained but rich colour and the fine feeling for design fit well with the surroundings, and in this case the whole effect is most successful. As is usual with Wren churches, the general colour is restrained, and relies on the mellow effect created by the deep coloured wood, light plaster, and rich gilding. The decoration of the dome consists of deep coffers, relieved with fine plaster and stucco decoration.

Wren was at work on St Stephen's in 1675, by which time he was already engaged in preparatory designs for the new St Paul's. As we have seen, association with the cathedral really began before the Great Fire, for in the summer of 1666 he had put forward a scheme for the repair and remodelling of the old structure, which was to include the building of a dome over the crossing. After the fire he reluctantly agreed to pull down the choir and tower and rebuild onto the more or less stable nave. Work on this project proceeded until the April of 1668, when a fall of masonry brought down some of the new structure and threatened further damage. It was then decided to go ahead with a

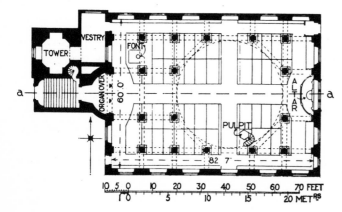

Fig. 189

St Stephen, Walbrook, London (1672–9), by Sir Christopher Wren

This plan is one of Wren's most subtle conceptions, achieving a feeling of 'nave' and 'transepts' without destroying the rectangular shape of the external walls

completely new building, and in the spring of 1670 the 'first model' was complete. No drawings of this scheme now exist, only fragments of a wooden model, but from these it is possible to see that it was to have been a modest affair.

As a result of the growing confidence and increasing prosperity of the City—fine churches, halls, and houses were beginning to rise—it was felt that some more ambitious cathedral was needed, and as a result of these factors Wren produced the 'great model' in September 1673. The model for this scheme is still preserved in the Cathedral, and shows a building which would have borne comparison, in all but size, with Michelangelo's St Peter's. The basic conception was that of a Greek cross, and the plan derives equally from St Peter's and, probably, from a drawing which John Webb made for Inigo Jones, which it is safe to assume that Wren had seen.

The most original part of the plan was the joining of the four arms of the cross by four concave segmental curves. Though this idea is original, it is far from certain that it would have been a success, for the perspectives of these great curves must ultimately have produced a weak effort. Such a completely centralized plan supplanted the medieval idea of a directional plan, and was too much of an intellectual exercise for the church authorities, who must have rejected the idea at once. In his insistence on a domed form (and it was never far from his mind), Wren was only being a man of the Renaissance. The principle of a centrally-planned church had been accepted as the 'ideal' church layout from Alberti onwards (see Chap. 3 for a further discussion of this

problem), and Wren was disappointed when his scheme met with such opposition.

After this rebuff he was forced to return to the idea of placing a dome over the crossing of what was, to all intents and purposes, a Gothic cathedral. In 1675 he produced the 'Warrant Design' probably in some haste, as the work of demolition of the old cathedral was then far advanced. The most important feature of this scheme is the plan, which bears a remarkable similarity to the one actually executed. There are only two essential differences: firstly, the nave was revised to consist of three bays, so balancing the choir; and secondly, additional compound bays at the west were provided to form a sort of vestibule and lateral chapels. The executed plan is therefore symmetrical on both axes, but has the addition of an imposing western approach and an apsidal termination in the east.

The dome over the intersection of the 'Warrant Design' is in some ways too much like a Gothic spire sitting on an upturned saucer. Nor are the elevations much more satisfactory; the detail is 'thin' and the whole design too 'skimped' to be fitting for the major cathedral in a capital city. However, from this design Wren's ideas slowly developed, and finally reached the fully matured form with which we are now familiar. E. F. Sekler* puts forward a most ingenious explanation of the method Wren may well have used to arrive at the proportions of the whole scheme. Sekler has found that by applying the well-known method that Serlio advocated for constructing the correct proportions of a Classical

* E. F. Sekler, *Wren—His Place in European Architecture* (Faber, 1956).

door (Fig. 190), it is possible to reconstruct all the salient points of Wren's plan. Wren had already used simple geometrical construction in the elevations of some of the City churches, so that it is possible to concur with Sekler when he says of the geometrical constructions of St Paul's, 'They are simple and so convincing that with all the caution necessary in dealing with such geometrical schemata it would be difficult to ascribe their presence to a mere coincidence'.

The external elevations, so much more rich and satisfying than those of the 'warrant' design, owe much to the work of Inigo Jones at the Banqueting Hall. The transepts are enriched by the addition of the semicircular porches, surmounted by a pediment, which makes a point of emphasis in a design which flows with ease along the entire length.

The final shape of the dome (Fig. 63) was probably not settled until 1697, and preparatory drawings suggest that Wren had two types of design in mind—one based on Bramante and the design of the Tempietto, and the other based on the Michelangelo dome at St Peter's. Wren finally settled for a compromise between the two, for the final design is in effect a peristyle such as Bramante used, except that the buttress effect that Michelangelo favoured is achieved by filling in every fourth intercolumniation. A brilliant solution! The task of placing a dome on the four corners of an intersection is difficult, as the outward thrust is so great; however, Wren solved it with his usual mastery. The dome is supported on eight piers, which form an internal octagon. Wren had never moved far from this basic idea either—it is present in the 'warrant' design,

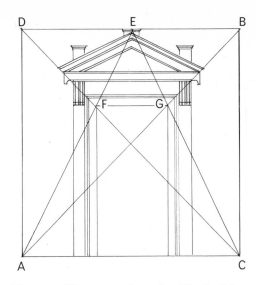

Fig. 190 The proportions of a Classical door, based on Serlio. The opening of the door is a double square, whilst the points F and G lie on the intersections of the $\sqrt{2}$ diagonals AB, CD and the $\sqrt{3}$ lines AE, CE

and also in the 'great model'—probably because this is the easiest transition from a square to a circle.

To support the outward thrust of nave vaults, Wren used the Gothic principle of the flying buttress, placing the buttresses behind an enormous screen wall running round the building. This feature has come in for some adverse comment from the purists, who claim that hiding the construction in this way is bogus design. Yet the intention is not perhaps so dishonest as would first appear, and can be defended on several points. The screen wall not only permits the designing of an imposing façade, suitable for such an important structure, but also provides enough weight to enable the lower part of wall to take the thrust of the nave vaults without further supports. Moreover, being in line with the main arches of the dome, it offers additional support for these as well.

Plate 35

St Paul's Cathedral,
London,
by Sir Christopher Wren—
west front

A comparison with the
west front of St Peter's,
Rome (Plate 14), reveals
two very different
methods of solving the
same problem

The design of the dome itself presents three problems: (i) it must look satisfactory from the inside; (ii) it must support the lantern; and (iii) it must present a satisfactory external silhouette. Externally the dome is certainly one of the finest things in English architecture, and its pre-eminence over St Peter's is always a rewarding topic for debate and discussion (Figs. 62, 63). The differences should be carefully considered, in relation both to the building as a whole and to the unit from the roof line upwards. As regards the internal aspect, Wren must have been acutely aware that a structure of such massive proport ons rising uninterruptedly would be unsatisfactory and that an internal dome with an 'oculus' was necessary to maintain a satisfactory sense of scale. This leaves the problem of the support of the lantern, and this Wren solved by building a cone-shaped structure of brick, between internal and external domes. By supporting the lantern on a separate structure he was then free to mould the external silhouette with maximum freedom. The beauty of the final solution is well shown in (Pl. 35).

By 1698 the cathedral was complete except for the dome, western façade, and towers, and it is to these features that we must now turn. It seems fairly certain that Wren wanted to employ a single colossal order for the western portico, but was prevented from doing so because he could not get hold of stones of a sufficiently large size. He was therefore forced to turn to the use of superimposed orders, following Roman precedent. There can be no doubt that the final composition is much more successful than the cramped and frankly uncomfortable front at St Peter's. The relation between façade and dome is also much more successful, for at St Paul's the dome dominates the design in the way it was intended to do. It is when one comes to consider the relationship between dome and the western towers that one becomes conscious of an odd contradiction. The splendid order and serenity of the dome is oddly at variance with the rather more wayward and wilful treatment of the towers. Wren seems to have indulged himself in one of those frivolous fancies which, as we have already seen, seemed to overtake him at St Stephen, Walbrook. The high seriousness of the dome is nowhere reflected in the two towers, which have a movement which is not even related to the composure of the façade beneath them. Are they then to be considered as a misconception in design, or as a point of relief—the seasoning which makes the more substantial body of the building more appetizing? Whatever the answer to this intriguing question, the towers reveal a strong element of the Baroque, and foreshadow the work of those two supreme masters of English Baroque, Sir John Vanbrugh and Nicholas

Hawksmoor both influenced by Wren.

By 1700 work on the drum of the dome was well in hand, and by 1709 the cathedral was structurally complete. In 1717, after some unpleasant wrangling with Wren, the commission insisted, for reasons best known to themselves, on erecting a balustrade round the parapet of the entire building. This move was made against Wren's wishes, and led to his dismissal from the post of surveyor-general—fine thanks for work on a building which must rank high in European architecture!

Wren lived to see the completion of his Cathedral, something that had never happened to a cathedral builder before. Whilst he was engaged on this work he was also responsible for other designs, many of them in his official capacity as surveyor-general. His Chelsea Hospital (1682–89) was a conception of almost monastic restraint. The plan was quadrangular, surrounded on three sides by buildings and open to the river on the fourth. The impressive portico (Fig. 191), foreshadows much that was to be designed in Queen Anne's time, and the dignified buildings with their simple lines were to be echoed in many collegiate and hospital buildings of the eighteenth century. Such poor records of his Palace at Winchester exist that it is impossible to reach a true estimate of its real value, and the building itself was destroyed by fire late in the nineteenth century. His work at the Palace of Whitehall suffered the same fate in 1698. At Hampton Court the portion of his work which still exists today is only a fragment of what he originally intended. The complete scheme, with its balanced accommodation on King's side and Queen's side, along with the usual courtyards, barracks, etc., is reminiscent of the Louvre. This scheme was not carried out, and the final result is a heavy mass, bordering on the monotonous. The passages of fine craftsmanship cannot relieve the measured tread of windows along the wall, and the *œils-de-bœuf* placed between 'piano-nobile' and attic storey are not really convincing from the point of view of proportion; even the pediment cannot assert itself, and is crushed into insignificance by the attic.

His work at the Royal Naval Hospital, Greenwich, however, is of more importance. The original plan, with its succession of courtyards and quadrant colonnades leading to a portico and dome, is a combination of Palladian and French inspiration (Pl. 36). This idea was taken up by Vanbrugh, probably through Hawksmoor's suggestion, and developed with such splendid results at both Castle Howard and Blenheim. Why this plan was never carried out at Greenwich is difficult to determine; it was probably because of a reluctance to close the vista through to the Queen's House. In the second plan, which is the basis of Greenwich as we know it, Wren left the vista open and pro-

duced two domed buildings which frame the Queen's House in the distance. Wren never saw the completion of the scheme, which was carried out by Hawksmoor, and probably Vanbrugh. Later work was added after Vanbrugh's surveyorship ended in 1726.

Prominent among the works Wren completed outside the sphere of the office of surveyor-general are those at the Universities of Oxford and Cambridge. The library at Trinity College, Cambridge (1676–84), is one of his most successful buildings. The designs were produced whilst he was busy hammering out the early ideas for St Paul's. The beauty of the library depends upon its simplicity and directness of statement. The

Fig. 191

*Chelsea Hospital (1682–9),
by Sir Christopher Wren*

Plate 36   The Royal Naval Hospital, Greenwich, showing:
The Queen's House (1616–35), top right
King Charles II block (completed 1665 by John Webb)
Queen Anne Block (completed 1715 by Nicholas Hawksmoor)
Main blocks and colonnades (completed 1716 by Wren, Vanbrugh and Hawksmoor)

façades are wonderfully unified, in the way that Jones's Banqueting Hall is unified, and the management of details subtle and refined. The two façades, one to the river and the other to Nevile's Court, are not the same, and the entrance from the court is unmarked, except for four figures over the centre columns.

At Oxford, his work at The Queen's College was probably modified by Hawksmoor, but he was responsible for the Tom Tower at Christ Church, in his own brand of Gothic. The *leit-motif* of the tower is the 'ogee' arch, but this building could never be mistaken for a Gothic tower; but the whole design is too carefully considered, and the horizontal accent too prominent, even though there are many vertical features. Wren chose the Gothic style because he felt it would be more appropriate to its surroundings than the classic. He then proceeded to design a classically domed building, using Gothic features. The result is a tower of interest and no little distinction.

Pratt, May and Talman

There is no private house that can with any certainty be ascribed to Wren, though, like Inigo Jones before him, his name has been associated with many houses from time to time. The development of domestic architecture owes more to Pratt and Hugh May than to Wren. Hugh May (1622–84) exerted considerable influence in his own day, though there now remains only one complete house that can be ascribed with any certainty to him, namely Eltham Lodge, London (c. 1664). Except in the plan it bears little resemblance to the work of Pratt at Coleshill. Eltham is built of brick and has four Ionic pilasters supporting a central pediment on the main front—material and devices that Pratt seldom if ever used. May had visited Holland, and whilst there he may well have studied the work of Pieter Post and Van Campen, two Dutch architects who had studied the work of Palladio and managed to combine with the Italian master's style something of their own national idiom. Eltham shows how much May was indebted to the Dutch Palladian style. He also built several other houses of which little or nothing is now known.

Part of his popularity as an architect may well be explained by the fact that he managed to show how brick, one of the country's principal building materials, could be used in the construction of a particular kind of house which was both sensible and very popular at that time. Between them, Pratt and May helped to introduce a type of house which is so often misleadingly called the 'Wren' type, though Wren himself had nothing to do with domestic building.

William Talman (1650–1720) was another of the more notable professional domestic designers. He was an enigmatic figure, and his designs, being more lavish than most, were very influential. His most important work was that which he undertook at Chatsworth, though he was not responsible for the famous west front. It is claimed that he designed Thoresby, Notts. (destroyed 1745). This was a most original design, and his later works were equally individual in conception.

Few houses of any consequence were built during the Civil War, and it was not until well into the 1650s that building was resumed on any scale. Those houses which were built owed more stylistically to the classicism of France and Flanders than they did to the classicism of Inigo Jones. Indeed, it seems likely that English builders would have arrived at much the same conclusions if Jones had never designed a building at all.

More and more homes, in both town and country, were being built of brick with sound roofs of tiles or thatch, and these must have been comfortable and convenient. Many of these houses were designed by their owners or the local builder, for this century and the succeeding one were the period of the amateur architect. However, wattle-and-daub huts were still in existence, and the people who were unfortunate enough to inhabit this sort of dwelling must have led a miserable life indeed.

FURTHER READING

E. F. Sekler, *Wren and His Place in European Architecture*. Faber & Faber, 1956.

A very thorough review of the great architect's work, with many plans, drawings, and photographs.

John Summerson, *Sir Christopher Wren*. Collins, 1953.

A good short introduction.

Viktor Fürst, *The Architecture of Sir Christopher Wren*. Lund Humphries, 1956.

A book full of many large-sized plans, drawings and photographs, and with an authoritative text.

J. A. Gotch, *Inigo Jones*. Methuen, 1928.

The Connoisseur Period Guides, ed. R. Edwards and L. L. G. Ramsey. National Magazine Co.
The Stuart Period: 1603–1714. (1957)
The Early Georgian Period: 1714–1760. (1957)
The Late Georgian Period: 1760–1810. (1961)

These books are particularly important for the articles on and illustrations of the minor arts, though each has a short section on the building of the period.

The reader is also directed to the books in the general bibliography at the end of the book.

9

INTERLUDE–ENGLISH BAROQUE

English Baroque was a short-lived style which flourished roughly between the last decade of the seventeenth century and the first quarter of the eighteenth century. The style was largely the product of two men, Sir John Vanbrugh and Nicholas Hawksmoor, both of whom had been associated with Wren, whose work provided the starting-point for many of their ideas.

The high points of the style are usually considered to be the London churches built during the reigns of Queen Anne and George I, and of course Blenheim Palace. There is about these buildings something of the restless movement, though not the complexity, which we associate with continental Baroque. They differ from the work of Wren in the basic quality of a feeling for the movement of mass. This was a quality that Wren had lacked, and on occasion his façades bordered on the monotonous, as at Chelsea and Hampton Court. He had a tendency to rely too much on beautiful detail and careful proportion for the achievement of a satisfactory architectural effect, but as we have already seen the architect must be something of a sculptor as well (Chap. 3, pp. 66–7). It was in the spires of his City churches that Wren came nearest to achieving this sculptural quality—though the interior of St Paul's shows that he had an appreciation of the dramatic vista—and his

use of light, both in St Paul's and in the churches, is often inspired. With the work of Sir John Vanbrugh and Nicholas Hawksmoor, however, there is a return to the feeling for the handling of mass which puts their creations back on to a more truly architectonic level. They had the ability to use classical detail and ornament to mould space and volume into a creation of great emotional intensity.

This restless quality can be seen in the gateway to the kitchen wing at Blenheim (Fig. 192). In many ways this feature is the epitome of Vanbrugh's style—the tremendous weight, made apparent by the heavy horizontal rustications and the squashed

Fig. 192 Blenheim Palace—gateway to the kitchen wing (1708–9), by Sir John Vanbrugh
This feature shows the awkwardness of Baroque

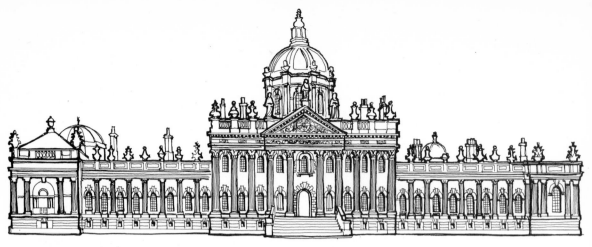

Fig. 193 Castle Howard, Yorkshire (1702–14), by Sir John Vanbrugh and Nicholas Hawksmoor—south front

segmental arch over the clock; the awkward relationship between the ascending series of arches, all of which seem to be on the point of crumbling under the weight of the masonry above. A careful analysis of this feature provides a key to Vanbrugh's art as well as a basis for understanding Baroque art in England.

The lives and characters of the two main protagonists could hardly be more of a contrast. Hawksmoor entered the service of Wren at about the age of eighteen and rapidly gained a position of responsibility. To read an account of his life and work is to gain the impression of a rather colourless

but sound record. He had not the advantage of being born a gentleman, and this, coupled with his fundamentally modest disposition, may well have accounted for his lack of worldly success. His association with Vanbrugh began in 1699, and he helped him with at least four of his great houses.

Vanbrugh, on the other hand, had the advantage of a prosperous family background and a less retiring nature. His career was full of adventure and incident. He joined the army, but resigned his commission, was arrested in Calais in somewhat mysterious circumstances and charged with spying. This resulted in two years imprison-

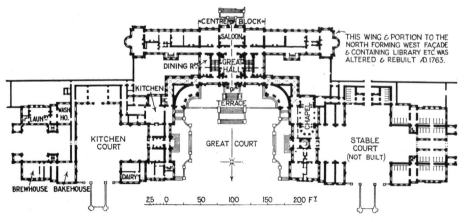

Fig. 194 Castle Howard—plan. (The south front is at the top)
This plan obviously owes much to similar layouts introduced by Palladio

ment in France. On his release he returned to England and obtained a minor post in the Household. During his spell in prison, which seems to have been a period of boredom and inconvenience rather than discomfort, he turned to play-writing. The first play to be produced was *The Relapse*; this was followed by *Æsop* and, in 1697, by his best play, *The Provok'd Wife*. He produced a further ten plays, but *The Provok'd Wife* and *The Relapse* are now the best-known, and rank high in the English comic tradition.

In 1699 he suddenly turned architect, by designing Castle Howard, Yorkshire (Fig. 193). This may seem like learning to swim by jumping in at the deep end, but Vanbrugh carried it off with enormous ease and panache. Hawksmoor certainly helped with the design, and may well have been responsible for suggesting the form of the plan — based on Wren's first idea for Greenwich Hospital, with which Hawksmoor must have been familiar. There is the central block containing the beautifully proportioned hall, one of the finest things that Vanbrugh

did, and to east and west of this block are the two courtyards, one for the stables and one for the kitchen accommodation. The principal apartments are ranged along the south front. As can be seen from Fig. 193, the cupola on the eastern end is missing, having been destroyed by fire and not replaced. From an architectural point of view it is sadly missed as a balancing feature in what was an extremely ordered design (Fig. 194). That it is the flattest façade that Vanbrugh ever designed must, presumably, be put down to inexperience, for he never did the same thing again. Even so, it is a façade which shows that the designer was a figure to be reckoned with, and this was to be borne out by his later buildings.

The grounds of Castle Howard also contain two delicious buildings, one by Vanbrugh, the other by Hawksmoor. The Temple of the Winds (Fig. 195), is one of Vanbrugh's most charming creations. The touch is light and sure, entirely lacking the ponderousness to which he was prone. More serious is Hawksmoor's design for the

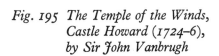

Fig. 195 The Temple of the Winds, Castle Howard (1724–6), by Sir John Vanbrugh

One of Vanbrugh's most delightful inventions

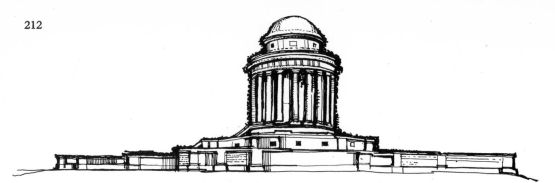

Fig. 196 *The Mausoleum, Castle Howard (begun 1731), by Nicholas Hawksmoor*
A noble structure which deserves comparison with the finest examples from the past

mausoleum (Fig. 196). Despite its comparatively small size the building dominates the landscape, and by a carefully regulated proportion the building manages to create a feeling of tremendous scale. These two buildings throw a new light on the work of both men, and seldom have such small buildings produced such memorable results.

In 1705 Vanbrugh was selected by the Duke of Marlborough to design the house which the Queen was going to confer on her Captain-General for his victory at the Battle of Blenheim. The plans of the two buildings, Castle Howard and Blenheim Palace, have many points of similarity. But Blenheim marks a step forward in that it is much more organized and the elements are more compact, even though it is a larger building.

Basically the elements are still the same, namely a central block, joined on either side by quadrant colonnades (Fig. 197) to a stable courtyard on one side and kitchen courtyard on the other. Again the principal apartments have a southerly aspect, an innovation which Vanbrugh had introduced at Castle Howard. A comparison of the way in which he organized the deployment of the various masses of the two courtyard elevations shows to what extent he had become master of the art of disposing masses in an interesting and dramatic way (Pls. 37, 38). The disposition of these masses is much more highly charged at Blenheim, and Castle Howard is by comparison much more relaxed and pastoral in concept. This change may be justified on the ground that one was a private house, whilst the other was a monument to a great soldier from a grateful nation.

Fig. 197

Blenheim—
the quadrant colonnades,
by Sir John Vanbrugh

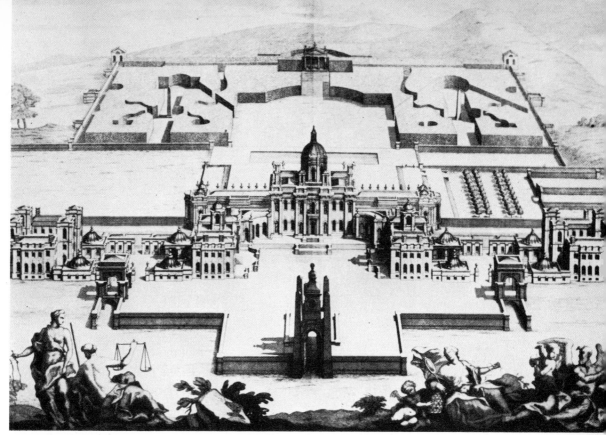

Plate 37 Castle Howard, Yorkshire (1699–1712), by Sir John Vanbrugh

Plate 38 Blenheim Palace, Oxfordshire (1705–24), by Sir John Vanbrugh

*Plates 37 and 38 should be looked at together and the differences carefully noted.
Vanbrugh uses very similar means to achieve very different ends*

Fig. 198

*Seaton Delaval,
Northumberland (1720),
by Sir John Vanbrugh*

Whatever the causes, however, Blenheim shows Vanbrugh's command of architectural rhetoric. The result is a building the like of which England had not seen before and was not to see again. One of the most striking features of the design is the vertical emphasis, despite the many strong horizontal elements. This verticality is achieved not only through the use of 'colossal' columns for the portico, but also through the use of the prominent and heavy attic storeys which surmount the blocks at the termination of his quadrant colonnades. This massive emphasis on the corners of the main block is largely responsible for the more compact feeling of the design. Lacking them, Castle Howard seems to spread, and its design is much more loosely knit.

Though many would call Blenheim the culminating point of Vanbrugh's art, it is at Seaton Delaval in Northumberland (Fig. 198) that we can find his most compressed and least rhetorical statement. This most beautiful house, situated not far from the sea, is on a much smaller scale than the two major works which we have just been discussing. In its present ruined state, the centre block having been completely gutted, one is constantly aware of two strongly conflicting emotions. One's first reaction is that

it should be restored as quickly as possible to what must have been its original splendid design, but as the atmosphere begins to assert itself one finds in the emotive ruins of the interior, roofless and rain-stained as they are, Vanbrugh's romanticism is thrown into even sharper relief.

This was one of the houses that Vanbrugh designed without the assistance of Hawksmoor, and it shows an even greater insistence on the arrangement of masses. The basic elements of the plan are the same as those which we have already studied, though this time the central block is of almost spartan simplicity—in fact it resembles the central block of some great Welsh concentric castle. From the four corners of the block spring octagonal turrets, and midway between them, on the east and west sides, are the great staircase towers. The entrance front has a small doorway flanked by triple columns, in heavy rusticated Doric, which support nothing but the entablature, which has to break out to contain them. The south, or garden, front has a massive unpedimented portico supported on Ionic columns. Decoration is kept to a minimum, and emphasis is by rustication, sparingly used. From these simple elements Vanbrugh achieves a closely integrated design of great force. This splendid little house tends to be over-shadowed by the more flamboyant of the architect's achievements; yet a visit confirms that a rare integration of the arts of architecture and sculpture has taken place there, and has produced a building of real distinction.

The relationship between Vanbrugh and Hawksmoor was so close that it is difficult to determine exactly how interdependent they were. It would seem to have been one of those associations where one man seemed to stimulate the other. There can be little doubt that in the early days of their association Hawksmoor's wide knowledge and long practical experience must have been of great value to Vanbrugh. It is only in recent years that Hawksmoor has emerged as an

important architect in his own right and that his originality has been appreciated.

It has been fashionable to scorn the excesses of Vanbrugh's work, and the excesses of his style are hard for the purist to stomach. Yet there must be a place for rhetoric in any art form, and in this form of display Vanbrugh was unique.

Hawksmoor's most important work is in the half-dozen churches which he designed as a result of the Act of 1711. There had been a lull in church-building since the completion of the City churches built after the Great Fire, and few were built between 1685 and 1712. Just as Wren's designs had dominated the post-Fire building, so the church designs of Hawksmoor dominated the period immediately after 1711.

Between 1712 and 1723 Hawksmoor designed six churches, of which the first two were St Alphege's, Greenwich, and St Anne's, Limehouse. These were followed some three years later by St George-in-the-East (gutted 1941), and St Mary Woolnoth, and lastly, in 1720 and 1723, St George's Bloomsbury and Christ Church, Spitalfields.

In each of these churches he is clearly indebted to Wren for some of his ideas, both in plan and in details, but he manages to give to his use of his master's ideas a point and emphasis that are entirely personal. Like Vanbrugh, he had a feeling for mass that Wren lacked, and he was able to conceive work which was both strong and unified. The two churches illustrated (Figs. 199, 200) show his eye for the bold and arresting shape and his ability to compose an arresting tower and spire.

Fig. 199 St Anne's, Limehouse (1712–24),
by Nicholas Hawksmoor

*Fig. 200 St Mary Woolnoth, London
(1716–19), by Nicholas Hawksmoor*

St Mary Woolnoth has a plan of particular interest (Fig. 201). It consists of a square open space in the centre, with three Corinthian columns at each corner supporting a richly carved entablature, above which rise four great semicircular clerestory windows. The colour scheme is much the same as that which Wren favoured, relying as it does on the contrast of dark wood and white walls enriched with gilding. The Corinthian

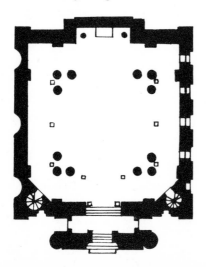

columns are set on pedestals to raise them above the level of the pews, and this idea he must have taken from Wren who, realizing that much of the beauty of the columns was lost if the bases were not visible, introduced this idea of putting the columns on raised supports. Internally, the church gives a much greater impression of spaciousness than is suggested by the outside, and the interior is indeed a splendid arrangement. The west front is a most solemn design, composed as it is of almost unrelieved rectangles. With true Baroque feeling the two semicircular arches stagger under the weight of the masonry massed above. The feeling of oppressive weight is emphasized by the long horizontal lines of rustication which embellish the lower storey. This is most uncompromising architecture, hardly beautiful, but stern and certainly striking.

Hawksmoor was also responsible for work at the Universities of Oxford and Cambridge. At The Queen's College, Oxford, the design of the south quadrangle is from his hand, and at All Souls College he essays a type of Gothic which is as personal in its own way as Wren's Tom Tower. With his work at the Colleges and the University Printing House (now Clarendon Building), he began to think in terms of a complete replanning of the city, but this plan never came to fruition.

It is plain, then, that Hawksmoor must be looked upon as an important creative figure; his churches bear comparison with those of Wren and any of the other architects of the time. His only domestic architecture seems to be that which he undertook in collabora-

*Fig. 201 St Mary Woolnoth—plan
A very spacious effect is achieved
internally by this design*

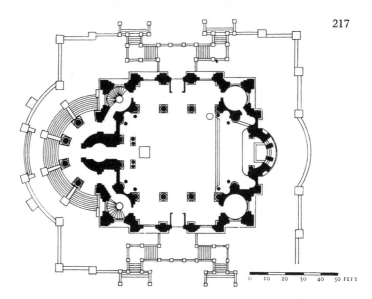

Fig. 202

St Paul's Deptford (1730), by Thomas Archer

A most original plan, which breaks up the square shape with great ingenuity

tion with Vanbrugh, and Easton Neston, Northants., on which he was working before Castle Howard was started. This is to be regretted, for his work suggests that he would have produced some designs of distinction.

Among a number of interesting churches which were built as a result of the Act of 1711, those of Thomas Archer may be mentioned. He produced two, St Paul's, Deptford, and St John's, Westminster, both of which owe something to Hawksmoor and also to the influence of Roman Baroque. This latter influence is doubtless due to a visit which Archer paid to Rome whilst still a young man. Like Hawksmoor's, these churches are bold in conception, and the plan of St Paul's is particularly interesting because, despite its square shape, it shows a remarkable plasticity in the handling of space (Fig. 202).

The Baroque movement in England was short-lived, and there are only a handful of buildings to which the term can be applied. The main stream of architecture continued without reference to the architects we have just been discussing, and it is to this greater body of work that we must now turn.

FURTHER READING

Robert Smith, *Baroque Architecture*. Clarendon Press, 1953.

H. S. Goodhart-Rendel, *Nicholas Hawksmoor*. Benn, 1924.

L. Whistler, *Sir John Vanbrugh: Architect and Dramatist*. Cobden-Sanderson, 1938.
—*The Imagination of Sir John Vanbrugh*. Batsford, 1953.

There are not a great number of books on the English baroque. All the above volumes are therefore useful, and the reader is further directed to the general histories for further reading. Both Tapié's book and that by Bazin mentioned in the bibliography for Chapter 4 contain sections on English architecture of the period, as does Summerson's *Architecture in Britain 1530–1830*.

10

THE EIGHTEENTH CENTURY

The eighteenth century is usually looked upon as the Golden Age of English architecture. Certainly the level of design reached a consistently high standard, though there were some aspects, such as hygiene and sanitation, which would not be acceptable today. Without the disturbance caused by the Civil War, building proceeded at a much more even rate throughout the country, and the result was a style that was uniform without being monotonous, harmonious and at the same time diverse.

The houses themselves were comfortable and well-appointed, and a system of design had been evolved which perfectly suited the needs of the family in every way. The design of the houses reflected the taste and substance of the middle class for which they were built, and this accord between the style and the needs of the occupier must go a long way towards explaining the success of the architecture which it produced.

Not only did architecture flourish: other aspects of life were developed by a people both energetic and intelligent. The minor arts, in particular, reached a standard of design the excellence of which is still highly regarded for its elegance and practicability. Many pieces of Georgian silver-ware and pottery possess that timeless quality of design that is so often the product of a combination of intelligent use of material and fitness for purpose. Like their medieval forebears, the gentry and middle class kept an excellent table. Meals were lavish, and over-eating and gluttony common. This love of the table must have created the demand for fine table-ware, just as the growing popularity of tea-drinking not only led to the rise in the imports of sugar, but also to the founding of many potteries. The Derby, Worcester, and Staffordshire potteries were all started during the fifties of the century.

The need for the products of expanding commerce to be transported from place to place led to some improvement in the roads. These had fallen into a bad state during medieval times, though it was of little importance then, as the movement of goods was almost non-existent. During Stuart and Hanoverian times, however, as a measure towards a more efficient transport system, a number of turnpike roads were built. By means of a levy on those who used these roads, the onus of maintenance was removed from the parish through which the road passed. This freed parishioners from the irksome duty of having to keep the roads in repair by voluntary labour, as had been the custom in the past. Even with these improvements, however, passage by wheeled traffic was still difficult, especially in winter, and the pack-horse train still survived. For heavy merchandise, the most efficient method of transportation was by water, and so the eighteenth century saw not only the broadening and deepening of existing waterways, but also the building of completely man-made canals.

The chief method of heating in towns was by coal, and this was one of the main commodities transported by water. In London, where it had been taxed to pay for the building of St Paul's and for the French wars, coal was expensive, though nearer to the collieries it was quite cheap. Lighting was by candle, and though in the poorer houses this was often dim and inadequate, in the larger mansions, especially where it was reflected from the myriad facets of the crystal chandeliers, the effect was quite brilliant.

The growing prosperity of the country was due to many causes. The cotton cloth industry was now beginning to rival the older and well-established woollen trade; and the trade of the great East India companies, coupled with the gradual emergence of London—after the débâcle of the South Sea Bubble—as a centre for world trade and financial transactions, enriched the pockets of aristocracy and professional class alike. With the money so gained the aristocracy, who set the example for the bourgeois to follow, set out to enrich their houses, as well as their minds.

The increase in trade with foreign parts saw the introduction of new woods of exciting colour and fineness of grain. Designers and craftsmen soon realized the potential of these new materials, and the advantage they gave them in creating a more refined style. The heavy and elaborately carved furniture of the reign of George I gave way to the lighter and more elegant work of Chippendale, who dominated furniture design during the middle decades of the century.

A well-stocked library was an important part of every gentleman's house, and so the publishing trade flourished. Publishing houses sprang up throughout the country, and were not confined to the capital. Thomas Bewick's beautiful wood engravings were first published as far north as Newcastle upon Tyne. Reading was extremely popular, so popular in fact that some of the larger cities founded their own circulating libraries. The works of such authors as Pope aroused interest in classical subjects, and this, coupled with the influence of foreign travel on artists, architects, and men of letters visiting the remains of classical antiquity in Italy, led to the classical revival at the end of the century and its full flowering in the early part of the nineteenth century. The acquisition of the Elgin Marbles for the British Museum gave an added fillip to the movement.

If the library was filled with well-read books, the walls were hung with pictures, whether by foreign masters, bought on their owner's travels, or by English artists. Sir Joshua Reynolds's move to found the Royal Academy in 1769 encouraged the purchase of pictures by the middle class, anxious to give the appearance of gentility.

Not only did growing medical science help the rise in population through the introduction of vaccination, but doctors also became aware of the healthful properties of sea air, bathing, and 'taking the waters' at such spa towns as Bath. Coupled with the pursuit of leisure activities, these factors saw the development of spa and seaside towns like Brighton and Lyme Regis in the south and Scarborough in the north.

The theatre was also popular; in London

Fig. 203 The Dowry House, Bristol (c. 1730)

Fig. 204 No. 32 St James's Square, London (1792), by S. P. Cockerell

Fig. 205 No. 72 High Street, Marlow, Bucks. (c. 1805). An early Regency façade of great charm

Fig. 206 Church Langton Rectory, Leics. (late eighteenth century). A house showing the influence of the Adam brothers

Fig. 207 No. 20 St James's Square, London (1775–89), by Robert Adam

Fig. 208 Newby Hall, Yorks.

The work of an anonymous architect, this façade shows the restraint which came about through the influence of Greek architecture

Garrick, and later Mrs Siddons, had what must have amounted to 'star' value by present-day standards, and in the provinces the theatre was no less popular and active. The Theatre Royal, Bristol, and the charming little theatre at Richmond in Yorkshire are both products of this period. English music, though popular as a form of entertainment, did not fulfil the promise of the work of Purcell in the previous century. Handel, a naturalized Englishman, occupied the central position during the first half of the century. Arne, a native composer, set many of Shakespeare's songs to music, and Dibdin was a successful composer for the theatre. Perhaps the vigorous ribaldry of *The Beggar's Opera* was the most important contribution of native composers, tilting as it did against the affectations of the Italianate creations of Handel.

For the wealthy, life must have been lived in an atmosphere of luxury and elegance. There were, however, many social injustices and hardships; and the standard of living for the peasant and worker, whether in the cottage industry or in the new factories, was very low indeed. During the second half of the century especially, when the effects of the Industrial Revolution were just beginning to make themselves felt, the lot of the poor must have become very hard; in some of the larger towns, particularly, conditions must have been dreadful, though not so bad as those of the next century, which are dealt with more fully in later pages. Now, however, it is time to return to a consideration of the architecture which the society we have just been looking at produced.

For the greater part of the eighteenth century, domestic architecture was unaffected by the work of Wren, Vanbrugh, and Hawksmoor. Instead, the emergence of the Palladian school, under such men as Burlington, Campbell, and Kent, led to a reawakening of interest in Inigo Jones. Under the influence of these major figures, the amateur architect flourished, and rich squires and country gentlemen, with a keen interest in architecture and a well-stocked library of pattern books, often designed their own houses. They may well have had the advice of the local builder to help in matters of construction, but as the plans of various types of house had by this time become standardized, no great technical knowledge was necessary. And not only did the pattern books help the gentleman; they were equally useful to the small builder himself, and many of our most charming but modest houses must be the product of his labours. The use of these pattern books did not, as might easily be assumed, lead to dull repetition and monotony of design: on the contrary the houses and mansions of the period show a tremendous variety. Great originality and ingenuity was shown in the use of the orders and in the application of detail, which was generally tastefully used (Figs. 203–8).

The leading figures of the early part of the period were, as has been mentioned, the EARL OF BURLINGTON and his two protégés, Campbell and Kent. The extent to which Burlington and Campbell were dependent on Palladio is seen in the two houses, Mereworth, Kent (1723), and Chiswick House, London (1725; Fig. 209). Both these houses obviously owe their origin to Palladio's Villa Capra or Rotonda (Fig. 90), with which they should be compared.

WILLIAM KENT worked in close association

with Burlington, and he also made important developments in furniture-design and landscape-gardening. Kent had started his career as a painter, though he proved to be an indifferent practitioner. However, through Burlington's guidance he gradually turned to architecture, and to this art he gave something of significance. Holkham Hall is typical of the Palladian type of plan, with a central block from which spring four wings. The hall of this house is one of the finest things that the Burlington school produced, and the apsidal structure, with a fine staircase, makes a memorable entrance. The exterior shows the designer's ability to reduce a grandiose scheme to its bare essentials, for there is not an unnecessary ornament or detail on it (Pl. 39). This ability to reduce decoration to the minimum is one of the striking features of Kent's style, and his building at the Horse Guards, London, has a similar treatment.

Though the typical Kent façade may be stark to the point of brutality, he did introduce an element of contrast in his handling of the garden. The schematization of garden-design was beginning to prove unacceptable to the eighteenth-century gentleman, and Kent was the first to begin to soften the hard regularity of formal garden-planning. The more 'naturalistic' or 'romantic' aspects of the countryside were becoming more attractive, and even the Lake District was gaining popularity as a holiday resort. Previously the wild and rugged nature of the countryside had been dismissed as uncouth and uncivilized. Now mountain scenery was sought after, and paintings of mountains were popular. In this respect Kent was only mirroring the taste of the time by introducing a more informal element into the landscape environment of his houses. He was, of course, followed by the most well-known of all landscape gardeners, 'Capability' Brown, who saw such 'capability' of improvement in his patrons' estates that he

Plate 39 Holkham Hall, Norfolk (begun 1734), by William Kent

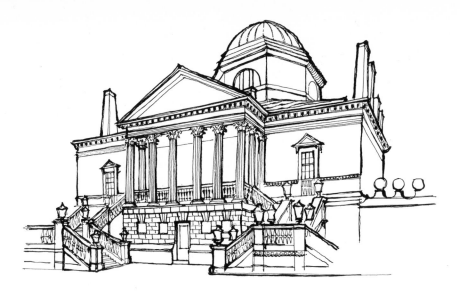

Fig. 209 Chiswick House, London (1725), by Lord Burlington, whose work marks the revival of interest in both Palladio and Inigo Jones. This house shows the influence of Palladio's Villa Capra (Fig. 89), with which it should be compared

often put them in debt. So enthusiastic were many of these eighteenth-century builders that they often had to mortgage their property to the hilt in order to pay for their improvements. It is from Burlington and Kent that this new concept of house-and-garden relationship stems. Under their influence the house became much more part of its environment, the two being partners on equal terms.

One of the most individual architects of the eighteenth century was JAMES GIBBS. His contribution does not fit smoothly into the main stream of Palladianism, but retains a rugged independence, exhibited in a number of remarkable buildings. His church, St Mary-le-Strand (1714–17), designed under the same act as produced the Hawksmoor churches, shows his dependence on Roman Baroque. This remarkable little building is quite different from anything else designed at the time. The shape is limited by the site, which is cramped, but the façades are intensely dramatic, even

though the use of a double order in preference to a single colossal one does give an air of smallness to the whole. His other church, St Martin-in-the-Fields, is much more successful, combining as it does a monumental portico with a splendid steeple. The plan of the existing church was preceded by an even more striking design, which unfortunately was turned down—this was based on a huge circular structure, with prominent additions to east and west. If it had been carried out it would have provided one of the most original churches in England (Fig. 210).

Both schemes for St Martin's owe much to Wren; the circular plan derives from St Stephen Walbrook, and doubtless from some of the oval churches which Gibbs had seen in Italy, whilst the existing church draws inspiration from much of Wren's work in the city churches, though Kent takes these ideas a stage further in their working out.

At Cambridge, Gibbs was responsible for the Senate House and the Fellows' building at King's College. Both of these are buildings of distinction, but it is to Oxford that we must turn to find the building which, along with St Martin's, gives Gibbs his lasting claim to fame.

In the Radcliffe Camera (Fig. 211) Gibbs turned once again to Italian Mannerism for his inspiration, and the result is striking. This great circular building is one of the most rhythmically complex to be found in England. At no point does the emphasis fall just where expected. The bays themselves are alternately wide and narrow, with the double columns standing awkwardly above the corners of the pediments round the rusticated base. Even the buttresses on the drum do not fall over the columns, as one would expect, but mid way between. The result is a design of enormous vitality and richness of effect.

Though Gibbs belonged to no school, and retained an intensely individualistic approach throughout his life, he had a widespread influence. This was not only through his buildings but also through the numerous books which he published, providing models on which many country gentlemen based the designs of their houses.

The second half of the century was dominated by WILLIAM CHAMBERS and the ADAM brothers, of whom Robert is the most important. Both Chambers and Robert Adam came from comfortably wealthy families, and both travelled extensively. Chambers studied architecture in Paris and Italy, and also visited the Far East, and on his return to England in 1755 he set up his practice, which was to prove immediately successful. Not only his buildings, but also his writings, were widely influential—he published two

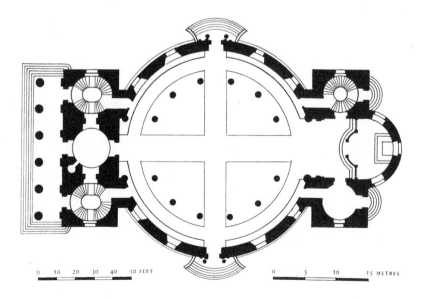

Fig. 210 St Martin-in-the-Fields, London, by James Gibbs—preliminary plan
This shows Gibbs's original idea, which was unfortunately rejected

Fig. 211

*The Radcliffe Camera, Oxford
(1739–48), by James Gibbs*

*This striking building
shows the influence of
Roman Mannerism*

books, one on Chinese buildings and the other entitled *Treatise on Civil Architecture*, and these were widely read. During his early years of practice he built largely town- and country-houses of the Palladian type (he was a great admirer of Inigo Jones), and also a number of gateways and stables. But his most important commission was to be the scheme for Somerset House, which he began in 1775. The idea was to unite a number of government offices under the same roof, and Chambers's social standing made him the natural choice for the architect. Like so many architects of the past it seems that Chambers was unable to think on a large enough scale, and so in the last analysis the design is not really as great as the sum of its parts. The river front is a façade of great dignity, but it lacks the broadness of vision and the ability to conceive a bold arrangement of masses that a building on such a scale demands. Several of the other façades are similar to those of many of the houses standing in London at the time. The detail is beautifully

conceived, but the total effect is wanting.

Chambers was the most important official architect of his day: Robert Adam the most daring innovator. Robert was the second son of a Scottish architect, and he had three brothers—John, who remained in Edinburgh; James, who worked with Robert; and William, who acted as business manager of the firm of which Robert was the prime force.

Like Chambers, Robert travelled widely, and in his designs he drew on the knowledge gained in these travels. He was not in any way unique in this penchant for travel; indeed it was the rule rather than the exception for those who could afford it to make the 'grand tour'. On his travels Robert made many drawings of the buildings he saw, and

Plate 40 The Adelphi, London (1768–72), by Robert Adam

of particular importance are the drawings he made of Diocletian's Palace at Spalato. These were not only important in themselves, but they also indicate the fact that artists and architects were starting to look even further afield for inspiration than before. In fact Robert was insatiable in his search for new material, and he drew inspiration not only from the home-based Palladianism of Burlington and Kent, but also from France and from the many French architectural books he collected during his stay in that country. His interest in archaeology provided further new material, and he also admitted to influences from the Italian Renaissance. With such wide and varied ingredients he managed to produce a style which was at once personal and immensely popular. He had the ability to take a style and abstract from it the essential ideas which he required and then to produce a design which presented the old style in a new light. In this respect he was aided, not only by his powers of invention and innovation, but also by a keen eye for proportion and a fastidious sense of refined detail and ornament.

He was also one of the first to believe that the architect's task did not end with the fabric of the building but extended to the decoration of the rooms, the furniture and carpets, and all fittings. This amplification of the architect's responsibility is important; too often in the nineteenth century, and the twentieth century too for that matter, the further ramifications of the architect's function have been overlooked or ignored. Yet surely, especially in important schemes, to separate architecture and decoration is to force a division which does not exist.

It always seems slightly surprising that, although Adam's influence was so widespread, the bulk of his work was confined to restoration and remodelling, rather than original building. Even one of his most ambitious and successful schemes, Syon House, Middlesex, constitutes a rebuilding within the existing quadrangular Jacobean shell.

The remodelling is a scheme of great splendour, and the transformation of the early plan into a series of rooms of varying proportions and shapes is skilfully carried out. The apsidal entrance hall gives at one end on to an oval ante-room (a favourite shape for Adam), and at the other on to a rectangular ante-room skilfully made square by a screen of free-standing columns. The dining room also has apsidal ends, this time squared off by placing twin columns on the chords. The courtyard was to have contained a huge rotunda, but unfortunately this was never built. The idea was based on the Pantheon, and one can imagine that Adam would have made a magnificent job of it. The northern side of the block is occupied by a gallery. The decoration of this extremely long 'long gallery' is carried off with considerable panache. He had decorated the hall on an almost heroic scale, with free-standing figures above the columns; the gallery, however, is much more intimate in feeling, with almost every space covered with a delicate filigree of decoration. The ceiling, almost Jacobean in complexity, is a good example of the Adam's manner before it underwent a process of simplification and elimination of detail around 1775–80. The shape of this gallery is by no means classical, but by dividing the long wall into bays with thin flat pilasters Adam has made interesting a shape that could easily have been monotonous.

The figures, standing on the entablature which projects over the columns in the hall at Syon, are reminiscent of a Roman triumphal arch. On the south front at Kedleston, Adam is much more forthright in his statement of the same theme. Within the limits of the already existing plan, laid out by James Paine, this front is pure Adam. The central block is clearly based on Roman models, and this version of the triumphal arch makes a fine centre-piece to the design, at the same time giving expression to the dome behind, which forms the roof of the main apartment. The portico at Osterley Park shows a similar regard for a classical feature, and again provides relief to a rather severe design.

Adam worked on several other country houses, and his designs for the Adelphi (c. 1768–72; Pl. 40) and Portland Place (from 1773) set the pattern for London housing until the work of John Nash and the Regency period. The Adam brothers poured great sums of money into the Adelphi scheme, and the result, though ultimately unprofitable, provided a number of houses on a monumental scale. The façade overlooking the river is simple and dignified, and the thin pilaster decoration was at once taken up by other builders. Indeed the Adams used it again on their less ambitious project at Portland Place. The semicircular arches, which pierced the base on which the main structure stood, contrasted well with the measured rectangles of the windows of the block above. Unfortunately time, bombs, and the speculative builder have all played their part in the almost complete destruction of these two schemes.

During this period the Adam brothers were responsible for three more houses which were to prove important in setting the style of the smaller London house, with its peculiar requirements—the high price of land demanding that houses should be deep, narrow, and high. One of these three houses has disappeared, but the extremely beautiful ones at 20, St James's Square (Fig. 207), and 20, Portman Square, still exist. The interior decoration of these houses shows an advance on that of the Gallery at Syon. Though there is still evidence of the liking for linear pattern, it has now undergone significant transformations. The detail is more restrained, and the feeling for exquisite proportion and the utmost refinement is at once apparent. In less vigorous hands the effect would have been too 'precious', but there is evidence of a great deal of experience in the placing of the accents of the design, and this prevents any suggestion of the effete.

By 1780 the career of the brothers was rapidly on the decline, and they undertook little work that was of first importance. The many thousands of drawings which they left bear testimony to the wide range of their interests and their unflagging ability to develop new ideas. They had created their own particular brand of classicism, based on a very catholic knowledge of past styles. From this knowledge they had forged a style which was followed by many, who managed to make out of the 'Adam' style something workable and at the same time pleasurable to look at.

Before leaving the eighteenth century a word must be said about the work of the two Woods in Bath. By the end of the first quarter of the century the reputation of the city was high; it was becoming a fashionable summer resort for society, who went there when the court left London, to amuse themselves and 'take the waters'. The importance of this royal patronage created the demand for a suitably impressive style of architecture.

JOHN WOOD the Elder (1704–54) was responsible for the first plans of Queen's Square, which was built between 1729 and 1736. The idea was related to the London estates of the times, though Wood's passion for Roman antiquity made him want to provide Bath with a Forum, Circus and Imperial Gymnasium. Only the circus was a success and came to full fruition. The intention was to provide the city with a number of town houses conceived on a monumental scale, and at the same time to impose a unity of design on the whole façade. The result was startingly successful, though Wood's son was to produce a scheme of even greater impact. The elder Wood used the three superimposed orders of antiquity, doubling the columns to give the necessary weight and emphasis necessary for such a wide sweep. The horizontal division of the façade in this manner diminishes the scale, but gives an overall effect of great charm (Pl. 41).

His son, JOHN WOOD the younger (1728–81), in partnership with another, acquired a piece of land to the east of the Circus, and there built the Royal Crescent (1767–75). This semi-elliptical block not only improved on his father's work but also set the pattern for many similar schemes. The elder Wood had attempted the monumental and not quite brought it off, but his son managed the task with considerable *élan*. By the simple expedient of using a single colossal order, and standing the columns on a high base, he achieved the effect, at once simpler and more monumental, which his father had just missed. The elimination of the middle entablature, which had weakened his father's design, gives the façade more sweep, and the single columns are of sufficient weight to

Plate 41 The Circus, Bath (begun 1754), by John Wood
This shows how by good proportion a terrace house can achieve dignity

provide the vertical emphasis which gives the design its strength.

The whole of this scheme, comprising the Circus, the Royal Crescent, Gay Street, and Queen Street, is an urban complex of great originality. The Crescent was to provide the model for similar buildings at Buxton, Brighton, and other spa towns, which did, in fact, form the basis of many town-planning projects until early in the next century. Developments in the more industrial towns have obliterated many of the eighteenth-century schemes, and it is in the spa towns and seaside resorts that they are best seen. Of work in the Scottish capital we shall have more to say later, but the work of

JAMES CRAIG was important in the lay-out of the 'new town' at Edinburgh.

Although the actual Regency lasted only from 1811 to 1820, the Regency style in architecture is generally considered to cover roughly the first thirty years of the century. The period saw not only the continuing refinement of detail and decoration of the late eighteenth century but also the introduction of the 'picturesque' style, of which JOHN NASH was one of the most important leaders. From about 1795 to about 1802 he worked in close collaboration with Humphry Repton. During this important partnership Repton was responsible for the 'improvement' of the estates, whilst Nash either

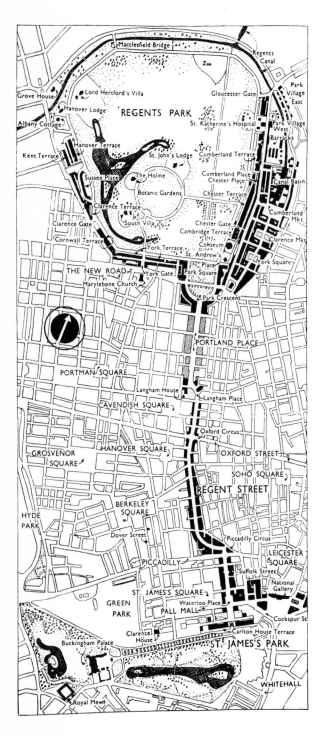

rebuilt or altered the houses. In addition he added summer-houses, lodges, and other fripperies to the grounds.

Up to the time of the Regency Nash was mainly concerned with such work in a variety of styles—some in classic, but the majority in Gothic. The closing years of the eighteenth century saw the beginning of the fashion for cottage-building, and also the sudden spurt in the number of garden shelters, pavilions, verandahs, and balconies which blossomed over the estates, great and small. These trifles were all the product of the interest in the picturesque, and the greatest of all these fancies is the Royal Pavilion at Brighton. This represents the style of a moment, but it is at the same time the summation of the taste for exotica which swept the country.

Nash took over the remodelling of the building from Repton in 1815, and it was complete by 1822. At the turn of the century S. P. Cockerell had essayed an Indian design at Sezincote in Gloucestershire, but Nash supplied the last word. In the past the Pavilion has come in for much criticism, and the strictly partisan functionalist will presumably continue to scorn its extravagances. To the less bigoted, however, the Pavilion will remain a sheer delight. This is the architecture of the fabulous dream world, a build-

Plate 42 The Royal Pavilion, Brighton (1815–22), by John Nash

ing of unparalleled riches. The exterior (Pl. 42), with its agglomeration of onion domes and minarets, is the epitome of picturesque design. The interior—with its glittering chandeliers, immense wall paintings, and scarlet, gold and yellow lacquer—presents an even more sumptuous spectacle. The opulence of the decoration, however, is not allowed to detract from the overall proportion of the rooms themselves. Indeed two of the apartments, the Banqueting Room and the Music Room, are particularly fine in this respect. The Banqueting Hall, with its great domed ceiling from which hangs a flying dragon carrying the central chandelier, is the more ornate of the two, the Music Room being comparatively restrained and less fanciful in decoration.

The Great Kitchen still retains much of its original equipment, and is spacious and workmanlike in appearance. The cast-iron columns are an example of the early use of the metal in building, though the palm leaves which sprout from the top defy function; they carry the building's general extravagance into its more remote parts.

The other striking achievement of Nash was his plans for Regent's Park and Regent Street. Work began in the Park in 1812, and the following year his plan for Regent Street was accepted. By 1835 the greater part of the scheme had been carried out, St James's Park had been brought into the design and so had the new Buckingham Palace. The whole concept is one of striking originality (Fig. 212). It is essentially the design of an urban landscape in the picturesque manner of which Nash was such an able

practitioner. Little of his work now remains, except for the plan and some of
the terraces around the Park (Fig. 213).
The few other remaining buildings show
that the whole scheme must have been one
which maintained with great skill a balance
between variety and uniformity.

Nash was not liked by his fellow architects; small wonder, for he used classical
trappings with more freedom than his more
archaeologically minded contemporaries,
such as Soane and Smirke, could stomach.
The work of these architects was in laying

the foundations of the Greek revival style
that was to gain such a hold in this country
during the latter part of the eighteen twenties
and the early 'thirties.

JOHN SOANE (1753–1837), after a notable
studentship, had been awarded the surveyorship of the Bank of England, and in this
capacity had designed the Bank Stock
Office in a style which, in its economy of
detail, was extremely original. In 1806 he
was elected professor of architecture at the
Royal Academy, and his lectures there did
much to establish the classical style. His

own work has a certain austere quality (Pl. 43), coupled with a rather uncertain feeling for proportion. The figures round the dome of the Consols Office are curiously cramped, and the placing of the semicircular arch on the end wall is uncomfortable. This slight awkwardness of placing may account for, or be the result of, his liking for the work of Vanbrugh. Ultimately, despite many originalities, it weakened his work.

ROBERT SMIRKE was articled to Soane for a short period, but left after a disagreement. After a long visit to the Continent he returned to England and was given his first great opportunity when he designed the new theatre at Covent Garden. This was London's first Greek building, though he later abandoned the Doric order in favour of the Ionic which he used with such overpowering effect on the British Museum. He also used the Ionic order on his other major building, the General Post Office (demolished 1913), though here he limited the use of the order to the porticos. Except for these features the façade was devoid of decoration and lacking in power.

Smirke was also responsible for the United Services' Club (redesigned by Nash in 1828). The professional man's club was a new type of building which came into favour after Waterloo and was rather different from the clubs for gaming and gambling, or the political clubs which were already in existence. But the more influential clubs are more the concern of the period after 1830, and so fall into the next chapter.

Fig. 213 Cumberland Terrace, London (1827), by John Nash

FURTHER READING

Walter Ison, *The Georgian Buildings of Bath.* Faber & Faber, 1948.

Valuable illustrations, and many details and plans in the text.

John Gloag, *Georgian Grace 1660–1830.* Adam & Charles Black, 1956.

This book deals with the architecture and minor arts of the period and contains much background material.

John Summerson, *Georgian London.* Pleiades Books, 1945.

This invaluable book is now available as a paperback published by Penguin Books.

Christopher Hussey, *English Country Houses.* Country Life, 1957.

Vol. 1 *Early Georgian 1715–1760* (1955)
Vol. 2 *Mid Georgian 1760–1800* (1956)
Vol. 3 *Late Georgian 1800–1840* (1958)

Like the many other beautiful books on the English House produced by this company, the present volumes contain detailed accounts of the houses, accompanied by numerous photographs and drawings in the text.

Dorothy Stroud, *The Architecture of Sir John Soane.* Studio Books, 1961.

A comprehensive review, well-illustrated.

PART THREE

The Nineteenth
and Twentieth Centuries

11

THE NINETEENTH CENTURY

This century was, of course, one of intense and rapid development, for it saw the change from a primarily agricultural society to an industrial and urban one. This rapid industrialization, with the consequent growth of towns, is responsible for much of the squalor prevalent in the industrial centres of today. Advances in engineering and technology were many and varied, and it is always a sobering reflection on man's creative ability that he was generally so slow to take advantage of scientific and technological developments in order to improve the standard of housing and the amenities of towns. Some of the inventions which affected architecture more directly are listed below; many presented the architect with new problems because they needed new types of building, and there are many more which had less direct effects on architecture.

Probably the most spectacular developments took place in the fields of travel and communications, for this was the great period of railway expansion. The new method of transportation grew up from the necessity of finding an efficient and economical way to move the coal, so essential to Britain's booming iron trade. This concentration on rail transport is probably responsible in a large measure for the lack of improvements to Britain's road system, for we were probably slower to realize the potential of the internal-combustion engine than any other major European country.

The 1850s and 1860s saw the traditional methods of sea-travel replaced by the much faster and more reliable steamship. Further improvements were the development of the electric telegraph and the introduction of the penny post.

1801–2 Trevithick's steam carriage
1821 Iron steamboat
1824 Portland cement
1825 Stockton and Darlington railway
1827 Jacob Perkins's high pressure steam boiler
1830 Compressed air used for sinking shafts under water. Elevators used in factories
1831 Faraday's dynamo
1834 Liquid-refrigerating machine
1838 Morse's electro-magnetic telegraph
1840 First steel cable suspension bridge at Pittsburgh
1851 Crystal Palace (First International Exhibition of Machines and the Applied Arts)
1853 The 'Great Eastern' steamship
1856 The Bessemer Converter
1860–3 The London 'Underground'
1867 Reinforced concrete
1878–9 Swan and Edison electric light bulbs
1879 Electric railways
1883 Daimler's petrol engine
1893–8 Diesel engine
1896 Marconi's radio-telegraph*

* For these and many other useful inventions, see Lewis Mumford, *Technics and Civilization* (Routledge, 1934).

By 1848 Britain was producing half the pig-iron of the world, and in the next thirty years her output was trebled. Coupled with this came the growth of the wool and cotton industry, which developed rapidly after the various spinning and weaving processes patented at the end of the eighteenth century. As already pointed out, this industrial expansion led to the rapid growth of towns, where conditions during the earlier part of the nineteenth century must have been appalling. Sanitation was bad or almost non-existent, sewage accumulating in a cesspool sometimes situated under the floor of the house. In a *Report on the State of Large Towns and Populous Districts* (1845) it was stated that in 1843-4, 700 inhabitants were supplied by 33 necessaries only, i.e. one toilet to 21·2 people.* Cellars were used as dwelling places, and the lack of light coupled with the dank, stale atmosphere provided ideal breeding-grounds for germs and disease. After a particularly bad outbreak of cholera the first Public Health Act was introduced in 1848, but seems to have had little effect for the next twenty years. There were published at this time a number of novels giving graphic descriptions of the social conditions of the period. Prominent amongst these were *Coningsby* and *Sybil*, by Benjamin Disraeli; *Alton Locke, Tailor and Poet*, by Charles Kingsley; *Mary Barton*, by Mrs Gaskell; and last—but by no means least important—*Oliver Twist*, by Charles Dickens.

Nor is there any reason to believe that England was alone in enduring these miser-

* For this and many other facts on nineteenth-century town-dwelling, see Lewis Mumford, *The Culture of Cities* (Secker & Warburg, 1938).

able conditions. There is ample evidence that conditions in Paris, New York, and Berlin were very much the same as London. Indeed, conditions were aggravated during the second half of the century by the rapid growth of towns and by the apparent inability of architects, for one reason or another, to deal with the problem. The rapid increase—indeed, almost explosion—of population which took place in the larger industrial cities from 1850 onwards was due not only to the increasing numbers of people making their way into the towns from country areas but also to the vast increase in the birth-rate in the towns themselves. In 1800 not a city in the western world had a population of over 1,000,000. By 1850 London had over 2,000,000 and Paris over 1,000,000—and by 1900 over eleven major cities throughout the world had a population of over 1,000,000. To contain the increased population within the ancient walls and fortifications which still existed around many cities was impossible, and so these were pulled down and the towns began to spread outwards, usually without much attention to planning. So fast did these developments take place that architects found the problems they had to solve too great. Previously they had been concerned only with the erection of one building, or perhaps some small scheme involving a limited number of buildings; consequently they found themselves unable—and this is as much a reflection on the training they received, as on the individuals themselves—to work to the necessary scale.

In England, in an attempt to gain some sort of control over the standards of living conditions in towns, the Municipal Corporation Act of 1835 was passed. This led (unintentionally, it must be admitted) to the modern municipalities, with their many powers and responsibilities. More far-reaching was the Local Government Act of 1888, for this not only established the London County Council (which began at once to undertake many schemes of social welfare) but also created the county councils to administer the affairs of rural areas.

The provision of a decent standard of housing and a reasonably pleasant environment in which to live was not the only aspect of urban living that was allowed to languish. The new and more complicated machinery housed in the rapidly growing factories (which were largely responsible for the rapid urban growth) demanded more and better educated operatives to work them. But the State seemed very wary of venturing into what had been virtually a system of voluntary schools until Gladstone's Act finally established elementary education. England had to wait until the twentieth century before secondary education on a national scale was introduced. This lack of foresight in educational progress may account for the barrack-like buildings which passed for school architecture in the Victorian age and which, even 70 years later, are still far too much in evidence.

Architectural development during the nineteenth century is complicated, but generally speaking the buildings produced fall fairly naturally into three groups.

The first group comprises those buildings which were built in a revival style. We have already seen that an interest in historical and exotic styles had already begun to manifest itself in the last years of the previous century; now, however, revivalism began to dominate the architectural scene. In the early part of the century the classical architecture of Greece and Rome provided the inspiration, but as these styles gradually lost their novelty, architects began to look further afield to more and more unfamiliar sources. The second half of the century saw interest mainly centred on the Gothic style, not only for ecclesiastical architecture but also for domestic building as well. Buildings designed in the revival styles included the houses and clubs of the rapidly growing upper middle class, as well as the town halls, civic buildings and banks, etc., erected by prospering businesses or local authorities. To many, much of the architecture and design of the period seems bogus, and doubtless much of it was, for reasons we must consider in due course. Nevertheless, there was much work of merit, if not of the first order of greatness, in the revival styles.

The second group is made up of speculative houses built to accommodate the rapidly expanding working class who were flocking to the towns in their thousands. These miserable dwellings are the basis of the modern slums, and these, too, can be broadly divided into two classes, those built before 1875 and those built after.

The third and last of the groups, and the one most likely to be of real interest to the modern student of architecture, comprises the early industrial buildings. Into this group can be placed those buildings which were primarily places of work. Many of them employed traditional techniques, of brick and stone, and fine and forthright examples can still be seen today in such places as Boston (Lincs.), Bradford, Wakefield, etc. But some of them began to exploit the new materials—namely glass and iron. The new mills, warehouses, factories, bridges, and exhibition buildings can all be gathered into this last category, which, at the time, was hardly considered important enough to warrant the term 'architecture' at all.

The revival styles and the new industrial buildings will concern us at greater length later; for the moment, let us turn our attention to the second group. Living conditions for the working class in the towns have already been touched upon. The lack of any real planning was a national disaster, resulting in nothing but discontent, misery, and disease. The endless proliferation of the miserable mass-produced dwellings for the working class has made it all but impossible, in such towns as Leeds (Fig. 214), Wakefield, and Bradford, to tell where one town ends and the next begins. The countryside was turned into a slum—dull, dirty, and uninspired. The houses built before the great Public Health Act of 1875 were particularly

Fig. 214 Nineteenth-century housing at Leeds

grim. Found mainly in the industrial mid-lands and north, these hovels had neither water-closet nor running water. Sanitary arrangements were in the form of a communal closet, pump, and wash-house in the rear courtyard. A kitchen, or adequate provision for the storage of food, was lacking. Many of these houses have gone, but many still remain, though admittedly with added amenities.

The Public Health Act of 1875 established public control of housing, and enabled local authorities to enforce certain minimum standards. The bad old habits were banned and the result was a distinct improvement. Under the new Act walls had to be over a certain thickness, and properly damp-proofed. Sewage and drainage were improved, and each house henceforth had its own private closet, and water laid on to a sink inside the house; there would also be a copper for washing clothes. Rooms were normally lit by candles or oil-lamps, though the best room might have had the luxury of a gas-jet. Although these new houses placed England in the forefront of public housing in Europe,

Fig. 215 Modern development at Leeds

they suffered from being narrow (14 feet to 17 feet was the most common measurement for the frontage), and light and space were restricted at the back. In the twentieth century these houses had hot water systems and bathrooms added, and they have remained in demand, for they are generally near the city centre and give more opportunity for social life than the far-flung and sprawling housing estate or garden city.

As the towns grew, naturally some sort of plan had to be adopted. A minimum width and length of street was prescribed, though blind adherence to these minimum standards led to a deadly uniformity, especially where the block plan or 'grid' system of layout was used. This economical system consisted of a grid of roads and streets crossing at right angles without any regard for topography. Middlesbrough is a good example of this type of plan, which is often referred to as being American in origin. This method of extending towns by blocks was, however, well known in Europe before the nineteenth century; the Romans used such a method, and of course, Wren, Evelyn, and Hooke all produced block plans of one sort or another for London after the Great Fire.

Though it is easy to be scornful about the way these depressing areas were allowed to develop, and though we decry the absence of any humanizing influences—the largest open spaces were railway sidings and marshalling yards, not parks, gardens, and playgrounds—and the lack of any consistent zoning of living-space and working-space, it must be remembered that builders and architects were trying to cope with a problem of a magnitude not known before. Further, we must not forget that even today, compared with the highly sophisticated techniques of rocketry, our building techniques remain comparatively primitive. The time for criticism is now past; we need to learn from previous mistakes and develop a more dynamic approach to the problem of providing a civilized and visually stimulating environment. One is bound to wonder whether the twentieth-century 'square keep' rearing its head above the morass of wasteland (Fig. 215) is really the answer to our housing problems. Even in its dilapidated state the street shown in Fig. 214 suggests a sense of community. Will 'vertical streets' succeed in areas like this?

People who did try to do something constructive in the way of providing better standards of living for the factory hands were such idealists as Lord Shaftesbury and Edwin Chadwick, who fought in Parliament for reforms in housing standards. On the practical level of housing and health, Octavia Hill and George Peabody also made an outstanding contribution to the alleviation of hardship for the working class in London. Other reformers turned their attention to building completely new towns, and gradually developed the idea of a garden city. Early examples of this type of development were Edensor in Derbyshire and Saltaire near Bradford. More ambitious was the scheme at Port Sunlight near Liverpool, 1888–1910, and at about the same time George Cadbury began his town at Bournville. In 1890 local authorities were empowered to build houses for the first time, and the immediate results were large schemes in London and Liverpool, though it was not until after the First World War that local-authority

Fig. 216 A late-Victorian middle-class house in Harrogate

building was carried out on a large scale.

But whilst this type of building was going on, large areas of more commodious dwellings were going up in such towns as Edinburgh, Cheltenham, Brighton, and other seaside and spa towns. The work of such builders as Thomas Cubitt is to be seen in many of our larger towns. The houses such builders put up were well made, with large rooms and good windows, for the Victorian father was proud of his home and liked to show his affluence to the world. In the larger towns the high price of land made these houses tall and narrow, as can be seen in the squares and terraces of Earl's Court and South Kensington in London, and in the larger provincial towns. Accommodation was on four or five storeys, with a basement below ground level. Where pressure on land was not so great, however, the houses spread and became very fanciful in their treatment (Fig. 216).

Architecture in Britain 1830–1890

THE GREEK REVIVAL

As we have already seen, the Greek revival was already well established in this country by the end of the second decade of the century, Smirke, Soane, and Wilkins having been responsible for work which was both important and influential.

A prominent feature of revival architecture in the 1830s was the London club. The twenty-odd years between Waterloo and Victoria's accession were the heyday of club building, though many were built after 1837. We need concern ourselves here with only four. The earliest, Nash's United Services Club of 1828, is a design of great character. The façade is based on Roman models, and the superimposed orders and sculptured frieze produce a scheme of great richness. The rectangular pedimented windows set in the stucco of the first floor provide a nicely managed contrast to the ground-floor windows, with their broken pediments and ashlar masonry setting.

Although the Athenaeum Club of 1830 lacks the richness of the United Services

Plate 44 The Reform Club (1838–40),
by Sir Charles Barry

Fig. 217 The British Museum, London (1823),
by Sir Robert Smirke—south front

façade, it shows a sure sense of proportion and a feeling for restrained decoration. Decimus Burton chose to follow a severely Greek style, and it is to be regretted that the later addition of an attic storey spoils the lightness of his original conception, for now the façade appears rather squashed and cramped.

The two clubs of Sir Charles Barry, The Travellers' of 1832 and The Reform of 1838-40, are both based on Renaissance models (Pl. 44). The earlier building bears some resemblance to Raphael's Palazzo Pandolfini in Florence, whilst the Roman Palazzo Farnese was the obvious model for the later one. Both are designs of great elegance and fine proportion, and both make a strong feature of the cornice.

It seems appropriate that museums should, as they often do, provide the best example of classic revival buildings. The gigantic south front of Smirke's British Museum (1823-47; Fig. 217) and Schinkel's Altes Museum (Fig. 218) in Berlin are two of the finest examples. As the British Museum is not marred by the dullness and slight uneasiness of proportion which detracts from so many of Smirke's façades,

Fig. 218 The Altes Museum, Berlin (1824-8), by K. F. Schinkel

it is possible that the two architects met and exchanged ideas, for Schinkel was in Britain in 1830 visiting the industrial areas around Manchester and the north of England. The domed central reading-room of the museum was carried out by Smirke's brother Sydney. The dome is of cast-iron construction, and although it does not equal Labrouste's work in the Bibliothèque Nationale, it is neverthe-less one of the last major monuments in this material in the country. With a span of 140 feet it was the largest to be constructed since the Pantheon, which had a span of 142 feet 6 inches.

The Fitzwilliam Museum at Cambridge (1837–47) gives an example of splendour and opulence that is hard to match. The style is eclectic, and it is sad that the architect, George Basevi, did not live to see it com-pleted. During the course of construction he was called over to Ely for consultations on certain repairs to the cathedral, and while carrying out the survey on the tower he fell to his death. Work on the museum was car-ried on by C. R. Cockerell, and later by the younger Barry. Basevi was also responsible for some fine squares and streets in London's Belgravia.

Nor are all the best examples of the classic revival confined to the southern counties. The work of Cuthbert Brodrick in Leeds, for example, is worthy of atten-tion. His Town Hall (1853–58) is a fine conception, and it is to be regretted that the site has become so congested. The scheme is a broad one, and shows a feeling for the imposing effect—though this is somewhat spoiled by a tower and clock which when seen from some angles tend to lack the authority required by the building beneath.

The Corn Exchange of 1860 is a bold and solemn design, whilst the Grand Hotel at Scarborough (1863–7) has just the right amount of respectable flamboyance for a prosperous spa town of the late nineteenth century. Despite the screaming amusement arcades beneath its feet, the hotel still manages to dominate the bay which it over-looks.

There can be little doubt that one of the finest of all classic revival buildings in England is St George's Hall, Liverpool (Fig. 219). Designed in 1839 by H. L. Elmes, whose early death was a sad blow to English architecture, this compact yet monumental building shows the revival style at its most impressive. The Corinthian order gives the façade a richness which relieves the rather stark attic block, and the play of column and pilaster gives added variety. In the treat-ment of a long façade both Elmes and Schinkel had similar problems to solve, and a comparison with the Altes Museum is both interesting and rewarding.

C. R. Cockerell was an architect of great discrimination, and his designs for several of the branch Banks of England are worthy of study. One of the best of these is the Liver-pool branch, and here the classic orders are used with great imagination. There are, of course, many other fine buildings in the classical revival manner which are also worthy of mention: Birmingham Town Hall, by J. Hanson and T. Welsh; Barry's Bur-lington House; the National Gallery in Trafalgar Square, by William Wilkins; and Decimus Burton's Triple Archway at Hyde Park Corner. There were, however, im-portant developments in Scotland and to these we must now turn.

British phlegm and stolid admiration for anything foreign in matters artistic tend to produce a consistent underestimation of indigenous achievements. Early in the century, developments in the layout of Edinburgh on largely classical lines placed it quite firmly amongst the finest cities in Europe. The site of the city is, in itself, one of great interest, and fortunately the architects took full advantage of the natural surroundings. To say, as some do, that if you took away Princes Street, nothing would be left, is an exaggeration. Nevertheless, its loss would be a serious blow to a magnificently-managed scheme. Indeed it is a sad reflection on modern entrepreneurs that they have so little sense of environment and occasion. The large multi-storey shops, in the course of erection on this splendid street in the mid-twentieth century, show little respect for the grandeur of their setting.

Princes Street itself runs east and west, while to the south, on its grim crag, stands the castle, a splendid reminder of medieval castle-building. Eastwards the vista is closed by Calton Hill and, a little to the south of it, Arthur's Seat. To the west the vistas are closed by a series of spires and domes, belonging to St George's Church, Gilbert Scott's St Mary's Cathedral, and St John's Church. To the north lies the gracious new town. As the streets here run either at right-angles to, or parallel with, Princes Street, one is constantly presented with a magnificent set of closed vistas to east, west, and south, whilst to the north the land falls away towards the Firth of Forth. This succession of vistas gives to the new town a vivid sense of compactness and scale. The eye, after exploring the street, always finds something to admire at the end of it. But the qualities of this part of the town are endless, and the whole layout is a fine example of late eighteenth-century and early nineteenth-century planning. As a contrast to the orderliness of the new town, the older

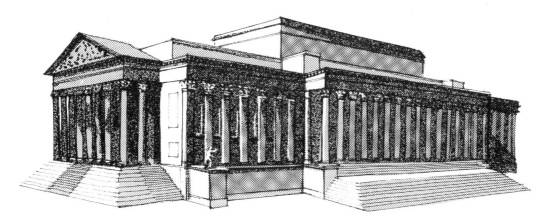

Fig. 219 St George's Hall, Liverpool (1839–54), by H. L. Elmes

Figs. 217–19 show some of the more impressive aspects of the Classic Revival style

medieval town huddles round the castle, the streets following the contour of the land rather than an ordered pattern.

For most of the notable nineteenth-century buildings we are largely indebted to C. R. Cockerell and W. H. Playfair (1789–1857). Arthur's Seat has been kept clear of buildings, but Calton Hill has become a Scottish acropolis. The largest structure there, the National Monument by Cockerell and Playfair, was never completed—probably a blessing in disguise, for in its present apparently ruined state it adds a dramatic touch to the romantic picturesqueness of the scene. The group is completed by Thomas Hamilton's Choragic Monument to Robert Burns, Nelson's Monument, and some minor structures which add interest and excitement to the whole. Playfair's terraces, erected between 1820 and 1860, supply an impressive base to the whole composition.

The local stone weathers a rather deep grey, but its original beauty and mellowness of colour can now be seen on the Royal Scottish Academy building (1822–36), which was cleaned and restored in 1962–3. The building, an essay in massive Doric, was crowned just after completion by a splendid seated figure of the young Victoria (Fig. 220).

Another of Playfair's buildings, his Scottish National Gallery, stands behind it, and this time he uses the Ionic, with consequent lightness of touch. It is difficult to decide which is the finer building, for each shows a splendid understanding of the qualities of the different styles, and together they make a fine group. Behind and above these two classic buildings is Playfair again—this time in a vaguely Tudor mood—with the Free Church College (1846–50). The crisp detail and verticality of the twin towers provide relief and variety to the foreground classicism. These towers provide a frame for the graceful spire of Tolbooth St John's (1843) by J. G. Graham.

Out of the centre of the town, but beautifully sited on the south side of Calton Hill,

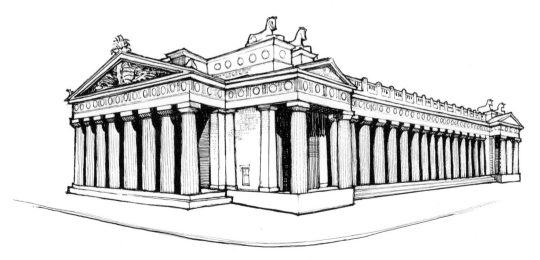

Fig. 220 The Royal Scottish Academy (previously The Royal Institution), Edinburgh (1822–36)—from the south. Architect, W. H. Playfair

is the High School (1825) by Thomas Hamilton, who was also responsible for the highly original Hall of Physicians in Queen's street. Two great banks, grander than anything in London when they were built, are worthy of mention: Rhind's Commercial Bank of Scotland in George Street (1846), and Bryce's British Linen Bank in St Andrew's Square (1852).

Before we leave Scotland altogether, the work of Alexander Thomson in Glasgow is well worth consideration. His Caledonia Road Free Church (1856–7), with its diversity of levels and Ionic mock portico on a heavy podium block, all dwarfed by a monolithic tower, produces a most picturesquely 'off-beat' ensemble (Fig. 221). It was gutted by fire, however, in 1965.

Too often we tend to dismiss these apparently heavy, black smoke-begrimed buildings without a second look. If we could see them cleaned to their original colour, as is now possible in the case of the Academy and National Gallery buildings in Edinburgh, we might be persuaded to think again about their merits.

THE GOTHIC REVIVAL

The Gothic Revival in England is important not only for the buildings it produced but also for the influence it had on a great deal of subsequent architecture. During this very industrious period a number of immensely hardworking architects, together with the critic John Ruskin, not only developed a style based on Gothic, but also formulated a way of looking at, and thinking about, buildings which was to colour our way of thinking about architecture for generations to follow. If the acquisition of the Elgin Marbles for the British Museum had given a tremendous boost to the Greek revival, then the design of the new Houses of

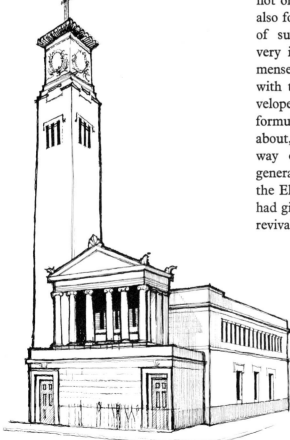

Fig. 221 Caledonia Road Free Church, Glasgow (1856–7), by Alexander Thomson

Parliament gave official recognition and encouragement to the Gothicists.

Throughout the early years of the century interest in the Gothic style had been growing. Indeed many writers claim, with some justification, that the style had never really died in this country. As far back as 1760 Horace Walpole, with his own house, Strawberry Hill in Twickenham, introduced the style into polite society, and this house, with its carefully arranged picturesque outline and accurate detail, is usually taken as the beginning of the revival proper.

By the 1830s the ground had been prepared and the climate was right for some major work to be carried out in the style. Romantic literature was popular, and Sir Walter Scott, who had lived in a modern Gothic house himself, was at the height of his fame. Steel engravings of cathedrals and medieval antiquities sold in vast numbers, and books on painting, including the Italian Primitives for example, were being published. Thomas Rickman, in his *Attempt to Discriminate the Styles of Architecture in England* (1817), gave names and dates to the periods of English Gothic which are still used.

On 16 October 1834 the Old Palace at Westminster was burnt down, and in June of the following year a competition was announced for a new design. The site was to be that of the Old Palace, and because of the surroundings—namely Westminster Hall, the ruins of St George's Chapel and the Abbey itself—the style was to be either Gothic or Elizabethan. The Gothic Revival had 'arrived', and the most important public building in the country was to set the standard.

That the choice fell on the Gothic style appears, in retrospect, to have been something of a foregone conclusion. Certain sections of the public had already decided that a taste for Gothic showed a well-formed and independent judgement, and it was also a widely-held belief that Gothic was the national style, which sprang from native soil. The few dusty pedants who insisted that Gothic originated in France were swamped in oceans of patriotic rhetoric.

Those who tried to defend classical architecture on various vague and quasi-philosophical grounds were likewise deflated. Not that their arguments were strong in the first place. The words 'natural' and 'manly' were bandied about, the classical architects claiming that the classical column had sprung from the idea of a tree growing sturdily out of the ground and quoting as further evidence of this 'naturalness' the Corinthian capital with its leaf-forms. Not only, according to the classicists, were these orders based on forms occurring in nature, but their chaste and pure shapes were more 'manly'. The Gothicists, however, retaliated with the argument that if the classic column represented a tree then the columns in a Gothic nave were a veritable forest, and the gloom and massive solemnity of a Gothic structure were far more 'manly' than the openness and arid formalism of a classic façade.

Despite these long wordy arguments and the flashes of inspiration and perception of both Pugin and Ruskin—two key figures in this period—these earnest Victorians seem to us today to have been singularly lacking in critical faculty. The imitation became, for them, more important, and of greater worth, than the original. Two quotations, one from *The Gentleman's Magazine* of 1818, another from Dallaway's *Anecdotes on the Arts in England*, illustrate this quite clearly.

A contributor to the magazine, commenting on the desirability of using Gothic moulding made from cast-iron, says: '. . . As lightness and elegance are the leading and most desirable characters in this class of building [i.e. Gothic], these might be carried to a much higher degree of perfection than they ever were capable of with so fragile and destructible a material as stone . . . and the iron-work ornaments, being covered with an anti-corrosive of stone colour, would be rendered indestructible for ages!' The view of the writer in Dallaway's *Anecdotes* that 'a happy imitation is of much more value than a defective original' is equally unacceptable to the modern student. The full implications of these two quotations hardly need comment; they are mistaking the shadow for the substance with a vengeance.

The Houses of Parliament

But to return to the Houses of Parliament, there can be little doubt that the choice of the Gothic style gave official recognition to a gathering force, and from then on Gothic was the recognized style for public buildings until the fracas between Gilbert Scott and Palmerston over the government offices nearly a quarter of a century later.

Barry is always named as the architect of the Parliament buildings, and there can be no doubt that he was responsible for the plan. It seems equally certain that Pugin was entirely responsible for the façades.

Barry was, after all, trained in the classical tradition and could use the classic style with freedom of expression and individuality, as his clubs show. The size of the commission made it legitimate for Barry to employ an assistant, and it must have been awkward indeed when the assistant turned out to be an architect of near genius. Pugin himself seems to have been indifferent as to whether Barry recognized his part in the designs or not, and Barry on his part would appear to have tried to ignore Pugin's contribution. It is unfortunate that the whole affair should have degenerated into a bitter feud between the two families after Pugin's death. The whole scheme was so successful that each could have recognized the other's part without any loss to personal pride or prestige (Fig. 222).

Pugin freely admitted that he could not have produced the plan, which, with its enforced symmetry and dummy windows, was classical in conception. Working to this, however, Pugin managed to devise a façade of great richness, which became not only a national monument, but the symbol of London, the capital of a large empire, as well. The importance of the Houses of Parliament as the largest and most important building of the neo-Gothic style, is obvious. Yet this familiar and well-loved silhouette represents a combination of architectural styles which would normally be considered incompatible. Barry had hoped that a building of this importance would help to give impetus to the revival of interest in fine craftsmanship, and in this he was not altogether disappointed. However, the gradual formation of a rigid body of doctrines governing the new style imposed such a

Fig. 222 The Houses of Parliament, London (1840–66)—river front
Architects, Sir Charles Barry and A. W. N. Pugin

straight-jacket on practitioners, that all hope for the growth of a spontaneous style was lost. Pugin was largely responsible for the formation of these doctrines, which were so strict as to rival even the carefully worked out proportions of the classic orders.

Pugin

The facts of Pugin's life can be summarized in a few brief sentences. His father fled from France during the Revolution and obtained a position in Nash's office, where he became an authority on the Gothic style. By the time his son was fifteen he had manifested a gift for drawing and a passion for Gothic architecture. At about this time he became friendly with George Days, son of Edward Days, the portrait painter, who introduced the young Pugin to the world of the theatre. His enthusiasm was so great that he con-

verted one floor of his father's house into a model stage, and after two years' work brought off a triumph by designing the sets for the ballet 'Kenilworth', presented at Drury Lane. This passion for the theatre horrified his parents, and to add to their consternation Pugin then developed an equal fervour for the sea. There is 'nothing in life worth living for except Gothic architecture and a boat', he said. By 1833, after a disastrous business venture, which landed him in a debtors' goal, he had begun to make some progress, and built himself his first house, near Salisbury. But the real turning point in his life was the year 1834, when he became converted to the Catholic faith. Despite the dislike and distrust of Catholicism in this country at the time, his conversion did not affect his architectural practice, for he always had more work than he could comfortably cope with. In 1835 he began to publish the first of the long stream of books which were to be so influential. He published *Contrasts* at his own expense, and though he lost financially on the transaction his reputation was greatly enhanced. In 1837 he was appointed professor of architecture at Oscott College, and later published the lectures he delivered there under the title *True Principles of Christian Architecture.* His *Glossary of Ecclesiastical Ornament*, published in 1844, was a work of great learning and would have employed a normal person for many years. During this time he also managed to design a dozen churches and another house for himself, this time at Ramsgate. This house had its own private chapel, St Augustine's, which he later considered to be his most successful work.

It is unfortunate that his buildings tend to be overshadowed by his writings, though admittedly the former are somewhat disappointing. That they should have been so was not altogether Pugin's fault, for the phenomenal speed at which he worked, and at which the church authorities expected him to work, seldom allowed for second thoughts or revisions. Added to this is the fact that many of the schemes were carried through on a very limited budget. Here Pugin's religious fervour did him some disservice, for he was so anxious to get a church opened and working that he was prepared to sacrifice architectural standards. At his best, however, he did produce work of character and individuality. St Barnabas at Nottingham, later to become a cathedral, and some of his work for monastic and collegiate foundations, are well worthy of mention and consideration.

In 1851 he was commissioned to design the Medieval Court at the Great Exhibition, but the strain of coping with unsympathetic commissioners and public bodies proved too much for his already overworked and overstrained mind, and in the following year he became insane and was removed to Bedlam, where he died on 14 September.

In considering some of Pugin's ideas about the theory and practice of architecture it is interesting to see how close to an acceptable theory of aesthetics he comes. Yet so often he falls short in the application of these theories. Not that he is alone in this, for it seems a common failing of the Victorians. Ruskin, as we shall see, was capable of the most perceptive analyses, yet ended in disaster when he tried to put them to practical use; and that ill-fated alliance, the Pre-Raphaelite Brotherhood, was based on sound principles, yet lapsed when it came to apply its beliefs.

There seems little doubt that Pugin grasped only too clearly the importance of structure in architecture. This is well illustrated by these quotations from his book, *The True Principles of Pointed or Christian Architecture.* Firstly: 'That there should be no features about a building which are not necessary for convenience, construction, or propriety; second, that all ornament should consist of enrichment of the essential construction of the building.' And later: 'There is no reason why noble cities, containing all possible convenience of drainage, water courses, and conveyance of gas, may not be erected in the most consistent yet Christian character. Every building that is treated naturally, without disguise or concealment, cannot fail to look well.'

This latter statement is a most remarkable

piece of architectural thinking, and could have been written almost sixty years later and still been considered *avant-garde*. He had also seen the organic connection between architecture and society, as is shown in this passage: 'The mechanical part of Gothic architecture is pretty well understood, but it is the principles which influenced ancient compositions, and the soul which appears in all ancient works, which is so lamentably deficient; nor, as I have said before [this is the crux of this statement], can anything be regained but by the restoration of the ancient feeling and sentiments; 'tis they alone can restore Gothic architecture.' Here he sees with absolute clarity the essential requirement, not only for the Gothic Revival but for any revival at all, at least if it is to be a complete revival such as Pugin and his followers had in mind. There can be little doubt that an architect trained by, or living in, the Classical tradition thought that a competently trained architect could design in any style he pleased. The idea of equating the architecture of any given period with the society which produced it was entirely foreign to him.

Having seen so far into the nature of architecture, where did Pugin go wrong? The answer to this question seems to be in the next stage of his development of ideas. He went on to claim that, 'The history of architecture is the history of the world'. So far so good, but from there he deduced that good building depended on the condition of society and the conviction of the architect. For Pugin this meant Christian architecture, or the architecture of the Gothic period; hence classical architecture, being the product of a pagan society, was insufferable and unworthy of serious consideration. It is this attribution of moral values to architecture which is the weak link in the chain of Pugin's argument. Unfortunately this line of reasoning was developed by an even more ardent and persuasive champion and one who in the long run was to have more influence, namely Ruskin. In his *Seven Lamps of Architecture*, he made the two following pronouncements:

(i) The value of a building depends on the moral value of its creator.
(ii) A building has a moral value independent of, and more important than, its aesthetic value.

Of Ruskin we shall have more to say later. In the meantime we must turn to another of Pugin's disciples—and one who did more to change the face of England than any other architect—Gilbert Scott.

Scott (*1811–78*)

Sir George Gilbert Scott may not be the greatest architect of the period, but he is the most representative. He had a very large practice; in 1878 a published list named 730 buildings by him, and it was not complete. Like other architects of the period, he was interested in the problem of how to apply the Gothic style to domestic buildings, and which period of Gothic to choose; and his other interest was the restoration of the great English cathedrals and churches.

In 1844 he was elected to represent this country in an international competition for the new St Nicholas' Church in Hamburg. Despite the fact that his design came third it was finally decided to carry it out, instead of the classical temple which won first place.

This success led to an ever-growing number of commissions to restore the great churches throughout this country. It is difficult to determine the exact amount of damage done to our architectural heritage by these restorations. Doubtless Scott often receives the blame for the crimes of slipshod clerks-of-works and bad stonemasons, and in all probability his clients were not as generous as they might have been. Scott himself remained adamant over the fact that he was strictly conservative in the amount and manner of his restorations. He also claimed that without his work many of our finest churches would have fallen down, as they were in such a bad state of repair.

Conservative restoration, is, however, a very relative term. The churches at that time were confronted with two types of restorer: the local builder and mason who would simply replace anything that looked old and worn, and the 'Camden Society', who spent much of their time debating the various merits of their two systems of restoration, namely 'eclectic' and 'destructive'. By the first system the whole building was pulled down and rebuilt in the style that was most prevalent in that particular church, and the second method was to pull down the whole building and rebuild it in the 'best' style, i.e. 'Decorated'. The Camden Society had in fact a scheme afoot, and plans drawn up, to pull down the whole of Peterborough Cathedral and rebuild it in the Decorated style, and had funds been forthcoming they would no doubt have made a serious attempt to carry out their ideas. By such standards, Scott was indeed a conservative restorer.

Today such attitudes must seem arrogant beyond belief, but there can be little doubt that these earnest Victorians were convinced that they were doing a thoroughly worthwhile and noble task in looking after these great buildings so well. We just cannot escape the fact that though we think Scott built rather bad Gothic, Scott himself and many of his contemporaries thought that he built very good Gothic.

It was when Scott was at the height of his powers that he sustained his bitterest blow and humiliation. In 1857 he published his book *Remarks on Secular and Domestic Architecture*, which did a great deal to establish the Gothic style as the right and proper style for domestic use. In the same year a competition was announced for two new government offices in Whitehall. Naturally Scott entered, with a scheme based on French Gothic. However, the judges 'knew amazingly little about their subject', and Scott's designs were passed over. It was not until Scott heard that Lord Palmerston had decided to set aside the results of the competition and appoint a non-competitor, namely Pennethorne, that Scott thought himself 'at liberty to stir'. So successfully did he 'stir' that he got himself appointed architect for both buildings. But no sooner had he gained approval for his new plans than a certain Mr Tite (a classical architect and M.P. for Bath) objected to them—and the Battle of the Styles was on.

A change of government brought Palmerston to the head, and he was a firm classicist. He sent for Scott and insisted that any new design must be in the Italian style, for, if left to his own devices, he (Scott) would Gothicize the whole of the country. Palmerston even went so far as to say that he would welcome a new order of architecture, specially designed to meet modern needs—a remarkable statement, and one wonders exactly what he meant by it.

The arguments dragged on for some months and finally Palmerston again summoned Scott, and after much smoothing of the way and giving Scott to understand that the Gothic style had won the day, Palmerston quietly suggested that he had been thinking of appointing a coadjutor, who would in fact make the designs. Scott was so stunned by this latest development that he felt himself unable to do justice to his case by word of mouth, but retired to write a strongly worded protest. We do not know the outcome of this letter, for Scott said 'I forget whether he replied', and he also remarked 'I also wrote, if I remember rightly, to Mr. Gladstone'.

After this exchange Scott, for the first time in twenty-four years' practice, took a holiday. He then prepared new designs in the Byzantine manner, which he thought 'both original and pleasing in effect', but Palmerston would have none of them and referred to the scheme as a 'regular mongrel affair'. Scott then decided that rather than let the project fall into the hands of the enemy he would make at once a hero and a martyr of himself, and study the Italian style. So ended the 'Battle of the Styles'. Scott had in fact, one more humiliation to suffer, namely that of the Law Courts, but here it was clearly a matter of the better man winning.

After the Whitehall débâcle Scott could never again be looked upon as being the chief representative of the Gothic Revival style, and his culminating success, the

Fig. 223

St Pancras Hotel,
London (1866–71),
by Sir George Gilbert Scott

An example of the Gothic Revival

Albert Memorial, has had many rude things said about it. One of the kindest that has been said about it is that it should be regarded as a valuable document of mid-Victorian taste. Yet the very stridency of the design and colour of this extraordinary shrine imparts a compelling quality which is memorable, whilst the assemblage of past genius which so boldly parades round the base, romantic rubbing shoulders with classicist, medieval architects with Renaissance ones, philosophers and thinkers discoursing and gesturing with equal authority, shows either a sublime sense of humour or such uncommon broadness of mind and culture, that we have cause to revise our opinion of its creator.

Scott, as we have already noted, was representative of the period, and before we leave him altogether it may be worth while to examine the more professional side of his career in greater detail. Of his industry there can be no doubt; it was said during his lifetime that he could take a train to any part of the country and be within easy reach of one of his buildings, or the site where work was in progress. In medieval and Renaissance times the architect had been content to rest his fame on two or three buildings, but in mid-nineteenth-century England architects had huge practices. Street, who worked at a phenomenal speed, together with Shaw and Waterhouse, to mention only three, put up a very great number of buildings. Scott was also representative of his age in the self-confidence and energy with which he went about his business, for there can have been few ages in which so much sheer hard work was done.

Perhaps two statements that Scott made can be used to throw light on the way architects regarded their work and practice. Of his drawings for the first competition for the government offices he says, 'With all its faults, however, it would have been a noble structure; and the set of drawings was perhaps the best ever sent in to a competition, or nearly so'. It has been a common belief that these drawings were later used for the St Pancras Hotel, but this has now been disproved. Of this building (Fig. 223) he said, 'It is often spoken of to me as the finest building in London. My own belief is that it is possibly too good for its purpose'. The first of these statements seems to suggest that an architectural scheme should be judged by the quality of the drawings on paper. But this can lead to a very superficial assessment of an attitude to the problem of building. After all, the quality of a building is not what it looks like on paper, but how it works, whether it serves its purpose efficiently and whether it looks good from all angles. For, as we have seen so many times, fine architecture is primarily the efficient organization of space, not the application of pleasant washes of colour to paper. The second statement, '. . . that it is possibly too good for its purpose', shows again the Victorian passion for imposing arbitrary values on architecture. No building can be too good for its purpose. We shall see in due course that many of the buildings which were considered to be not worth the name of architecture, namely bridges, warehouses, and office blocks, were the very buildings to which the architects of future generations were to turn for inspiration.

Ruskin

He who was probably the greatest of the Victorian arbiters of taste, and whose work we must now examine, was not an architect at all, but an art critic. John Ruskin (1819–1900) was the child of rich parents, who appreciated him and encouraged him to express his genius from the earliest age. They considered him too delicate to go to school and too brilliant to be subjected to any rigid system of tuition. His early life was sheltered, almost isolated, and during his years at Oxford he took tea with his mother every day. His religion was rigorously Protestant, with fixed hours each day for Bible-reading and religious study. On Sundays, whilst he lived with his parents, screens were erected in front of his paintings in case their bright colours might distract the mind from its sinful state.

There are thirty-nine volumes of the library edition of his works, of which the five volumes of *Modern Painters*, *The Seven Lamps of Architecture*, the three volumes of *The Stones of Venice*, *Lectures on Architecture and Painting*, and *The Two Paths*, contain his best work. It is almost impossible to summarize the contents of these works, for so uneven is the writing, so mixed the quality of the thought, that by taking carefully selected passages it would be possible to prove almost anything. The best examples would show a rare and perceptive intellect, with a profound grasp of fundamental principles; others, however, would suggest the wanderings of a muddled, almost incoherent mind, or the capriciousness of blind prejudice. Yet for all this he was widely read and admired in his own time and had great influence on public taste. For

our purposes the *Seven Lamps* is probably the most important of his writings, though the section on 'The Nature of Gothic' in *The Stones of Venice*, contains magnificent passages on the fundamentals of the style.

It is paradoxical that Ruskin should be looked upon as the champion and instigator of the Gothic Revival in this country, for he wrote *The Seven Lamps* with little knowledge of the movement, and what little he did know of it he did not like. Later, when he realized what the result of his championship of Venetian Gothic had been, he bitterly regretted the influence he had had, and decried the ugliness which he saw all around him, but to little avail. The 'streaky bacon' style, so splendid in Pisa and Venice, persisted, and the alternate red and yellow bands of brick can still be seen in plenty in our towns today.

It was not until the mid-fifties, after long and careful study of Gothic, that Ruskin became interested in the Gothic Revival in England. He was particularly interested in ornament, and this aspect is developed in the *Lamp of Life*. This is one of the best, perhaps the most 'illuminating', of the *Lamps* and is well worth close study. It is this emphasis on ornament that constitutes his most important and vital point of difference from Pugin. To Pugin, structure was always the paramount consideration; to Ruskin, the most important feature was decoration and ornament. Ruskin probably came to this conclusion because, in his study of Gothic architecture, he had found that however crude the ornament might be, it had a life and vitality which he did not see in work going on around him at that time. He saw, moreover, that it was these very imperfections and irregularities which gave Gothic ornament and planning its interest and virility. By comparison, the mechanical regularity of nineteenth-century mass-production was dull and lifeless.

The only building with which Ruskin had any direct connection was, unfortunately, a failure. This was the Oxford Museum, and despite all his enthusiasm and optimism the building remains unfinished. It was to have been a grand essay in the Venetian Gothic style. Ruskin had promised to get members of the Pre-Raphaelite Brotherhood to work on it, and he himself designed some windows. However, after much wrangling the University authorities withdrew their financial support, and the building—never very successful as a design—came to a halt.

Ruskin's complex life and activities present a most perplexing subject for discussion. He certainly exerted a wide influence in his own day, unfortunately not always for the best. His writing was an inspiration to William Morris, with whom he shared an interest in social conditions of the day, and Ruskin did in fact write pamphlets and books of social criticism, such as *Unto this Last*. His ideas on basic artistic principles were sometimes profound, but occasionally faintly comic. In the *Lamp of Beauty*, for example, his criticism cannot fail to strike the modern reader as amusing, and the passage where he considers the relationship between the Greek fret and bismuth crystals is equally naïve. Yet might there not be a premonition here of the interest that micro-photography and the structure of crystals was going to arouse in artists and designers in the mid-twentieth century? These examples could be

multiplied almost ad infinitum, and the best advice is to read one or two passages from the works, for they are always stimulating reading.

Morris

William Morris was another influential force on the development of nineteenth-century taste and there is cause for unending regret that he misunderstood the nature of the machine so completely. He had seen the Great Exhibition and had been revolted by the poor standard of the goods which had been exhibited there. Seldom had such a fine building housed such a collection of poor design and bad workmanship. Morris realized the poor quality of the designs and, mistakenly, began to hold the machine responsible for it. Like the romantics of the period, he believed in the dignity of labour and the value of sound craftsmanship. Morris himself joined the ill-assorted Pre-Raphaelite Brotherhood, which the painters Millais, Holman Hunt and D. G. Rossetti had formed in 1848. As their name suggests, they tried to get back to the honesty and truthfulness-to-nature of the early Italian painters. But the association was short-lived and hardly lasted ten years before it broke up completely.

During his time at Oxford Morris studied theology, ecclesiastical history, and medieval poetry, and—amongst the modern poets—Tennyson and Ruskin. When he left Oxford he studied architecture in the office of G. E. Street, and in 1862 set up the business of Morris, Marshall and Faulkner, 'Church Furnishers'. The firm specialized in church decoration carving, stained glass and metal work, and they also designed paper hangings and carpets. The firm prospered, and in 1875 Morris became sole manager. In 1881 he managed to enlarge the business, and established a tapestry factory at Merton. Six years later he published his own version of the *Odyssey* and became interested in typography. This interest led to the founding of the Kelmscott Press, and to one of his most outstanding achievements, the Kelmscott *Chaucer*, which took five years to plan and two years to print.

Morris's interests were not confined to the arts, however, for in 1884 he became an early and enthusiastic member of the Socialist movement, and throughout his life he was interested in radical politics. If he had carried this radicalism into his work in the fields of industrial design, the whole course of design in the latter part of the nineteenth and early twentieth centuries might well have had a different complexion. There can be little doubt that Morris was a brilliant designer; even today the freshness and virility of his designs cannot be denied. Few designers of any generation have been able to impart such beauty and sense of natural growth to plant forms. Many of his designs would be completely acceptable to contemporary eyes, with a little simplification and a rather fresher scheme of colour, as his own would often seem dowdy to modern eyes. Above all, his designs never lost their sense of purpose, and he always recognized that his wallpapers and carpets were intended to go on a flat surface. This is in strong contrast to many of the extremely naturalistic designs of fruit and flowers, which had been in such evidence at the Great Exhibition, and which look as if you could squash them if you put your foot down or touched a wall. He had, above all, a passion for beauty, which was to be achieved irrespective of cost or speed of manufacture; and the stress he placed on the 'hand-made' has given a lasting value to the articles which he designed.

Perhaps it may be felt that we have spent too long on these mid-Victorian figures, and yet they were important not only for what they did but for the influence they have had on present-day thought. There can be little doubt that much of our modern thinking about architecture and the allied arts is the result of ideals and prejudices built up in this period. Perhaps if we understand some of the causes of much of the muddled thinking which still goes on we may be able to do something more constructive about it.

Of the other architects working at this period, several are worth mention and study. It is difficult to attempt to put them into any kind of order of merit, and each student will have his own particular favourite.

William Butterfield (1814–1900) has been considerably underrated, and is now coming in for the kind of attention he deserves. His church architecture is always striking, with its rich kaleidoscopic use of colour. Some may find this aspect of his work too strident, but working within the limits of the Gothic Revival style he managed to concoct an architecture which is at once personal and intensely expressive. His best-known work is All Saints' Church, Margaret Street, London. Here his sense of rich decoration both inside and out is seen to best advantage, and produces a scheme of great force and originality.

J. F. Bentley (1839–1902) must be men-

Plate 45 The Roman Catholic Cathedral, Westminster (begun 1894), by J. F. Bentley

tioned, if only for his very impressive Westminster Cathedral (1894–1903; Pl. 45). The design is based on a close study of Italian Byzantine models and Santa Sophia, though the plan bears a strong resemblance to French Romanesque examples. The management of the interior recaptures something of the grandeur and massiveness of the earlier churches, though the exterior is less successful.

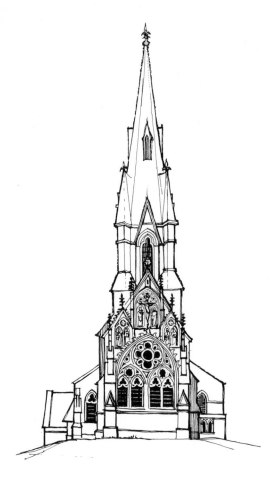

Fig. 224 St Mary's, Studley Royal
(1871–8), by William Burges
—east end

The work of William Burges (1827–81) is also of interest, as he was a considerable scholar and admired particularly the work of Villard de Honnecourt. His work as a designer has an aggressive quality and his best interiors approach the grandiose. St Mary's Church, Studley Royal, Yorkshire (Fig. 224), has a particularly fine east-end and a beautifully domed chancel.

DOMESTIC ARCHITECTURE

The last decades of the century in England produced some of the most remarkable domestic architecture in Europe. The three leading figures were Shaw, Voysey, and Webb. They all had much in common, yet all produced work of marked individuality. They shared a respect for, and appreciation of, the raw materials of their trade, a desire to build in the traditional methods and materials, and the ability to plan simply and efficiently.

Shaw

Of the three, Richard Norman Shaw (1831–1912) was the most versatile, though not necessarily the best architect. Like so many other architects, he worked in Street's offices, where he succeeded Webb as chief draughtsman. Sometime in 1862 or 1863 he set up his own offices and went into partnership with the younger Nesfield (1835–88). It seems safe to assume that in their early years together Nesfield had a great influence on Shaw, and may well have been the stylistic instigator in many instances. At his best, Shaw reintroduced a feeling of delicacy, and his work shows a fine sense of composition. This can be seen in the Old Swan House, Chelsea (Fig. 225). His own house, 6, Ellerdale Road, Hampstead, London (Fig. 226), is also a piece of carefully-considered design. In both these houses he uses his favourite device, the Ipswich window. This is a three-light window, the central light being double the width of the side lights and having a semicircular arch in place of the transoms which divide the adjoining openings. In 1888 and 1890 Shaw built 170, Queen's Gate, London (Fig. 227),

*Fig. 225 Swan House, Chelsea (1876),
by Norman Shaw. A design of
rare distinction*

*Fig. 226 No. 6 Ellerdale Road, Hampstead
(1875), by Norman Shaw
A novel design with carefully
considered proportions and
detail*

Fig. 227

*No. 170 Queen's Gate, London
(1888), by Norman Shaw*

and also Bryanston, Dorset, and here, with his unornamented use of brickwork, he paved the way for the English domestic neo-Georgian style of 1910 and after.

Although in his early years he reacted against the grossness of High Victorian, he was later to introduce, to quote Pevsner, '. . . the more reprehensible Baroque-Edwardian-Imperial-Palladianism of official architecture.' Of this phase nothing is more Baroque than the Piccadilly Hotel of 1905.

During the '80s and '90s his studio was a most influential school; many of the next generation of architects were working with him and some of these were to become teachers.

Voysey and Webb

Neither C. F. A. Voysey (1857–1941) nor Philip Webb (1831–1915) was so prolific as Shaw, nor did they design on such a grandiose scale. But in their quieter way each had a valuable contribution to make to the development of domestic architecture, not only in England but also on the Continent, where their designs were eagerly awaited, and studied with enthusiasm. Webb was probably the more retiring and self-effacing of the two.

Webb's reliance on strictly practical planning and respect for local materials and methods of construction is illustrated in his collaboration with William Morris over the Red House, Bexleyheath (Fig. 228). Smeaton Manor, Yorkshire (Fig. 229), was one of his most influential designs, and well in advance of anything designed at that time. Here he shows that respect for local materials which had been evident from his earliest major work, Arisaig, near Fort William, in Scotland. To appreciate just how far Webb was in advance of his time, it is worth putting some of his designs beside houses built in the late 1920s or early 30s; they do not look at all out of place.

His greatest work was 'Clouds', near East Knoyle, Wilts. (Fig. 230). Unfortunately this splendid house has suffered a major reconstruction, and is now much mutilated. It was designed for a particular purpose, and Webb laboured over it for five years—almost to the exclusion of all else. The house was built to provide a setting for the great house-parties that were so fashionable a part of the society life of that day. The owners, the Honourable Percy Wyndham and his wife, were noted for their hospitality, and their parties were frequented by artists, writers, and statesmen. The plan, like that of all his larger houses, is based on a two-storey central hall with a gallery giving access to the bedrooms. In 1887, after many delays and difficulties, the house was completed at a cost of between £75,000 and £80,000, only for the greater part of the interior to be gutted by fire two years later. However, this was carefully reconstructed by Webb himself. Lighter and less gloomy than some of his earlier work, the interior rejoices in some delightfully crisp plaster decoration which Webb designed himself. Externally the house has that uncluttered, workmanlike appearance that is so typical of the architect. Throughout his life he would only accept a commission if it appealed to him, and as his work was much sought after, unsuccessful clients often insisted that their own architects should design in the Webb style.

Webb had begun his career by making a great success of designing wallpapers, textiles and carpets, and it was through coming to regard this as too transient an art-form that he turned to the more lasting and permanent medium of architecture. His houses made an immediate impression on the Continent, and he was widely appreciated in this country, though his output remained comparatively small. It was a great disappointment to him that during the 1890s, when the Gothic Revival was a spent force, the younger generation of architects turned not to first principles, as he would have wished, but to the neo-Georgian style in the manner of Shaw. During the last years of his life he withdrew into almost complete retirement.

In a paper to the Design Club in 1911, and published in *The British Architect* of 17 January that year, C. F. A. Voysey summarized human needs in relation to domestic architecture. Amongst the list of qualities that he thought a house should possess we find: cheerfulness, simplicity, breadth, warmth, economy of upkeep, evenness of temperature, and making the home the frame to its inmates. These admirable

THREE

WEBB

HOUSES

Fig. 228 The Red House, Bexleyheath, Kent (1859) — the house designed for William Morris

Fig. 229 Smeaton Manor, Yorkshire (1887)

Fig. 230 Clouds, East Knoyle, Wilts. (1880)

TWO

VOYSEY

HOUSES

Fig. 231 Moor Crag, near Windermere (1898)

Fig. 232

The Pastures,
North Luffenham,
Rutland (1901)

qualities would make a very desirable dwelling, and there is cause for regret that they have not been more widely observed—not only by his contemporaries, but by later generations of designers as well.

The essence of a Voysey house can easily be summarized: it is white and its windows are grouped in long horizontal bands. Moor Crag, near Windermere (1898; Fig. 231), was one of his most influential houses, and was the beginning of the best period of his work. It is so simple a house and so direct in its statement that it is difficult to say anything about it. Equally attractive is 'The Pastures', North Luffenham (1901; Fig. 232). The design is direct and unpretentious but the whole aspect is enlivened by the beautifully placed arch of the porch. This relieves the otherwise austere rectangles of

the windows and brings the whole composition to life.

THE USE OF IRON, AND THE CRYSTAL PALACE

Throughout the period we have just reviewed there were important developments taking place which cannot be ignored any longer, for ultimately they were to prove of more importance in the development of twentieth-century architecture than those we have just been considering. So far, the architects we have studied had been content to use the traditional building-methods and materials. But as we have already seen, there was also a group of buildings which were the work of engineers, rather than architects, using the new material—iron. In their

TABLE 3

SOME EARLY STRUCTURES WHICH EXPLOITED THE USE OF IRON

Date	England	Date	America	Date	The Continent
1771–81	Coalbrookdale bridge				
1793	Bridge across river Wear, Sunderland				
1795–6	Buildwas Bridge, Shropshire				
1796	Flax-spinning mill at Ditherington, Shrewsbury (cast iron columns)				
1801	1801 Telford's design to replace London Bridge (600′ span)				
1815	Brighton Pavilion (Nash)				
1818	Telford's Menai Straits Bridge (first suspension-bridge; 579′ span)			1824	Seguin bridges on Rhône near Toulouse (with suspension-bridge)
1836	Brunel's Clifton Suspension-Bridge designed (not completed until 1864)	1837	Store in Gold St., New York (Lorillard)	1843	Bibliothèque Ste Geneviève, Paris (Labrouste)
		1848	Cast iron factory in New York (Bogardus)		
		1849–50	Jayne Buildings, Philadelphia		
1851	Crystal Palace				
1852	King's Cross Station				
1853	Saltair Mills				
1854	Paddington Station	1854	Harper Bros. Store, New York (Bogardus)		
1855–6	Jamaica Street, Glasgow				
1857	Reading Room, British Museum (dome only 2′ less than Pantheon)				
1858	Boat store, Naval Dockyard, Sheerness			1858–68	Bibliothèque Nationale, Paris (Labrouste)
1859	Bridge at Saltash (new system of construction)			1871–2	Chocolate Factory at Noisel-sur-Marne (Jules Saulnier; early steel-frame building)
1864–5	Oriel Chambers, Liverpool				
1868	St Pancras Station (240′ span)			1889	Eiffel Tower

own day these buildings were too often overlooked as not being worthy of the name 'architecture'. Nash had, of course, used cast iron in the Royal Pavilion at Brighton as early as 1815, but the way he used it there was not likely to give rise to a new aesthetic. It was the more industrial and utilitarian uses that were to provide the outlet for a new style.

As usual, it was the changing social conditions which gave rise to the need for new building-types. The rapidly growing railways needed not only bridges to carry the lines over rivers and canals but also stations where people could board this new and very fashionable mode of transport. The new machines of mass-production, largely in the spinning and weaving industries at first, needed factories to house the machines and warehouses to store and handle the materials which the machines produced. To sell and display the greater quantities and varieties of merchandise which the machines were producing, department stores, with large open selling spaces, were necessary.

Another important building-type which began to appear in the latter part of the nineteenth century was the imposing office-block, which housed the highly specialized and profitable concerns which carried on the expanding commerce. These concerns — banks, insurance companies, etc. — wanted not only to provide accommodation for their offices but also to provide buildings which had prestige value and suggested affluence, in order to inspire confidence in their clients. The following table lists, in chronological order, important buildings which made use of iron and steel.

The early use of cast iron in bridge-construction certainly produced some designs of refreshing simplicity. The famous bridge at Coalbrookdale, in Shropshire (1777–81), which spans 100 feet in one single arch, is surprisingly modern in conception considering its date (Fig. 233). From the 1790s onwards there was a rapid increase, both in number and length of span, of iron bridges in this country. Thomas Telford (1757–1834) was responsible for a number of very beautiful bridges one example being Craigellachie Bridge, Banff (Fig. 234). The Buildwas Bridge in Shropshire designed by him had a span of 130 feet, and his design to replace London Bridge with a single arched span of 600 feet of cast iron had great delicacy and poise.

At the same time as the development of the arched bridge came that of the suspension-bridge. This was an idea of great antiquity, and had been known in China for some centuries. In the 1740s a tiny bridge over the Tees was built just above Middleton, with a span of only 70 feet and a walk only 2 feet wide. This bridge was replaced by the present structure in 1802, but there were no other attempts at suspension-bridges in this country until 1818, when Telford's Menai Strait bridge, with its main span of over 570 feet, was constructed (Fig. 235).

The most impressive of all British suspension-bridges, however, is the Clifton Suspension-Bridge at Bristol (designed 1829–31, begun 1836); this was the work of Isambard Kingdom Brunel. The majesty and power of the design is best appreciated from the road beneath, where the massive pylons are seen to make a perfect foil to the lighter tracery of the iron work. In the original design it was proposed to have

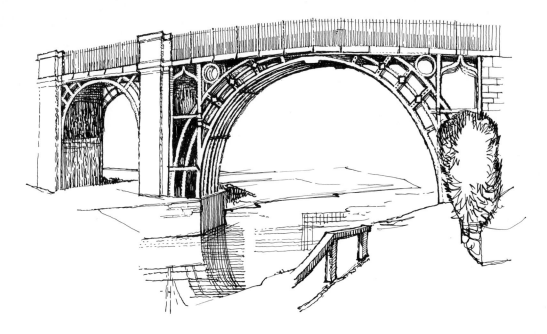

Fig. 233 Coalbrookdale Bridge (1777–81). Designer doubtful

Fig. 234 Craigellachie Bridge (1815), designed by Thomas Telford

Fig. 235 The Menai Suspension Bridge (1818), designed by Thomas Telford

Fig. 236 The Clifton Suspension Bridge (begun 1836),
designed by I. K. Brunel

These early iron bridges (Figs. 233–6) show the way in
which the engineer approached the problem of design

Egyptian detailing on the pylons, but fortunately this idea came to nothing. Any worrying detail on the massive, battered end-pieces would sadly detract from the stark simplicity of their well-managed proportions (Fig. 236). On the Continent the work of Marc Seguin is worth mentioning. His suspension-bridge across the Rhône uses wire ropes instead of chains. This idea was taken over by the Americans, and the German immigrant Roebling designed several bridges using this technique. His bridge at Niagara Falls no longer exists, and his most famous work is the Brooklyn Bridge, New York, which is still one of the city's landmarks.

Aesthetically pleasing as many of these early bridges are to the modern student, it must be realized that their refreshing simplicity was the outcome of common sense and good engineering practice. After the excesses of much of the 'architecture' of the period, it is simply the straightforward use of material which makes them significant in the development of subsequent building.

The same qualities are to be found in the use of iron in the new warehouses and factories that were going up at the same time. The interior of the flax-spinning mill of Benyon, Bage and Marshall, at Ditherington, Shrewsbury (1796; Pl. 46), shows great refinement and cleanness of line. The use of cast iron columns, of subtle shape, gives the interior an openness and lightness which is remarkable for its date. The use of cast iron on the exterior of a building such as the

Plate 46 The Benyon, Bage & Marshall flax-spinning mill at Ditherington, Shrewsbury (1796)

Plate 47 *Warehouses, Jamaica Street, Glasgow (1855–6)*

Plate 48

*The Oriel Chambers,
Liverpool (1864–5),
by Peter Ellis*

Jamaica Street Warehouses in Glasgow (1855–6; Pl. 47), or the Oriel Chambers, Liverpool (1864–5; Pl. 48), imparts to these façades a quality of lightness and delicacy which is new. The way Peter Ellis managed the contrast between advancing and receding masses on the Oriel Chambers shows a most advanced piece of architectural thinking. Another uncompromising façade is that which G. T. Greene designed for the Boat Store at Sheerness Naval Dockyard (1858–61; Pl. 49). The structure here is expressed with complete frankness and, as in the Liverpool and Glasgow examples, glass is used with great success.

There can be little doubt that Sir Joseph Paxton's work on Crystal Palace had given some impetus to the use of the new material, and in this way he provided another milestone on the way towards a new architecture. It is often implied that the Crystal Palace was a turning-point in Paxton's career. This is far from the truth, for he was already well established by the time he came to make the designs. He had been building in glass for 20 years before 1851, and his designs included those for the Lily House at Chatsworth. He had speculated successfully on the rapidly growing railways, had had experience of conventional building, and was a consultant on public parks and suburbs. Like so many of his contemporaries,

Plate 49   The Boat Store, Royal Naval Dockyard, Sheerness (1858–61), by G. T. Greene

Plates 46–9 show the remarkable forward-looking quality of a certain section of British architecture of the period

he seems to have had an insatiable appetite for hard work, for besides the activities already mentioned he was the head gardener at Chatsworth, and generally held to be the 'greatest gardener of his time', to quote *The Times* obituary notice. His work at Chatsworth included a very successful series of botanical experiments, particularly with the more exotic plants, and his interest in trees resulted in the introduction of several new species to this country.

When the competition for a building to house the new exhibition was announced, Paxton did not compete. There were, however, several schemes of great interest, all of them using ferro-vitreous construction. Two of these, an Irish entry from Richard Turner (who had been Burton's collaborator in the design of the glasshouses at Kew), and a scheme by the Frenchman, Hector Horeau, were particularly interesting and noteworthy. However, the commission, which consisted of the Duke of Buccleuch and the Earl of Ellesmere, the architects Charles Barry, C. R. Cockerell, and Prof. T. L. Donaldson, and the engineers Robert Stephenson, I. K. Brunel and William Cubitt, turned all the entries down and decided that the commissioners' own building committee should produce a project.

Despite the fact that the best practitioners in the country were employed on the scheme, the result was completely impracticable. A large part of the structure was to have been of brick, and it is difficult to see how they intended to get the building completed in time. The tenders were already out when Paxton submitted his scheme in July 1850. His idea was an extension of the methods he had used in the Lily House at Chatsworth. His first sketch had been done on a piece of blotting paper, and a more complete sketch was published in the *Illustrated London News*, along with a low bid by the constructors Fox and Henderson. This new idea proved acceptable, and work was put in hand. The cost was to be £150,000—or £79,000 if the materials remained the property of Fox and Henderson after dismantling.

Turner's scheme was to have cost £300,000 and would have consisted of a rectangular glass-and-iron frame building, 1,440 feet by 1,060 feet, with four small domes and a fifth one larger than the others, rising to a height of 200 feet. Paxton's design was a vast structure, consisting of a tall central nave, galleried aisles, and arched transept. The overall dimensions were 1,848 feet long by 408 feet wide, with an extension on the north side 936 feet by 58 feet wide, making a total width of 466 feet. The ground floor covered an area of 772,784 square feet, and with the addition of 217,100 square feet for the galleries, a total of 989,884 square feet was available for exhibition space. The enormous roof area of $17\frac{3}{4}$ acres was drained by Paxton's own design of guttering, with the rain running away through hollow columns acting as down-pipes. There were 3,000 tons of cast iron and 300 tons of wrought iron, 3,300 columns, 2,150 girders, 372 roof-trusses, 24 miles of Paxton guttering, 205 miles of sash-bars, 900,000 square feet of glass and 600,000 cubic feet of timber. This may seem a very large amount of wood in a building which has become a landmark in the development of metal construction. Yet it had been part of the

Plate 50   The Crystal Palace, London (1851), by Sir Joseph Paxton

specification, for this was, after all, primarily intended as a temporary structure. The many influential critics of the building, however, seized upon this apparently excessive amount of timber as a possible fire hazard after the Exhibition. The vast amount of material was finally assembled in seventeen weeks (Pl. 50).

This apparently miraculous achievement was the result of a carefully worked-out schedule and a vast amount of planning beforehand. The whole building was designed to a 24-foot module, and all the elements were so designed that they could be mass-produced and then erected on the site. The value of this method of working was further proved when the entire building was taken down and re-erected on a new site when the exhibition was over.

The whole scheme was given a very mixed reception. Pugin, Ruskin, and the ecclesiologists detested it. The critic of the Ecclesia-

stical Society did admit the admirable quality of the design, but found it formless and the infinite duplication of the same component parts destructive of its claim to high architectural merit. This accusation of formlessness is not hard to understand when we consider the type of building, with its very rigid definition of space, to which the architectural critics and the public of the day were accustomed. Today, with our more fluid conception of form and space, the merits of Paxton's achievement are easier to grasp. There can be no doubt that Paxton had created a new space-concept. The huge areas of shimmering glass supported on flimsy iron columns must have come as a complete surprise to the Victorians, with their liking for substance and solidarity.

Quite apart from its aesthetic merit, which was considerable, the Crystal Palace also proved a triumph for the new techniques of standardization and mass production. This was in every way a building of the machine-age produced by the machine-age. Unfortunately the machine was not to be accepted quite so readily as that. The new inventions came to be looked upon either as a quick way of producing cheap and shoddy ornament covering bad workmanship or as an enemy of creative design. There was plenty of evidence that the machine-made products were of bad design; but nobody seemed capable of realizing that the machine could only produce the sort of design that was fed into it, and that if the design was good then the end-product would be good as well.

In the past it has been the custom to dismiss the Victorian period as of little consequence, architecturally speaking. In the worst examples the standard was low, particularly in the fields of applied design, but there were a few buildings which did advance the course of architectural development in this country, as well as having influence abroad. The pity of it is, however, that in too many cases these buildings were not recognized in their own country, and despite our lead in design the most important developments were to be found on the Continent and in America.

Developments in Europe

England was not alone in experiencing a wave of architectural revivalism during the nineteenth century; the fashion swept through Europe with the same energy and enthusiasm. The movement, though it took slightly different forms in each country, remained remarkably uniform, and indeed whether the city were London or Paris, Munich or Milan, mattered little architecturally; a street or square lifted bodily from one European city would not have looked too much out of place in another. The widespread circulation and popularity of the many pattern books and important architectural writings of such men as J. N. L. Durand, whose *Précis des leçons d'architecture données à l'École Polytechnique* became almost a bible of architectural styles during the 1840s, doubtless account in a large part for this uniformity.

In a review such as the present many omissions must be made, and to some degree the choice of buildings becomes almost a personal one. However, there are some examples which are important in the sense that they point the way to the style of the twentieth century or show particular aspects of the revival style at its best.

THE GREEK REVIVAL

We have already seen that, generally speaking, the best examples of buildings in the Greek-revival style were museums, and that Smirke's British Museum and Schinkel's Altes Museum in Berlin were undoubtedly two of the finest examples of Greek revival buildings in Europe. Both use the Ionic order, and the south front of the British Museum (Fig. 217) provides the most overwhelmingly impressive use of the classic façade in England.

Karl Friedrich Schinkel (1781–1841), like Inigo Jones before him, made his first impression not as an architect but as a designer for the stage; he was also a painter of some distinction. At first glance the long unpedimented façade of his Altes Museum in Berlin (1824–8; Fig. 218) appears merely a correct archaeological exercise. On closer acquaintance, however, its regard for sound constructive principles becomes apparent. The Ionic columns are certainly most beautifully proportioned and detailed. The weakness at the corners, so difficult to avoid where long rows of columns are used, is overcome by the flat buttresses which replace the outer columns. In this way a firm containing frame is built up around the structure. Comparison with Brongniart's Paris Bourse of 1808–15 shows clearly the strength given to the façade by Schinkel's method. The huge columns of the Altes Museum suggest immediately a single storey, and it is only as we begin to penetrate the gloom of the portico that it is made clear by the double flight of stairs and the dark mural (Schinkel's own design) that it is, in fact, a double-storey building. It is then that we become conscious of the rectangular attic arising over the centre of the giant portico. It is in this way that we realize that this façade, at first sight so dull and academic, does in fact, tell us something of the building behind. Underneath this attic is a domed central space to provide room for a sculpture gallery. To accommodate the pictures, Schinkel, with an almost prophetic touch, provided screens at right angles to the windows, so much like the movable screen in the art galleries of the mid-twentieth century. Schinkel also worked in Potsdam and Berlin on various schemes of reconstruction and enlargement.

RUNDBOGENSTIL

Another important example of the influence of Durand (and he appears to have had more influence outside his country than inside) is the *Rundbogenstil* movement in Germany. Most popular during the 1830s and 1840s, it could well be called the German counterpart of the Victorian Gothic style in England—for the latter style never achieved the popularity on the Continent that it did in this country. Broadly, the style was based on the round arched styles of Early Christian, Byzantine, and Romanesque. The style spread to other countries, but it is particularly Germanic in flavour. Burklein's Railway Station at Munich, now partially rebuilt, and the Johanneum at Hamburg (unfortunately destroyed in the Second World War) were examples of the style.

ARCHITECTURE IN FRANCE

During the first half of the nineteenth century, France exerted little influence on European developments, but during the 1850s there was a revival of interest in French work. This was largely due to the influence of the École des Beaux Arts, and during the second half of the century ever-increasing numbers of architectural students made their way to Paris to study. The influence of the school was enormous, and students from the Beaux Arts filled many important teaching posts in schools of architecture throughout Europe. Such training was particularly favoured in both North and South America, and the first schools of architecture founded in North America were on very similar lines to those of the Beaux Arts. Throughout the nineteenth century, however, architecture in Paris showed very little development. As in other European capitals, the most exciting building was that done for public bodies; private building was, on the whole, carefully correct in detail but uninteresting. During the first decades of the century the piety of the restored Bourbons had led to something of a revival in church-building, most of it undistinguished. The adoption of the basilican plan, however, tended to produce richer and more interesting interior arrangements than the open-galleried arrangements so popular in England.

During the middle decades of the century the work of Eugène Haussman in Paris at once transformed the city and made it the model on which many European cities based their development and replanning. Haussman concentrated his efforts on the *street*, firstly as a means of communication and secondly as part of a uniform scheme. The first of his objectives he achieved by making his boulevards straight and wide (cannon-shot boulevards, as they are often called). Napoleon III had first seen the advantages of long straight streets for the rapid movement of troops when quelling riots, but it took the dynamic energy of Haussman to carry out his ideas. The second he achieved by imposing a uniform design on the façades of the blocks which lined his boulevards. Though the design of the detail of these façades may have been nondescript they

were well proportioned, and as no one block was allowed to dominate, the result was homogeneous. The arrangement of accommodation was also standardized. The ground floor was usually given over to shops, which had extra storage or work-room space in the mezzanine floor; above the mezzanine there were three floors providing living-space for middle-class families; whilst attic floors accommodated the servants.

These attic floors also gave these blocks a very characteristic feature, the mansard roof, which was frequently concave or convex in profile.

There are many buildings which could be chosen to illustrate the architectural achievement of nineteenth-century Paris: the Madeleine, with its imposing Roman exterior and Corinthian columns; the Romanesque inspiration and magnificent site of the Sacré-Cœur; or E. E. Viollet-le-Duc's church St-Denys-de-l'Estrée, which is perhaps as near to the High Victorian revival style of England as France ever reached.

But perhaps the most interesting of the buildings, because it is the most French and at the same time marks the end of an epoch and a style of living that we shall never see again, is the Paris Opéra (1861–74; Pl. 51). The work of J. L. C. Garnier, the building epitomizes the style of the third quarter of the century. Others have tried to copy the lushness and the bombast, but none has succeeded completely. The plan is one of great complexity, yet the exterior with its well-placed sculpture and its semi-dome, which expresses the auditorium, shows great plasticity of feeling. The richly coloured marbles, the gilt, and the glitter, make this

Plate 51

*The Opéra, Paris
(1861–74),
by Charles Garnier
—the foyer*

*The magnificence
caught the spirit
of the age,
the like of which
we shall never
see again*

Plate 52

*The Bibliothèque
Sainte-Geneviève, Paris
(1843–50),
by Henri Labrouste*

*Revivalist architecture
at its most tasteful*

an unforgettable building. There is only one other building to rival the Opéra—and that again is by Garnier—the Casino at Monte Carlo. Right at the end of the century Charles Girault designed the Petit Palais for the Exhibition of 1900. A building of great charm, which has a central entrance with semicircular entablature abutting onto a dome, it has influenced many examples of twentieth-century revival architecture.

There are two buildings which are of particular significance, for in them can be seen the beginnings of the twentieth-century approach to the problem of architecture: the Bibliothèque Sainte-Geneviève (1845–50) and the reading-room of the Bibliothèque Nationale (1862–8). They are both the work of Henri Labrouste and both are remarkable. The exterior of the Sainte-Geneviève draws inspiration from the Italian Renaissance and shows a splendid sense of restraint and a sure sense of proportion and placing between the various parts (Pl. 52). But it is the reading-room of the Bibliothèque Nationale which is of the greater interest, and gives the deeper satisfaction to the modern student.

In the earlier building Labrouste had used iron construction in the interior with imagination and daring. In the later building he shows mature mastery of the medium. The sixteen cast iron pillars one foot in diameter and thirty-two feet high, which support the roof of the reading-room, are connected by semicircular arches made from light girders, which help to form the nine domical vaults. At the top of each dome there is a circular opening to give a perfectly even light over the reading-desks ranged beneath. The effect of lightness and grace that he manages

to create is well in advance of the period, and the decoration is equally light and tasteful.

Fine though the reading-room is, the stack room or *magasin central* as Labrouste called it, with its free and undecorated use of iron, shows perhaps more clearly the direction architecture was going to take. In his attempt to give maximum light over the four stories of racks (there was also a basement, as originally the library was planned to accommodate 900,000 books), Labrouste resorted to using open iron grilles. The play of light, falling from the glass roof, through these open grid-iron floors and passages, and across slender bridges connecting one floor to the other for direct communication, gives at once the impression—so characteristic of twentieth-century architecture—of fluid structure. In this simple and direct solution to a problem Labrouste comes near to anticipating the ideas and theories current nearly half a century later.

ARCHITECTURE IN AUSTRIA AND ITALY

Of the nineteenth-century developments, perhaps Vienna is the single European city which rivals Paris in the splendour of its reorganization. The city had been architecturally dormant during the first half of the century, but when Francis Joseph came to the throne in 1848 he determined that his capital should rival Paris. In 1857 the fortifications round the old town were removed and a year later Ludwig Förster won the competition for the layout of the Ringstrasse. His scheme took the next three decades to complete and underwent several modifications. The scheme comprises not only tree-lined boulevards but also open spaces with well-designed groups of public buildings in them. The buildings show a great variety of style, and the small group of architects which worked on them have managed to convey an impression of splendour and grace throughout the whole area.

Italy's contribution to the century's architecture need not detain us. The astonishing monument to Vittorio Emanuele II, which dominates the Imperial City from its vast platform at the end of the Corso Umberto, makes our own much-maligned Albert Memorial pale into insignificance. Of real interest, however, is the Galleria Vittorio Emanuele in Milan. Designed by Mengoni in the 1860s, it is the greatest of several of these arcades. There were over forty in Paris alone at one time, but none of them equalled the one in Milan. It is a remarkable piece of glass and iron work—light and spacious, and a superb addition to the town's amenities.

Developments in America

Early in the nineteenth century, American architects had given a new 'twist' to the classic revival by translating details into wood instead of using the more traditional stone-construction. This produced buildings which had a lightness and elegance that is novel in European eyes. The work of Wren, who had little influence on domestic design in England, proved more popular as a source of inspiration to the architects of the new world. In some cases, it is true, the American architects used the familiar recipes merely to give an effect, and to conceal a lack of real creative ability, but both Jefferson and Latrobe produced work of distinction in the Wren tradition.

However, the skyscraper is to be our main concern in this chapter, for this was the building which was to prove the most significant contribution to modern architecture that America had to offer. Exactly why the multi-storey building developed into a major art form on the American continent is hard to explain; it must be due to a number of deep and involved reasons. It may be possible to explain the phenomenon as a reaction against the flatness of the surrounding terrain, for most of the important early work on skyscrapers was done in Chicago, of which somebody once remarked that when there was a wind over the lake the waves formed bigger hills than were to be found on the land. The school of architecture formed there was certainly both important and influential.

A further reason why the Chicago school should have developed where it did may be that the city was almost razed by fire on 8 October 1871. The fire broke out on the west side, near lumber yards. The summer had been particularly rainless and the wooden houses were tinder dry. In six hours the fire had spread over two miles and was only brought under control with the help of heavy rain which began to fall after about twenty-seven hours—but not before two-thirds of the city had been destroyed, 17,500 buildings lost and 100,000 people made homeless. Wooden buildings had been so popular prior to the fire that they had given rise to a particular style of construction known as the 'balloon frame'. This consisted of a simple wooden frame on which planks were nailed. These simple buildings had satisfied the needs of a rapidly growing community and were really the product of early mass production, because they presupposed, firstly, the facilities to saw vast amounts of wood and, secondly, the machinery to produce thousands of nails. After the fire, wood was banned as a building material in the centre of the city and some years later in the outskirts as well.

Huge sums of money were raised both in America and abroad for the relief of hardship after the disaster, and helped to make Chicago one of the richest cities in the world. As the initial shock of the catastrophe wore off, a mood of unbounded optimism prevailed, and this, coupled with the flatness of the surrounding terrain, may have induced the builders to push their buildings upwards—in much the same way as the Egyptians 5,000 years before had pushed up their great pyramids from the flat plains of Egypt. Not that the architects did not have difficult technical problems to overcome, for the solid bedrock was too far down to provide a firm foundation, so a special method had to be evolved of floating the buildings on a raft of metal beams set in the mud.

The need and the means were there, and it only remained for the architects to supply the demand. The early buildings were not of great architectural merit, for the centres of architecture were still in New York and Boston. The Chicago style had been emerging in these two cities from the 1820s, in the work of such men as James Bogardus, who has been experimenting with metal construction. It is difficult to say exactly when the steel frame came into general use. Bogardus had used metal in façades and in the internal structure of buildings as early as 1848. The Chocolate Factory at Noisel-sur-Marne (1871–2) is also quoted as an early example of the steel frame, as is the Home Insurance Building, Chicago (1883–5). Iron had, as we have seen, been used in industrial and commercial buildings in this country as early as the end of the eighteenth century, and the work of English engineers and mill-wrights was certainly not unknown to American designers. This question is of great importance in the development of the skyscraper because, strictly speaking, a multi-storey building is not a skyscraper if it has bearing walls.

Before we go on to discuss the development of the skyscraper proper there are some multi-storey buildings with bearing walls which are important. The earliest of these is the Marshall Field Store (1885–7) by H. H. Richardson (Fig. 237). Richardson was a most influential architect not only in civic architecture (see Fig. 238), but also in domestic work (see Fig. 239), where he was a prime force in rejecting the antiquarian influences that were prevalent, and establishing in their place the importance of the basic necessities of construction and planning. In this respect he occupies a similar position to Voysey and Webb in England.

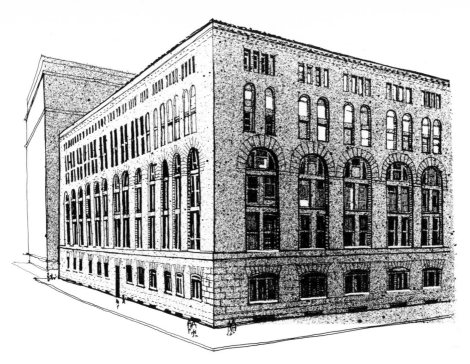

Fig. 237 The Marshall Field Store, Chicago (1885–7), by H. H. Richardson
A bold design owing much to Romanesque models

Fig. 238 The Allegheny Courthouse and Gaol, Pittsburgh, Pennsylvania (1848–88),
by H. H. Richardson

*Fig. 239 Stoughton House, Cambridge, Mass. (1882-3),
by H. H. Richardson*

*Fig. 240 The Watts Sherman House, Newport,
Rhode Island (1874), by H. H. Richardson*

*These two houses show the return to traditional building, which was
being practised by such architects as Voysey and Webb in England*

Fig. 242 *The Home Insurance Building, Chicago (1883–5), by William le Baron Jenney*
The first building to utilize a steel frame

Fig. 241
The Monadnock Block, Chicago (1890–1)
Architects, Burnham and Root
The last of the great weight-bearing wall blocks

Their work was followed with the greatest interest in America, and in his Watts Sherman House, 1874 (Fig. 240), Richardson shows something of the same freshness of approach as his English counterparts. In the Marshall Field Store, however, he takes the Romanesque style and interprets it in a new and straightforward manner. The walls are of the traditional weight-bearing type, but the freedom from ornament and the massive simplicity are exciting, and were to have a profound influence on the development of the Chicago style. In the same class and even simpler in treatment is the sixteen-storey Monadnock block, 1891 (Fig. 241), by Burnham and Root. This beautiful weight-bearing wall block is the last office building of its type in Chicago. It is completely devoid of ornament and relies for its effect on

Fig. 243 *The Reliance Building, Chicago (1890–4)*
Architects, Burnham and Root
A fine example of the Chicago style

Fig. 244

The Auditorium Building,
Chicago (1889),
by Louis Sullivan

Fig. 245   The Walker Warehouse, Chicago (1888–9), by Louis Sullivan
An early Sullivan work of striking simplicity and force

the interest created by the pattern of window openings in the solid wall. This pattern is enhanced by the rhythm of the slightly projecting bays, the only hint of ornamentation being the suggestion of an Egyptian cavetto moulding which crowns the building.

In the Home Insurance Building (1883–5; Fig. 242), one of the first true skyscrapers, William le Baron Jenney accepts the rigidity of the structural system and does not allow the rather heavy historical ornament of the masonry to obscure the gridlike pattern created by the steel frame. The Reliance Building (1890; Fig. 243) was by Burnham and Root, already mentioned. In this, the structural aspect of the building is made evident in the clear rectangles of the windows and terra-cotta bands of decoration. The contrast between the smooth clear surfaces of the glass and the decorative treatment of the horizontal bands between them is particularly pleasing. With its frank insistence on verticality, this is one of the most impressive of the early 'glass towers' of the Chicago school.

Sullivan

It is to Louis Sullivan, however, that we must turn to find the really dominant figure of the school. Sullivan was one of the great forces in American architecture, for not only was he an architect of genius, he was also a powerful teacher. His summary of the function of the skyscraper is both concise and clear. He saw the building divided into a number of clearly defined strata: (i) a storey below ground which contained the boilers, engines, etc., necessary to run the building —this was the 'service' area, if you like; (ii)

a ground floor devoted to stores, banks or other establishments which required large open areas, windows for display if necessary, and complete freedom of movement and access; (iii) a second storey, easily accessible by staircase, again with large subdivisions and unencumbered by large structural members; (iv) an indefinite number of storeys of offices, piled one on top of the other, rather like a honeycomb, all similar in shape and size; (v) a top storey containing the lift mechanisms and tanks for the heating system in the basement, to which it is linked by the vital pipes and cables that constitute the whole building's spinal cord. Expressed in this way, the analysis of the problem seems remarkably simple, but it requires a great mind to achieve this degree of analytical thinking.

Sullivan came to Chicago in 1879, when he joined the firm of the Danish architect Dankmar Adler. But his first major work was not undertaken until seven years later, when he designed the Auditorium Building (Fig. 244). The influence of Richardson is clear in the great round-headed arches (also to be found in the impressive Walker Warehouse, Fig. 245) of the entrance front; the line of ten of them makes a powerful feature of the design. The building is ten storeys high and covers two acres of ground, and at the time was the largest and most impressive building in America. Since it was built it has served a number of purposes, including hotel, office-building, and opera house.

Sullivan was also one of the first and most successful exponents of Art Nouveau in America, and this aspect of his work can be seen in much of the decoration of his buildings. It is possible that the young Frank

Lloyd Wright had some hand in the detailed decoration of the Auditorium Building, and Sullivan's Art Nouveau influence made a strong and lasting impression on the young architect.

The 1890s see the maturing of the sky-scraper as an art form, and it was during this period that Sullivan produced his best and most refined work. This trend is clearly apparent in the Wainwright Building (1890–1; Fig. 246). The lines are more clear and the proportion more exact than in the Auditorium block. The division into the various stages of the building are more evident, yet the sense of unity of design is not lost. The influence of Art Nouveau is seen in the richly decorated cornice, and this provides the foil to the simplicity and angularity of the storeys below.

The Wainwright Building was, however, only a step in Sullivan's development, for in 1894 he produced the Guaranty Building, which was to be his masterpiece (Fig. 247). The basic conception is similar to that of the earlier block, but now the form reaches greater refinement and presents a design of complete unity. The definition of the parts is even clearer, and the vertical members lighter in weight. It seems that here Sullivan manages to combine the simple monumentality of the Egyptians with a feeling for proportion that is Greek in its purest form. The block is poised on a base which is largely composed of glass, and there can be no mistaking that the internal steel frame is taking the weight of the storeys above. The corner pilasters are much reduced in weight, and the thin pilaster strips are decorated, as well as the horizontal divisions. In this respect the Guaranty block differs from the Wain-

wright, and this all-over treatment of the decoration on the later building acts as a unifying agent. Again he uses the semi-circular arch as a termination of the vertical window strips—and note how much more lightness and grace they give the building—and then sets circular windows, deeply recessed into an Egyptian cavetto moulding at the top of the block. This form of termination may well be an echo of the Monadnock block, and the semicircular arches a well-digested Richardsonian influence, but Sullivan managed to give to both a personal treatment that is entirely his own. Again, the Art Nouveau decorations on cornice and pilasters are pure Sullivan, but he manages to use them like some rare spice which enhances the flavour. He also manages to give the block a strong vertical emphasis, despite the horizontal bands of the windows, by setting them back behind the level of the pilasters.

In his last major building, the Carson, Pirie, Scott Store (Fig. 248), built between 1899 and 1904, Sullivan carried even further his attempts to create an unobstructed sales-space. The first two storeys are clearly stated, and are embellished with his own particular brand of ornament. The storeys above, however, with their new and even clearer statement of the steel grid that supports the building, mark a new phase, not only in Sullivan's development, but in the development of twentieth-century architecture. The windows are again recessed, but this time the horizontal strips are on the same plane as the vertical, thus creating an all-over pattern for the whole of the upper storeys; added definition is given by the sharp, precise ornament which runs round

Fig. 246 The Wainwright Building, St Louis (1890–1), by Louis Sullivan

Fig. 247 The Guaranty Building, Buffalo (1894), by Louis Sullivan

The Guaranty Block is Sullivan's masterpiece; the Wainwright shows a step in the evolution of the design

Fig. 248

The Carson, Pirie, Scott department store, Chicago (1899–1904), by Louis Sullivan

the window frames and is supported by horizontal bands at top and bottom. Emphasis to the final floor is given this time, not by decorated cornice, but by moving the whole top floor back, thereby creating a deep shadow at the top of the building, which is relieved by the light verticals of the roof supports. The rigid pattern of the framework Sullivan created may well foreshadow the functionalism of Le Corbusier, but there is not the same sense of aesthetic satisfaction in this late work that he achieved with his Guaranty block.

In the latter part of his life Sullivan designed several small-town banks throughout the mid-western states (Fig. 249). He referred to these small buildings as his 'little gems' or 'little jewel boxes'. They have a freshness of approach that even today is delightful. In these minor works he favoured the use of dark red brick, contrasted with green-blue terra-cotta decoration, and in some of them stained glass is used with effect. Even in these buildings he indulged in his favourite brand of lush decoration, which never seems to have had any influence either inside or outside his native country.

In the great 'World's Fair' held in Chi-

cago in 1893 he designed the Transportation Building. This was in strong contrast to the official imitation Greek and Roman buildings which dominated the grounds. A notable feature of the design was the Golden Door, a brilliantly coloured and richly decorated entrance which was enhanced by the brilliant white of the surroundings. Of all the buildings in the Fair, Sullivan's was the only one that aroused international interest. It is rather tragic that the one architect who had made such a contribution to the modern movement should have been so neglected, for in his later years Sullivan lived in poverty and loneliness.

It was not until well into the twentieth century that the skyscraper in New York achieved architectural significance, for many of the early ones were completely lacking in any real architectural qualities. The intention to impress by size was too much in mind, and the result was oppressive in the extreme. Purity of form was lost in the effort to create an impression of wealth and financial security. Why these mighty buildings developed in the city is difficult to say. The lack of space on Long Island is often given as the principal reason, but this is not borne out by the facts, for the tall buildings are situated only in a single line which roughly follows Broadway. If an average were taken all over the island the buildings would need to be in the region of only five or six storeys high. It is probably simply a question of industrial efficiency, for in an area of high density, personal contact between business-houses becomes simple and quick. This ease of communication between business-men may explain the rapid spread of multistorey buildings, once the materials and building techniques were at hand. Although the introduction of the electric lift by W. von Siemens in 1850 (elevators had been in use in factories for half a century before this date), was an important contributory factor in the design of tall buildings, another important consideration was the very high return the financier could get for such a building on a comparatively small site. This tends to imply that high buildings forced up the price of land in city centres, rather than, as many suggest, that tall buildings are the result of the high prices of sites.

The study of the skyscraper shows that this form of building can be a genuine vehicle for architectural expression of the highest order, and it is sad that many of them descend to a display of commercial vulgarity.

FURTHER READING

Henry-Russell Hitchcock, *Architecture: Nineteenth and Twentieth Centuries*. Pelican History of Art; Penguin Books, 1958.
Indispensable to any study of the modern movement.

H. S. Goodhart-Rendel, *English Architecture since the Regency*. Constable, 1953.

Reginald Turnor, *Nineteenth Century Architecture in Britain*. Batsford, 1950.
Both these books form a valuable introduction to developments in this country.

Hugh Casson, *An Introduction to Victorian Architecture*. Architectural Press, 1948.
A very brief and concise introduction to the subject; a good book to start with.

Sir Kenneth Clark, *The Gothic Revival*, 3rd ed. Murray, 1962.
Some of the discussion of Victorian aesthetics and opinion is very valuable.

Henry-Russell Hitchcock, *Early Victorian Architecture in Britain*. Architectural Press, 1954.
These two volumes (Vol. 1 devoted to the text and Vol. 2 to the illustrations) form a most detailed study of the period.

J. M. Richards, *The Functional Tradition*. Architectural Press, 1958.
Excellent photographs of early industrial buildings in this country, accompanied by concise commentary.

Peter Ferriday, ed., *Victorian Architecture*. Cape, 1963.
A collection of essays on many of the prominent Victorian architects; there is also a good selection of photographs.

Nikolaus Pevsner, *Pioneers of Modern Design*, rev. ed. Penguin Books, 1960.
An important book on the artistic theories and important practitioners from Morris to Gropius.

G. F. Chadwick, *The Works of Sir Joseph Paxton*. Architectural Press, 1961.

A good introduction to this great Victorian engineer's work; plenty of illustrations.

Carl W. Condit, *The Rise of the Sky-scraper*. C.U.P., 1952.

A very interesting book with illustrations of many early buildings now, unfortunately, pulled down.

Wayne Andrews, *Architecture in America*. Thames & Hudson, 1960.

A fine collection of photographs of notable American buildings from the seventeenth century to the present, accompanied by a concise text.

John Gloag, *A History of Cast Iron in Architecture*. Allen & Unwin, 1948.

A comprehensive survey, well illustrated.

Lewis Mumford, *The Roots of Contemporary American Architecture*. Grove Press Evergreen Profile Book, 1959.

A collection of essays by various authors on the problems of the American architect. Many are of particular value to those interested in the rise of the skyscraper.

Mention should also be made of two little books, *Bridges* and *Follies*, published by Chatto & Windus for the National Benzole Co., Ltd., and edited by Sir Hugh Casson. They are packed with information and attractively illustrated. There is also one on *Castles* in the same series.

For those wishing further reading on Louis Sullivan there is an excellent volume on the master in the 'Masters of World Architecture' series mentioned in the main bibliography at the back of the book.

12

THE MODERN MOVEMENT

The history of architecture is the history of man's ability to organize space. As we have already seen, the more sophisticated the society the more complex and numerous will be the types of buildings required to satisfy the needs of that society. From the simplicity and subtlety of the Greeks, the organization of space becomes gradually more complex until, in medieval times, space is manipulated with great dexterity and almost intuitive genius. After the decline of medievalism the organization of space falls broadly into three phases: Renaissance, Baroque and Twentieth-Century. Each approach has its own very distinct character, the later ones growing naturally out of the earlier.

Generally, in architectural history books, the importance of the influence of developments in painting is insufficiently stressed or completely ignored. Yet with few exceptions —notably the work of Frank Lloyd Wright in America—innovations in architecture are preceded by, or go hand-in-hand with, developments in painting. It will be remembered that the artists of the Renaissance were not specialists in any one field: Leonardo, Michelangelo, and Bernini were skilled in many aspects of art. In England, Wren, Vanbrugh, and many others were not trained as architects, and began to design buildings almost by accident, or as a hobby. The Renaissance was preoccupied with the science of picture-making perspective, anatomy, the Golden Mean, ideal proportion and so on. This predilection for perspective, with the projection of horizontal lines back to the vanishing-points on the horizon, seems to explain, in part at any rate, their liking for long straight lines. Many Italian Renaissance buildings and piazzas look just like perspective drawings made real. The designers would certainly have had formal training, and it is reasonable to suppose that this form of drawing influenced their designs. This highly formalized approach placed limitations on the Renaissance concept of space. The vista, the axis, the right angle, and the carefully balanced façade are the characteristics of Renaissance design.

Into the ordered symmetry of the High Renaissance, Michelangelo threw the first disturbing qualities which were to lead to the Baroque. The importance of this movement has already been stressed, for it is not, as many have claimed in the past, merely the continuation of the Renaissance into decline. It is a new and revitalizing force, using Renaissance motifs, but giving them a new meaning. If the Renaissance is the period of the straight line and the right angle, Baroque is the period of the oval and the S curve. The clear definition of space, so typical of the fifteenth and sixteenth centuries, is very different from that of the seventeenth century, which sees the opening-out of space. Wall merges through curves and decorative mouldings into other walls or ceiling.

Trompe-l'œil painting was very popular, and often it is difficult to differentiate between painted and modelled decoration. The freedom of handling of space and the sense of continuous movement in a Baroque building would have been unthinkable in a building of the previous period. The strong sense of a central axis disappears; the flat façade, with clearly defined planes, which is a piece of static design, gives way to the curved façade and the broken pediment, which create a sense of movement across and into the building.

Before further developments could take place in the free organization of space, new materials had to be available. The structural possibilities of stone and brick are limited, and it was not until the introduction of iron and steel in the nineteenth century that new materials became available. Iron and steel made possible the new techniques which architects required to enlarge their command of spatial relationships.

In the visual arts of painting and architecture, and to a lesser degree in the other arts of literature and music, the nineteenth century was a period of revolution and revolt. A search for new values to replace the dry academism which many felt to be the anathema of the creative spirit was evident. In painting, Delacroix led off the revolt against classicism by starting the Romantic movement, from which came realism, leading in turn to impressionism.

But these movements are of importance to the student of architectural history only insofar as they provide the background to emergence of the figure who is protean in the history of twentieth-century art. For it is Paul Cézanne (1839–1906), with his attempts to 'realize his sensations', who made possible the advances in painting and architecture which are characteristic of this century. This fumbling, almost inarticulate old man, living in seclusion and painting his beloved Mont-St-Victoire, or jugs and bottles, laid the foundations of the twentieth-century movement. As far as the architectural student is concerned, Cézanne is perhaps less important for what he did as for what he made it possible for others to do. Cézanne broke with the classical concept of perspective; he found that the third dimension could be represented without the paraphernalia of the perspectivist—vanishing points, picture plane, horizon, etc. Cézanne's drawing often looks clumsy, but it never looks flat.

From middle- and late-period Cézanne to the Cubism of Picasso and Braque is but a small step. Cubism, with its complete breakdown of surface appearance, is the starting-point for the twentieth-century approach to the problems of spatial relationships. There can be no doubt that early Cubism had a profound effect on such architects as Gropius and Le Corbusier, for example. The Cubists, in their attempt to represent form, broke the surface up into small facets. In many Cubist paintings, for instance Picasso's 'Portrait of Uhde' 1910, or 'Man with a Pipe' 1911, and in many of Braque's portraits and still lifes of the same period, it is difficult to determine which is the object and which is the background, so complete is the disintegration of the image.

Now all this may seem a far cry from developments in architecture, but on closer examination it is seen to be very relevant. Just as painters were destroying the surface of objects in an attempt to lay bare the structure beneath, so architects began to lay bare the structure of their buildings. Walter Gropius, in the Fagus factory buildings at Alfeld a.d. Leine (1911), set the new style. Here the interior structure is quite clear, owing to the extensive use of glass walls. These walls are reduced to providing a screen against the elements, and are in no way weight-bearing. This clear statement of function and frank acceptance of new materials make this factory a landmark in architectural development. The American critic, Henry-Russell Hitchcock, in calling it 'the most advanced piece of architecture built before the First World War, is not overstating its importance.

Not only has Gropius exerted great influence by the buildings he created, but he has also influenced many young architects and designers by his work as a teacher. The Bauhaus, criticised and abused on political as well as aesthetic grounds, was widely misunderstood during its hey-day. Subsequently, however, the wisdom and value of the revolutionary teaching methods which Gropius introduced there have been vindicated.

Le Corbusier, possibly the most spec-tacular and controversial architect of the first half of the twentieth century, continued the process of providing the architect with a new vocabulary of forms and new methods of manipulating space. For him a house should be open for entry from all sides, even the roof. Few architects have paid so much attention to this feature. To most it is simply a lid over the top of a structure, but Le Corbusier, constantly aware of changing conditions, realized that with the growing numbers of aircraft, the possibility of seeing houses, or even entering them from the top instead of ground level must not be ignored. This new attitude to the roof is well illustrated in the splendid Villa Savoye, where Le Corbusier's treatment of this new dimension shows that he considered the roof as important as the plan or elevation.

The foregoing is an attempt to summarize the influences and aims of the modern architect. It will be seen that modern architecture is not so much a style as a new way of handling space. Just as the pointed arch and flying buttress were necessary to the Gothic masons, so today the architect uses the steel joist, the cantilever, and the strength of reinforced concrete to realize his aspirations.

Europe and America

The architecture of this century had its roots in a movement of the last century that we have not so far mentioned. The curious movement known as Art Nouveau in this country, and 'Jugendstil' and 'Style Mod-erne' in Germany and France, was an international movement which sprang into existence throughout Europe almost simultaneously. It differed in essence from other nineteenth-century movements in that it was not a revival style in any sense of the word, and its exponents tried to fashion a style which owed nothing to the past.

Art Nouveau

In its purest form the movement was short-lived, for it hardly survived the last decade of the century. But in a broader sense the work produced under its influence was both wide and varied, and embraced some aspects of the work of such architects as Hoffmann, Wagner, and Olbricht, as well as the more obvious Horta and Mackintosh.

The exact beginnings of the movement are hard to define. In France from the 1860s various experiments with iron and metal construction had been going on, and without the use of metal it is doubtful if the movement could have taken shape in architecture at all. In England in the 1880s certain developments in the decorative arts contained inklings of the style. Indeed even the lush interiors of the Brighton Pavilion, with their rich colouring and exuberant decoration, seem to contain more than a hint of the artificiality and preciousness that runs through so much of the movement.

The chief characteristic of Art Nouveau is the curve. The curve was used by the Baroque artists and architects, but that was a virile curve; the curve of Art Nouveau is languorous and all-embracing and, especially in the work of Aubrey Beardsley, it is a curve of decay. In the painting and graphic arts particularly, a strong sense of self-destruction pervades the entire *œuvre*. Some would liken this curve to a flame, and at first glance this seems appropriate, yet the flame is a curve of burning and intensity;

Art Nouveau uses the curve of the lily and the lily is the flower of death. Once one has started on the pursuit of Art Nouveau, the practitioners amongst painters are not hard to recognize. Burne-Jones, Toorop, and Munch come easily to mind, and—most characteristic of them all—Aubrey Beardsley. This strange figure proved to be the high-priest of the movement. Seldom has an artist been able to establish a reputation with such limited means; for Beardsley's strength was based on his uncanny ability to manage black and white. His early drawings showed little promise, and yet in a few years he had gained such mastery of his chosen medium that he was to remain unequalled. Although he is most famous for his illustrations to poems and plays, the actual content of his drawings often bore little relationship to the subject he chose to illustrate. He caught the spirit rather than the letter of the passage he was portraying. His meticulous technique enabled him to control the tone relationships very exactly whilst at the same time suggesting rich and varied colour, as well as texture.

It may well be asked, at this point, what all this has to do with architecture. A glance at the staircase of the house designed by Victor Horta at No. 6, rue Paul-Émile Janson (formerly 12, rue de Turin), Brussels, shows Beardsley's curves drawn in three dimensions with iron (Pl. 53). This particular house brought Art Nouveau, fully developed, into the architectural scene, and proved to be one of the most influential buildings of the movement. The plan does show some advances in the arrangement of levels that are new to the architectural vocabulary of the day, but essentially Horta was a decorator.

One of the most important British figures of the movement was the Scottish architect, Charles Rennie Mackintosh, who was responsible for the remarkable Glasgow School of Art (1896–1909) and also for the tea-rooms which he designed in Sauchiehall Street and Buchanan Street in the same city. These last two buildings have something of that *outré* quality which is such an integral part of some aspects of the movement.

The front of the Art School is notable for the bold handling of mass. The contrast between large areas of glass and rugged stone is relieved by the fine tracery of the iron railings, which are almost playful after the solemnity of the rest. He added the Library wing some years later (1907–9), and to this

Plate 53 The staircase at No. 6, rue Paul-Émile Janson, Brussels (1893), by Victor Horta

Fig. 250

Glasgow School of Art, by C. R. Mackintosh— library wing (1907)

The form echoes the great Scottish highlands; the decoration is Art Nouveau

Plate 54

*The Cathedral of the
Sagrada Familia, Barcelona,
The Nativity Transept
(1903–26),
by Antoni Gaudí*

aspect he brings something of the crag-like quality of Scottish Baronial style, to which he manages to add something of the natural majesty of the Scottish Highlands (Fig. 250). The jutting angularity suggests the remoteness and pride which is so much part of the great sweeping mountains beyond Fort William. In that respect this part of the building is as much a product of its environment as are the long low prairie houses of Frank Lloyd Wright.

In Austria, the work of such architects as J. Hoffmann, J. M. Olbrich, and Otto Wagner represented a distinct trend towards a more geometric and angular quality within the international Art Nouveau movement. The buildings which these architects designed were certainly elegant, but they also had a certain aura of extravagance and excess. Between 1894 and 1911 Wagner designed many of the stations for the Vienna subway, Olbrich designed the Sezession Palace in Vienna, and Hoffmann built the Stoclet house in Brussels. All these buildings show, to a greater or lesser degree, something of the fantasy, and to a certain extent the awkwardness of this aspect of Art Nouveau design.

Antoni Gaudí

The early buildings mentioned above all show a very individualistic approach to building, and, further, they hold a balance between, on the one hand academicism, and on the other the picturesque, which was, as we have seen, a fashionable product of the latter part of the nineteenth century. The architect who was at once the most individual, the most fantastic, and the most extravagant was the Spaniard, Antoni Gaudí i Cornet. Gaudí (1852–1926) was a great eccentric who used his eccentricity to fashion a style of building that was at the same time unique, personal, and inimitable. To many he is one of the two indisputably great figures to emerge from the Art Nouveau movement. His style is at once outrageous and irrational—many would say downright freakish and intolerable—and yet one

Plate 55

A house in rue Franklyn, Paris (1903), by Auguste Perret

A façade which is full of movement

cannot help but admire his audacity and sheer inventiveness. All his work was done in the area of Barcelona, and when confronted with it for the first time one thinks of the Land of the Sugar Plum Fairy or the witch's house from Hansel and Gretel (Fig. 251). The forms and colours are so unbelievably fantastic that it seems the buildings stand by a miracle, not by building science. Further acquaintance with the buildings, however, reveals a logic and force in their apparent thoughtlessness. Few architects seem to have been allowed the freedom to make such personal statements through their art.

Despite the apparent novelty of his forms and methods, Gaudí's art has deep roots in the past. To find his antecedents it is necessary to turn to the buildings of the primitive tribes of Africa, as well as to the practices of the medieval master-masons. But, not only does he look back. To give his buildings life and variety of surface-pattern, he often faced the walls with bits of pot and crockery, glazed tiles, and such bric-à-brac as came to hand. In this respect he looked forward to the surrealist outbreak which shook the artistic world in the 1920s.

The two housing blocks which he erected in Barcelona, the Casa Milá (Fig. 252) and the Casa Battló, show his curiously undulating sense of form. The stone seems to have been poured rather than quarried. The wave-like form of the roof, coupled with the irregular shape of the windows, produces an effect of instability and an almost amoeba-like movement across the façade. His masterpiece, and the culmination of his life's work, is that extraordinary fragment, the Sagrada Familia at Barcelona (Pl. 54). He began

Fig. 251

The Park-keeper's House in the Parque Güell, Barcelona, by Antonio Gaudí

work on the building in 1884, and it is still incomplete, as he left only a few drawings and models, many of which were damaged by the ravages of war. Whether it will ever be finished is a matter for conjecture. Like the medieval master-mason, Gaudí worked on the site of the church, designing it as it was built. There seems to have been no final plan, and problems appear to have been solved as they arose, by means of sketches and models. The façade shows Gaudí's change of attitude as he built higher and higher. The lower part is a fairly obvious piece of Gothic Revival architecture, but as the stages progress, the style departs more and more from the original intention and becomes progressively personal. With the four spires, new and strange lands are entered, and the pinnacles which surmount the spires can only be compared with the most advanced sculpture of the period. If it had been finished, this must have become one of the great churches of the twentieth century.

From a structural point of view the building shows not only Gaudí's grasp of Gothic principles but also his ability to turn those principles to his own ends. It also becomes clear that, however outlandish the forms Gaudí employed, they were the direct solution of the structural problem involved. Stylistically, the portals of the cathedral façade contain more than a hint of the portals at Reims and other French work, though Gaudí does not manage to relate his ornament to the structure of the building in the way the French masons had done. Or is this perhaps the closing pages of Spanish rococo?

The sculpture encrusted round the lower parts of the Sagrada Familia bears some resemblance to the sculptural convolutions of figures round the *transparente* of Toledo Cathedral of 1732. This latter work, whilst unmistakably baroque, shows as clearly as anything the underlying Gothic feeling which underpins so much Baroque architecture. The Gothic impulse is much more overt in the Gaudí, but this is the link between the two works. Gaudí was possessed of an uncomfortable genius; only a country that could give birth to a Goya and a Picasso could nurture such a spirit.

The period before the First World War saw European architecture in a state of flux. Experiment was in the air. In Paris, for instance, Auguste Perret was making a number of interesting experiments in reinforced concrete, though his lead was never really taken up and developed (Pl. 55). Despite the various innovations which were made, however, no architect was able to show the same depth of invention that was taking place in the field of painting. Here the old academism was being not only attacked, but replaced by a new set of standards and values. Leading the revolution were painters of the calibre of Marcel Duchamp, Paul Klee, Piet Mondrian and Wassily Kandinsky, all of whom had made major contributions to the new aesthetic before 1914. Picasso and Braque had invented cubism between 1910 and 1912, and during the 1920s the new vision was to put Europe in the forefront of architectural development.

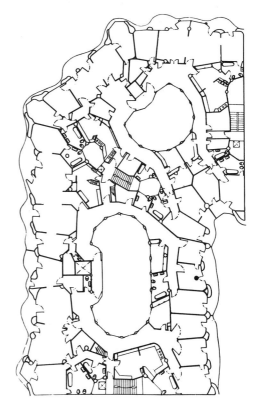

Fig. 252 Casa Milá, Barcelona (1905–10) by Antonio Gaudí. The plan shows Gaudí's fluid conception of space

Frank Lloyd Wright

In America, however, Frank Lloyd Wright, working in isolation, was arriving at very much the same conclusions about the organization of space as the painters were reaching in Europe. Wright began his career in Chicago in 1887 in the office of two of the best men in the country, Louis Sullivan and Dankmar Adler. Both of these men were then approaching the height of their creative power, and Sullivan's clear thinking must have had a profound effect on the young apprentice. However, when he began to work on his own Wright did not follow the Chicago tradition and in his first major commission (Fig. 253) he showed both his independence and, if anything, a return to the monumental forms of Richardson. He did not use the new materials, and rejected the iron frame and large areas of glass. It was

not until the 1930s that he began to use ferro-concrete to any extent at all, one of his finest examples of the use of this material being 'Falling Water' in Pennsylvania (Fig. 254).

In 1910 a monumental study of his entire output to that date was published in Germany, and from that time onward he was accepted in Europe, his progress was noted with interest, and his influence became widespread. Wright's freshness of approach and radical thinking can probably be explained by two influences; firstly, the fact that his parents believed in the most advanced educational theory and for that reason only allowed him the simplest of toys, mainly consisting of rectangular bricks; and secondly, the fact that, being born in the American Middle West, he was able to see

Fig. 253 The James Charnley House, Chicago (1891), by Frank Lloyd Wright

In his first house Wright asserts his independence and originality

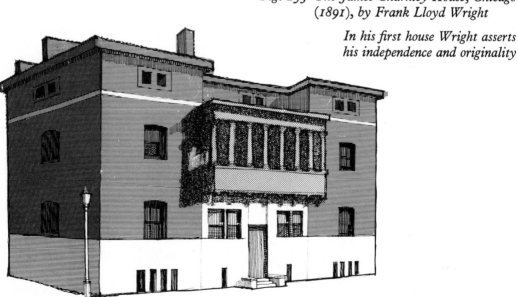

Fig. 254 Falling Water, Bear Run Park, Pa. (1936), by Frank Lloyd Wright
Wright did not use reinforced concrete until late in his career, but he then
used it with daring and imagination

little architecture of either historical importance or significance. This meant, of course, that he came to architecture with a fresh mind uninfluenced by imposing historic examples.

From the outset Wright concentrated his energies on solving the problem of the house as a shelter. He took as his point of departure the traditional hunting-lodge, and he worked with the idea of the house as a single room clearly in the forefront of his mind. It was his declared intention to treat the floor as one room, which was then divided off into sections for various activities, such as dining and reading; to this he added the kitchen with servants' quarters as a semi-detached block.

The other important influence on Wright was the Japanese house, which he studied in great detail and from which he learned much about the art of suppressing the unnecessary. There is nothing in a Wright plan which is not important; the insignificant is entirely eliminated.

The plans of many of Wright's houses, especially the smaller ones, assume the shape of the four outspread arms of a windmill. In this type of plan he took as his starting point

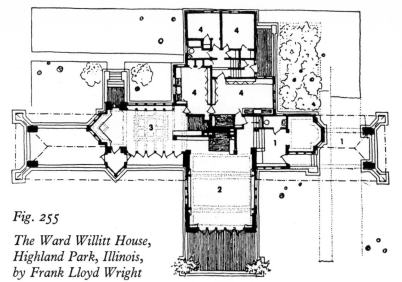

Fig. 255

The Ward Willitt House,
Highland Park, Illinois,
by Frank Lloyd Wright

the idea of a huge central fireplace which formed the kernel of the plan. From this central point the rooms spread out in a cruciform shape. The advantage of this type of plan is that by putting the fireplace at the centre of the house, instead of on a wall, the fire can give heat all round instead of in one direction only. Another advantage is that the rooms can receive light from three sides. This type of layout is well illustrated in the Ward Willitt House (Fig. 255).

The idea of a central fireplace was by no means new; it had been used in various houses in nineteenth-century America, and, of course, ultimately it is very similar in intention to the central fire of the English great hall. Further analogies with the great hall are to be found in Wright's custom of making the living room the full height of the house. Again, this arrangement is to be found in the early American settlers' houses of the seventeenth century. To divide this space and introduce a new sense of plasticity Wright introduced the use of the balcony around the central living space. This is to be found in the Isabel Roberts House, and

not only does it give a greater sense of internal movement, but it also expresses another of Wright's devices for introducing new spatial relationships, that is, planning the house on two horizontal planes which interpenetrated at different heights. These planes were usually gathered round a solid masonry block, which provided not only the solid basis for the whole structure but also the necessary vertical member which stabilized the otherwise unconnected horizontal planes of the rest of the house.

Wright also emancipated the porch. This feature was common in the cotton and rice-growing areas of the south, but Wright both gave this feature a new prominence and finally made it an important element in the appearance of his houses. The long, hovering, cantilevered eaves of the Robie House (Fig. 256) show exactly what a dominating feature this could be. Not only is the appearance of the house vitally affected, but the actual area which the house covers is extended. As we have seen, Wright was concerned with the house as shelter; these broadly-expanding eaves beckon man into

Fig. 256

The Robie House, Chicago (1909), by Frank Lloyd Wright
This shows Wright's use of the verandah as an extension of the house and the space
which surrounds it

the shelter and protection of the building which lies somewhere, almost concealed, behind them. For Wright's houses provide shelter in the most primitive sense. This is the animal's lair, where he can seek protection and comfort against a merciless environment. The porch and eaves are not an addition, but an integral part of the concept. They are important aesthetically, and they help to express the psychological mood of a Wright house.

By the use of these revolutionary concepts Wright had achieved by 1910 a freedom of planning unknown in other countries. In addition, without the help of the painters, Wright was coming to very much the same conclusions about new concepts of space and vision. In his fearless and unprecedented way of dividing a vertical wall plane, he was almost a decade in front of Europe. There was, however, one essential difference between Wright and the Europeans. Wright regarded the house as a self-contained spatial unit; the interior was often rather dark and the entrance hard to find. In Europe, on the other hand, architects were preoccupied with the problem of the interpenetration of inner and outer space. This gives the European house an appearance of greater vulnerability and renders it less of a protective cloak.

The typical Wright house is long and low, and crouches close to the earth (Fig. 257). His Larkin Building on the other hand is almost medieval in its verticality and solemnity. This building was designed in 1904, and makes an interesting comparison with the Stock Exchange which Berlage designed in Amsterdam (1898–1903). Both buildings make much use of brick and both have about them a massive uncompromising quality. Wright employed unbroken brick towers to support a flat roof pierced by skylights, which give the interior the even light required for office work.

He used a similar top light in the Johnson

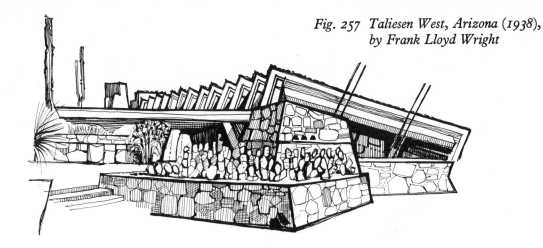

Fig. 257 Taliesen West, Arizona (1938), by Frank Lloyd Wright

Wax Building, Racine, Wisconsin, of 1936–9, but this building is most remarkable for the giant columns which support the roof (Pl. 56). Wright was slow to adopt the new structural techniques, but when he did, it was with considerable imagination and daring. The columns in question were severely criticized as being too fragile to carry the load that was to be placed upon them. Each column was 22 feet high and was to carry a load of 12 tons on a 9-inch base. This was in flagrant disregard of the code of building which called for a base of 30-inch thickness for a column of such a height. A demonstration column was built, and after seven days successfully bore a load of 60 tons.

Plate 56 S. C. Johnson & Son, Inc., Wisconsin (1936–9), by Frank Lloyd Wright— interior of Administration Building

This roofing system cannot be defended on grounds of strict functionalism, but the end justifies the means

It was then estimated that after a twenty-eight-day period the column would carry a load of 80 tons. This demonstration convinced the doubters, and the columns were allowed to stand. Their strength is produced by the internal wire mesh which is welded into a cone and then further bonded by concrete.

Pyrex glass tubes are used in the roof, as they disperse light evenly and do not discolour. But they are both expensive and difficult to fit. It is said that the building cost twice the amount first estimated, and the apparent pointlessness of the design annoys many people. There is about the building, however, an intensely poetic vision which renders it memorable and at the same time places Wright amongst the great romantic architects of all time. For Wright *was* a romantic, and it is this quality that pervades his architecture and places it among the greatest that this century has

so far produced. The Guggenheim Museum of Art in New York (1943–59) not only proves Wright's romanticism but is also the culmination of the movement with which this chapter began, namely Art Nouveau. Throughout his life, Wright's decoration had retained distinct affinities with the movement and this attitude to decoration had doubtless been acquired in the studio of Sullivan. The Guggenheim Museum is based on the spiral, the Art Nouveau curve in three dimensions. The idea of using this form was that, by taking the lift to the top of the building, one could then walk down the descending ramp, looking on the way at the art collection which the museum was designed to house. The spiral structure is at once apparent in the external appearance of the building, where one again senses Wright's organic sense of form (Fig. 258). This continuation of the Art Nouveau influence places Wright along with Gaudí as

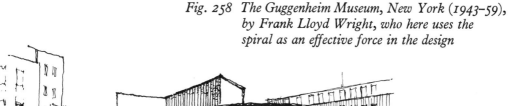

Fig. 258 The Guggenheim Museum, New York (1943–59), by Frank Lloyd Wright, who here uses the spiral as an effective force in the design

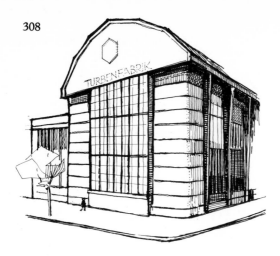

*Fig. 259 The A.E.G. Turbine Factory, Berlin
(1909), by Peter Behrens*

one of the great products of the movement.

Though Wright was one of the great romantics, his grasp of structure was sound. This is clearly shown in the way he handled the design of his Tokyo Hotel. The problem was to build a structure that would withstand the earthquakes which frequently damaged many of the conventionally designed buildings. He managed a successful solution to the problem by building the hotel in sections which could move independently of each other—a solution which has so far proved successful, as the building has withstood several tremors.

Peter Behrens

After the interruption of the First World War, developments in Germany created a new attitude to both architecture and the applied arts. Amongst the most important architects working in Germany before 1914 was Peter Behrens, and his influence was wide, both as practising architect and as teacher. His buildings reflect the clear logical method he used in his attempts to solve the basic problems of architectural design. He was mainly concerned with factories, and he made a determined effort to raise the standard of industrial buildings so

that they became both dignified and architecturally significant places of work. His A.E.G. Turbine Factory in Berlin (Fig. 259) combines a classical severity of design with a feeling for the proper use of the new materials, steel and glass. The heavy corner piers contrast with the light, tight skin of the window, and the whole façade is imbued with a feeling of simple grandeur.

Whilst in the employ of the A.E.G. Behrens became their artistic consultant, the first time an architect had been called upon to fill such a post. In this capacity he was able to supervise the output of the factory and advise on the design of their entire range of commodities. He was even responsible for the design of the trademark. This opened up a completely new sphere of influence for the architect, putting him in much closer contact with the output of the industry for which he worked. Such a position obviously demanded a person of the widest interests and abilities, combined with a sound technical knowledge. To the field of applied design Behrens brought the same analytical approach which had marked his architectural work, and he heralded that return to first principles which was to play such an important part in the curriculum of the future art school headed by Gropius, one of his most brilliant pupils. By understanding the industrial processes involved, Behrens was able to design forms which were well suited to mass production methods and so went some way towards the vindication of the machine as a means of producing high-quality design.

His methods of work and attitude to the fundamental problems of architecture and

Fig. 260 The Fagus Works, Alfeld a. d. Leine (1911–16), by Gropius and Meyer The new aesthetic asserts itself in this important building

applied design must have had a deep effect on his pupils. Le Corbusier was for a time in his studio, but he did not remain long; Walter Gropius and Mies van der Rohe also worked there, and all were to achieve international status. Gropius began his career when the Deutscher Werkbund was in the ascendent. This was a body rather similar to the Art Manufacturers' Guild which had been founded in England in 1847, some sixty years before the Werkbund. The German institution tried to stimulate public taste and raise the standard of design of mechanically produced goods.

Walter Gropius

Gropius's first important commission was the Fagus Factory at Alfeld a.d. Leine, in Germany (Fig. 260). Immediately the differences between the work of master and pupil are apparent. Behrens had used rather heavy solid forms; Gropius uses light transparent surfaces, which are obviously screens. The structure of the building is laid bare behind the elegant glass façades, and the lightness of the whole conception announces at once a new aesthetic. The building he designed

for the Werkbund Exhibition at Cologne in 1914 is equally frank (Fig. 261). Again the nature of glass is made quite evident, and the two brick wings, which appear to rise through the glass wall, create a new feeling for architectural composition and space relationships. Gropius was laying open the structure of the building in just the same way as the painters were laying open the structure of the objects they were painting.

These two buildings ushered in a new movement with both conviction and success. The work Gropius did at the Bauhaus was to prove his eminence as leader and teacher. In 1919, after the interruption of the war, Gropius was called to the Weimar School of Art. He succeeded Henry van de Velde and founded the Bauhaus, the 'High School of Creative Art'.

Fig. 261 The Werkbund Exhibition Building, Cologne (1914), by Gropius

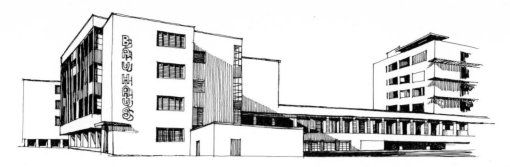

Fig. 262 The Bauhaus, Dessau (1925–6), by Walter Gropius

The Bauhaus School

Immediately after the war, Germany was a shattered and depressed nation. The feeling of despair manifested itself in the Expressionist painters of the immediate post-war period. Before the war, even before the turn of the century, there had been a number of painters interested in expressionism, but ultimately the aims of this movement were too limited to form the basis of a major advance in the visual arts. Though the intentions of the painters were deeply felt, they were only an outcry against transitory conditions. The products of expressionism were topical but they were tinged with too great an element of self-pity to be of lasting value. When Gropius came to Weimar he set about creating a new and more constructive atmosphere in which the artist could create. He seemed instinctively aware of the limitations of the contemporary painters, and he began the task of a complete reorientation of artistic training. To this end he gathered about him a young and energetic staff, most of whom had not had experience in the field of applied art.

The school at Weimar originally consisted of two schools, a school of design and a school of applied art; Gropius combined the two to form the Bauhaus. Amongst the first to join the staff was the young Johannes Itten. He had been teaching in Vienna and had developed a completely new method of educating the tactile sense. Gropius put him in charge of the preliminary course. This initial period was considered of vital importance, as it was during this time that the young designer's senses and powers of perception were to be sharpened, and his ability to think creatively awakened. Other members of the staff were Gerhard Marcks, the German sculptor, and the American, Lyonel Feininger, one of the few Expressionist painters interested in the new concepts of space and spatial relationships. Between 1921 and 1923 Paul Klee, Oskar Schlemmer, Wassily Kandinsky and Moholy-Nagy joined the staff. With artists of this calibre it is not difficult to imagine the intensely active and creative atmosphere that must have been generated.

In 1925 the whole school was moved to Dessau, and Gropius designed the new buildings, which had to meet a variety of requirements (Fig. 262). The whole complex had to contain accommodation for the school of design itself, and provision had also to be made for the continuation of trade courses for the industries of the city. Combination studio-and-dwelling quarters for the full-time students had to be available, and in addition there were the administrative offices, dining-hall, and stage. There were

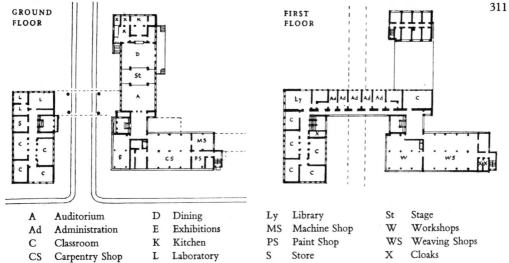

GROUND FLOOR

FIRST FLOOR

A	Auditorium	D	Dining
Ad	Administration	E	Exhibitions
C	Classroom	K	Kitchen
CS	Carpentry Shop	L	Laboratory

Ly	Library	St	Stage
MS	Machine Shop	W	Workshops
PS	Paint Shop	WS	Weaving Shops
S	Store	X	Cloaks

Fig. 263 The Bauhaus—plan. The use of a series of inter-related cubes gives an impression of moving out into space which is quite new

workshops for cabinet-making, weaving, theatrical design, printing, and metal work, etc., and also exhibition space and lecture theatres (Fig. 263). Gropius had his own private studio, and the teaching staff were given Gropius-designed houses in a wood near by. Though today the form of the buildings which Gropius designed may appear rather thin and papery, the design as a whole was much more mature and advanced than anything done to that date. As usual, Gropius made full use of the new materials, and the large glass curtain is now famous. The whole scheme is an expression of the aesthetic which the school was trying to establish.

At its height the Bauhaus must have been one of the greatest educational ventures ever devised. But during its entire life-time it was under constant attack from all sides. The general public were baffled by the revolutionary teaching. The expressionists condemned its approach, whilst the academicians found its aims equally repugnant. Further criticism came from the political

parties of both right and left wings. In retrospect it is possible to appreciate the work of Gropius and what his team were trying to do. In their attempts to integrate the training of artist, architect, sculptor, and industrial designer they were only trying to affirm the fundamental unity of the problems which all creative designers have to solve. Each branch of the arts may approach these problems from a slightly different direction, but in the end, each must make his creation work. Despite constant criticism, the Bauhaus influence began to infiltrate into industry. Manufacturers began to seek Bauhaus-trained designers to supervise the design of their products. Lighting fixtures, carpets, textiles, and furniture began to assume new and more thoughtfully conceived forms and colours. Like the new and advanced painting, Bauhaus design began to be accepted. But by this time Hitler was assuming power, and in 1933 the school was disbanded and most of the creative talent in Germany sought refuge outside the country.

Plate 57

*The Einstein Tower,
Potsdam (1920–1),
by Erich Mendelsohn*

In radical opposition to the rational geometry of the Bauhaus school were the Expressionist architects, and of these Erich Mendelsohn, Hans Poelzig, and Otto Bartning were most influential. After the rationalist building of such designers as Oud, Gropius, and Mies van de Rohe, their buildings seem freakish and the forms senselessly distorted (Pl. 57). It is the architecture of Le Corbusier and Mies van der Rohe that continued the line of development.

Le Corbusier*

Charles-Édouard Jeanneret, better known as Le Corbusier, came from a Swiss family who had been painters and engravers for generations. He worked with Perret in Paris between 1908 and 1909, learning to use reinforced concrete. He then spent a short time in Berlin with Behrens, and as a result of this association he published his first book on the German industrial art movement. He then visited Greece and the Near East. From the study of classical architecture he found the stimulus he needed, and he returned to Europe ready to begin his work with renewed enthusiasm. Le Corbusier is one of the most advanced architectural thinkers and theorists that the twentieth century has produced. His early books were both important and influential, for he was one of the first to preach the machine aesthetic. He gave to the word 'functional' much of its present meaning when applied to architecture and objects of everyday use, and he was the first to instance the aeroplane and the steamship as examples of functional design and beauty. The medium in which Le Corbusier expressed his architectural ideas is reinforced concrete, and the language of his architecture is that of simple geometric shapes. From these basic ingredients he managed to forge a style which is at once highly personal and lucid. His theory of contemporary architecture and construction is formulated with typical clarity of thought. The basic ingredients of his theory of structure are the pillar and the reinforced concrete skeleton. The pillar must be left free to rise through the building, taking all the load of the structure, leaving the walls nothing to support. Closely allied to the pillar is the skeleton which supports the

*Since this passage was written Le Corbusier has died. He was given a State funeral at the Louvre in Paris on 1 September 1965.

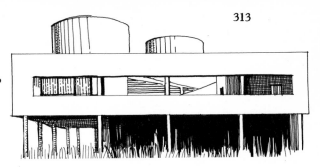

Fig. 264 The Villa Savoye, Poissy (1928–30), by Le Corbusier. A striking house of great originality

horizontal planes of the floor. This leaves the interior space quite free to be moulded at will by light screen walls placed according to the demands of the building. This achieves absolute freedom of planning, for if necessary the floors can be divided independently without reference to the disposition of space either above or below. Further, as the walls become simply protective screens, they can be arranged and pierced at will. This is what Le Corbusier meant by *le plan libre.* He also paid much more attention to both the roof of the house and the space beneath. As the pillars rose right through the house from ground to ceiling it was possible to suspend the house in the air, utilizing the space under the house to let the garden continue. Similarly the roof achieved a new significance. He quickly realized that with the new structural technique a pitched roof was no longer essential and so he adopted the flat roof, to add new amenities to the house in the form of a recreation space enlivened by a roof-garden.

It is now possible to grasp the difference between the American idea of open-planning, as formulated by Frank Lloyd Wright, and the European concept as practised by Le Corbusier and his followers. A Wright house is a lair, freely planned inside but offering protection to its occupants. Indeed, so well does the building merge with the

landscape that it becomes almost an example of natural camouflage. A Le Corbusier house, on the other hand stands out strong and clear and can be entered with freedom from almost any side. Wright allowed his houses to spread over the landscape; Le Corbusier liked to contain his house within a cube, but it is an open cube, in which space and solid are freely moulded.

These basic elements of design are given almost perfect expression in the Villa Savoye at Poissy, France, (1928–30; Fig 264): the pillars rising through the building, the screen walls pierced by the long panoramic windows, which form such a typical Le Corbusier feature, the free space under the house, and the flat roof giving space for garden and recreation area. Progress from floor to floor is by ramp, and these ramps, though not strictly 'functional' in terms of space-saving, give that freedom of movement and smooth transition from level to level that Le Corbusier was so keen to achieve (Fig. 265). The pair of houses for

Fig. 265 The Villa Savoye—side elevation

The use of the ramp instead of a staircase gives a new sense of movement through the floors from ground to roof

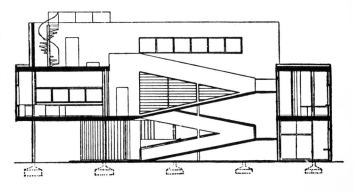

Fig. 266 The Weissenhof Housing Scheme, Stuttgart (1927), by Le Corbusier

the Weissenhof housing scheme at Stuttgart (Fig. 266) again show his ability to design blocks of great plastic beauty, with plans as compact as the exterior elevations would suggest. In the Villa Garches, near Paris (Fig. 267), of 1927, the garage, servants' quarters and utilities are situated on the ground floor, and by raising the living accommodation to the first floor, a return to the Renaissance 'piano-nobile' is effected, with the long strips of windows right across the façade. In 1927 the competition for the Palace of the League of Nations building took place. The results of this competition were as illuminating as they were disappointing. For the first time architects working

in the contemporary idiom challenged the dull routine of the Academic tradition. As it happened, the Academy won, but it was a hollow victory. Over 330 projects were submitted, and it was evident that the scheme submitted by Le Corbusier and his cousin Pierre Jeanneret, was of especial significance. This scheme was contrary to the established style of contemporary office-building, which had held sway for decades. But so novel were the needs of the new building that traditional methods were inadequate to meet the new demands. As set out by the commission the programme for the scheme was divided into three sections; firstly, there was the Secretariat, where the daily work of the League was to be carried on, secondly, there was the provision of meeting-places for the committees of various sorts which met at irregular intervals; and thirdly, there was the large hall necessary for the yearly meeting of the General Assembly. There was also a vast library to be housed in the layout. And in addition to these requirements, there were the problems of movement of traffic, which would naturally be very heavy at times.

*Fig. 267 The Villa Garches, near Paris (1927),
by Le Corbusier*

*Fig. 268   The Swiss Students' Pavilion, Paris
(1930–2), by Le Corbusier
This building shows clearly
Corbusier's ideas about a building
being a 'floating cube'*

*Plate 58   Unité d'Habitation, Marseilles
(1946–52), by Le Corbusier—
his attempt to put his ideas on
mass-dwellings into practice*

The jury consisted of six eminent architects, Berlage from Holland, Hoffmann from
Austria, Moser from Switzerland, Horta
from Belgium, Lemaresquier from France,
and Sir John Burnet from England. The
first three favoured a modern design, and
the last three supported the more traditional
styles. It is most curious that Horta, himself a revolutionary in his younger days,
should on this occasion have thrown in his
support with the reactionary forces. The
result of the voting was an impasse and,
completely abdicating its responsibilities,
the jury awarded nine first prizes.

Though Horta's vote lost Le Corbusier
the competition, his plan and the way he
had managed to evolve a building excellently
suited to the complex purpose it had to serve,

showed that the new architecture was a
force to be reckoned with. The Swiss
Students' Pavilion at University City in
Paris, which Le Corbusier designed in
1930–2 (Fig. 268), is a complete expression
of his 'floating cube' idea. The building is
raised quite clear of the ground on 'pilotis',
giving absolute freedom of pedestrian movement. The six massive pilotis are joined
together by a joist which supports the four-
storey block above.

The two later buildings which are of the
greatest interest and importance are, however, the Unité d'Habitation at Marseilles
and the Chapel of Notre-Dame-du-Haut at
Ronchamp. The Marseilles block (1947–52;
Pl. 58) is a complete housing-scheme in one
building. The building is the epitome of Le

Fig. 269 Notre-Dame-du-Haut, Ronchamp (1950–5), by Le Corbusier
The various views of this chapel show Corbusier's transition to a more free and plastic form

Corbusier's ideas on the problem of the mass dwelling. The design of the long façade is punctuated by the middle storey, which is occupied by shops. As in the Swiss Pavilion, the building is supported on stilts, and the technique of using poured concrete gives perfect expression to their weight-bearing function. In his earlier buildings he had finished the exterior surfaces of concrete with hard precise edges, but time, and the effects of weathering, had soon made the mechanical precision of the slabs look ragged and untidy. In his later work, therefore, he left the concrete surfaces rough from the marks of the timber shuttering. Both the Swiss Pavilion and the Unité d'Habitation are examples of this treatment. The rough

texture so achieved is both remarkably robust and varied.

The roof of the Marseilles project is turned into recreation space, and the concrete forms which the architect evolved are remarkably sculptural in concept. Le Corbusier had always regarded architecture, sculpture, and painting as merely three different ways of expressing the same things. Throughout the years his architecture became increasingly sculptural in form. The plan and the buildings for the entirely new capital for the State of the Punjab at Chandigarh in India are even more sculptural than the Marseilles block. The most sculptural single building, however, is the chapel at Ronchamp, France (1950–5). The form of

Mies van der Rohe

this is remarkably plastic, and from any point of view it represents a most satisfying arrangement of forms and shapes (Fig. 269). The geometrical rectilinearity of the earlier buildings is replaced by a series of freely sculptured forms which have remarkable cohesion. The south wall is pierced by a number of casually scattered window-openings. Though the placing of these openings appears accidental, their shape and proportion are evolved from his own system of measurement, which he called the 'Modulor'. The effect is both intense and dramatic. Though Le Corbusier's architecture is often thought of as arid and intellectual in content, the Ronchamp chapel has about it a strongly romantic appeal. In his other work too it is possible to discern a latent romanticism. Though this element is rigidly in hand, there is at times a certain dramatic quality in his handling of shape and mass which is highly evocative.

The architecture of Ludwig Mies van der Rohe, on the other hand, is entirely intellectual in its appeal. Both Mies van der Rohe and Le Corbusier started from a very similar point of departure—the 'de Stijl' movement in Holland. This was primarily a painters' movement, the chief practitioners being van Doesburg and Mondrian. The movement did, however, influence both architecture and the applied arts. Mies van der Rohe, however, has remained more faithful to the tenets of 'de Stijl' than many other architects. His Farnsworth House at Plano, Illinois (Fig. 270), reduces the dwelling to a glass cube. This is architecture reduced to its fundamentals. The proportion is beautiful, and the structure revealed, but one begins to suspect that in laying bare the bones of the building, he has also laid bare the bones of the occupants. The interior of the Tugendhat House, at Brno, Czechoslovakia (Fig. 271), has a similar, almost ruthless, quality about it. The keynote of Mies van der Rohe's architecture is simplicity. By a

Fig. 270 *The Farnsworth House, Plano, Illinois (1950), by Mies van der Rohe*

Fig. 271

The interior of the Tugendhat House, Brno (1930), by Mies van der Rohe careful analysis of the function which the building has to fulfil, the simplest form the building can take can be arrived at. Form and function are then expressed with the strictest economy of means. Though both Mies van der Rohe and Le Corbusier divided the internal space of their buildings according to the functional requirements, their concepts of total space were rather different. Whilst Le Corbusier had maintained maximum freedom within the building, the

Fig. 272

Plan of a projected brick country house (1923), by Mies van der Rohe

There is a strong similarity between this plan and the paintings of Mondrian and other members of the 'de Stijl' movement

block was kept to a compact shape. Mies van der Rohe, on the other hand, spread his building out and over the site. The result was a much looser definition of internal and external space. The resulting freedom of movement is well shown in the plan of a project for a brick country house (Fig. 272). Here the walls spread far out, completely breaking the feeling of a compact, self-contained unit. This plan also shows the influence of such painters as Mondrian, for the severely rectangular arrangement of lines and blocks is very similar to many 'de Stijl' paintings.

Throughout his career Mies van der Rohe has adhered to his first ideas on architecture. His forms remain spartan in their severity, and the attraction of his work lies purely in the refinement of proportion. Decoration is utterly lacking, and the materials with which the building is constructed are allowed to make their maximum impact. The Seagram Building (Fig. 273) in New York and the Chapel for the Institute of Technology at Chicago (Fig. 274), illustrate this very well. There is no pretence here; form and structure combine to give perfect expression to his intentions. The Chapel and the Farnsworth House have much of the Greek temple

Fig. 273 The Seagram Building, New York (1956–7). Architects, Mies van der Rohe and P. C. Johnson

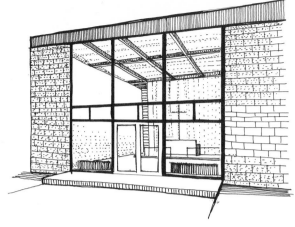

Fig. 274 Chapel for the Illinois
Institute of Technology,
Chicago (1952),
by Mies van der Rohe

Alvar Aalto

about them. But, and this is the important point, it is the Greek temple stripped of all its decoration. This raises one of the fundamental problems of architectural design, which is that it is the architect's task to build beautifully, not beautify buildings. That Mies van der Rohe builds beautifully none can deny (Fig. 275), though some find this architecture too inhuman, its perfection too forbidding—and this quality may in time detract from his reputation. There is nothing of the romantic about Mies van der Rohe; the intellect rules supreme, whereas the romanticism of both Wright and Le Corbusier gives their buildings contact with humanity.

Before leaving developments in Europe and turning to twentieth-century developments in England, the important Finnish architect Alvar Aalto must be mentioned. Aalto did not appear on the European scene until the 1930s. By this time the new architectural language had been formulated and its basic principles accepted. Finland remained remote from European advances, though before the First World War there had been a strong school of architects headed by such figures as Lars Sonck, Eliel Saarinen and J. S. Siren. Sonck was responsible for some striking churches in the Art Nouveau manner, and Saarinen's railway station at Helsinki was a design of some elegance. Aalto

Fig. 275 The National Theatre, Mannheim (project, 1953), by Mies van der Rohe

The work of Mies van der Rohe illustrated here shows his insistence on simple basic shapes and beauty of proportion. The result is both frank and original—though some may well find the result too uncompromising for real aesthetic satisfaction

was, however, the first Finnish architect to achieve international status. Though Aalto used the new methods and materials, it is his use of timber which marks his real contribution to architectural development. He discovered in this traditional material new potentialities for creative design. Unfortunately Aalto's career coincided with the most troubled period of Finland's history. Shortage of public money curtailed building activities, and therefore important public buildings are not part of Aalto's output. His first building to be known outside Finland was the Turun–Sanomat offices at Turku. The most striking feature of these newspaper offices was the handling of the mushroom piers inside the building. His Tuberculosis Sanatorium at Paimio of 1929–33 was a complex building, and the first example of the modern style being applied to hospital architecture. In this building the special requirements of the patients were catered for and provision was made to encourage the patients to meet together in small groups. In the City Library at Viipuri, Aalto designed a lecture theatre which was provided with a roof of irregular wave forms to aid the acoustic properties. Aalto was also interested in the design of furniture, and some of his designs in laminated plywood are both sensible and elegant.

If developments in Europe are to be summarized we must return to the works of Le Corbusier and Mies van der Rohe. The work of these two architects continued the development in the handling of space which we have seen developing from the Renaissance, through Baroque, down to the present century. The Baroque saw the loosening up of the axial emphasis of the Renaissance. The treatment of space became more plastic, and the interior and exterior began to diverge. In the present century we are presented with a complete integration of the two aspects of a building. Interior and exterior are so interwoven that it is sometimes difficult to separate the two. The gradual emergence of the modern concept goes back to the beginnings of the exploitation of iron in building—to the Crystal Palace and Labrouste's library-stacks in the Bibliothèque Nationale, and also to the work of the leading painters of the period.

Great Britain

At the end of the nineteenth century England was leading Europe both architecturally and in the realm of the decorative arts. The work of Morris, Voysey, Webb, and Mackintosh was watched attentively on the Continent. The twentieth century unfortunately saw a relapse into the most arid conservatism relieved only occasionally by the odd shaft of light. One of the few creative talents to continue active during the early years of the century was Sir Edwin Lutyens (1869–1944), who, during the 1890s, produced work which rivalled in quality and quantity that of Shaw, Voysey, and Webb.

Fig. 276

*The Deanery Gardens,
Sonning, Berks.,
by Sir Edward Lutyens*

His early work was traditional, characterized by a feeling for fine proportion and beautifully executed detail. The Deanery Gardens, Sonning, Berks. (1899; Fig. 276), may be considered the culminating point of his early work. He was also responsible for the design of Hampstead Garden Suburb, London, 1908, but his most important commission was doubtless the design of the layout of New Delhi, as the capital of India. The scheme was one of some grandeur, and the buildings not only have an importance suitable to their purpose but also manage to include some reference to the architectural heritage of India herself.

Nevertheless the tone of the general architectural scene in this country was one of unrelieved boredom. The various 'styles' of preceding architectural periods were churned out with almost unending monotony, and apparently without thought or understanding. The 'tooth-and-gap' effect of a line of semi-detached houses sporting the matchboard imitation 'half-timbering' of 'stockbroker's Tudor' gave an air of respectability as shallow as it was bogus. Architecture sank into a characterless morass of conformity in which such houses as Behrens's 'New Ways' at Northampton, built in 1926 (Fig. 277), shone out like a lighthouse. This important

Fig. 277 New Ways, Northampton, by Peter Behrens

house was to set the trend in architectural design in England, and architects such as Thomas Tait and the MARS (Modern Architectural Research) group began to work in the new idiom.

These architects were the exception rather than the rule. The general trend was a debasement of the form of past styles which descended at times almost into caricature, with ugly and ill-considered proportions. A fine example of this architectural hotchpotch is Vincent Harris's Civic Hall in Leeds, Yorkshire, built between 1930 and 1933. The inspiration for the façade seems to be Wren, but the use of the classical canon is rendered senseless and inappropriate by the awkward triangular site. The classicism of the façade is almost reduced to high comedy by the protrusion of two great gilded clocks which stick out like twin time-telling ears.

It was during the decade of the 1930s that the influx of architects from Hitlerite Germany made such an impression on this country. Architects of the stature of Gropius, Mendelsohn, Chermayeff, and Marcel Breuer were an invigorating influence; the force of their example and teaching—and they were all powerful teachers—explains why much of the work of native architects of this period was so clearly influenced by continental models. Gropius came to England in 1934 and in partnership with Maxwell Fry designed the Impington Village College, Cambs., in 1936. This was one of the first schools to be designed in the modern manner, and the pavilion-type of building which they used provided the model for many subsequent school layouts. Mendelsohn and Chermayeff designed the De la Warr Pavilion at Bexhill in 1935. This is a building of many attractions and is perfectly suited to its purpose. The strong horizontal

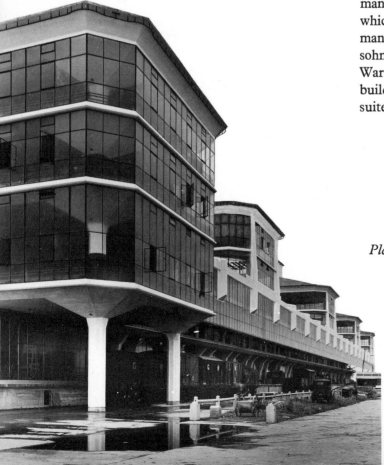

Plate 59   The Boots Factory, Beeston, near Nottingham (1930–2), by Sir Owen Williams

This structure makes use of the 'mushroom' type of concrete construction developed by Maillart before the First World War

emphasis echoes the long sea-scape horizon, and the rounded projecting staircase—a favourite device of Mendelsohn—suggests the form of waves and relieves the formalism of the rest of the building.

Some industrial buildings fared rather better than domestic projects. One of the most influential of these was Owen Williams's chemical plant which he built for Boots, at Beeston near Nottingham, 1930–2 (Pl. 59). Mushroom construction provided the maximum floor space, and completely glazed walls spread an even light over all parts of the building.

In 1938, the firm of Tecton, which was founded by Lubetkin and was already responsible for the delightful Penguin Pool in the Regent's Park Zoo, designed the Finsbury Health Centre. The design of this building owes something to Le Corbusier,

and though the site is cramped the building manages to give an air of spaciousness. In the same year William Crabtree designed the Peter Jones Store in Sloane Square, London. The gently curving façade of the building is refreshingly simple, and this was an early attempt to provide uninterrupted floor space for sales-areas and store-rooms in this country (Fig. 278).

The outbreak of war in the autumn of 1939 interrupted building in this country, and for the next six years building was brought to a standstill, except for that of airfields and military installations. The cessation of hostilities, however, presented the architect with many new and exciting

Fig. 278

The Peter Jones store, Sloane Square, London (1938), by William Crabtree, in association with Slater & Moberly and C. H. Riley

problems. The most important of these were the rebuilding of the vast areas in towns which had been laid waste by enemy air attacks and the building of completely new towns in an effort to replace the slum property, now long overdue for demolition. Many towns prepared extensive schemes for the complete replanning of their city centres and the systematic zoning of their residential areas. None of these schemes was the product of one man, but the combined effort of a team comprising architects, sociologists, and engineers, who produced a complete social survey. The best-known pioneer in this field was Sir Patrick Abercrombie, and he was responsible for the master-plans of such cities as Bath, Bristol, Sheffield, Plymouth, and London. The scope and foresight of his plans were far in advance of the times, and forecast with great accuracy many of the problems which are with us to this day. Despite the wisdom of his findings, many of his ideas were never carried through, and a number of cities are now struggling with the problems his planning would have avoided. Towns such as Coventry and Plymouth, which did take some notice of the planners' advice, are now reaping the benefits. The shopping precincts at Coventry provide shoppers with traffic-free areas where they can browse at leisure. Built on two levels, the roughly rectangular areas are

Plate 60   The Roehampton Estate, London, by L.C.C. architects (Hubert Bennett, in succession to J. L. Martin & R. H. Matthew). A modern example of low-cost housing, to accommodate 9,500 people on a site of 128 acres

Fig. 279 The Royal Festival Hall, London (1951), by the L.C.C. Architecture Department

arranged so that interesting perspectives of buildings within and without the area can be seen.

The formation of new towns created other problems, and it was decided that these satellite towns were not to be regarded purely as dormitory-areas but were to be complete communities in themselves. All aspects of modern life were to be catered for, and all the amenities of modern living were to be provided. The people who were to live in these communities were to represent a cross-section of society at large and were to include both manual workers and professional people. This idea has been put into practice in such towns as Stevenage, Harlow, Crawley, and Hemel Hempstead.

London presented its own problems, and here such housing estates as Roehampton and the Alton estate at Wandsworth are notable. Advantage has been taken of the site, and the nature of the terrain has been respected, making trees and green areas important features of the schemes (Pl. 60).

Though much valuable work has been done in the field of school-building, too often designs have been spoiled by the use of too much glass and too thin partition walls;

the first leads to extremes of temperature, and the other means that the noise penetrates from one class-room to the other. In the larger schools and colleges multi-storey blocks are used, but in the smaller primary and secondary schools single-storey buildings are more popular. Many schools make use of prefabricated components, which may be an advantage financially but tend to impose a certain uniformity on the appearance.

One of the most important single factors to influence post-war design was the Festival of Britain, held in 1951. Though most of the buildings erected in connection with this event were of only a temporary nature, this sort of function does give some opportunity for both experiment and display. Many of the features of this exhibition were both new and exciting, and it provided the opportunity for some of our young designers to try their wings. Two buildings of more lasting importance did emerge from the Festival, however. One was the Dome of Discovery, by Ralph Tubbs, a daring construction in aluminium. The other was the Royal Festival Hall (Fig. 279), designed by R. H. Matthew and J. L. Martin. Though the

Plate 62 *Guildford Cathedral (begun 1936), by Sir Edward Maufe*

Plate 61 *Liverpool Cathedral (begun 1903), by Sir Giles Gilbert Scott*

Plates 61 and 62 represent the last of the 'traditional' type of religious architecture. Both have a certain natural beauty, but the question is, 'Do they serve the times for which they were built?'

acoustic qualities of the concert hall have proved disappointing, the design of the building as a whole was successful. The problem was to provide a concert hall on the south bank of the river so that advantage could be taken of the constantly changing river-scenery from the lounges and restaurants which were to form part of the amenities. The difficulties were the elimination of external noise both from the Hungerford Bridge, which carries main line rail-traffic, and from the river. The problems of sound insulation were finally solved by making the auditorium a separate box surrounded by a bigger box which contained the various facilities—restaurants, bars, lounges, booking and administrative offices, and artists' changing-rooms. Though great care was taken over the design of the auditorium and the acoustic qualities of various materials were carefully considered and varied throughout the interior, the sound proved at first to be too dry and clinical for the performance of orchestral works, and extensive alterations were made in 1965. Despite these shortcomings, the design has had some influence on concert halls in other countries.

During this century three major cathedrals have been built. The earliest of these was that at Liverpool, designed by Sir Giles Scott; later, Sir Edward Maufe designed one for Guildford; and after the war one at Coventry was designed by Sir Basil Spence. Construction also began on a most interesting Roman Catholic cathedral at Liverpool, designed by Frederick Gibberd. The first two of these cathedrals are on traditional lines and in the Gothic style, which has undergone a certain simplification and modernization. Scott's design can safely be

regarded as the last of a line, for there are no longer the masons available to carry out the stone-carving and masonry necessary for a building of such magnitude. Although construction began in 1903 the work was still continuing in 1965, and owing to the dwindling number of masons it will be many years before the final stones are laid. The conception has, however, a certain magnificence, and it is a lasting monument to a particular school of thought (Pl. 61).

The Guildford cathedral is built of brick, and has been carried through in something like thirty-five years. The exterior is a simple and dignified design with tall lancet-like windows, and the interior has a solemn grandeur (Pl. 62).

Though both Liverpool and Guildford are products of the present century they both reflect the pre-war outlook and architectural climate; their form and style are what, traditionally, we would expect a a cathedral to look like. The cathedral at Coventry, however, is a product of the post-war generation of architects. The old cathedral was completely gutted by enemy action, and only the tower and shell of the original building still stand. The new cathedral was sited so as to include what remains of the original building, and is therefore orientated north and south, not east and west, though to save confusion the usual terminology of 'east-end' and 'west-end' is adhered to. Though at first sight the cathedral appears to be in the modern idiom, closer examination soon reveals a conventional plan and, to a certain extent, close affinities with traditional styles. The simple cliff-like walls of the eastern end, for example, are reminiscent of the fortress-like quality of Norman work, just as the light and effective vaulting of the ceiling suggests Perpendicular fan-vaulting.

The plan actually carried out differs only in minor points from Spence's first idea, which was that of a simple open nave, made to appear more spacious by the use of very light columns supporting the roof. From the west-end no windows are visible down the length of the nave, as they are carefully angled to throw the light forward onto the altar. The whole effect is very simple, and the only relief is provided by the series of very beautifully lettered panels, which are one of the most outstanding achievements of the whole scheme.

As we progress a short way up the nave towards the east-end the brilliance of John Piper's baptistery window on the right makes an immediate impression. The marvellously-judged tone and colour-design which, starting from the deeper colours of the spectrum, works up to a pitch of astonishing brilliance in the centre of the window, is perhaps the most memorable feature of the whole cathedral. The nave-glass, which can only be seen from the east-end, is also impressive; these windows were designed at the Royal College of Art by Lawrence Lee, and in retrospect it is the glass that lingers in the memory when details of the building itself begin to fade.

The eastern end is, of course, taken up by the great tapestry designed by Graham Sutherland and woven in France. Technically the work is a miracle, the colours and textures of a Sutherland painting have been caught with complete verisimilitude, yet one feels that this was not conceived as a tapestry but as a painting. The design of the Christ in Majesty, like that of the whole cathedral, is quite traditional; the particular form which Christ takes, and the shapes and beasts which surround him, occur frequently in Romanesque and medieval church decoration. In the last resort, however, the tapestry must be counted a failure, though a magnificent one.

Whether the whole cathedral is a success is a matter for debate. There are certainly many felicities of design, and only time can decide whether the idea was forward-looking enough to be completely successful. When the new Roman Catholic cathedral in Liverpool is finished, a comparison of the two buildings will be at once interesting and instructive, and may help to clear our minds on both what a cathedral is for and how the problem of design should be approached.

The design of the smaller churches which have been called into existence to serve the new towns has raised many problems concerning the function of the church in the twentieth century. Should it be traditional or contemporary in style? Should it be centrally-planned, so that the altar is placed in the centre of the congregation and not far removed, as in the more usual plan? Should there be provision for a social centre, so that the church can once again be drawn into the life of the community, or should it be a special place for religious worship only? These are only some of the problems that the modern church architect has to face. Is the frequent failure of the design simply due to the failure of the church authorities to brief the architect thoroughly enough before he began his task? At the present time church-architecture is going through a period of transition and indecision. Whether a truly new and vital style will eventually emerge is a fascinating subject for speculation.

On a rather more utilitarian level, the problem of providing new offices and factories has received a rather more positive solution. Many of the new office-blocks in city centres are more exciting than in the past, and the entirely new building problems presented by atomic power stations must have called for the closest collaboration between architect, scientist, and technician.

There are two bridges which must be mentioned, both of them are major engineering achievements. These are the Runcorn–Widnes road bridge and the new Forth road bridge in Scotland. The Runcorn–Widnes bridge has a span of 1,000 feet taken by one single arch, and the Forth bridge has a main span of over 3,300 feet and is the fourth longest suspension-bridge in the world. The design of both these bridges continues the tradition of English metal bridge-building which began so long ago at Coalbrookdale.

Since the war, architecture in Great Britain has improved a great deal, and a more characteristic style is beginning to emerge. This improvement in architectural standards is doubtless due to the influence of the continental architects who emigrated to this country during the 1930s. Their attitude must have influenced that of those who are now teaching architecture, for the curriculum is now much more realistic than in pre-war days. In addition, the general public is now much more tolerant of innovation, and new styles are more readily accepted.

Nevertheless there are still certain factors which detract from modern architecture in this country. Mass production has revolutionized the building industry, but it has left in its wake a uniformity which spreads throughout the country. The variety and vitality which was bred from the use of local materials has now vanished. It is unfortunate that the loss of the local craft-tradition is the price that has had to be paid for economy and speed of construction.

The finish of modern buildings also leaves much to be desired. Already there are long streaks of discoloration from the metal supports on the porch of Coventry Cathedral, and too often stories of bad finishing and warped woodwork in new buildings are heard. New materials, which are said to withstand the smoke and grime of the modern city, seem ineffective. The new blocks of flats which are now appearing in many northern industrial cities, such as Leeds and Bradford, look most attractive when first completed, yet within a few months they look dirty and stained. The solution to these problems is important if the new style is to develop into something of lasting worth.

The scope of the modern architect is enormous, since new types of buildings are coming into existence every year. This sense of adventure and discovery makes the study of architecture exciting and rewarding, for buildings are the mirror of the society which produces them, and they are much more part of our environment than any other art-form. Paintings, poetry, literature, sculpture, and music we can ignore if we wish; architecture we must experience almost every moment of our lives. This places an enormous responsibility on the architect, for his work can enliven or spoil our cities for generations to come. One is bound to pose the question 'What will our architecture look like in 300 years time?' The outlook sometimes seems depressing; though with the new 'throw-away' society perhaps this problem will not arise as we seem to be on the verge of seeing 'throw-away' architecture come into being.

Whether or not a new style is emerging in Europe it is difficult to say. Perhaps the creative force has worked itself out there, and it is to new countries that we must look for future developments. The attempt by Brazil to create a new capital city has suffered many vicissitudes, but if the project comes to full fruition this may be the country which makes the most important contribution to mid-twentieth-century architecture.

FURTHER READING

Arnold Whittick, *European Architecture in the 20th Century*, 2 vols. Crosby Lockwood & Sons, 1950.

A thoroughgoing survey, and the writing is lively and interesting.

J. M. Richards, *An Introduction to Modern Architecture*. Penguin Books, 1940; rev. ed. 1962.

This book has remained fresh throughout its long life and is still very necessary reading. The chapter on construction techniques is especially useful.

Jürgen Joedicke, *A History of Modern Architecture*. Architectural Press, 1959.

A splendid book, with plenty of illustrations and a country-by-country review of developments.

Eric de Maré, *New Ways of Building*. Architectural Press, 1948.

A very comprehensive survey of modern building methods.

Neville Conder, *An Introduction to Modern Architecture*. Art & Technics, 1949.

A good short introduction.

Peter Blake, *The Master Builders*. Gollancz, 1960.

Three long articles on Le Corbusier, Frank Lloyd Wright, and Mies van der Rohe. All of them are equally good and are both enlightening and informative. They are now available separately, published by Penguin Books in three volumes.

Henrique E. Mindlin, *Modern Architecture in Brazil*. The Architectural Press, 1956.

An informative book, well illustrated.

The reader is also directed to the book by Vincent Scully in the 'Great Ages of World Architecture' Series, and to the 'Masters of World Architecture' volume on Gaudí, which are mentioned in the General Bibliography. There is also a useful book on Mackintosh by Thomas Howard, published by Routledge in 1952.

GENERAL BIBLIOGRAPHY

WORLD ARCHITECTURE

Banister Fletcher, *A History of Architecture on the Comparative Method*, 17th ed., rev. R. A. Cordingley. Athlone Press, 1961.

In its modern form this is still probably the best single-volume work on the subject. Earlier editions are very lacking in information and are biased in opinion on late nineteenth-century and twentieth-century architecture.

World Architecture by various authors. Hamlyn, 1963.

This is a very attractive and well illustrated volume which one finds oneself referring to with increasing regularity. Useful glossary.

H. Heathcote Statham, *The History of Architecture*, 3rd ed., rev. H. Braun. Batsford, 1950.

A very useful volume, particularly as regards structural techniques.

Nikolaus Pevsner, *An Outline of European Architecture*. Penguin Books, 1943; 7th rev. ed., 1963.

This old friend keeps turning up. In its new format it forms a comprehensive and wise survey of European architecture. This is not an easy book for the complete beginner.

F. M. Simpson, *Simpson's History of Architectural Development*, new ed. Longmans, 1954–6.

Vol. 1 *Ancient and Classical Architecture*, by Hugh Plommer

Vol. 2 *Early Christian, Byzantine and Romanesque Architecture*, by Cecil Stewart

Vol. 3 *Gothic Architecture*, by Cecil Stewart

Vol. 4 *Renaissance Architecture*, by J. Quentin Hughes and Norbert Lynton

Vol. 5 *Nineteenth and Twentieth Century Architecture*, by Thomas Howard

These are all very useful volumes and have recently been revised. Illustrations are good and the texts full of factual information.

John Gloag, *Guide to Western Architecture*. Allen & Unwin, 1958.

A sound guide to the subject, very well illustrated with carefully chosen examples of great character.

The Great Ages of World Architecture Series. Prentice Hall International, New York, 1961–3.

Each book in this series deals, as the title suggests, with one particular period of world architecture. The illustrations are very useful indeed, but the texts suffer for the British reader from being written in American English. They should be used with care; some are very useful, but by no means all.

F. E. Brown, *Roman Architecture*
R. Branner, *Gothic Architecture*
H. A. Millon, *Baroque and Rococo*
V. Scully, Jr., *Modern Architecture*
R. L. Scranton, *Greek Architecture*
W. MacDonald, *Early Christian and Byzantine Architecture*
H. Saalman, *Medieval Architecture*
Bates Dowery, *Renaissance Architecture*
J. Hoag, *Western Islamic Architecture*
Nelson Wu, *Chinese and Indian Architecture*
D. Robertson, *Pre-Columbian Architecture*

Masters of World Architecture Series. Mayflower Books, 1960.

The books in this series are well illustrated and contain both factual information and informed opinion. They form a valuable addition to the architectural shelves in any library.

F. Gutheim, *Alvar Aalto*, 1960
F. Choay, *Le Corbusier*
G. R. Collins, *Antoni Gaudí*, 1960
J. M. Fitch, *Walter Gropius*, 1960
W. von Eckardt, *Eric Mendelsohn*, 1960
A. Drexler, *Ludwig Mies van der Rohe*
A. L. Huxtable, *Pier Luigi Nervi*, 1960
E. McCoy, *Richard Neutra*
S. Papadaki, *O. Niemeyer*
A. Bush Brown, *Louis Sullivan*, 1960
V. Sculley, Jr., *Frank Lloyd Wright*

Buildings of Europe Series, ed. Harald Busch and Bernd Lohse. Batsford, 1959–62.

Romanesque Europe, with commentaries on the illustrations by H. Domke, 1960
Gothic Europe, with commentaries on the illustrations by H. Domke, 1959
Renaissance Europe, with commentaries on the illustrations by Hans Weigert, 1961
Baroque Europe, with commentaries on the illustrations by Eva-Maria Wagner, 1962

These books are particularly valuable for many beautiful photographs.

Patrick Geddes, *Cities in Evolution*. Williams & Norgate, 1915; new ed. 1949.
A good introduction to the problems of city planning.

Lewis Mumford, *Technics and Civilization*. Routledge, 1947.
— *The Culture of Cities*. Secker & Warburg, 1938.
— *The Condition of Man*. Secker & Warburg, 1944.

These three volumes form a valuable source of reference material for the social background. They are also an attempt to link the technological developments with the social ethos of the time and show how one influenced the other.

The Oxford History of English Art, ed. T. S. R. Boase. O.U.P., 1952–.

A history of the art of this country in 11 volumes by various authors. These volumes are useful on occasion for their comments both on architecture and on the social background to many of the artistic movements of the time.

The volumes are:

I To A.D. 871 *   VII 1553–1625, 1962
II 871–1100, 1952 VIII 1625–1714, 1957
III 1100–1216, 1953 IX 1714–1800 *
IV 1216–1307, 1957 X 1800–1870, 1959
V 1307–1461, 1949 XI From 1870 *
VI 1461–1553 *

* Not yet published.

Literary Sources of Art History, ed. Elizabeth Gilmore Holt. Princeton University Press, 1947.

Full of fascinating information.

S. Giedion, *Space, Time and Architecture*, 3rd ed., O.U.P., 1954.

An interesting and stimulating book.

John Summerson, *Heavenly Mansions*. Cresset Press, 1949.

A delightful collection of essays on a variety of subjects, each good of its kind.

Geoffrey Scott, *The Architecture of Humanism*. Methuen, University Paperbacks, 1961.

An old book, first published in 1915, but still very stimulating.

Pierre Levedan, *French Architecture*. Penguin Books, 1956.

A splendid introduction, well illustrated, and with a useful section of biographical notes on the architects mentioned in the text.

Sidney Toy, *A History of Fortification 1600 B.C.–A.D. 1600*. Heinemann, 1939.

R. Fedden and J. Thompson, *Crusader Castles*. John Murray, 1957.

This is an enlarged version of an earlier work and a useful short introduction to the subject.

BRITISH ARCHITECTURE AND ITS BACKGROUND

F. Gibberd, *The Architecture of England from Norman Times to the Present Day*, 5th ed. Architectural Press, 1944.

A very good short introduction; the illustrations are well chosen and the book has stood the test of time very well.

N. Lloyd, *A History of the English House*. Architectural Press, 1931.

A most authoritative book.

R. Turnor, *The Smaller English House*. Batsford, 1952.

A valuable guide to the smaller homes. Well illustrated, and should be read in conjunction with one of the books which deals with the more imposing showplaces.

E. A. Fisher, *An Introduction to Anglo-Saxon Architecture and Sculpture*. Faber, 1959.

A well illustrated volume which fills in the ground only touched on in this present book.

John Harvey, *Gothic England*. Batsford, 1947.

A sound guide to the period.

Geoffrey Webb, *Architecture in Britain in the Middle Ages*. Penguin Books, 1956.

> One of the Pelican History of Art series, and therefore a most valuable addition to the library shelves.

John Summerson, *Architecture in Britain 1530–1830*. Penguin Books, 1963.

> This is now (like all the other books in the Pelican History of Art) the authoritative work on the subject—indispensable for any serious study of the period.

J. Alfred Gotch, *The English Home from Charles I to George IV*. Batsford, 1918.

> An old book, but containing many useful illustrations and plans. The text is now out of date in parts and must be used with care.

Doreen Yarwood, *The English Home: A Thousand Years of Furniture and Decoration*. Batsford, 1956.
—*The Architecture of England*. Batsford, 1956.

> Both these volumes have many valuable drawings and photographs, and the text is both clear and concise.

Sacheverell Sitwell, *British Architects and Craftsmen*. Pan Major, 1959.

> A delightfully written work.

Patrick Abercrombie and Derek Plumstead, *A Civic Survey and Plan for Edinburgh*. Oliver and Boyd, 1949.

> A complete analysis of the city.

Visual History of Modern Britain, ed. Jack Simmons. Vista Books.

> Geoffrey Martin, *The Town* (1961)
> Jack Simmons, *Transport* (1962)
> M. W. Barley, *Home* (1963)

> These are stimulating books, well illustrated, and give a good deal of information on the social background.

Steen Eiler Rasmussen, *London; the Unique City*. Penguin Books, 1960.

> A fascinating study.

> In addition to the books listed above there is the monumental 'Buildings of England' Series, edited by Dr Pevsner and published by Penguin Books, a county-by-county survey of all buildings of merit.

G. M. Trevelyan, *A Shortened History of England*. Penguin Books, 1959.
—*An Illustrated Social History*. 4 vols., Longmans, 1944.

> There is much useful material in these volumes. The *Illustrated Social History* is now available in Penguin Books.

The Pelican History of England, ed. J. E. Morpurgo, 8 vols. Penguin Books, 1950–5.

> This series of histories is useful, for each volume has a section on the artistic and social developments of the period with which it deals.

D. Hartley and M. M. Elliot, *Life and Work of the People of England*, 6 vols. Batsford, 1925–31.

> A useful work for details of social background.

ABACUS (Latin: *abacus*—table, tablet) a square slab placed between capital and architrave. The precise form varies from order to order. The square abacus continues in early Gothic, especially in France.

ABUTMENT Solid masonry block from which an arch springs. It must be solid enough to resist outward thrust of arch.

ADYTON Secluded room—often behind cella of temple.

AEDICULE Architectural treatment of opening—usually two columns complete with entablature and pediment.

AGORA Greek version of Roman forum. As the two types are not exactly similar the terms should not be interchanged.

AISLE Division running parallel with nave in a basilica or church. Basilican-type churches on the Continent usually have two aisles on each side of nave—in England this is exceptional.

ALA (Latin: *ala*—wing) a recess for conversation in a Roman house.

AMBULATORY Aisle round apse or circular building. In French Gothic, a continuation of aisles to form processional way.

AMPHIPROSTYLE *See* Temple.

ANNULET (Latin: *annulus*—a ring) small flat fillet round a column. Prominent part of the Doric order.

ANTA Greek equivalent of pilaster. When forming the termination of a temple wall the capital and base differ from those of adjacent columns. Also found in Egyptian temples.

APSE Semicircular or multi-angular termination of a building—usually of a church sanctuary. The apse is a continental device; the term (Latin: *apsis*—arch or vault) referred in classical times to curved seats in theatres, niches in walls and arches and vaults.

APTERAL (Greek: without wings) a temple without columns at the sides.

ARAEOSTYLE *See* Intercolumniation.

ARCADE A row of arches, supported on piers or columns, which may be free-standing or attached to a wall.

ARCHITRAVE The beam, or lowest member of the three principal divisions of the entablature. Loosely applied to any moulding round door or window.

ARCHIVOLT A moulding which follows the line of an arch.

ASHLAR Rectangular blocks of hewn stone in regular courses.

ASTYLAR Without columns (term used of a façade so designed).

ATRIUM (i) In Roman architecture, the main courtyard in a house. (ii) In early Christian architecture, the forecourt of a large church.

ATTIC   In Renaissance architecture, a term applied to a storey above the main cornice of a building. The term is now applied to any rooms in the roof space.

BALDACHINO   A canopy supported by columns, generally over an altar—also known as ciborium.

BALUSTER   Small pillar or column, generally with a swell in it, supporting hand rail or coping. Introduced in Renaissance —but there is a form of baluster peculiar to the Saxon period. A row of balusters is known as a balustrade.

BARBICAN   An extension of the gateway of a castle or town to give added fortification.

BARGE BOARD   Facing-board fixed on gable end.

BARREL VAULT   *See* Vault.

BASE   The lower portion of a column or any architectural feature. The bases of columns fall into three main types: (i) Attic; (ii) Tuscan; (iii) Ionic, Corinthian and Composite. The structural object is to distribute the weight of the column over a larger area.

BASILICA   Roman hall for administrative and judicial functions. The plan of a Roman basilica, which consisted of an oblong hall, with aisles and apsidal ends, became the prototype of the early Christian church. This consisted of a nave with three or five aisles, and an apse at one end.

BATTER   Inward slope (of wall) towards the top.

BAY   In Gothic the term refers to one complete unit, usually the area between columns or piers, stretching across the building from wall to wall, thus forming one unit of repeat. It may also be applied to a unit of arcading on a wall, both internal and external. Not applied to colonnaded architecture, presumably because upper portion is continuous. It is also used of a projecting window.

BERM   Clear space surrounding the outer curtain of a castle.

BOSS   Projecting stone placed at intersection of vaulting-ribs or ends of hood-moulds in Gothic architecture. Often delicately carved with angels or natural forms.

BROACH   Pyramidal structure which is placed at corners of square tower to fill space caused by placing octagonal tower on square base. Popular in thirteenth-century Gothic work in which the whole is often referred to as a broach spire.

BUCRANIA   In Roman architecture the ox-heads found in metopes of a Doric frieze.

BUTTRESS   Generally any projection from the face of a wall designed to resist the outward thrust of upper storeys and roof. The design varies with each period. In French Gothic this becomes a very important feature, and the flying buttress, which is a free-standing member, achieves remarkable development and skill in design and placing.

CALDARIUM   The hot-baths chamber of a Roman thermae.

CAMPANILE A bell tower, especially in late medieval and Italian Renaissance architecture. Usually detached from main building.

CANCELLI In pagan basilicas, a screen or railing dividing off a semicircular court. Later adopted in basilican form of church —cognate with 'chancel'.

CAPITAL Crowning member of a column or pier. Each of the classic orders has its own distinctive capital.

CARAYTID Sculptured female figure used in place of a column. The Erechtheum and the Louvre show these features at their best.

CAULICOLI The eight stalks which support the volutes in Corinthian capitals.

CAVETTO Simple concave moulding. Egyptian and Greek buildings show the moulding in its most refined form; in Renaissance times it became a simple quarter-circle.

CELLA Small rectangular room in the centre of a Greek temple.

CENTERING Temporary framework on which an arch is supported until the keystone is in place. Until modern times wood was generally used, but now iron centering has often been used on bridges, etc., of wide span.

CHANCEL Space for clergy and choir, often separated by a screen from the nave. See Cancelli.

CHEVET A circular or polygonal apse surrounded by an ambulatory which opens on to side chapels: a term applied to a particular type of eastern termination of French cathedrals. The form is not common in England.

CHOIR See Chancel.

CIBORIUM See Baldachino.

CINQUEFOIL An arrangement of five foils terminating in cusps, in Gothic tracery.

CLERESTORY OR CLEARSTORY The highest part of a building, with windows above the general roof level. In churches it applies to windows lighting the nave above the level of the aisle-roofs.

CLOISTERS Covered passages around an open quadrangle. In a monastic building they provided sheltered communication between church, chapter house, refectory, and other parts of the monastery. They were generally situated on the south side of the nave, presumably to catch the maximum of sunlight and warmth.

COFFERS Sunken panels formed in ceilings, vaults and domes.

COLONNADE A range of regularly spaced columns with entablature. If the columns support arches it is called an arcade.

COLOSSAL ORDER Any order where the columns extend from the ground through more than one storey.

COLUMN A free-standing vertical support, usually comprising capital, shaft and base.

CORBEL A projecting block of stone built into a wall to support beams of roof, vault, or floor. In Gothic times corbels were often elaborately carved.

CORBEL TABLE Range of regularly spaced corbels carrying an over-sailing feature or moulding. Generally seen at base of spire or roof parapet in Gothic architecture.

CORBELLING Method of roofing an enclosed space by a series of overhanging courses without recourse to arch or vault construction.

CORNICE In classic or Renaissance architecture, the upper part of entablature, or crowning feature of wall, which projects beyond the face. It can be loosely applied to almost any horizontal moulding which is decorative in character.

CRENELLATION Opening in upper part of parapet for the purposes of fortification and defence.

CROCKET In Gothic architecture a carved projecting block on angle mouldings of spires or gablets (reaches finest development in English Decorated). Design usually consists of conventionalized leaves and foliage.

CROSSING In medieval church architecture, the area where nave, chancel, and transepts intersect. The piers at this point are called crossing piers, and the principal arches which spring from them the crossing arches.

CRYPT A cell partly or entirely under a building—often used as an early burial place. In churches it is usually beneath the chancel.

CUPOLA Small domed erection above general line of building. The dome may be over a circular or a multi-angular apartment.

CURTAIN The wall enclosing a courtyard. The term is usually applied to ramparts around a castle.

CUSP The point formed by the intersection of foils in Gothic tracery. This is an important feature of Gothic architecture for it gives much of the character to the style.

CYMA Originally a classic moulding made up of reverse curves. Where the concave curve is uppermost it is known as cyma-recta; where the convex curve is uppermost, as cyma-reversa.

DADO Term usually applied to the lower portion of walls when treated as a separate part of the decorative scheme. It may also be applied to the block of a pedestal between base and cornice.

DAIS Originally referred to the raised platform in a medieval great hall, where the master and his family and guests dined. Now applied to any raised portion of a room.

DENTIL BLOCKS Tooth-like blocks or cubes in Ionic, Corinthian and Composite cornices.

DIAGONAL RIBS In medieval vaulting, those ribs which spring from the four corner supports and cross the vaulting-apartment diagonally. These are the earliest of the vaulting-rib family. See also 'lierne' and 'tierceron' ribs.

DOME A roof, circular on plan and either semicircular or arch-shaped in section. Strictly, the structural characteristic of a dome is that the masonry should form an arch both horizontally and vertically. Many domes, such as the one on Florence cathedral, do not observe this principle and are, therefore, not true domes,

DONJON Old French word for square tower or keep. N.B. The modern word 'dungeon' derives from this word, but has a very different meaning.

DOSSERET In Byzantine architecture, the deep block placed above the capital. It may have originated from the need to level the tops of unequal columns brought from older buildings.

DRIPSTONE Projecting moulding over windows, doorways, etc., to throw rain clear of the wall. Also known as a hood-moulding.

DRUM (i) The circular wall on which a dome is placed. (ii) The separate sections which make up a complete shaft.

ENCEINTE The outer walls of a group of temples or other buildings grouped together. Castles of enceinte is a term applied to Scottish castles, especially of the thirteenth century, when the walls and towers together are known as the enceinte.

ENTABLATURE The upper part of a classical order. Consists of architrave, frieze, and cornice.

ENTASIS The convex curve which is used in classical columns to counteract the optical illusion which would make straight-sided columns appear to curve inwards.

EXTRADOS The outer curve of an arch formed by the upper edges of the voussoirs.

FAÇADE The face or elevation of any building. Usually applied to the entrance front, implying a large and imposing composition.

FAN-VAULT System of English vaulting. The ribs lose their structural importance and become merely surface decoration resembling a fan.

FASCIA Vertical face or broad moulding usually found in the architrave or entablature of the Orders. Ionic and Corinthian have architraves divided in this manner.

FILLET Narrow flat band used to differentiate one moulding from another.

FINIAL The culminating decoration of a pinnacle or any other architectural feature.

FLÈCHE A slender, usually wooden, spire rising from a roof, especially in French Gothic. It must be a light structure, and many modern flèches are made of wrought-iron.

FLUTE AND FLUTING Vertical channel(s) carved in classical columns. Also occasionally applied to horizontal channelling on capital or base of classical columns or pedestals. Its main purpose is to emphasize the verticality of some upright member.

FLYING BUTTRESS *See* Buttress.

FOIL A small arc opening in Gothic tracery. A cusp separating two foils. The number of foils per opening is signified by Trefoil, Quatrefoil, Cinquefoil, etc.

FOREBUILDING Additional building against a castle keep. Contains the stair to the main entrance and often the chapel.

FRIEZE The central of the three primary divisions of the classical entablature. In Doric it is made up of alternating triglyphs and metopes; in the other orders it is a running band carved with appropriate decoration.

FRIGIDARIUM Cold chamber in the Roman thermae.

GABLE The triangular portion of a wall formed by sloping lines of the roof. In Gothic architecture it becomes as important as the pediment in classic architecture. In its smaller form in Gothic it is often known as a Gablet.

GALILEE Chapel, or porch used as a chapel, in medieval architecture. Origin is uncertain, but may come from the last place the celebrant stopped at in the Sunday procession.

GARDEROBE The latrine, usually in a castle.

GARGOYLE In medieval architecture a projecting water spout, designed to throw rain-water well clear of building, and decorated with grotesque head.

GROIN The edge left by the junction of two intersecting surfaces of a vault.

HYPO-STYLE HALL In Egyptian architecture, a hall of many columns. The two centre rows are higher than the rest, so forming a clerestory which provides illumination. Beyond this gloomy and impressive place the general public was not allowed.

IMPOST Any point from which an arch springs.

INTERCOLUMNIATION The distance between columns, usually expressed in diameters and measured from centre to centre. The following are Vitruvius' types: Pycnostyle—$1\frac{1}{2}$ diameters; Systyle —2 diameters; Eustyle—$2\frac{1}{4}$ diameters;

Diastyle—3 diameters; Araeostyle—4 diameters. Eustyle is the most common, but other intercolumniations are used in the Doric order, owing to the placing of the triglyphs.

JAMBS The sides of door and window openings.

KEY-STONE Central voussoir of a semicircular arch. Often larger than the others and sometimes decorated.

KING-POST A vertical post, of wood or metal, in trussed roof, which extends vertically from ridge to centre of tie-beam beneath.

LANCET ARCH A sharp-pointed arch resembling a lance. Very common in the Early English period, which is often called 'Lancet' in architectural usage.

LANTERN Small glazed structure on the top of dome or tower to provide extra illumination. In some Gothic cathedrals, e.g. York and Ely, the central tower provides a lantern.

LIERNE OR LIERNE RIB In Gothic vaulting, a minor decorative rib which does not spring from the impost and is not a ridge rib. Very common in English Decorated period.

LINTEL A horizontal stone or timber member, sometimes called an architrave, which spans an opening.

LISTS The space between inner and outer walls in medieval castle-design.

LOGGIA A gallery behind a colonnade or arcade, usually on the ground floor. Common in Italian Renaissance palaces. Occasionally introduced under the roof, where it adds interest as well as convenience in outlook.

MACHICOLATION In castle architecture, a corbelled gallery with slits in the floor through which boiling pitch and other delights were poured on the attackers beneath. Although originally strictly military in intention it was often introduced as a decorative feature in later buildings.

MANSARD ROOF A roof in which the lower division is at a steeper pitch than the upper. Named after the elder Mansart, who introduced this feature.

MEGARON The principal hall of a Minoan or Homeric house.

METOPE The rectangular space between triglyphs in Greek Doric order. Sometimes left open in early examples but later filled with decorative carvings.

MEZZANINE A low storey between two lofty ones.

MISERICORD A hinged seat made so as to support a standing person, the underside often grotesquely carved.

MODULE A measure of proportion which is used throughout a building. In classical architecture the module is usually half the diameter of a column at the base. This module was itself divided into 30 parts.

MULLION Vertical division of a window.

MUTULE Projecting inclined block in the Doric cornice. May have derived from the rafter-end in wooden construction.

NAOS Principal chamber in Greek temple —contained the statue of the deity.

NARTHEX A porch in front of west-end of a church, forming an entrance. Common in Early Christian churches.

NAVE The term is applied to the western arm of a church to differentiate it from choir and transepts. Also applied to central aisle of basilican, medieval or Renaissance church, as opposed to side aisles.

NEWEL The central shaft round which wind steps of a circular staircase—also applied to post in which hand-rail is fixed.

OCULUS The eye-like opening at the centre of a dome.

OGEE Moulding comprising a convex and concave curve. The name is also applied to an arch of a similar shape. Introduced in the Decorated period in English architecture, where it was very popular as a decorative feature over door and window openings.

OGIVAL Adjective used to describe French pointed Gothic architecture.

ORDER A term in classical architecture meaning the column and base with entablature. The pedestal is not necessarily part of the order—though it is usually included by architects from Serlio onwards. SUPERIMPOSED ORDERS One order placed vertically over another on a façade. This decorative use of the orders was introduced in Roman times. The sequence is always Doric at ground level, Ionic at first storey, Corinthian or Composite at the top.

ORIEL A window projecting from the wall, usually on an upper storey, supported by corbels or brackets.

ORIENTATION Strictly, a pronounced axis running east–west, but can be used loosely to mean any alignment with points of the compass.

OVERSAILING Any course of stone or brick which protrudes beyond the face of the wall beneath is described as 'oversailing'.

PARIAN MARBLE A fine marble of a waxy appearance; it was the marble most commonly used in Greek sculpture.

PEDESTAL Square, circular or polygonal block used as a support. Originally used as a base for statues but extensively employed as a support for columns and pilasters.

PENDENTIVE The domed triangular shape which results from the transition from a square base to the circular base of a dome. A dome so supported is called a dome on pendentives.

PENTELIC MARBLE A fine-grained white marble in which it was possible to carve the delicate precise detail which the Greeks admired. The Parthenon is of Pentelic marble.

PERI-APSIDAL The term used, in connection with medieval church-building, to describe an eastern termination in which the central eastern apse is surrounded by a continuation of the aisle (known as an ambulatory).

PIANO NOBILE The first floor of an Italian palazzo, containing the principal rooms.

PIER A mass of masonry (as distinct from a column, which is a simple cylindrical, or octagonal, shaft).

PILASTER A flattened rectangular projection in the form of a classical column. The pilaster is a decorative rather than a structural feature.

PILOTIS Posts or stilts supporting a whole building clear of the ground.

PINNACLE In Gothic architecture, a small spiral-like termination to a buttress. Although often highly decorated, pinnacles have the additional function of bringing extra weight on to the buttress.

PLINTH The lowest square member of a column, or any projecting base which runs round a building.

PODIUM The heavy base on which a classical temple stands.

PORTICO A covered entrance porch, supported on at least one side by columns. Particularly applied to classical architecture, though it can be used with reference to certain grand Gothic entrances, such as the one at Peterborough.

PRESBYTERY A term often applied to the whole eastern arm of a church.

PROPYLAEUM (also PROPYLAEA, PROPYLAION, PROPYLON) In Greek architecture, the monumental entrance to a sacred enclosure.

PURLIN A horizontal beam resting on the principal rafters and supporting the subsidiary ones.

QUADRIPARTITE Adjective used to describe the simplest form of cross-vaulting. The two transverse and two diagonal ribs divide the plan into four segments.

QUATREFOIL In Gothic tracery, a four-leaved motif formed by cusps.

QUEEN-POSTS The two upright beams in a roof, standing on the tie-beam, and supporting principal rafter and purlin.

QUOIN Large rectangular stone on the corner of the main wall plane. The decorative nature of quoins is often emphasized by making them protrude slightly, and also by rustication.

RESPOND Half-pier attached to wall to support an arch, or placed at the end of arcade.

RETICULATED Term often applied to English Gothic of the Decorated period, where the openings in the tracery give a net-like effect.

RIDGE RIB The rib running along the apex of a pitched roof.

ROSE-WINDOW In Gothic architecture, a round window filled with tracery.

RUSTICATION A method of giving the appearance of added strength to a building by leaving the stones rough-hewn. The edges of the block are often cut back to give added emphasis.

SEDILIA Seats for the clergy, formed in the wall on south side of chancel.

SEMI-DOME A half-dome set against a building which is fully domed. In this way the semi-dome becomes a kind of extended flying buttress.

SEXPARTITE Adjective describing method of vaulting introduced in both France and England in an attempt to give added strength. The quadripartite bay was further divided by an extra vaulting rib springing from the wall of the compart-ment, thus giving six divisions instead of four.

SGRAFFITO A method of producing wall decorations by laying a thin coat of light plaster over a thicker coat of dark-coloured plaster. The light colour was then scratched away to reveal the dark colour underneath. In this way effects of light on dark or dark on light could be produced.

SHINGLES Pieces of wood used in place of tiles.

SOFFIT The underside of any architectural member or arch or lintel. The soffit was often elaborately decorated in classical architecture.

SOLAR A medieval term for an upper chamber. Usually applied to the private apartment at the upper end of the great hall.

SPANDREL The roughly triangular space at the head of an arch between the curve of the arch and the rectangular wood-mould. The spandrel is often elaborately decorated.

SQUINCH ARCH Arches built diagonally across the corners of a square to convert them to circles or octagons to facilitate the erection of a spire or dome. The alternative method is by pendentives.

STOA In Greek architecture, a long open colonnaded space for the transaction of public business.

STRING-COURSE A horizontal moulding used to mark divisions in the composition of a façade, or to give external expression to an internal division between storeys.

STUCCO Fine plaster applied internally and moulded into decorative features, or used to cover the whole exterior walls with a smooth uniform surface.

STYLOBATE A continuous base on which a row of columns is placed. In Greek architecture it means particularly the upper part of the stepped base on which the Doric columns stand.

SUPERIMPOSED ORDERS *See* Order.

TEMPLE A place or space marked off for the observation of worship, or for meeting. The disposition of the columns around the temple has been given the following terminology:

> *Prostyle* Having a portico at the front only.
> *Amphiprostyle* Having porticos at both ends.
> *Peripteral* Having porticos connected by open colonnades along the sides.
> *Pseudoperipteral* Having porticos only connected by pilasters or half-columns.
> *Dipteral* Having porticos connected by a double range of columns along the sides.
> *Pseudodipteral* Having the same arrangement as Dipteral as regards spacing, but with the inner ranges of columns omitted.

TIE-BEAM The horizontal beam across a roof which prevents the principal rafters from spreading. The tie-beam may be flat or slightly arched.

TIERCERON Intermediate ribs rising from the same capital as the diagonal ribs but not rising to the central boss.

TRABEATED Style of architecture which relies on the use of the post and beam not of the arch and vault, e.g. Greek as opposed to Roman or Gothic.

TRACERY The ornamental stone-work in the upper part of a Gothic window. It may be 'plate' or 'bar' tracery.

TRANSOM The horizontal bar, whether of wood or stone, across a window.

TREFOIL In Gothic tracery, a three-leaved motif formed by cusps.

TRIFORIUM The middle division between nave arcade and clerestory in Romanesque and Gothic church architecture. There is usually a passage-way behind the triforium arcade and above the aisle-roof.

TRIGLYPHS Vertical blocks separated by metopes in the frieze of the Greek Doric entablature. The triglyphs have three vertical flutes or channels.

TYMPANUM The triangular area formed by the sloping and horizontal cornices of a classical pediment. In medieval architecture, the space between lintel and arch of a doorway.

VAULT An arched covering made of stone or brick over any building. There are several types of vault, each with its special characteristics:

> Barrel vault
> Fan vault
> Quadripartite vault
> Segmental vault
> Tunnel or waggon vault
> Corbel vault
> Groin vault
> Rib vault
> Sexpartite vault

VOUSSOIRS   The truncated wedge-shaped stones used in forming an arch.

VOUTAIN   Thin stone slab used as in-filling between the ribs of a Gothic vault.

WALL ARCADE   *See* Arcade.

WALL-SHAFT   In Gothic architecture, a decorative rather than structural feature. The half or three-quarter shaft projecting from the wall is most often used to lead up to the springing of arch or vault.

WATTLE-AND-DAUB   A primitive method of walling whereby vertical timber stakes are woven together by horizontal branches or reeds. This framework is then covered by mud, which is allowed to dry in the sun to form a simple enclosure.

WHEEL-WINDOW   A circular window in which the mullions radiate like the spokes of a wheel.

ZIGGURAT   Stepped pyramid supporting an altar, or temple. This type of building is found in Mesopotamia and Mexico.

INDEX

Notes: The numerals in italic type refer to the page numbers of the illustrations. Buildings, churches, and monuments are generally given under the cities or towns in which they are situated.

Aalto, Alvar (b. 1898), 319–20
abbey church, definition of, 104
Abercrombie, Sir Patrick (1879–1957), 324
Aberystwyth Castle, 151
Abingdon, church of St Helen, 126, *127*
Adam, Robert (1728–92), 224–8
Adler, Dankmar (1844–1900), 287, 302
Agrigentum, Temple of the Olympian Zeus, 14
Alberti, Leon Battista (1404–72), 19, 54, 58, 59–65, 73, 84, 87, 201; *De re aedificatoria*, 59; *De statua*, 59; *Della pittura*, 59; design of church façades, 61; ideas on the function of the column, 61, *62*; town planning, 59
Alfeld a.d. Leine, Fagus factory, 295, 309, *309*
Alnwick Castle, 172
Amesbury House, 193
Amiens Cathedral, 31, 32, 36, 37, *37*, *39*, 40, *46*, 47
amphitheatre, Roman, 21, 23
Amsterdam Stock Exchange, 305
Anglo-Saxon style, characteristics of, 134
Angelico, Fra (Guido di Pietro), 71
Anne, Queen of England, 184, 209
Anne of Denmark, wife of James I, 184
apse, in Norman building, 108; in Roman basilica, 21; in Romanesque cathedral, 108; in French Gothic cathedral, 36
arched braced roof, 131, *131*
Archer, Thomas (1668–1743), 217
Arisaig House, near Fort William, 264
Armada, 144
Arne, Thomas, 221
Art Manufacturers' Guild, 309

Art Nouveau, 287, 288, 295, 296–301, 307
Arundel Castle, 189
Ashleworth, Glos., *171*, 182
Asolo, Villa Maser, 81, 82, *82*
Athens: Acropolis, 15
    Agora, 15, 19
    Erechtheum, 3, 8, 9, *11*
    Lysicrates, Choragic Monument of, 10, *11*
    Nikè Apteros, Temple of, 8, *11*
    Parthenon, 6, 7, *7*, *8*, 10, 12
    Stoa of Attalus, 15, *17*
    Temple of Zeus, 10, *11*
Augustine, Saint 118
Augustinian Canons, 104 n., 118
Aulnay, Saint-Pierre-de-la-Tour, 30
Autun Cathedral, 30
Aydon Castle, 159

ballista, 142
'balloon frame' construction, 282
Bamburgh Castle, Northumberland, 145
barbican, 153, 154, 155, 156, 157
Barcelona: Casa Battló, 299
    Casa Milá 300, *301*
    Sagrada Familia, *298*, 300, 301
Baroque style, characteristics of, 86–88; concept of space, 89–91; English, 209, 210
barrel vault (waggon vault), introduction of, 17
Barry, Sir Charles (1795–1860), 245, 251, 274
Bartning, Otto (b. 1883), 312
Barton-on-Humber, 106

Basevi, George (1794–1845), 246
basilica, early Christian, 28; Roman, 19–21, *21*
bastard feudalism, 158, 162
Bath: Cathedral, 108
    The Circus, 228, 229, *229*
    Gay Street, 229
    Queen Street, 229
    Royal Crescent, 228, 229
battering-ram, 142
Battle Abbey, 119
'battle of the styles', 255–6
Bauhaus, Dessau, 295, 309, 310–12, *310*, *311*
Beardsley, Aubrey (1872–98), 296
Beaumaris Castle, 151, 154, 155, *155*
Beauvais Cathedral, 31, 40, *46*, 48, 114
Beggar's Opera, 221
Behrens, Peter (1868–1940), 308–9, 312, 321
Belsay Tower, Northumberland, 161
Belton House, 193, *193*
Benedict, Saint, 118
Benedictine Order, 118
Beni Hasan, Egypt, 5
Bentley, J. F. (1839–1902), 260–1
Benyon, Bage and Marshall mill, Ditherington, Shrewsbury, 271, *271*
Berkhamsted Castle, 144
Berlage, H. P. (1856–1934), 305, 315
Berlin: A.E.G. turbine factory, 308, *308*
    Altes Museum, 245, *245*, 276, 277
Bernini, Gian Lorenzo (1598–1680), 68, 77, 94–95, 96, 293
Bess of Hardwick, 180
Beverley Minster, 32, 33, 116, *117*
Bexhill-on-Sea, De la Warr Pavilion, 322
Bibury, Glos., 175
Birmingham Town Hall, 246
Black Death, the, 41, 125, 136
Blenheim Palace, 205, 209, *209*, *212*, *213*, 212–14
Boccaccio, 52
Bodiam Castle, 158, *158*, 160
Bogardus, James (1800–74), 282
Boleyn, Anne, wife of Henry VIII, 175

Bolton Abbey, 105, 122
Bolton Castle, 160
Boothby Pagnell Manor, 166, *166*
Boots Chemical Plant, Nottingham, *322*, 323
Borromini, Francesco (1599–1667), 94, 96, 98
Boston, Lincs., St Botolph, 128
Bothwell Castle, 161
Botticelli, Sandro, 71
Bourges, Saint-Étienne, 40, *49*, 50, *50*
Bournville, 242
Bradford, Yorks., 175
Bradford-on-Avon, Saxon church at, 106, *106*
Bramante, Donato (1444–1514), 59, 66–69, 70, 76, 77, 78, 84, 95, 202
Braque, Georges (1882–1963), 294, 301
Breuer, Marcel Lajos (b. 1902), 322
bridges, development of, 268–71
Brighton, 219, 229, 243
    Royal Pavilion, 230–1, *231*, 268
Bristol: Clifton Suspension Bridge, 268, *270*
    St Mary Redcliffe, 125, *125*
    Theatre Royal, 221
Broderick, Cuthbert (1822–1905), 246
Brongniart, Alexandre-Théodore (1739–1813), 277
Brown, Lancelot ('Capability') (1716–83), 222
Brunel, I. K. (1806–59), 268, 274
Brunelleschi, Filippo (1377–1446), 52, 57–58, 59, 71
Bruni, Leonardo, 52
Brussels: Rue Paul-Émile Janson, No. 6, 296, *297*
    Stoclet House, 299
Bryanston House, 263
Buffalo, N.Y., Guaranty Building, 288, *289*, 290
Buildwas Bridge, 268
Builth Castle, 151
Burford, Oxon, 175
Burges, William (1827–81), 262
Burlington, Lord Richard Boyle (1695–1753), 221–3, 226
Burne-Jones, Sir Edward, 296
Burnet, Sir John James (1857–1938), 315

Burnham and Root, 285–7
Burton, Decimus, 245, 246
Butterfield, William (1814–1900), 260
buttress, flying, 31, 34, *36*
Buxton Spa, 229
Byland Abbey, 107, 119, 120, 122

Cadbury, George, 242
Caen: La Trinité (Abbaye-aux-Dames), 108, *109*
    Saint-Étienne (Abbaye-aux-Hommes), *38*, 40, 108, *109*, 114
Caerlaverock Castle, 162
Caernarvon Castle, 151, *152*, *153*, 154
    fortified town, 144
Caerphilly Castle, 149, 151, 154, 155
Cambridge: Fitzwilliam Museum, 246
    King's College Chapel, 31, 57, *138*
        Fellows' Building, 223
    Pembroke College, 194
    Senate House, 223
    Trinity College, 168, 205
Camden Society, 255
Campbell, Colin (d. 1729), 221
Campen, Van, 207
canals, 219
Canons, Augustinian, 118; Regular, 104n; Secular, 104n.
Canterbury Cathedral, 37, 106, 108, 110, *111*, 113, 118, 138, 169; foundation of, 118
Caracalla, thermae of, 25
Carmelite Friars, 118
Carthusian Order, 123
castle, decline of, 143, 144, 157–9; definition of, 140; cost of building, 141; of enceinte, 161; of livery and maintenance, 157–9
Castle Ashby, 189
Castle Hedingham, 146, 147, 148
Castle Howard, Yorks., 205, *210–12*, 211–12, *213*, 217; Mausoleum, 212, *212*; Temple of the Winds, 211, *211*

Cathedral, English, characteristics of, 110–12
    French, characteristics of, 36–37
cathedral church, definition of, 104
Catherine de Médici, 41
Caus, Isaac de, 188
cella, 3, 12, 14
central plan in Renaissance church, 54–55, 176
central tower in greater English church, 112
Cézanne, Paul, 294
Chadwick, Edwin, 242
Chambers, Sir William (1723–96), 224–5
    comparative 'orders', *18*
Chandigarh, India, 316
chantries, 124, 125, 128
chapter-house, 121
Charles I, king of England, 193
Charles II, king of England, 196, 197
Chartres Cathedral, 30, 33, 37, 40, 49, 50
Chatsworth House, Derbys., 180, 207; Lily House, 273, 274
Cheltenham, 243
Chermayeff, Serge, 322
Chevening House, 189, *189*
chevet, 36, 45, 48, 110
Chicago: Auditorium Building, *286*, 287
    Carson, Pirie, Scott Store, 288, *289*
    Gaol, *283*
    Great Fire of, 281–2
    Home Insurance Building, 282, *285*, 287
    Illinois Institute of Technology chapel, 318–19, *319*
    James Charnley House, *302*
    Marshall Field Store, 282, *283*, 285
    Monadnock Block, 285, *285*
    Reliance Building, *285*, 287
    Robie House, 304, *305*
    Walker Warehouse, *286*, 287
    World's Fair, 290
    Golden Door, 290
Chicago school, 281–91
Chipchase Tower, 161
Chippendale, Thomas, 219
Chipping Campden, Grevel House, 169, *170*

Chiswick House, 221, *223*
Chiswick Park, 189
Choir: alterations to, 108–10; peri-apsidal, 108–10, *109*; parallel-apsed, 108, *108*
Choragic Monument of Robert Burns, 248
Choragic Monument of Lysicrates, 10, *11*
circle, symbolism of, 54, 55
circus, Roman, 21, 23
Cirencester, church of St John, 126
Cistercian Order, 118, 119
Cîteaux, 118
city-state, rise of Italian, 52
Civil War, 175, 185, 189, 190, 192, 207, 218
classical revival in the nineteenth century, 239
Claypotts Castle, 162
Clifton Suspension Bridge, 268, *270*
Clouds House, 264, *265*
Cluny Abbey, 118
coal tax, 219
Coalbrookdale Bridge, 268, *269*, 329
coastal defences, 144, 159
Cockerell, C. R. (1788–1863), 246, 248, 274
Cockerell, S. P., 230
Colchester Castle, 146
Cold Ashton Manor, *171*, 176
Coleshill House, 189, 192, *192*
Cologne, Werkbund Exhibition, 309, *309*
colour, in Greek temple, 13; in Gothic cathedral, 32; in medieval house, 164
Composite Order, *18*, 19
Compton Wynyates House, 176, *177*
concentric castle, 151, *155*, *157*
concrete (or pozzolana), used by Romans, 17
Conisborough Castle, 150, *150*
constitution of greater English church 103–5
Conway Castle, 151, *152*, 154
Corbridge Tower, 161
Corbusier, Le (C. E. Jeanneret) (1887–1965), 290, 295, 309, 312–17, 318, 319, 320, 323; and League of Nations competition, 314; and *le plan libre*, 313
Corinthian Order, 6, 10, *18*
Cortona, Pietro da (1596–1669), 89, 94

Cothay Manor, 167, *167*
Coutances Cathedral, 40
Coventry Cathedral, 32, 327–8
Crabtree, William, 323
Craigellachie Bridge, Banff, 268, *269*
Craigievar Castle, 162
Craig, James, 229
Crane, Sir Francis, 189
cruck construction 165, *165*
Cubism, 294–5
Cubitt, Thomas, 243

da Vinci, Leonardo (1452–1519), 53, 55, 58, 293
Dalyngrigge, Sir Edward, 158
Dante, 52
Days, Edward, 252
Days, George, 252
Deal Castle, 159
Deanery Gardens, Sonning, 321, *321*
Decorated style, characteristics of, 136
Dekker, Thomas, 184
Delacroix, Eugène, 294
De la Warr Pavilion, Bexhill-on-Sea, 322
Dessau, Bauhaus, 295, 309, 310–12, *310*, *311*
de Stijl, 317, 318
Deutscher Werkbund, 309
Dibdin, Charles, 221
Dickens, Charles, 238
Diocletian's Palace, Spalato, 226
Dirleton Castle, E. Lothian, 161–2
Disraeli, Benjamin, 238
Dissolution of monasteries, 105
dome: developed by Byzantines, 27, *27*, *28*; of Pantheon, 23, *24*; of Florence Cathedral, 56, 57; of St Paul's, London, 57, 200–3; of St Peter's, Rome, 56, 67–68; Renaissance concept of, 57, 78; Baroque concept of, 97, 99
Dominican Friars, 118
Donatello (Donato de Betto Bardi), 52, 53
Donne, John, 184

d'Orbais, Jean, 47
Doric Order, 6, 7, 8, *18*
Doune Castle, 162
Dover Castle, 141, 151, *154*, 155, 156, *156*, 157
Duchamp, Marcel, 301
Dundonald Castle, 162
Dunstan, Archbishop of Canterbury, 118
Dunstanburgh Castle, Northumberland, 159
Dürer, Albrecht, 55
Durham: Castle, 145
    Cathedral, 29, 31, 36, 37, 103, 106, 107, *107*, 108, 110, 112, 114, 122, 134
    St Cuthbert, shrine of, 110
Durand, Jean-Nicolas-Louis, 276

Earls Barton tower, 106, 134
Early English style, characteristics of, 135
Easton Neston House, 217
Ecclesiastical Society, 275
École des Beaux Arts, Paris, 277–8
Edensor, Derbys., 242
Edinburgh: Arthur's Seat, 247, 248
    British Linen Bank, 249
    Calton Hill, 247, 248
    Choragic Monument of Robert Burns, 248
    Commercial Bank of Scotland, 249
    development in the nineteenth century, 247–9
    Free Church College, 248
    George Street, 249
    High School, 249
    National Gallery of Scotland, 248–9
    National Monument, 248
    Nelson's Monument, 248
    Physicians' Hall, Queen Street, 249
    Princes Street, 247
    Royal Scottish Academy, 248, *248*, 249
    St Andrew's Square, 249
    St George's Church, 247
    St Mary's Cathedral, 247
    Tolbooth St John's, 248

Edward the Confessor, king of England, 108
Edward I, king of England, 151
Egyptian architecture, 3
Eleanor of Castile, wife of Edward I, 164
Elgin Marbles, 219, 249
Elizabeth I, 184
Ellis, Peter, 273
Elmes, Harvey Lonsdale (1814–47), 246
Ely Cathedral, 31, 36, 37, 106, 107, 108, 112, 246
enclosure of common land, 175
entasis, 10
Epidaurus, theatre of, 16, *16*
    Tholos, 12
escalade, 142
Escomb Church, Durham, 106
Ethelwold, Bishop of Winchester (Æthelwold), 118
Etruscans, 16
Evelyn, John, 194, 196, 242
Exeter: Cathedral, 31, 110, 112, 116
    Guildhall, 168
Eyck, Jan Van, 30

'Falling Water' House, Bear Run Park, Pennsylvania, 302, *303*
fan-vaulting, 34, 138, *138*
Farnsworth House, Plano, Illinois, 317, *317*, 318
Festival of Britain, 1951, 325
Festival Hall, Royal, 325, *325*
Field of the Cloth of Gold, 103
Finchale Abbey, 123
firearms, introduction of, 142
Firste and Chief Groundes of Architecture, 176
Fish House, Meare, 166, *166*
flèche, 37
Flint Castle, 151, 159
Florence, 52
    Cathedral, 56, 57
    Foundling Hospital (Ospedale degli Innocenti), 52, *53*, 57, 71
    Hospital of S. Maria Nuovo, 53

Florence—(*continued*)
  Laurenziana Library, 66, *67*, 72
  Medici Tomb, 57, 66, *66*, 67, 71, 78
  Palazzo Medici, 64, *64*
  Palazzo Pandolfini, 69, 245
  Palazzo Rucellai, 59, *60*
  Palazzo Strozzi, 64
  SS. Annunziata, 58
  S. Lorenzo, 71
  S. Maria degli Angeli, 58
  S. Maria Nuovo, 53
  S. Spirito, 57, 58
Florentine palazzo, characteristics of, 64–65
flying buttress, 31, 34, *36*
Fontana, Domenico (1543–1607), 77
Forth Road Bridge, 329
Förster, Ludwig, 280
Forum Romanum, 19
fountains, Roman, 25
Fountains Abbey, Yorks., 107, 114, 119, *120*, 122, 123
Francis Joseph, Emperor of Austria (1848–1916), 280
Franciscan Friars, 118
friars, entry of, into England, 124
Fry, Maxwell (b. 1899), 322
Fulbroke Castle, 176

Galilee chapels and porches, 110, 112, 114
Garnier, Charles (1825–98), 278–80
Garrick, David, 221
Gaskell, Mrs Elizabeth Cleghorn, 238
Gaudí, Antoni (1852–1926), 299–301, 307
George I, king of England, 209, 219
Ghiberti, Lorenzo (*c.* 1378–1455), 52
Gibberd, Frederick (b. 1908), 327
Gibbs, James (1682–1754), 223–4
Giocondo, Fra, 77
Giorgi, Francesco (also Zorzi), 63
Giotto di Bondoni (1276–1336), 52, 53
Gladstone, William Ewart, 256

Glamis Castle, 162
Glasgow: School of Art, 297, *297*
  Caledonia Road Free Church, 249, *249*
  Jamaica Street Warehouses, *272*, 273
  Tea Rooms in Sauchiehall Street and Buchan Street, 297
Glastonbury Abbey, 119, 122; kitchen at, 172
  St John's, *133*
Glenbuchat Castle, 162
Gloucester Cathedral, 37, 106, 108, 110, 114, 123, 138
golden section (golden mean), 54, *54*, 293
Goodrich Castle, 157
Gothic architecture, in Europe, 30–51; in Britain, 103 f.; French origin of, 40
Gothic art in Italy, 55
Gothic cathedral, French and English plans, 36–37, *37*
Gothic: a linear art, 30; a term of derision, 30
Goya (Francisco José de Goya y Lucientes) (1746–1828), 301
Graham, J. G., 248
Great Chalfield Manor, 172–4
Great Exhibition of 1851, 253, 259
great hall, description of, *167*, 167–9
Greek fire, 142
Greene, G. T., 273
Greenwich: Queen's House, 185–6, *185*, *186*, 187, 188, 189, 205
  Royal Naval Hospital, 193, 205, *206*, 211
  St Alphege, 215
Grevel House, Chipping Campden, 169, *170*
Gropius, Walter Adolf Georg (b. 1883), 294, 295, 309–12, 322
Grünewald, Matthias (1475–1528), 30
Guaranty Building, Buffalo, N.Y., 288, *289*, *290*
Guarini, Guarino (1624–83), 98–99
Guildford Cathedral, *326*, 327
Guildhall: Exeter, 168
  London, 168
  York, 168
Gunnersbury House, 193
gunpowder, 142

Haddon Hall, 167, 172–4, *173*
Hadrian, Roman emperor, 22
Halicarnassus, Mausoleum, 15, *15*
Halifax, Yorkshire, 175
Hamburg, St Nicholas, 254
Hamburgh, Johanneum, 277
Hamilton, Thomas, 249
hammer-beam, construction of, 131, *132*; at
    Westminster Hall, 168
Hampstead garden suburb, 321
Hampton Court Palace, *130*, 204, 209
Handel, George Frederick, 221
Hardwick Hall, 64, 178, 180–2, *181*
Harland, Hugh, 168
Harlech Castle, 151, 155, *157*, 159
Harris, Vincent, 322
Haussman, Eugène-Georges (1809–91), 278
Hawksmoor, Nicholas (1661–1736), 204, 205,
    206, 209–17, 221
Helsinki railway station, 319
Henry II, king of England, 145, 157, 158
Henry III, king of England, 104
Henry VI, king of England, 113
Henry VIII, king of England, 103, 105, 129,
    144, 159, 175, 177
Henry (Stuart), son of James I, 184, 192
Hereford Cathedral, 37
Herstmonceux Castle, Sussex, 161
Hexham Abbey, 120
Heywood, Thomas, 184
Hill, Octavia, 242
Hoffmann, Joseph (1870–1955), 296, 298, 315
Holbein, Hans (the younger), 190
Holkham Hall, 222, *222*
Hooke, Professor Robert (1635–1703), 196, 198,
    242
Horeau, Hector (1801–72), 274
Horta, Baron Victor von (1861–1947), 296, 315
house: cruck, 165, *165*; early Renaissance,
    175–82; fortified manor, 159–62; late
    Victorian, 262–6; medieval, 163–74; open
    plan, 313; Roman, 25, *26*
House of Raphael, Rome, 95

Hundred Years War, 113
Hunt, Holman, 259
Hunt's Farm, Kent, *171*, 182

Illinois Institute of Technology chapel, Chicago,
    318–19, *319*
Impington Village College, Cambs., 322
Industrial Revolution, 237–43
introduction of metal in building, 266–76
Ionic Order, 6, 8, 9, *18*
Ipswich window, 262
Isabel Roberts House, 304
Isenheim altar-piece, 30
Istanbul, S. Sophia, 28, 261
Itten, Johannes, 310

James I, king of England, 182, 184
Jeanneret, C. E., *see* Corbusier, Le
Jeanneret, Pierre, 314
Jefferson, Thomas (1743–1826), 281
Jenney, William le Baron (1832–1907), 287
Jervaulx Abbey, 119
Jew's House, Lincoln, 169, *170*
John of Gaunt, 172
Johnson Wax Building, Racine, Wisconsin, 306,
    306
Jones, Inigo (1573–1652), 80, 184–92, 201, 206,
    207, 225
Jonson, Ben, 184
Jugendstil (Art Nouveau), 295
Julius II, Pope, 77

Kandinsky, Wassily, 301, 310
Kedleston Hall, 227
keep, division of, 146–8
Kelmscott Press, 260
Kenilworth Castle, 172

Kent, William, 221–3, 226
Kew Palace, 190
Kidwelly Castle, 146, 151
Kildrummy Castle, 161
Kingsley, Charles, 238
Kirby Muxloe House, 161
Kirkham Priory, *121*, 122
Kirkstall Abbey, 108
Klee, Paul, 301, 310
Knaresborough Castle, 140
Knight, Capt. Valentine, 196, 197
Knook Manor, 167, *171*
Krak of the Knights, 150

Labrouste, Henri (1801–75), 246, 280, 320
Lady Chapel, in greater church, 108, 110; in
    parish church, 126–7
Lanercost Priory, 119
Lanfranc, Archbishop, 104
Laon Cathedral, 31, 37, *38*, 40, *44*, 45
Larkin Building, 305
Lateran Council, 104
Launceston Castle, 150
Lavenham Church, *128*
Laycock, cruck house, 166
Layer Marney Manor (or Tower), 176
Le Mans Cathedral, 40
Lee, Lawrence, 328
Leeds: Civic Hall, 322
    Corn Exchange, 246
    Town Hall, 246
    modern development, *215*
    nineteenth-century housing, *214*
Lemaresquier, 315
Lewyn, John, 160
Lichfield Cathedral, 31, 37, 108, 112, 114, 116,
    117
Lincoln: Cathedral, 32, 36, 37, 106, 108, 112,
    116
    Jew's House, 169, *170*
Little Wenham Hall, 160, *170*

Liverpool: Cathedral (Anglican), *326*, 327
    Cathedral (Roman Catholic), 327
    Oriel Chambers, *272*, 273
    St George's Hall, 246, *247*
Local Government Act, 1888, 239
Lochleven Castle, 162
London: Adelphi Terrace, *226*, 227
    Albert Memorial, 257
    All Saints', Margaret Street, 260
    Athenaeum Club, 244
    Bank of England, 232, *232*
    Banqueting Hall, Whitehall, 186–7, *187*, 188,
        189, 190, 206
    Beaufort House, Chelsea, 189
    British Museum, 219, 233, 245, *245*
    Chelsea Hospital, 204, *205*
    Chiswick House, 221, *223*
    Chiswick Park, 189
    Christ Church, Spitalfields, 215
    City churches, 198–200, *199–200*
    Clarendon House, 193
    County Council, establishment of, 239
    Covent Garden, 188, 233
    Crystal Palace, 273–6, *275*, 320
    Cumberland Terrace, *233*
    Drury Lane Theatre, 252
    Durham House, 193
    Earl's Court, 243
    Ellerdale Road, No. 6, Hampstead, 262, *263*
    Eltham Lodge, 207
    Finsbury Health Centre, 323
    General Post Office, 233
    Great Fire of, 188, 194, 200, 215, 242
    Greenwich, Queen's House, 185–6, *185–6*,
        187, 188, 189, 205
    Guildhall, 168
    Horse Guards, 222
    Houses of Parliament, 249, 251–2, *252*
    Hyde Park Corner, 246
    Law Courts, 256
    National Gallery, 246
    Peter Jones Store, Sloane Square, 323, *323*
    Piccadilly Hotel, 263

London—(*continued*)
Portland Place, 227
Portland Square, No. 20, 228
Queen's Gate, No. 170, 262, *263*
Reform Club, *244*, 245
Regent Street, *230*, 231
Regent's Park, *230*, 231
Regent's Park Zoo, the Penguin Pool, 323
Roehampton Estate, *324*, 325
Royal Academy, 219, 232
Royal Festival Hall, 325, *325*
Royal Naval Hospital, Greenwich, 193, 205, *206*
Royal Opera House, Covent Garden, 233
St Alphege, Greenwich, 215
St Anne, Limehouse, 215, *215*
St Bride, Fleet Street, *199*
St George, Bloomsbury, 215
St George-in-the-East, 215
St James's Park, 231
St James's Square, No. 20, *220*, 228
St John, Westminster, 217
St Martin-in-the-Fields, 223, 224; original plan, 223, *224*
St Mary-le-Bow, *199*
St Mary-le-Strand, 223
St Mary Woolnoth, 215–16, *216*
St Pancras Station Hotel, *256*, 257
St Paul's Cathedral, 57, *57*, 197, 200–4, *203*, 205, 209; Old St Paul's, 106, 108, 194; restoration by Inigo Jones, 187–8, *188*
St Paul, Deptford, 217, *217*
St Stephen Walbrook, 199–200, *200*, 204, 223
St Vedast, *199*
Somerset House, 225
South Kensington, 243
Stock Exchange, 197
Swan House, Chelsea, 262, *263*
Syon House, 226, 228
Tower, 146, *146*, *147*, 148, 151, 155, 156, 157; White Tower, 146, *146*, 148, 156
Travellers' Club, *244*, 245
United Services Club, 233, 244
Westminster Abbey, 105, 110, *111*, 113, 119, 250
Westminster Cathedral, 37, 261, *261*
Westminster Palace, 168, 188; destroyed by fire, 250
Whitehall, government offices, 255; 'battle of the styles', 255–6
Whitehall Palace, 188–9, 193, 204
Wren's plan, *196*, 196–8
long gallery, development of, 178
Longleat House, 64, 178, *179*, 180
Louvre, Paris, 205
Lubetkin, Berthold (b. 1901), 323
Lutyens, Sir Edwin Landseer (1869–1944), 320
Luzarches, Robert de, 47
Lyme Regis, 219

Mackintosh, Charles Rennie (1868–1928), 296, 297–8, 320
Maderna, Carlo (1556–1629), 77, 79, 94, 96
Maison Carrée, Nîmes, *20*, 31
Magdalen Laver, Essex, 124
mangon (or mangonel), 141
Mannerist style, characteristics of, 71, 74; decline of, 86
Mannheim, National Theatre (project), *319*
manorial system, 163
Mantua: Palazzo del Té, 72–3, *73*, *74*, 75, 84
    S. Andrea, 60, 61, *61*, 88
    S. Sebastiano, 60
Margat Castle, 151
market-towns, development of, 104
MARS (Modern Architectural Research) Group, 322
Marseilles, Unité d'Habitation, *315*, 315–16
Martin, Sir John Leslie (b. 1908), 325
Masaccio, 52
mason, medieval, 32–3
Matthew, Robert Hogg (b. 1906), 325
Maufe, Sir Edward (b. 1883), 327

Mausoleum of Halicarnassus, 15, *15*
May, Hugh, (1662–84), 207
Megaron, Mycenaean, 3
Menai Strait Bridge, 268, *270*
Mendelsohn, Erich (1887–1953), 312, 322, 323
Mengoni, Giuseppe (1829–77), 281
Mereworth Castle, Kent, 221
Michelangelo (Michelangiolo di Lodovico Buonarroti Simoni) (1475–1564), 53, 57, 66, 69, 71–2, 75, 77–9, 87, 94, 95, 176, 201, 202, 293
Michelozzo (di Bartolemmeo) (1396–1472), 58
Middlesbrough, Yorks., 242
Milan: Cathedral, 55
    Galleria Vittorio Emanuele, 281
    S. Maria delle Grazie, 66
Millais, Sir John Everett, 259
mine, 142–3
Minerva Medica, Temple of, 58
minster church, definition of, 104
module, 10
Modulor, 317
Moholy-Nagy, L., 310
Monadnock Block, Chicago, 285, *285*
monasteries, daily routine of, 121; dissolution of, 105; layout of, 120–3
Mondrian, Piet (1872–1944), 301, 318
Monte Carlo, the Casino, 280
Moor Crag House, Windermere, 266, *266*
Morris, William (1834–96), 259–60, 264, 320
Moser, Kolomon, 315
motte-and-bailey castles, 144–5, 159, 161
mouchette, 41, *43*
Mount Grace Priory, 123
Munch, Edvard, 296
Munich railway station, 277

Naos, 3
Napoléon III, Emperor of the French, 278
Nash, John, 227, 229–32, 233

Nesfield, William Eden (1835–88), 262
Neumann, Johann Balthasar (1687–1753), 99
Nevers Cathedral, 31
New Delhi, India, 321
New Ways House, Northampton, 321, *321*
New York: Brooklyn Bridge, 271
    Guggenheim Museum, 307, *307*
    Seagram Building, 318, *318*
Niagara Falls Bridge, 271
Nikè Apteros, Temple of, 8, *11*
Noisel-sur-Marne Chocolate Factory, 282
Nonesuch Palace, 177
Norman Conquest, 103
Norman style, characteristics of, 134
Norwich: Castle, 146
    Cathedral, 37, 106, 107, *109*, 110, 114
Nottingham: Boots' Chemical Factory, Beeston, *322*, 323
    St Barnabas, 253
Noyon Cathedral, 110

optical corrections, in Greek architecture, 10
Orders of architecture, characteristics of, 5, 6, 7–10, *18*; colossal, 76; decorative use of, 19, 61; origins of, 5; sequence of, 59–60; use of one order within another, 74; use of, in Renaissance, 55, 56
Orford Castle, 141, 150
Osterley Park, 227
Oswald, Archbishop of York, 118
Oxburgh Hall, 161, 172, 174
Oxford: All Souls College, 216
    Christ Church (college), 168
    Clarendon Building, 216
    Museum, 259
    New College, 168
    Queen's College, 206, 216
    Radcliffe Camera, 224, *225*
    Sheldonian Theatre, 194, *195*
    Tom Tower, Christ Church, 206, 216

Paestum, temples at, 7
Paimio Tuberculosis Sanatorium, Finland, 320
Paine, James (1716–89), 227
Palazzo Carignano, 98
   Chiericati, 81, *81*, 82, 186
   Chigi-Odescalchi, 95
   del Té, 72, 73, *73*, 74, 75, 84
   Farnese, 69, *69*, 70, 75, *75*, 245
   Massimi, 72, 74, *74*, 75
   Medici, 64, *64*
   Pandolfini, 69, 245
   Rucellai, 59, *60*, 64
   Strozzi, 64
   Vidoni Caffarelli, 68, *68*, 71
Palladio, Andrea (1518–80), 54, 64, 79–84, 176,
   185, 186, 187, 189, 207, 221; design of church
   fronts, 83–4; ideal shape of rooms, 79;
   I Quattro libri dell'architectura, 79
Palmerston, Henry John Temple, 3rd Visct.,
   255, 256
Paray-le-Monial Abbey, 30
Paris: Bibliothèque Nationale, 246, 280, 320
   Bibliothèque Sainte-Geneviève, *279*, 280
   Bourse, 277
   École des Beaux Arts, 277–8
   Franklyn, rue, house in, *299*
   Haussman's replanning of, 278
   Louvre, 205
   Madeleine, 278
   Notre-Dame Cathedral, 31, *38*, 40, 43, 45,
      45, 47
   Opéra, 278, *279*, 280
   Petit Palais, 280
   Sacré-Cœur, 278
   Saint-Denis Abbey, *38*, 40, 43, 103
   Saint-Denys-de-l'Estrée, 278
   Swiss Student's Pavilion, 315, *315*, 316
   Villa Garches, 314, *314*
Parthenon, Athens, 6, 7, *7*, *8*, 10, 12
Pastures House, North Luffenham, 266, *266*
Patrington, Yorks., church of St Patrick, 125,
   126
patronage in the Renaissance, 52, 53

Paul III, Pope, 76
Paxton, Sir Joseph (1801–65), 273–6
Peabody, George, 242
Peak Castle, Derbys., 145
Peel towers, 161
Pembroke Castle, 150
pendentive, 28, *28*
Penshurst Place, 167, *167*
'penthouse', 142
Perpendicular style, characteristics of, 136–8
Perret, Auguste, 301, 312
Peruzzi, Baldassare (1481–1536), 72, 74, 75, 77,
   84
Peterborough Cathedral, 106, 107, 108, 112,
   114, *115*, 116, 137
Petrarch, 52
Piano-nobile, 69, 314
Picasso, Pablo (b. 1881), 294, 301
Picola Farnesina, Rome, 70, *70*
Pierce, Edward, 191
Piper, John (b. 1903), 328
Pittsburgh, Pa., Allegheny Courthouse and
   Gaol, *283*
Plato, 62
Playfair, William Henry (1789–1857), 248
Pleshy Castle, 144
Poelzig, Hans (1868–1936), 312
pointed arch, 30, 31
Pollaiuolo, Antonio, 53
Pont du Gard, Nîmes, 23, *25*
Port Sunlight, 242
Porta, Giacomo della (1540–1602), 77
Post, Pieter, (1608–69), 207
post-and-lintel construction, 3, 16, 33
postern gate, 154
pozzolana, 17
Pratt, Sir Roger (1620–85), 189, 192–3, 207
Pre-Raphaelite Brotherhood, 253, 259
priory, definition of, 104
proportion, Palladio's theory of, 79–80; Pytha-
   goras's theory of, 62; Renaissance theory
   of, 56, 61–3
propylaeum, 12

Public Health Act, 1875, 240–1
Pudsey, Bishop of Durham, 110, 114
Pugin, Augustus Welby Northmore (1812–52), 250, 251, 252–4, 258, 275; *Glossary of Ecclesiastical Ornament*, 253; St Augustine's, Ramsgate, 253; *True Principles of Christian Architecture*, 253
Purcell, Henry, 221
Pythagoras, theories of proportion of, 62

Raglan Castle, 159
Raphael (Raffaello Sanzio) (1483–1520), 68, 69, 77, 78, 245; Marriage of the Virgin, 68
Raynham Hall, 190, *190*
Red House, Bexleyheath, 264, *265*
Reims Cathedral, 33, 37, *39*, 40, 47, *47*–48, 114
Repton, Humphry (1752–1818), 229, 230
Restormel Castle, 148, *148*, *149*
Reynolds, Sir Joshua (1723–92), 219
Rhuddlan Castle, 151, 155
Richard II, king of England, 168
Richardson, Henry Hobson (1838–86), 282–5, 287
Richmond, Yorks., the Georgian Theatre, 221
Rickman, Thomas, 250
Rievaulx Abbey, 121, 169
Rimini, S. Francesco, 60, 61, *61*
Ripon Cathedral, 114, *115*, 135,
Roberts, *see* Isabel Roberts House
Robie House, Chicago, 304, *305*
Rochester Castle, 146, *146*, 148, 149
Roebling, John A. (1806–69), 271
Rohe, Mies van der (b. 1886), 312, 317–19, 320
roman alphabet, 21
Romano, Giulio (1492–1546), 72–74
Rome: rise of, 16, 65
  Arch of Constantine, 22, *22*
  Arch of Titus, 19
  Arch of Trajan, *22*, 60
  Basilica of Trajan, *21*

Cancellaria, 65, *65*
Capitoline Hill, 76, *76*
Caracalla, Thermae of, 25, *26*
Colosseum, 21, *23*, 60
Fortuna Virilis, Temple of, 19, *20*
Gesù, Church of, 87, *87*, 88
House of Raphael, 95
Minerva Medica, Temple of, 58
palazzi, characteristics of, 69
Palazzo Chigi-Odescalchi, 95
Palazzo Farnese, 69, *69*, *70*, 75, *75*, 245
Palazzo Massimi, 72, 74, *74*, 75
Palazzo Vidoni Caffarelli, 68, *68*, 71
Pantheon, 22, *24*, 31
Piccola Farnesina, 69, *70*
Portunus, Temple of, 22, *22*
S. Andrea al Quirinale, 94, *94*
S. Andrea della Valle, 88
S. Carlo alle Quattro Fontane, *92*, 96, *96*
S. Ignazio, 88
S. Ivo della Sapienza, 97, *97*
S. Maria degli Angeli, 58
S. Maria della Vittoria, 95
S. Peter's, *56*, 67, 68, 70, 75–9, *77*, *78*, *93*, 94, 96, 97, 201, 202, 204; Piazza of, *93*, 94
S. Pietro in Montorio, 66, 67
S. Teresa in Ecstasy (by Bernini), 95
SS. Martina e Luca, 88, *89*, 89–91, *91*
Tempietto di S. Pietro, 59, 66, *66*, 67, 68, 202
Vatican Palace, 67
Villa Madama, 69
Vittorio Emanuele Monument, 281
Ronchamp, Notre-Dame-du-Haut, 315, *316*, 316–17
roof, timber construction of, 129–32, *130*, *131*, *132*
Rossetti, D. G., 259
Rouen: Cathedral, 31, 40
  St-Maclou, 43, *44*
Runcorn–Widnes Bridge, 329
Rundbogendstil, 277

Ruskin, John (1819–1900), 249, 250, 253, 254, 258–9, 275; *Lectures on Architecture and Painting*, 258; *Modern Painters*, 258; *The Seven Lamps of Architecture*, 258; *The Stones of Venice*, 258; *The Two Paths*, 258; *Unto this Last*, 259

Saarinen, Eliel (1873–1950), 319
St Albans Cathedral, 29, 105, 106, 107, 108, *108*, 119, 129
St Cuthbert, Durham, shrine of, 110
St George's Chapel, Windsor, 31
St Louis, Missouri, Wainwright Building, 288, *289*
Salisbury Cathedral, 31, 36, 37, *37*, 110, 112, 114
Saltaire, Yorks., 242
Salutati, Coluccio, 52
Sangallo, Antonio da (1485–1546), 69–70, 77
Sangallo, Guiliano da (1455–1516), 77
Sansovino, Andrea (called Contucci) (1460–1529), 83
Scalloway House, 162
Scarborough, Grand Hotel, 246
Schinkel, Karl Friedrich (1781–1841), 245, 246
Schlemmer, Oskar, 310
Scott, Sir George Gilbert (b. 1880), 254–7
Scott, Sir Giles, 327
Scott, Sir Walter, 250
Seaton Delaval House, Northumberland, *214*, 214–15
Seguin, Marc, 271
Selby Abbey, 129
semicircular arch, 34; introduction of, 16
Sens, William of, 110
Sens Cathedral, 110
Serlio, Sebastiano (1475–1554), 75
    proportions for Classical door, *202*
Shaftesbury, Anthony Ashley Cooper, 7th Earl of, 242

Shaw, Richard Norman (1831–1921), 262–4, 320
Sheerness, Naval Dockyard Boatstore, 273, *273*
shell keep, 148, *149*
Shrewsbury, Benyon, Bage and Marshall mill, 271, *271*
Shute, John, 176
Siddons, Sarah, 221
Siemens, W. von, 291
Siren, J. S., 319
Sixtus V, Pope, 94
skyscrapers, growth of, 281–91
Smeaton Manor, Yorks., 264, *265*
Smirke, Robert (1781–1867), 232–3, 244, 276
Smirke, Sydney (1799–1877), 246
Smythson, Robert (1535–1614), 178–82
Soane, Sir John (1753–1837), 232–3, 244
Somerset House, London, 225
Sompting Tower, 106, *106*
Sonck, Lars, 319
Sonning, Berkshire, Deanery Gardens, 321, *321*
Soufflet, 41, *43*
South Wingfield Manor, Derbyshire, 160
Southwell Minster, Notts., 114, *115*
spa towns, rise of, 219
Spence, Sir Basil Urwin (b. 1907), 327
springal (balista), 142
Stephen, king of England (1135–54), 145
Stephenson, Robert (1803–59), 274
Stirling Castle, 162
Stoke Bruerne Park, 189
Stokesay Castle, 160, 164
Stonehenge, 3, 5
Strasbourg Cathedral, 32
Strawberry Hill, 250
Street, George Edmond (1824–81), 257, 259, 262
Studley Royal, church of St Mary, 262, *262*
Stuttgart, Weissenhof scheme, 314, *314*
Style Moderne (Art Nouveau), 287, 288, 295, 296–301, 307
stylobate, 3, 10, 13
Suger, Abbot of Saint-Denis, 40, 43, 103

Sullivan, Louis Henry (1856–1924), 287–90
Sully, Bishop Maurice de, 40
suspension bridge, 268–71
Sutherland, Graham, 328
Synyards House, Otham, Kent, *170*, 175
Syon House, 226, 228

Tait, Thomas (1882–1954), 322
Taliesen West, Arizona, *306*
Talman, William (1650–1719), 207
Tantallon Castle, 162
Tattershall Castle, 159
Tecton Ltd., 323
Telford, Thomas (1757–1834), 268
temple, Greek, 3, *4*, 6–9, *12*, 12–13; Roman, 19
tenements, Roman, 25
Tewkesbury Abbey, 105, 114, 119
Texier, Jean, 50
thermae, Roman, 23
Theseion, Athens, 7
Tholos, Epidaurus, 12
Thomson, Alexander ('Greek' Thomson) (1817–75), 249
Thoresby Hall, 207
Thorpe, John (1563–1655), 182
Thorpe Hall, 193, *193*
Thynne, Sir John, 178
tie-beam, 12, 21, 129–31, *131*
Timaeus, Plato's, 62
Todi, S. Maria della Consolazione, 55, 58, *58*, 89–91, *89*, *90*
Tokyo Hotel, 308
Toledo Cathedral, 301
Toorop, Jan, 296
Toulouse Cathedral, 29
Tournus, St Philibert, 31
Tours Cathedral, 31
tracery, 135–6, *135–6*
trebouchet, 141–2
Trematon Castle, 148
Trent, Council of, 86

Tresham, Sir Thomas, 182
Trissino, Gian-Giorgio, Count, 83
triumphal arch, Roman, 19, 21, *22*
trompe-l'oeil, 99, 294
trussed rafter, 131
Tubbs, Ralph (b. 1912), 325
Tungendhat House, Brno, 317, *317*
Turin: Church of the Immaculate Conception, *92*, 98
 Palazzo Carignano, 98
 S. Lorenzo, 98, *99*
Turku, Turun-Sanomat offices, 320
Turner, Richard, 274
turnpike roads, 218
Tuscan Order, *18*, 19

Uccello, Paolo (1397–1475), 54
Unité d'Habitation, Marseilles, *315*, 315–16
Urbino, Palazzo Ducale, *63*

Vanbrugh, Sir John (1664–1726), 180, 181, 204, 205, 209, 215, 221, 233, 293
Vasari, Giorgio (1511–74), 30
vaulting, development of, 34, *35*; barrel (waggon), 17; English, 31; fan, 34, 138, *138*; rib, 136, *137*; semicircular, 34; sexpartite, 40
Vendôme, 'La Trinité', 41, *42*
Venice: S. Francesco della Vigna, *83*, 83–4
 S. Giorgio Maggiore, *83*, 83–4
 Redentore Il, 83–4, *84*
Vézelay Cathedral, 29
Vicenza: Palazzo Chiericati, 81, *81*, 82
 Villa Capra (Rotonda), 80, *80*, 81, 82
 Villa Thiene, 82
Vienna: Ringstrasse, 280
 Sezession Palace, 299
Vierzehnheiligen, pilgrimage church, 99
Vignola, Giacomo (1507–73), 77, 87, 176

Viipuri, (Vyborg), U.S.S.R., City Library, 320

Villa Capra (Rotonda), Vicenza, 80, *80*, 81, 82
    Garches, near Paris, 314, *314*
    Madama, Rome, 69
    Malcontenta, 82
    Maser, Asolo, 81, 82, *82*
    Savoye, Poissy, France, 295, 313, *313*
    Thiene, near Vicenza, 82

Villard de Honnecourt, 33, 262
Viollet-le-Duc, E. E., 278
Vitruvius, 55, 60, 194
Voysey, C. F. A., 262–6, 282, 320
voutains, 41, *41*

Wagner, Otto, (1841–1918), 296, 298–9
Wainwright Building, St Louis, *289*
Walmer Castle, 144, 159
Walpole, Horace, 250
Ward Willitt House, Illinois, 304, *304*
Warmington Church, 128, *128*
Wars of the Roses, 158
Warwick Castle, 172
Waterhouse, Alfred (1830–1905), 257
Watts Sherman House, Rhode I, *284*, 285
Webb, John (1611–72), 193, 201
Webb, Philip Speakman (1831–1915), 262–6, 282, 320
Webster, John, 184,
Weimar School of Art, 309, 310
Weissenhof Scheme, Stuttgart, 314, *314*
Wells Cathedral, 30, 33, 36, 112, *113*, 114, 116, *117*
Werkbund Exhibition, Cologne, 309, *309*
west front, of English greater churches, 114–16, *115*, *117*; of French cathedrals, *38*, *39*, *42*, *43*, *44*, *45*, *47*, *49*, 50

Westminster: Abbey, 37, 105, 110, *111*, 113, 119, 250; Chapel of Henry VII, 57
    R.C. Cathedral, 261, *261*
    Great Hall, 132, *132*, 168, 250
    Palace, 168, 250

Wilkins, William (1778–1839), 244
William I, king of England, 106, 108, 118
William of Sens, 110
William the Englishman, 110
Williams, Owen, 323
Wilton House, 187, 190–1, *191*
Winchester: Castle, 143
    Cathedral, 32, 107, 114, *137*
    Palace, 204

Windsor Castle, 143
Wollaton Hall, 178, 179–80, *180*
Wood, John the Elder (1707–54), 228–9
Wood, John the Younger (1728–81), 228–9
Worcester Cathedral, 114
Worksop Manor, Notts., 182
Wren, Sir Christopher (1632–1723), 168, 194, 206, 209, 210, 211, 215, 216, 221, 242, 281, 293; plan for London, *196*, 196–8
Wright, Frank Lloyd (1869–1959), 288, 293, 298, 302–8, 313, 319

Yevele, Henry (1320–1400), 168
York: Clifford's Tower, 150
    Five Sisters, 135
    fortified town, 144
    Guildhall, 168
    Minster, 32, 37, 106, 112, 114, *115*, 129, 138

Zeus, the Olympian, Agrigentum, temple of, 14
Zorzi, Francesco (also Giorgi), 63